Your Day in Wine Country

Touring the Wineries of Napa and Sonoma

Ralph & Lahni DeAmicis

Cuore Libre Publishing
Sonoma California

Your Day in Wine Country
Touring the Wineries of Napa and Sonoma
by Ralph & Lahni DeAmicis

Published by
Cuore Libre Publishing &
Space and Time Designing Inc.
19201 Sonoma Hwy #125
Sonoma, CA 95476

To Order Copies Phone 707-320-4274
Email: Lahni@SpaceAndTime.com
www.YourDayInWineCountry.com

Disclaimer: Even though we chose the wineries and restaurants in this book with great care and after extensive research, we make no guarantees for the accuracy of the information included herein. Even though we have made a huge effort to make the information and maps as correct as possible, we are dealing with information related to about five hundred independent businesses and they change things. Additionally, errors happen either in their transmission of the information or our recording of that information and that is often times beyond our control. We therefore accept no responsibility for any losses or inconveniences you may suffer from using this information.

Important: While these tours are designed to be as safe and enjoyable as possible, we accept no responsibility for your safety or satisfaction. Alcohol and driving are a risky mix that should be approached cautiously. We strongly recommend drinking in moderation, having a designated driver, or hiring a professional tour guide or livery service because we want you to be safe and have a fun day in Wine Country and come back again and again and again.

Ralph & Lahni DeAmicis, Cuore Libre Publishing, Space and Time Designing Inc

Contents

A Note about Why We Chose these Wineries

*"The challenge when coming to wine country is not 'finding good wineries',
it's figuring out which great wineries you're going to leave out".*
— *Ralph's often repeated refrain to clients.*

While our tours include many wonderful wineries and restaurants, we clearly left out many others and for that we are sorry. This was done for the sake of simplicity and convenience. The sheer number of wineries in Napa and Sonoma that you could visit can be overwhelming. This book was created to make a day trip enjoyable, educational and comfortable, and that meant selecting a manageable group of tours for visitors to choose from. To all of those wineries and restaurants that were left out please understand that we do love you and know that you're all great places to visit, *you just didn't fit into one of the tours selected for this edition.*

Why did we choose the wineries that we did? It was due to the way that the book was created. Over the course of two years of driving clients around Napa and Sonoma, Ralph recorded his tours. Some tours were the client's choices, or the hotel concierge, or from an in-house or associated travel department. The majority of the tours included were those that Ralph created based upon positive client feedback about the wineries over many visits.

For the book we selected the tours that Ralph's notes highlighted as exceptional with a high level of client enjoyment. The quality that makes a great tour is not just one stand-out winery, but a well-balanced collection of wineries enjoyed over the course of the day. The wineries in these tours have a lot to offer, good staff, great wines, scenery, architecture and a location that works well as part of a day trip. A satisfying tour needs to provide variety, comfort, safety and an efficient use of the visitor's time.

Finally our choices were based on one premise, 'Your Day in Wine Country' was designed for the needs of the visitor, not as an advertising tool for wineries. **None of the wineries or restaurants included here paid to be in this book.** They earned the right because they consistently do a great job for their customers. That takes a lot of work, creativity and commitment and we appreciate those qualities.

List of Photos

A Note about the Maps

The majority of the maps in this book don't even pretend to be drawn to scale. Many of the tour maps are also missing a whole bunch of roads and they pay only passing attention to the compass directions. They are a lot closer to maps drawn on napkins at some Wine Country café than anything produced by the National Geographic Surveys. Despite their deficiencies, or maybe because of them, you will find the maps tremendously helpful for navigating between the Sonoma and Napa wineries. When you are driving down the road most maps have a lot more information than you need to get where you are going. These are special purpose maps so they have been trimmed down to the essentials. Roads that you don't need to worry about are left out. Distances do matter when you are driving on a tour so mileage, along with navigation tips are recorded on the accompanying notes page. On the tour maps the best route is highlighted with a thick line. The overview maps are are more detailed and closer to scale but the tour maps are designed as simply as possible so that you can read them easily in a moving car in unfamiliar country, even if you've had a bit of wine to drink.

List of Maps

How to Fast Track this Book

Your Day in Wine Country is a practical book meant to be your friendly companion as you enjoy the North Bay Wineries. It is very relaxed and easy to use because we expect you to be reading this in a car, at a café table or lying on a hotel bed. There are three components. The first are a collection of chapters filled with helpful information to enhance your experience of Wine Country. The chapters are not very long, nor very complicated, but they will tell you what you need to know to feel comfortable and confident as you tour this beautiful countryside. Next are the tours. They are based on various themes and start from specific locations. The tours include simplified maps, along with notes and directions, so that you can safely navigate your way through daytrips to various groups of wineries. Third are the directories. They include both expanded information about the wineries mentioned in the tours, and information about other wineries and businesses in the area that you might want to visit.

Because you're on vacation and you don't want to waste time, you can fast track your way through this book. Here's how: Read 'Chapter 2: A Day Trip Strategy', for an idea about what winery touring is like. Read 'Chapter 4: How Many Wineries Can I Visit', for a realistic idea of the day ahead. Read 'Chapter 5: 'Clothing: Wine Country Casual?' to know what to wear. Read 'Chapter 12: Using the Mapped Tours' to use the tours most effectively. With this intro that's 3800 words. That won't take you very long to read, now will it? On the road it's the tour maps with their notes that you'll need.

Next look at the five categories of tours in the contents and select from the group that is most convenient to where you are staying. If this is your first visit to the area choose a tour that is close to your hotel. As much as you might want to go miles out of your way to some winery that you've heard of before, there are so many great wineries that you have never heard of, why spend the whole day driving when you could be making discoveries nearby? Pick out a tour that interests you and get going early.

Even though the tours are divided into five groups based upon where they start, that doesn't mean a tour is going to stay in that same area during the entire day. One of the qualities that make Napa and Sonoma so appealing is that the growing districts are close together so it is easy to see a lot of variety in the course of a day or two.

If you are staying in San Francisco choose from the lists for Southern Sonoma, Southern Napa and Central Napa. Look for the phrase 'A good day trip from San Francisco'. These work best from the city. If you are staying in Sonoma or Napa you can pretty much choose from any list, although starting with a tour that is close to your hotel is a smart choice.

Cost: The tours are listed sequentially from '$$ Moderately Priced' to '$$$$ Expensive'. This refers to the cost of the tasting and tour fees, rather than the prices of the wines. The shorter, simpler tours are listed first and the longer, more complicated tours, including those that require appointments, are listed last. The projected time for the day trip is based on an average of forty-five minutes per winery, and fifteen minutes between wineries. Appointment wineries and those with tours take longer. The estimates were adjusted for the actual routes. For any tour that starts in San Francisco you need to add at least an hour each way.

Some tours are marked as being 'Best with a Hired Car and Driver'. This recommendation is made in the interest of safety. Either the tour includes an excessive number of wineries, or the ones included make high alcohol wines, and then pour a lot of it for their guests. Some of the tours require a high level of punctuality and others go up roads that you don't want to navigate after having a glass or two of wine. A hired car and driver is a lot less stress and a lot cheaper than a DUI.

Most of the tours include three to six wineries. If you have a professional driver, or a designated driver, you can make it to all of the places listed on the tour. If you are driving and drinking, don't plan on making it to all of the wineries. On the other hand, if you limit what you consume by pouring the excess out, drinks *lots* of water, two to four ounces per ounce of wine, and eat after every two wineries, it's amazing how you can improve your tasting endurance. By the end of the day the palette is often saturated so the scenery, shopping and winery experience of the winery are more important than the tasting itself. By the way, make the time to read the rest of the book. You'll find it helpful for this trip, and very helpful for your next visit, because once you come here the first time the odds are that you are going to come back again.

After All, You have Friends in Wine Country!

Chapter One: Why You Should Visit Wine Country
And How to Use this Book!

To be sung on the way to Wine Country to the tune of
"Oh What a Beautiful Morning":
"Oh what a beautiful morning, oh what a beautiful day,
I've got a beautiful feeling everything's going our way.
There's a bright golden haze in the vineyards,
there's a bright golden haze in the vineyards,
and the grapes are as high as an elephant's eye and
the olive trees are reaching up to the sky.
Oh what a beautiful morning, oh what a beautiful day,
I've got a beautiful feeling everything's going our way."

Most people visit Wine Country for one or two days, and some lucky folks may stretch that out for a long weekend. But once they visit for the first time, the chances are that they're going to come back again. The reasons are simple: Sonoma and Napa are filled with good food, great wine, beautiful scenery and friendly people, and there's not a lot for kids to do, so you get to enjoy yourself like an adult. Of course, sometimes you do need to bring your children, but don't worry, there are hotels, wineries and other attractions that are quite kid-friendly. Some good ones: Sebastiani, Cline, Larson Chateau St. Jean, Benziger, Artesa, Domaine Chandon, V. Sattui, Beringer, Sterling, and Castello di Amorosa. It's just that Wine Country is really *Disneyland for adults*.

If you're visiting San Francisco you need to find a way to make the 45-minute trip North to where the first vineyards begin. Otherwise you're missing a great experience that's both enjoyable and educational. After all, how much do you really know about wine making and wine tasting, and wouldn't you like to know more?

Remember Benjamin Franklin's words, "Wine is constant proof that God loves us and loves to see us happy."

And no place is going to convince you of that truth more than Napa and Sonoma. The biggest challenge that visitors face is choosing where to go, where to eat and how to get there. Sonoma and Napa have so many great wineries that it's hard to decide which ones you're going to leave out.

If you're staying up in Wine Country, that's very smart of you and we congratulate you on your decision. The wine regions are so diverse that a week of day trips heading in every direction would just scratch the surface. Even though Sonoma and Napa are separate counties, and both are proud of their identities, this guide deals with them equally for a simple reason: They are equally easy to reach from San Francisco, that great tourist magnet that is the starting point for so many wonderful trips to Wine Country. The histories and economies of Sonoma and Napa are so linked they are clearly in a Yin Yang relationship. We could say that the bigger, moister, more fertile Sonoma is the Yin to the hotter, drier, more famous Yang Napa.

When we talk about wineries in the region the list often crosses county lines:
We have famous houses like Sebastiani, Beringer, and Mondavi.
We have glamorous ones like Ferrari-Carano, Rubicon, and Darioush.
We have convenient ones like Artesa, Cline, and Gloria Ferrer.
We have the elite winemakers like Shafer, Caymus, and Jordan.
We have the historic wineries like Buena Vista, Hanzell, and Beaulieu.
And we have the charming family wineries like Ceja, Passalacqua, and Arger Martucci.

Many of the over seven hundred wineries spread across the two counties are small, family-run affairs where the person pouring for you could be the winemaker, the owner or possibly one of the owner's children.

Even though we have so many wineries to choose from, they're spread over two big, agricultural counties and connected together by little, two-lane roads. Up in the mountains that overlook the valleys are some wonderful gems, but some of those roads are one lane and trail out into something that could charitably be called a goat path.

The secret to having a great tour is to connect the dots on the map together so that you spend more time enjoying the wineries than you do in the car. That's what the maps in our book will help you to do. So you can decide which tour is best for you, they are built around themes. That way, if you only like red wines, or you only like whites,

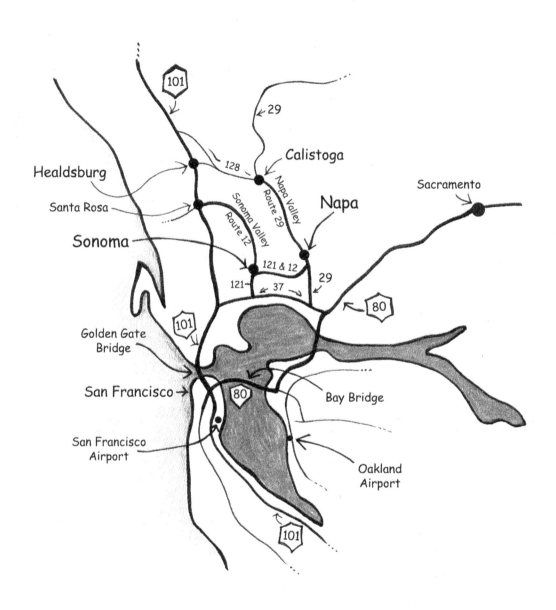

or you want the best gift shops, or art collections, or off the beaten track Mom and Pop tasting rooms, you can select a route based on your interests.

The maps are also organized by region. Depending on where you're staying certain wineries are more convenient than others, so the mapped tours are grouped together for Southern Sonoma, Northern Sonoma, Southern, Central and Northern Napa, although some tours cross over the county lines. The cross-county tours work most comfortably in the southern section of the two counties called Carneros. For example, from San Francisco you can make a very nice tour by leaving the city over the Bay Bridge and taking Routes 80 North, 37 West and 29 North to the Napa Valley (See map Page 12). Then you can visit wineries the entire width of Carneros, along the edges of Routes 121/12 East, crossing over into Sonoma in the process, and returning to San Francisco via Routes 121 West, 37 West and 101 South, that will take you over the very glamorous Golden Gate Bridge. By the way, this is a great tour in the hottest parts of the summer because it skirts the coolest sections of the two counties.

Chapter Two: A Day Trip Strategy
A Fast Track Chapter

Every great trip needs a great plan so let's talk about a strategy that you can use, one that will take the greatest advantage of the day. Start early! Winery tasting rooms normally open at ten and close about five. This is Vineyard Country where people work outdoors and the weather is beautiful most of the year, so everything important happens during the day.

If the idea of drinking at ten in the morning seems a little excessive, remember, they're called tasting rooms, not drinking rooms. The staff will pour small samples and hopefully encourage you to pour the excess out. And remember, you're on vacation. Early in the day the wineries tend to pour a little bit light, and that's a good thing. You don't want to be napping when you could be tasting wine. But after three in the afternoon, all bets are off and it becomes increasingly important to drink plenty of water to dilute all of that wine.

If you want to see more of the area and still enjoy as many wineries as possible, here's a plan that works great. Have a good breakfast, including plenty of protein and fat (No high carbs, AKA: Stacks of pancakes covered with syrup and fruit), and then leave your hotel in enough time so that you will arrive at the closest winery around ten in the morning. From San Francisco that's about forty-five minutes; from downtown Sonoma or Napa that's about five to ten. If you're staying in a hotel any place up in the Sonoma or Napa Valleys it is just minutes to a tasting room.

At the first winery enjoy a tasting, browse the gift shop, use the rest rooms and then head up valley to the farthest winery on your list. On the way there pick up some food for a picnic and put it in a bag with some cold bottles of water to keep them cool. Drink some of the water during the drive, at least four ounces for every ounce of wine. If it's hot, drink more water, since dehydration is one of the main causes of wine headaches and the unpleasant manifestations of intoxication, heavy–headed confusion and tiredness. It's not surprising that red wine will more often give people headaches because the tannins it contains are especially drying to the brain and pallet. Red wine headaches can often be resolved simply by drinking plenty of pure water.

The ride from the first winery to the second should be about half an hour to forty-five minutes, at the maximum. In Napa that's the distance from the Carneros district in the south to the town of Calistoga at the northern edge of the valley. The time between wineries could be less, but you want to allow your body some time to metabolize that first tasting, and you want to see some variety in the region. On the way you're going to be passing lots of other wineries, but don't worry, they're for the ride back. When you arrive at the next winery enjoy your second tasting, and assuming about forty-five minutes per winery that should bring you to just after noon, so now is a good time to find a picnic table and get out those sandwiches.

You never want to do more than two tastings without eating, unless you're pouring out lots of wine, and possibly spitting that out, which no one likes to do. So Eat!

When we say eating we don't mean just bar snacks. After that second winery you need a meal that includes some protein, fat and nice crusty bread to absorb a bit of that wine. Ideally the ride between wineries should be a minimum of ten to fifteen minutes. That way you have a chance to clear you taste buds with water and crackers. Otherwise the heavy reds are going to be stuck to your pallet and everything is going to taste the same.

So the plan is, visit two wineries and then eat lunch. If you try to fit in just one more winery before lunch your blood sugar, not to mention your alcohol level, will go all out of whack and it will tire you out. That's hard to come back from, although the main solution is a high protein meal and lots of water. Part of the secret that makes this system work so well is that alcohol is a great solvent for protein and fat, which are two of the best energy sources. By pausing after two wineries and giving all of that good wine something to work on, you're going to release that energy and you'll find that your afternoon endurance, and that includes your tasting endurance, is greatly improved.

Chapter Three:
What you Need to Know About the Region!

There is the historic town of Sonoma and the county of Sonoma. Likewise there is the town of Napa and the county of Napa. Both towns are in the southern parts of their respective counties, and while the town of Sonoma is a charming, historic Spanish style village, the town of Napa is a bigger, modern Californian town with a core of charming Victorian houses and great restaurants downtown. Note: Both centers, Sonoma and Napa are actually designated cities, but since the former barely tops 9,000 inhabitants and the later 70,000, from most people's perspective they are better described as towns.

Picnic Anyone?

When you're out wine tasting, one of the most pleasant things you can do is picnic. Now finding a place to picnic in Sonoma is easy, but trickier in Napa. Napa county has all kinds of regulations designed to rein in the onslaught of tourism, so while just about every Sonoma winery has some picnic tables, there are only a few dozen in Napa that are easily available and they're spread out. But don't worry; we noted them on the maps.

Of course there is the possibility that you don't want to picnic, although we have to tell you, picnicking is something that we do really well out here. But it does rain, and it even gets cool in the winter. Midday in January may find it in the fifties, and in August we've even seen times when it's been too hot to picnic, although that is pretty rare. In the summer it is hot and dry in the daytime and humid and cool in the evening. Even when the temperatures are in the nineties, because it is so dry, a little of shade and breeze goes a long way.

Of course, for many of us, eating at great restaurants is a wonderful pastime, and a joy onto itself. As you travel up valley there are plenty of fine restaurants to choose from, including some that are famous throughout the world, like 'The French Laundry'. But here's a little warning for you. Wine tasting is strenuous work; lots of walking, talking,

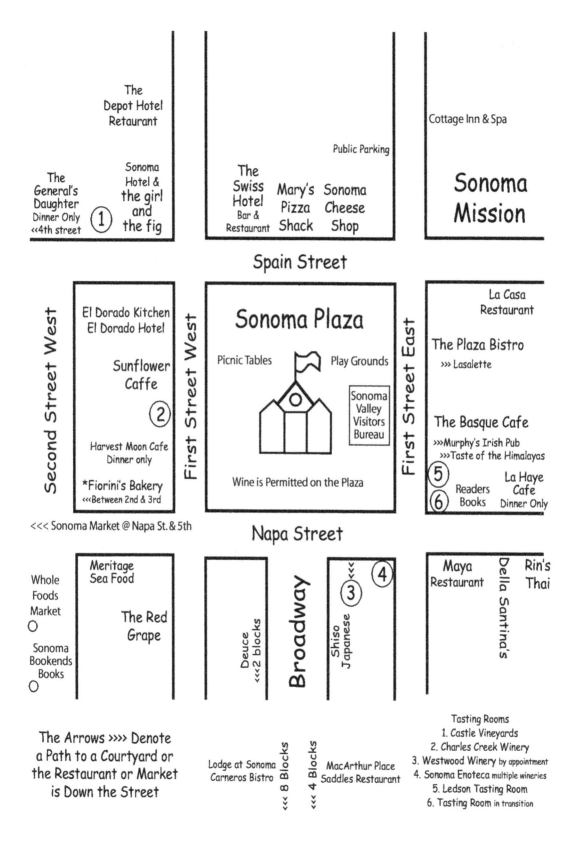

The Depot Hotel Retaurant

The General's Daughter
Dinner Only
<<4th street

(1) Sonoma Hotel & **the girl and the fig**

Public Parking

The Swiss Hotel
Bar & Restaurant

Mary's Pizza Shack

Sonoma Cheese Shop

Cottage Inn & Spa

Sonoma Mission

Spain Street

Second Street West

El Dorado Kitchen
El Dorado Hotel

Sunflower Caffe
(2)

Harvest Moon Cafe
Dinner only

*Fiorini's Bakery
<<<Between 2nd & 3rd

First Street West

Sonoma Plaza

Picnic Tables   Play Grounds

Sonoma Valley Visitors Bureau

Wine is Permitted on the Plaza

First Street East

La Casa Restaurant

The Plaza Bistro
>>> Lasalette

The Basque Cafe
>>>Murphy's Irish Pub
>>>Taste of the Himalayas
(5)
(6) Readers Books

La Haye Cafe
Dinner Only

<<< Sonoma Market @ Napa St. & 5th

Napa Street

Whole Foods Market
O

Sonoma Bookends Books
O

Meritage Sea Food

The Red Grape

Deuce
<<<2 blocks

Broadway

Shiso Japanese
(3)

(4)

Maya Restaurant

Della Santina's

Rin's Thai

The Arrows >>>> Denote a Path to a Courtyard or the Restaurant or Market is Down the Street

Lodge at Sonoma
Carneros Bistro

8 Blocks
<<<

4 Blocks
<<<

MacArthur Place
Saddles Restaurant

Tasting Rooms
1. Castle Vineyards
2. Charles Creek Winery
3. Westwood Winery by appointment
4. Sonoma Enoteca multiple wineries
5. Ledson Tasting Room
6. Tasting Room in transition

standing and elbow bending, not to forget carrying cases of wine back to the car. After all, a bottle of wine is the world's best souvenir. So, don't plan on a fancy dinner after an extended day of wine tasting, because you're going to spend that meal staring across the table at each other, trying to stay awake. If you're planning a very long day of winery visits, the best thing to do is have an early dinner with a nice piece of meat or fish, and then take a little nap. Get up about nine and go have a little snack with some Sparkling Wine. You'll be amazed how refreshed you feel. If you want to build a fancy dinner in, then start your wine tasting a little later in the day, eleven or twelve, or even after lunch.

For lunch there are plenty of places to catch a quick bite. Stop by the Sonoma Plaza, the largest in California, and you'll find a number of little restaurants along its edge. The Sunflower Café is one of our favorites. Up the Sonoma Valley, also known as the Valley of the Moon, you'll find restaurants in both Glen Ellen and Kenwood. In Northern Sonoma most of the restaurants are found around Healdsburg, although Sebastopol and Guerneville along the Russian River Valley host some lovely places. In the Napa Valley you'll find plenty of restaurants in the City of Napa, Yountville, Rutherford, St. Helena and Calistoga. Consult the restaurant directories in the contents.

The whole Napa Valley is only thirty miles long and five miles wide and there are many places where it's fence-to-fence vineyards. Sonoma County is much more diverse, their vineyards are often next to orchards, farms, pastures, and forests of eucalyptus and live oak. Sonoma is a much bigger county than Napa and while it actually produces more grapes, its identity isn't completely tied to the vines. Luther Burbank, the great botanist, called it the Redwood Empire and said that of all the places on Earth it was the spot most blessed by Nature. Napa is beautiful too, in a dryer, more spacious way that the grapes adore, but in Napa they make wine, very well, and that's what they do.

Chapter Four: How Many Wineries can We Visit?
A Fast Track Chapter

If you're careful about tasting and not drinking, you can visit four, maybe even five wineries in a day. If you're not as careful, then three is the maximum. The secret to visiting more wineries is to never go more than two tastings without eating, and in between consuming abundant amounts of water. Don't worry, most of these places have nice bathrooms. Some are nicer than are found in most homes.

Ideally, and typically, a tasting should be four, one-ounce samples. So, each winery tasting is equal to a glass of wine, if you drink it all. Most of the people who work in the wine industry are very responsible about their drinking, and they want to see you enjoy the wine, not get drunk. There are dumping buckets right there on the tasting bar for the excess and no one is insulted when you use them. Also, couples can share a tasting. That's not only practical, but also romantic, and no one in Wine Country is going to object to romance. *If you come to Wine Country with your honey and it doesn't make you feel romantic, you're not doing it right!*

Bring lots of water with you. When you drink plenty of water it dilutes the alcohol and diffuses it throughout your bloodstream, so that even your toes feel good and your head feels light. When you drink enough water, instead of feeling drunk you'll feel illuminated by the wine. If you want to visit more wineries and you're not prepared to spit, or you're simply worried about driving down country roads with a tummy full of wine, then hire a car and driver. If you have several friends, an SUV or limousine for a day is quite reasonable and it's a heck of a lot cheaper than a DUI. While most San Francisco-based drivers won't be winery experts, with a copy of this book in hand you'll be all set for a daytrip. There are also companies that specialize in winery tours, although they're mostly found in Wine Country. Many of them are prepared to pick up clients in the City.

In the high season there are so many black cars and stretched limos cruising around that you would think the Mafia was having a convention. But when you see people tumbling out of the cars wearing shorts and polo shirts you'll remember that the phrase 'Wine Country Casual' was invented here. The only neckties that you're going to see in Wine Country are those being worn by the limo drivers. It identifies them as guides and it gives them something to clean their ever-present sunglasses with.

Chapter Five: Clothing: Wine Country Casual?
A Fast Track Chapter

If you are Going to Taste Red Wine,
and Why Wouldn't You, Don't Wear White or Yellow or
Any Color That's Going to Show a Wine Spill Like a Red Wound.

Which brings us to what to wear? Or should we say, what NOT to wear. Leave the high heels at the hotel. Vineyards are farms and while the biggest wineries have Disney World-like paving, many of the others are a lot more suited to running shoes, flats, or sandals if it's really hot. Even when you're planning to tour the big shots; Rubicon, Artesa, Sterling, Beringer, Castello di Amorosa, Domaine Carneros and Domaine Chandon, keep in mind that even though they do have good sidewalks, they also often have lots of stairs. So, you have to choose between style and comfort.

Please leave behind the lipstick and the perfume. Tasting rooms are all about enjoying the senses and anything that competes with the flavors of the wine is best avoided. Also, the colors of the wine are part of the experience and since you're going to use the same glass for a winery's entire tasting you don't want it smeared with lipstick. The lipstick's oils will also affect the wine's subtle flavors. Additionally, getting lipstick off of fine crystal tasting glasses is a pain for the staff, so it definitely colors the way that they will treat you as they pour your wine. A friendly tasting room staff adds immeasurably to your enjoyment, so a little consideration is politic.

Wear loose fitting clothes. You're going to be sitting in cars, walking and sweating, so be comfortable. Sonoma and Napa are normally about fifteen degrees warmer than San Francisco, and the farther up the valleys you go the warmer it gets. At the same time it could be sixty-five degrees in Carneros, all the way in the South along the Bay, and ninety-five degrees in Calistoga at the top of the Valley. In Napa they claim that the temperature rises one degree for each mile you travel North.

You could start the day in the South at Artesa with their spectacular views and their constant, cooling Carneros winds and forty minutes later be thirty miles North, sweating, riding the gondola to the Sterling Winery perched on its hill within site of

Calistoga. There's also outside and inside. Some big wineries are air conditioned, but many are not. Some tastings are conducted in the cool barrel rooms. At the extreme, you could be taking a cave tour at Vine Cliff, Rutherford Hill, Kunde, Benziger, or even Spring Mountain, which could bring you from ninety degrees outside to fifty-six degrees inside. So, even if you're wearing shorts, bring a sweat jacket or a similar cover-up.

This area enjoys abundant sunshine, so good sunglasses are a must and the difference in comfort, temperature-wise between being in the sunshine and the shade is pretty dramatic. Finally, when the sun sets the temperature drops like a rock, so be prepared.

Wine Country Casual at its best means classy but comfortable. There's never a problem with looking too good, just too formal.

Travel Hint: If you're going to hire a car and driver, here's a little hint. If you want to enjoy the great scenery, then ask for an SUV or Town Car type vehicle. While limousines are impressive and social, the views out the windows don't compare to the taller cars. Also, in the SUV and Town Cars you're all facing forward, looking out the windows and no one gets carsick. In the limos you're facing towards the other people. This is good if the focus of the trip is the chance to talk and share, but someone is going to be sitting backwards and someone else is going to be sitting sideways. This isn't usually a problem unless it's too hot or someone's had too much to drink, which happens now and then in Wine Country. For a couple, a Town Car is the best option, it gives you great views, you're facing forward and you can talk with your guide.

Finally, if you do rent a limo, which can be a lot of fun, here's one clothing tip for the ladies: No short skirts. Your drivers are going to insist on opening the doors for you and you should let them. This is a safety issue. Wineries are busy places, with cars and fork trucks and workers coming and going. Your guide wants to make sure that you don't get run over. It ruins their tips. Well, the only graceful way to get in or out of a limo is to sit on the seat by the door and swing your legs around. It is impossible to do this modestly in a short skirt, when someone is holding the door for you and offering you an arm. And believe me, after a few wineries the reason they're standing there is to make sure that you don't fall out of the car. After all, you're not worrying about drinking too much, because you're not driving.

Winter

Unlike many vacation areas, Wine Country sees tourists year round, even during the rainy season from December through March. After all, it doesn't rain inside the tasting rooms, and the area is actually greener during the winter than the summer. During the summer Napa looks like Tuscany, golden and glorious, and during the winter it looks like Ireland, cool, green and misty.

If you're visiting in the winter wear a light, waterproof jacket and bring an umbrella. It might be wet but it won't be too cold during the day. Even though those visiting in the winter won't get to enjoy as much of our abundant sunshine, there are still many beautiful, sparkling days and the personal attention you'll receive at the wineries more than makes up for the lost opportunity to wear shorts.

Chapter Six: What to Expect Inside the Tasting Rooms

So, what's it like inside the tasting rooms? What are they going to expect from you? It depends on the winery. We've been in tasting rooms where the bar was some boards on top of a couple of empty wine barrels. We've been in others where the counter tops are marble and the building has been featured in Architectural Digest. But no matter where you go, the tasting room staff is going to do essentially the same things for you. They're going to pour from three to five wines for you. A typical pour is one to two ounces, and you're going use the same glass throughout the tasting. That's the reason for no lipstick. The only time they'll add an extra glass is if you're doing a side-by-side comparison, for instance, tasting wines from the same vineyard or a blend, but from different years. That's called a vertical tasting. That's the stuff of wine aficionados, people with great palettes and way too much experience drinking wine. An enviable position!

Good tasting room staff will talk with you about the wines, although not all tasting room pourers are equally knowledgeable. Also, many wineries have tasting notes about each wine, and some are very detailed, others not so much; like, 'Cabernet blend, great with steak'. How much time the staff takes with you depends on how busy they are. While a winery crammed with people can be fun, if you really want to learn about the place, visit them when the traffic is low. When you're driving around you can call them and find out how busy they are. Maybe they know that a tour bus is just about to arrive and they'll suggest that you come back later. During the week it's rare to find a winery crammed to capacity, but if you arrive in a parking lot and it's hard to find a parking space, it's also going to be hard to find a place at the tasting bar, so consider visiting one of their neighbors.

At the tasting bar they'll start with the white wine, and if they have more than one, the first one they'll pour will be the lightest, usually around here that will be a Sauvignon Blanc. Although, a winery like Signorello, up on Silverado Trail in Napa pours a Sauvignon Blanc, Semillon blend, because their winemaker, Pierre Birebent is French and that's the traditional blend. Pierre is unusual in Napa in that he's both the vineyard manager and winemaker, and all of their grapes come from within walking distance from the winery. So he guides those grapes from the fields into the bottles. Another example of vineyard manager and winemaker is Geoff Gorsuch of Goosecross cellars, just up the way from Signorello, on State road just off of the Yountville Crossroad. Both are small wineries that sell most of their wines through their tasting rooms and produce wonderful, properly priced products. Both also benefit from wonderful staff in their tasting rooms.

Here's a little insight about why you'll find certain grapes planted near each other. Sauvignon Blanc is a light, white grape that can range from quite dry to very sweet, depending on when it's harvested. Over the fence you'll find Cabernet Sauvignon, the King of the reds, deep, fruity, and complex. The reason that they like the same environment is because they're part of the same family. Sauvignon Blanc, a blonde, is the momma of Cabernet Sauvignon, and another red varietal, Cabernet Franc, is the papa. The 'Sauv Blanc', as its known to its friends, is very popular with winemakers because it harvests early and is ready to drink fast. That means it doesn't compete for tank space with the later harvested grapes, and it's ready to sell much earlier, which is always a nice quality.

Many wineries only make two whites, so the second one they'll pour will be their Chardonnay. The reason that everybody makes a Chardonnay is simple. It is the most popular white wine in the world and it's a very easy vine to grow. You could probably cultivate a nice one in your back yard. It's also very forgiving in the barrel, and capable of amazing variety. The fact that it has so dominated the market has coined a term among winemakers. They'll say, 'We're making ABC wines', for 'Anything But Chardonnay'. When they bring out the Chardonnay there is something to consider, to pour or not to pour out the excess? You see, the Sauv Blanc is harvested early before the sugars can go ballistic, and then its fermented in stainless steel, and maybe they show it to an oak barrel, or maybe not. And then, as soon as it's drinkable, it's bottled and sent to the tasting room. This produces low alcohol content.

Chardonnay though, is often handled like a red wine, they push for higher sugars, maybe use extra yeast, spend more time in the barrels to add some toastiness, and might do a second malic-acid fermentation to add a warm, buttery flavor. Some of their alcohol contents will rival the big reds. That's why they have pouring buckets on the tasting bar, so you can pour out the extra wine and the extra alcohol.

There are some times when you definitely will want to pour out the wine; if you don't like it! Don't expect everything to be to your taste. If you don't think it's special, save your taste buds for the next one! Not every winery has a great winemaker or access to fantastic grapes. And, if you feel like the alcohol is starting to percolate up to your brain, drink more water and less wine. You're there to sample the wines, not get drunk. It's more fun when you can actually remember the wineries that you've visited.

Helpful Hint: Take pictures of yourself in front of the winery signs. It's the best way to remember where you were. Most people are willing to take a photo for you, and if you see a tour guide or driver (watch for the necktie), they're almost always willing to snap a photo.

***It's helpful to understand that the winery staff is fine with you pour-
ing out the extra wine.*** They're not offended by it because when they go tasting, like
most professionals, they probably spit the excess out. It's the only way that they can taste
as often as they want without ruining their livers or their driving records.

This is also why they don't mind if a couple decides to share a tasting. We think it's
romantic; you share the glass, pass it back and forth, look into each other's eyes and dis-
cuss the wine, among other things. Remember, if you come to Wine Country with your
honey, and it doesn't make you feel romantic, you're not doing it right. Slow down, take a
deep breath, look around and delight in the beautiful surroundings, and then taste some
more wine.

After the Chardonnay, they're going to pour their lighter reds, a Pinot Noir, a
Sangiovese, a Merlot, or maybe a less common grape like a Barbera. Then they're going
to move on to the Cabernet Sauvignon. These are the big guns, la raison d'etre for many
and the reason that Napa exists as a world class wine region, although Sonoma can claim
some world class examples as their own.

Like Chardonnay, Cabernet Sauvignon is the most popular premium red wine grape in the world, and like Chardonnay, Cabernet Sauvignon is very popular with growers. That's because these two grapes will out produce most other varieties two to one. So if you're a grower and you're paid by the ton, and you can sell twice as many tons by planting Chard or Cab, what are you going to plant?

Most of the Cabernets that they pour will be a blend, but they won't tell you that unless you ask. The Cab is a big flavor and to help round it out they'll normally add smaller amounts of Merlot or Cabernet Franc.

As if the Cab wasn't enough, now they'll bring out their signature wine. This is their Red Blend featuring their best grapes. While the biggest players will be Cabernet Sauvignon or Merlot, it may include significant amounts of Cab Franc, Malbec, and Petite Verdot. Those are the main red Bordeaux varietals. If they are innovators maybe they'll include some Barbera, Zinfandel (like Paraduxx) or even Sangiovese, in the Super Tuscan style.

Some of the premium wineries, like Quintessa and Opus One, only make this signature blend. This is done in the style of the great wine houses of France where they typically make just one great blend. Of course there are small wineries that do this as well, but then you can pretty much figure that you arrived there by appointment, there was no sign on the gate, and you'll taste their wine at the kitchen table, and yes, the views are spectacular. The winery up on Spring Mountain called Paloma is a good example of that. They make spectacular wines in very small amounts from ridiculously steep vineyards, so steep that they have to hold onto the trellising wires to work the vines. They sample their wines on their patio overlooking the valley floor while the hummingbirds swarm to the bird feeders hung just an arm's length away.

Here's a system, although this will vary; generally little wineries have smaller lists of wines, and bigger wineries have grander lists, where you can select a tasting; normal or reserve, all whites or all reds, dessert wines, or vertical tastings. Beringer is in that big league. Some wineries specialize in the Rhone varietals like Landmark, just up the Sonoma Valley, others specialize in the Italian grapes, like Viansa and Jacuzzi in Carneros, Seghesio in Healdsburg, Benessere in Calistoga, and Luna on the southern end of the

Silverado Trail. In Carneros and the Russian River Valley many specialize in Pinot Noir and Chardonnay, and in the Dry Creek Valley Zinfandel is King. Then from year to year the lists will change depending on what the harvest favors and what looks good to the winemaker. It's never boring.

The preferred way to hold a glass during tasting is by either the stem or the foot. There are a couple of reasons for that and they really make sense. Wines are ideally poured at a specific temperature. Champagnes are the coolest, then sweet whites, then dry whites, then light reds and finally the deep reds are the warmest. But even at their warmest the temperatures are quite cool, so the tasting rooms have coolers to keep the wines at ideal temperatures. If your hand is heating up the glass you're not going to experience the wine at its best. The exception to that are the big reds, the Cabernet blends. The flavors can be so layered that letting it sit in the glass and gradually warm and oxygenate will dramatically change the experience of the wine, often for the better. That is why it is often poured into a decanter at least half an hour before tasting.

The second reason for holding the glass in what may seem an affected way is not a taste thing at all. It is to help you enjoy the colors of the wine. This is especially important here. The colors of Sonoma and Napa's wines are remarkable because of the way the vines are handled in the field. In this region the leaves are trellised up and the grapes hang below. Why? Because this region is much farther south than comparable vineyards in Europe, so we get a lot more sunlight. The brilliant colors are caused by the grapes exposure to sunlight. Why do they trellis up? Because more sunlight means higher sugar levels and if you add the moisture that the canopy promotes, it makes the vines more prone to the two biggest dangers, mold and fungus. Brighter sunshine also makes the skins thicker, resulting in better tannins for flavor.

When you swirl the wine you'll see red, blue, violet, gold, straw and on and on. So, you want a nice clean, un-smudged glass to enjoy that. When you hold it by the stem the person pouring for you recognizes that you know a bit about wine, and they treat you accordingly. On the other hand if you're more comfortable holding it by the globe, go ahead. It's not like anyone is going to complain.

Wineries have beautiful crystal goblets, and the fancier the winery the fancier the goblet. The reason they use crystal is that it's a little bit rougher than glass. Even though you may not feel it, at a molecular level there are these sharp little bumps that tear at the surface of the wine, breaking apart the molecules and mixing them with oxygen, and in the process, releasing the flavors and aromas for you to enjoy.

That's the reason that you swirl the wine, to open up the flavors. But there's a smart way and a silly way to swirl and the difference will show whether or not your dry cleaner has a sense of humor.

The smart way is to set the glass down on the tasting bar at arms length and vigorously swirl it for a few seconds, and then lift it to your nose and very gently sniff the bouquet in a series of little inhales. The sensory inputs are at the front of the nose, so inhaling a big bunch of the bouquet does no good. It's these little samples that tell your body the story.

Swirl and sniff the bouquet a couple of times before you take a taste.
That way you give the wine a chance to mix with some oxygen and open up for your palette. The best wineries will decant their high-end, signature wine about a half an hour or more before they pour it, but when things are hopping they can barely get the cork out before they're filling glasses. So, it's up to you to let that wine breathe.

With a Cabernet Sauvignon blend, the younger the wine is the more it will benefit from decanting. The whole structure of the wine is so much tighter that the liquid's motion in the crystal, as well as the exposure to oxygen, contributes to making the flavors more accessible.

Despite what you've seen in the movies, you do not want to hold the glass in front of you while you swirl. This massively increases the chance that the wine is going to end up on your shirt, and after you've done a couple of tastings, that risk increases exponentially. It's one of the reasons that people shouldn't wear white to a tasting, think burgundy, maybe blue, or a stain-concealing pattern, and of course black is always in style, although a little hot in the summertime.

They're going to pour you enough for two good sips. With the first sip hold the wine in your mouth and let it move around your tongue. There are many different flavors in wine and the taste buds are spread all over the place so get the wine into all of the nooks and crannies. If you like the wine have the second sip; if you don't, pour it out, the day is young.

Read the tasting notes. They'll often describe the flavors, so run those words through your mind while you taste the wine and see if any set off bells. That's how professionals taste wines. For each kind of wine they'll have a list of flavors, a big list, and they run the words through their minds while they taste to see what their palettes recognize. If that concept really intrigues you, check out the winery gift shops, you'll find flavor wheels that you can use as cheat sheets.

Most tasting bars will have water pitchers handy, which are for rinsing the glasses out, but you don't have to do that unless you feel that the flavors of one wine are going to interfere with another. They pour the delicately flavored wines first and the strongly flavored wines last so that's not usually a problem. The only time that we think it's necessary to rinse the glasses is when you are sampling a very sweet, sticky wine that will cling to the glass and affect the flavor of the following, dryer (less sweet) wine.

The higher end wineries sometimes rinse out the glasses with wine, normally a dry Sauvignon Blanc. They feel that it seasons the glass, like you'd season a frying pan. That may seem a little bit extravagant, but when you're charging two hundred dollars or more for a bottle of their big red, well, you get the point.

We find that in hot weather it's helpful to bring a bottle of water into the winery with you. That allows you to flush your palette now and then, and at the same time stop yourself from becoming dehydrated, which is the biggest cause of headaches and tiredness. If you forgot to bring water, many wineries keep bottled water handy so just ask.

Very few wineries do tastings for free, although some of the smaller wineries (especially in northern Sonoma) will forget about the fee if you buy wine. Most of the fees are reasonable, although some, like Coppola's Rubicon seem high, because they necessarily include the tour, whether or not you want it. But it is a magnificent place with lots of history, a great gift shop, and paying for the day grants you access all weekend.

What a winery really likes is when you to buy wine, and if you join their Wine Club they'll be your best friend. Wine bottles really are the best souvenir. They're portable, store well, make a great gift, and later when you enjoy the wine it reminds you of the trip. Then, you can stick a candle in the bottle until you replace it with a newer bottle from your next visit. While tucking a bottle in your luggage isn't hard, if you're buying more than a few bottles, the winery will ship it for you.

Your Day in Wine Country

If you're assembling bottles from numerous wineries you'll find local shippers who are well experienced at shipping wine safely, ask at the winery for a recommendation. But shipping wine is not cheap. You're not going to save money by sending it home, but that's not the point. It's the experience of picking it up yourself at the winery and enjoying it later at home with all the memories that makes it well worth the price. We've never come back from a winery trip and thought to ourselves, "Oh, we should have bought less wine." Quite the opposite!

If you're traveling light (with one suitcase), then get a shipping box designed for bottles, most of the wineries will have them, and check it as luggage. It is a very economic way to get your wine home.

The Wine Clubs are the secret treasures of every winery. Where the tasting is their one chance to sell their wines at retail, the Wine Club is their chance to establish a loyal clientele that will hopefully buy their wines for years to come. If you like the wines, the Wine Club is really a good deal. They normally give you a twenty percent discount and reasonable shipping. Depending on the club they may ship every couple of months, or four times a year. Normally there are months when they don't send simply because they're waiting for the next vintage. They'll send you a variety of wines so this is a chance to try wines that you wouldn't necessarily taste. Some of the bigger wineries will give you the option of all whites or all reds. Also, if you're planning on coming back soon, most clubs include free tastings for you and a certain number of guests. We love wine clubs, and we've joined a number for various periods of time because we never want to run out of wine, and it gives us access to wines that are not available to the general public.

Because these are tasting rooms and not bars, tipping is not expected. Now and then, with some of the high traffic places you'll see a tip bowl on the bar, but that's very rare. On the other hand I've never seen them turn down a gift!

Some wineries are famous for their great tasting room staffs, like Imagery and Loxton in Sonoma Valley, Peju and Arger Martucci in Napa Valley, Frank Family in Calistoga, Hop Kiln in Russian River, Passalaqua in Dry Creek just to name a few of our favorites. Some of these folks are tremendously knowledgeable and they add a great deal to your experience. ***The best way to say thank you is to buy their wine.***

Chapter 7: The Easy Way to
Wine Country from San Francisco

Tasting Hint: Before you leave your hotel for Wine Country, have a good breakfast, including plenty of fat and protein, but go light on the carbohydrates and sugar. In other words, lean towards bacon and eggs with some whole-wheat toast, but stay away from the waffles covered with syrup and strawberries. It will make a big difference in **'Your Tasting Endurance'.**

If you're starting in San Francisco, Route 101, which runs through the center of the city, first as Van Ness and then as Lombard, will bring you over the Golden Gate Bridge. This is a pretty spectacular way to leave the city and you'll get great views of Alcatraz, Angel Island, the Marin Highlands and the houseboats of Sausalito on the way.

In Sausalito there is very little land and most of that's vertical, so an amazing number of houseboats have accumulated. For years the police resisted their expansion, after all they don't pay real estate taxes. Once a year they would cut everyone's mooring ropes and set the homes adrift. Most of them are built on barges so they don't have engines. But this is Sausalito, one of the great havens for iconoclastic ultra-liberals, so as soon as the police left, all of their neighbors would help them back to their berths. The police don't do that anymore. Now the houseboats are so established that you can buy one with a mortgage.

After about twenty minutes of driving through the rolling Marin hills you'll see the exit for Route 37. It only goes East from here skirting along the northern edges of San Pablo Bay, which is the northern reach of San Francisco Bay. The signs will say Sonoma, Napa, Vallejo and Sacramento. Route 37, like Route 101 is another high-speed road but there are traffic lights, and after you past the first one you'll see the first vineyards on the edges of the hills up ahead.

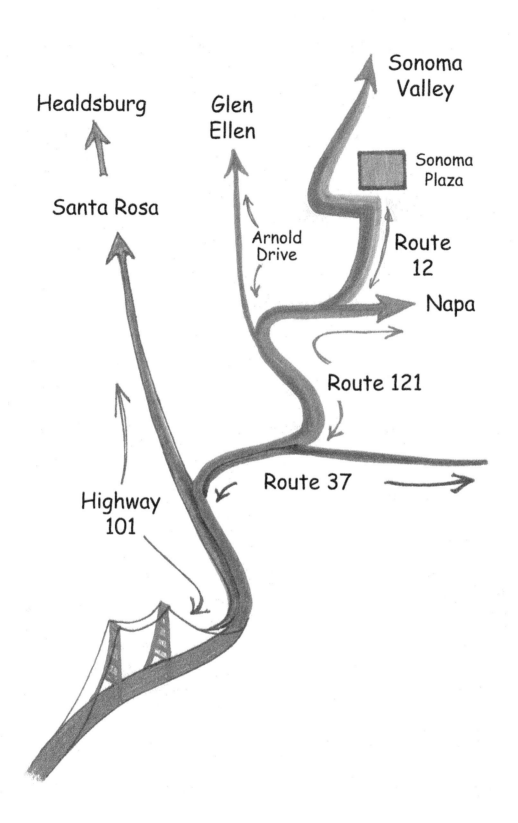

After you go over that hill you'll come to a second light and there you'll turn left onto Route 121. Look for the Racetrack sign on the left side. The intersection is very obvious with two left-turning lanes at a light. After that light the road narrows down to two lanes as it crosses the causeway that connects to the city of Vallejo across the wetlands, but that's not where you're headed. You're turning left and heading up into Carneros.

As you head North up Route 121 you'll encounter the first wineries open to the public. Plan on making a stop at one of these. After all, you just had breakfast and how many cups of coffee? Whether or not you taste wine here, this is a beautiful site for a rest stop and a stretch of the legs. These wineries are the closest to San Francisco so they are very popular, and rightfully so.

Some First Stop Options

For an old time, small winery you could visit Roche. They specialize in Carneros style Chardonnay, clean, dry, with a great structure. If you'd like a wider variety of wines there are three great choices just another mile up the road: Viansa, Cline and Jacuzzi. If you left the city without enough breakfast then stop at Viansa. Not only is this a beautiful Italian style winery with great views, they also have a deli, and plenty of snack samples. Viansa also makes a wide variety of wines so there is something for everyone. Another snack option is the Blue Tree Cafe just up the road across from Gloria Ferrer.

If you were smart and had a good breakfast, then just up the road is the Jacuzzi Winery and its older sister the Cline Family Winery. Jacuzzi, on the right side, like Viansa, specializes in Italian varietals. It is also home to the Olive Press with its wonderful gift shop. Cline, just across the street, also offers a wide variety of wines, but they include more of the French varietals as well. At Cline, early in the day you have a better chance of tasting their selections without a crush of visitors. Because they're on the southbound side of the road, late in the day, as everybody is heading back to the city, Cline often fills to capacity, which doesn't stop even more people from coming in.

If you'd like to start the day with some Sparkling Wine, then just past those wineries, on the left-hand side is Gloria Ferrer, a beautiful Spanish style winery, where you can buy a glass of a Sparkler and enjoy the beautiful view from the patio.

Let's Continue On...

Going to the Sonoma Valley

From any one of those wineries, continue North to the next light and bear right. This is still Route 121 (See map page on 41). Fairly quickly you'll see a large sign for Sonoma, Route 12 North. At the next left you can follow Route 12 North towards downtown Sonoma. This northbound section of Route 12 is part of the Camino Real, or Royal Highway from Spanish times. It will become Broadway and in several miles bring you to Sonoma's charming, historic Plaza, the largest in California. After that, following Route 12 North will bring you up the Sonoma Valley, also known as the Valley of the Moon and of course to the wineries there.

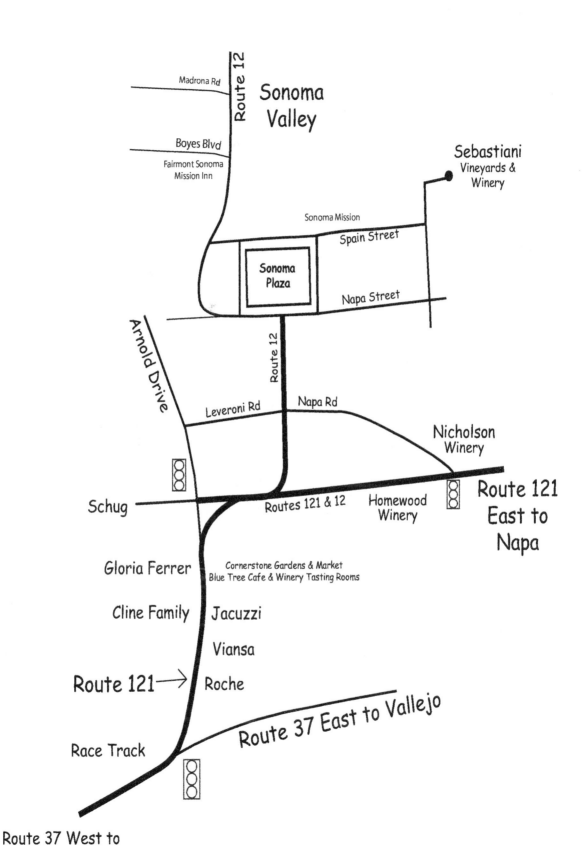

Madrona Rd

Route 12

Sonoma Valley

Boyes Blvd

Fairmont Sonoma Mission Inn

Sebastiani Vineyards & Winery

Sonoma Mission

Spain Street

Sonoma Plaza

Napa Street

Arnold Drive

Route 12

Leveroni Rd

Napa Rd

Nicholson Winery

Schug

Routes 121 & 12

Homewood Winery

Route 121 East to Napa

Gloria Ferrer

Cornerstone Gardens & Market
Blue Tree Cafe & Winery Tasting Rooms

Cline Family

Jacuzzi

Viansa

Route 121 →

Roche

Route 37 East to Vallejo

Race Track

Route 37 West to

Your Day in Wine Country

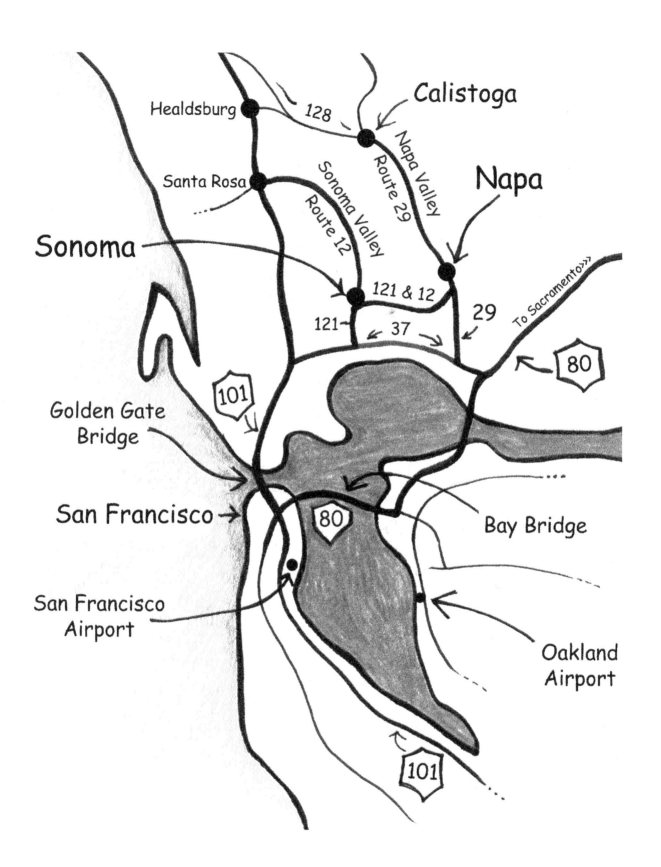

Going to the Napa Valley

If instead of turning left onto Route 12 North, you continue straight on Routes 121/12 East, that will bring you across the southern edges of the Mayacamas Mountains to Napa County. Eventually you'll come to Route 29. This is a traffic light at a T-intersection. Turning left onto Route 29 North will bring you up into the Napa Valley and the wineries there.

Using the Bay Bridge

If you're going to Napa from San Francisco, and points south, you can also cross from the city over the Bay Bridge and follow Route 80 North to Route 37 West and then to Route 29 North. This is a little bit shorter in terms of miles. But since the Bay Bridge consistently experiences the worst traffic jams in the Bay area, and since the other route through Marin and over the Golden Gate is so much more beautiful, we suggest that you go that way. If it is the weekend, and you're really in a hurry, then the Bay Bridge is a good route to return to the city. Dialing 511 gives you access to real time traffic reports.

Healdsburg from San Francisco

Because it is surrounded by three wonderful growing regions, The Russian River Valley, The Dry Creek Valley and the Alexander Valley, the little town of Healdsburg has become an epicenter for the wine world. Reaching it from the city is easy, although a fair stretch of the legs. You'll follow Route 101 North past the exit for Route 37, past the towns of Novato, Petaluma, Santa Rosa and Windsor, all the way to the exit for Downtown Healdsburg. Depending on traffic it could be one and a half to three hours. The key there is to carefully choose the time when you're starting out. During the week the rush hour traffic flows south towards the city in the morning and North towards Santa Rosa in the afternoon. On the weekends, especially during the summer, there is a small rush hour leaving the city in the morning and quite a bit of traffic heading south to the city at the end of the day. Traffic can back up approaching the Golden Gate Bridge.

From downtown Sonoma you can reach Healdsburg by following Route 12 North through Santa Rosa to Route 101 North.

From the Napa Valley the easiest route to Healdsburg is to go North on Route 29 to Calistoga, then go straight on Route 128 for a short distance, and then turn left on Petrified Forest Road. Follow that to the turnoff for Mark West (a right-hand turn) and that will lead you to an entrance for Route 101 North just above Santa Rosa. Alternately, you can stay on Route 128 North through Knight's Valley and Alexander Valley. At Alexander Valley Road you'll turn left to Healdsburg Avenue. There you'll turn left and in a few miles it will bring you to the middle of Healdsburg. This second route is a beautiful, winding road that is a lot of fun during the daytime and not so much at night. See the chapter on Touring Northern Sonoma for more details and maps.

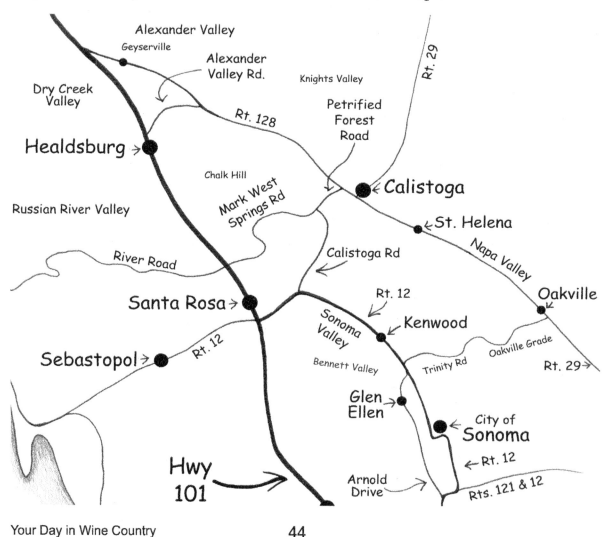

Chapter Eight: Touring the Sonoma Valley

A Sample Tour: This is based on the idea that you stopped for a tasting at one of the Carneros wineries. So, at the point where this tour is commencing you probably have one wine tasting under your belt.

If you're visiting Sonoma's Valley of the Moon, you'll follow Route 12 North to the Sonoma Plaza (See map on page 41). When you get to the Plaza, Route 12 turns left for a few blocks before turning right and heading up valley. It's clearly marked. Before you go up valley you might want to stop and take a walk around the Plaza. This is where the Bear Flag rebellion took place when California first established its independence from Mexico. After 25 days as an independent Republic, California became part of the United States of America. Besides some great history, it is also the site of some wonderful restaurants and shops, as well as a place to pick up picnic supplies.

The Sonoma Cheese Shop, on the North side of the Plaza, is a feast of picnicking supplies and cheese samples (See map on page 18). The Basque Boulangerie Café makes great sandwiches and salads and is a favorite bakery. The Sunflower Café is located in an historic adobe and their enclosed patio is a delight on a hot day. There are picnic tables right on the plaza, or you can wait until the next winery, which is just up the road. If you want something a bit different, then follow Route 12 for a few blocks past the Plaza and stop in at Fiorini's Italian Pastry Shop (See map on page 18). They also have a nice selection of sandwiches ready to go. Now, get back on Route 12 and head up into the Valley of the Moon. That's supposedly what Sonoma means in the local Indian language, the "Valley of the Seven Moons", and to call it a scenic drive is to damn it with faint praise. It's a gorgeous ride and it is home to some world-class, yet remarkably friendly wineries.

As you head North you're going to see a pretty place on the left side surrounded by olive trees and vines, the B.R. Cohn Winery. You can stop here and enjoy their wonderful wines and gift shop, or less than a mile farther, on the right side, after a rising curve you'll see the signs for Imagery. Watch for the banners. There's actually a second winery that shares this driveway, Arrowood. That's also a charming place and they make some

excellent reds, but Imagery is unique for a number of reasons, and for the sake of everyone's appetites, they also have picnic tables (See map on page 48).

There's a funny story about Imagery, which was started by the Benziger family, who has a spectacular Biodynamic winery and vineyard just up the road in Glen Ellen. Well, one of the secrets of winemakers is that many of them love beer. Some of them actually drink beer while they're blending their wine, claiming it clears the pallet. Since the Benzigers are originally from Switzerland, by way of Long Island, a love of beer is to be expected and so they decided to open a micro brewery, which they did on that site, installing a large, imported copper brewing vessel that stood two stories tall.

The one thing they didn't count on was that people come to Wine Country to drink wine, not beer, so when that sunk in they converted Imagery to a winery and tasting room, offering their small lot wines, often times those in which they only make three to five hundred cases. When you consider that some of their neighbors up valley make 200,000 cases of a single label, you can see that this is special.

But why do they call it Imagery? A little over twenty years ago Joe Benziger, the winemaker, was at a polo match talking with artist and critic Ted Nugent. They came up with the idea of commissioning artwork for each new vintage of each varietal. Now, twenty years later, they have the world's largest collection of art specifically created for wine labels, and large sections of the collection are displayed in their winery gallery. The only time that the artwork is used more than once is for the single vineyard designated wines. They'll have a portrait done of the vineyard, and use that every time they make wine solely from there, such as their Sunny Slope vineyard just behind the winery. But Imagery pulls grapes from all over both Sonoma and Mendocino counties and the Imagery wines are only available at the winery. They specialize in bringing lesser-known grape varietals to their clients. The staff will often recommend the Benziger Winery, which is just a short distance away in Glen Ellen, and that's a good recommendation. Their tour has been voted the best in the county again and again.

After the tasting take some time for lunch. If you have a good-sized party, buy a chilled bottle of wine from them and borrow some glasses from the tasting room. In the smaller wineries they're pretty good about that. Just make sure that you return the glasses.

After Imagery, continue heading North up the Valley of the Moon, drinking a bottle of water as you go. You're going to pass through the town of Kenwood, and see several wineries, Kunde, Kenwood, and Blackstone, as well as a number of smaller tasting rooms. Just across the street from Blackstone you'll see the signs for Chateau St. Jean on the right-hand side. This was the only winery to ever have four wines on Wine Spectator's top one hundred list at the same time. It's now owned by Beringer Blass, which in turn is owned by Fosters, but they still make great wines and they understand hospitality. They have beautiful gardens, a great gift shop and two tasting rooms. As you walk through the gardens to the end of the pathway, the more modern tasting room is to your right. That's where they pour their larger list of wines, and that also houses the deli, the wonderful gift shop and rest rooms. To the left is the mansion. This was built many years ago by a wealthy couple from Michigan so they could escape the winters.

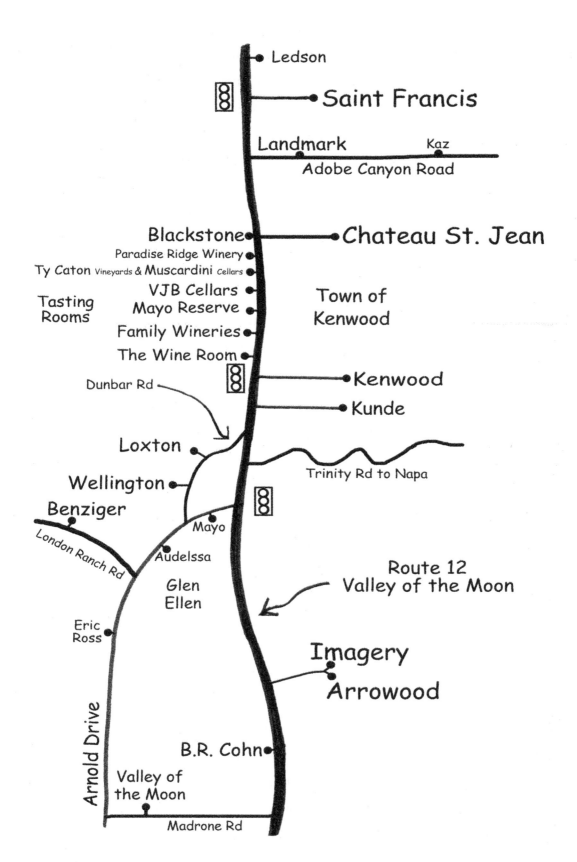

Ledson

Saint Francis

Landmark · Kaz
Adobe Canyon Road

Blackstone · Chateau St. Jean
Paradise Ridge Winery
Ty Caton Vineyards & Muscardini Cellars
VJB Cellars   Town of
Mayo Reserve   Kenwood
Tasting
Rooms
Family Wineries
The Wine Room

Dunbar Rd   · Kenwood

· Kunde

Loxton

Trinity Rd to Napa

Wellington

Benziger
London Ranch Rd   Mayo

Audelssa

Glen
Ellen   Route 12
                    Valley of the Moon

Eric
Ross

Imagery

Arrowood

Arnold Drive

B.R. Cohn

Valley of
the Moon

Madrone Rd

That's where you find the reserve tasting room, and if you like fine wines, the reserve tasting is worth paying for. Considering the quality of the wines it's quite reasonable. In the warmer weather they often do the reserve tasting sitting down, outside on the patio. We suggest that you call up and make an appointment for that. It's a very pleasant experience.

At this point you have to decide if you've had enough wine to drink. Of course, if you have someone driving for you who's not drinking, hey, take advantage of the situation. If you decide that you've had enough then head South again. If the traffic is light, this is easy. Even though these are just two lane roads, in front of every winery and major turn there is a center lane specifically for that purpose. So, you can turn left into this center lane and then merge into the southbound lane, and people are pretty nice about letting you in. If the traffic is heavy, or you're ready for another winery, then turn right out of St. Jean's driveway and head North, drinking a bottle of water as you go. In a mile and a half you'll come to an intersection with a light. You can either use this to turn around, or you can turn right and pull into the St. Francis winery. This is a mission-style building and a delightful tasting room, with beautiful views to the south over the vineyards towards Sugar Loaf Mountain. You can see their winery up the hill from the tasting room. They do a nice selection of wines priced from quite reasonable to very high end and the staff is always friendly.

St. Francis is at the northernmost edge of this particular tour, so whether you're tasting or just turning around here, we have one more winery for you to check out, that's quite different from anything else that we've visited.

As you head back south, drinking a bottle of water as you go, you'll pass through the little town of Kenwood again. Just after that you'll pass the Kunde Winery on the left-hand side. The winery is housed in a building modeled after the Georgian-style cow barn that sat on the site for many years. Kunde is another wonderful winery, but that's not the one we're looking for today. Just after passing Kunde start looking for the next

big road on the right side, Dunbar. It cuts off to the right on an easy angle. You're going to turn right there and very quickly you're going to see the quite small signs for the Loxton Winery, again on the right-hand side.

This is a small, hand-made winery where you walk past the pressing equipment to get in the door, and you can smell the oak of the barrels over your shoulder while you're tasting their excellent wines. There's a good chance that Chris Loxton, the winemaker, will be pouring for you, or at least he'll be close at hand. If it's during harvest he'll be every where. The wines are extraordinarily good, and a good deal, so it's common to see people carrying cases out of there.

By the way, don't be surprised by the Australian decorations. Chris hails from down under, and in fact his family has grown grapes there for three generations.

From there you go back onto Route 12 and head South, back towards downtown Sonoma, drinking a bottle of water as you go. Since you've now been to at least four wineries, and maybe five, you should get something to eat. This is an especially good idea if you're touring during the week, and your hotel is in San Francisco, because the Bay area has raised rush hour traffic to a high art form. Even though you'll supposedly be going in the opposite direction of the rush, the cross-county traffic is considerable. Sometimes the best solution is to stop for a light dinner, and head back after the rush is over, which is about six-thirty or seven o'clock. Then you'll have clear sailing.

As you leave Chris Loxton's you have two great dining opportunities. As you head South on Route 12 you'll quickly come to a traffic light. Turning right there onto Arnold Drive will bring you into the charming town of Glen Ellen. There are a number of nice restaurants there including the Fig Café and Wolf House, the latter being named that because the author Jack London had his ranch just up the hill from here. If you decide to eat in Glen Ellen you don't need to double back after your meal, just continue South on Arnold Drive, at the T intersection with the light bear left and this will bring you back to the intersection just North of Viansa, and from there go straight (South) to Route 37. However, Arnold is smaller and slower, so you might want to backtrack to Route 12 and follow that South. Arnold Drive is a good alternate route to know to get around the traffic that can build up going through the town of Sonoma.

You can also go to downtown Sonoma for dinner, by just continuing South on Route 12. When you get to the Plaza, go to the far side and turn left on First Street East. Then find a place to park. We have a wonderful variety of restaurants, including the Girl and the Fig for California French, Maya's for high brow Spanish, The Plaza Bistro for California cuisine, not to mention Taste of the Himalayan's, The Swiss Hotel, as well as informal places like Mary's Pizza Shack, Murphy's Pub and The Red Grape. If it's a weekend night make reservations. People in this area love to eat out (List on page 110).

Then after dinner, just head South on Route 12, also known here as Broadway, which is the large street at the base of the Plaza, in front of the town hall. Then stay on Route 12 all the way out of town to Route 121, where you're going to turn right and go to the light, where you're going to turn left and that will bring you to Route 37. But it is easier and quicker than it sounds because all the signs will point you towards San Francisco (See map on page 39).

Touring Northern Sonoma:
The Three Valleys Around Healdsburg

The area around Healdsburg is a wine lover's delight. It is the junction of three wine growing valleys that are distinctly different in their qualities and so they favor different grapes. The Russian River Valley favors Chardonnay, Pinot Noir and Syrah. The Dry Creek Valley is famous for Zinfandel and also grows some very interesting Cabernet Sauvignon. Alexander Valley is renowned for its Cabernet and Merlot.

Each of these areas is just a fifteen-minute ride from the Healdsburg Plaza, a charming place filled with great restaurants, hotels and shopping. It is also home to the area's best collection of tasting rooms, all within strolling distance from each other. While many of the wineries in the area close early, 4:00 to 4:30 PM, the tasting rooms in town stay open to 6:00 or 7:00 PM. It makes for a festive place late in the day.

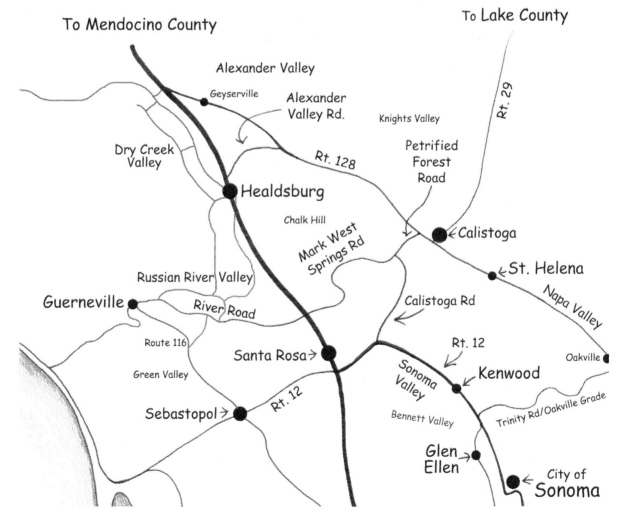

To Mendocino County

To Lake County

Alexander Valley

Geyserville

Alexander Valley Rd.

Knights Valley

Rt. 29

Dry Creek Valley

Rt. 128

Petrified Forest Road

Healdsburg

Calistoga

Chalk Hill

St. Helena

Mark West Springs Rd

Napa Valley

Russian River Valley

Calistoga Rd

Guerneville

River Road

Rt. 12

Oakville

Route 116

Santa Rosa →

Sonoma Valley

Kenwood

Green Valley

Rt. 12

Bennett Valley

Trinity Rd/Oakville Grade

Sebastopol →

Glen Ellen →

City of Sonoma

If you're day tripping from either San Francisco or southern Sonoma, you can reach Healdsburg by taking Route 101 North to the downtown Healdsburg exit. Alternately, from Sonoma, you can also follow Route 12 North through the Valley of the Moon to Santa Rosa where it meets Route 101 and continue North from there. If you're visiting from Napa, the most interesting route is to follow Route 29 North to Route 128 North (at Calistoga) and follow that up through Knights Valley and Alexander Valley. When Route 128 becomes Alexander Valley Road you'll see signs that will take you to Healdsburg, while Route 128 continues North through Geyserville (See map page 59).

It is about one and a half hours from San Francisco to Healdsburg, if you leave in the morning when the traffic is moving in your favor. It's about one hour from both downtown Sonoma and downtown Napa. The first Russian River Valley wineries are about twenty miles South of Healdsburg so the impatient can head northwest from Santa Rosa to start their tour.

Each of the valleys could consume an entire day of wine tasting, so if you have a preference for a particular type of wine, stay in one area. However, if you're coming to the area for the first time you could do a survey of the three areas in the course of a long day. This works best if you have a professional driver.

Note: While the Russian River Valley has a number of towns where you can find some nice places to eat, the other two are so agricultural that most of the convenient restaurants are found in Healdsburg. There are, however, plenty of picnic areas and nice area markets to pack your picnic basket. Here are three basic tours, one for each area. However, you can combine the route together to make one, extended tour.

Russian River Valley

Let's start from Route 101 North heading towards Santa Rosa. Exit at Route 12 West and head towards Sebastopol. At the center of town, head North on Route 116 towards Guerneville. As you wind through town you'll see a Whole Foods Market, so if you're planning on having a picnic this is one good place to pick up supplies.

About seven miles outside of town you'll see Ross Station Road on the left-hand side. Look for the small winery sign on a post pointing towards Iron Horse Winery.

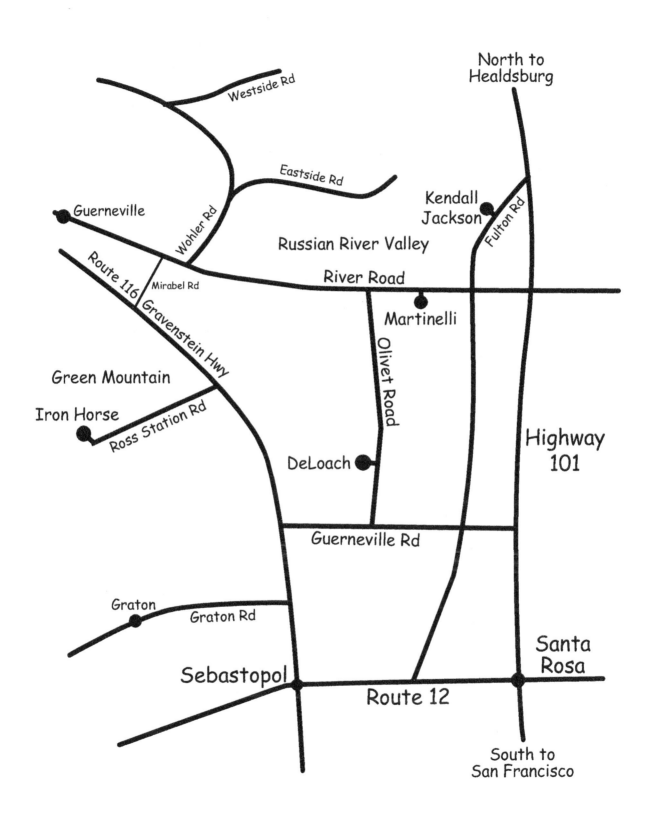

Follow Ross Station Rd. to the end and it will lead up the hill to beautiful views and delicious wines, both sparkling and still. This is the Green Mountain section of the Russian River Valley and Iron Horse is almost the only winery there. The tasting is conducted outside under an overhang and it is a delightful experience.

Now head back to Route 116 and turn right towards Sebastopol. Quite quickly you'll turn left on Guerneville Rd. In just over four miles you'll turn left on Olivet Rd. Look for the DeLoach Vineyards a short distance up on the left-hand side. This is a charming winery with great Chardonnay and Pinot Noir grown and made with Biodynamic methods. They also have a very nice courtyard in front of the building and a couple of picnic tables.

From here, continue up Olivet to River Rd. Turn right there and quite quickly again you'll see the Martinelli Winery. This family has been growing grapes for many, many years and quite recently, with the arrival of a new winemaker, their reputation has soared. They have a cute gift shop with lots of snacks, a very informal tasting room with a very knowledgeable staff and it's so convenient.

Even though three tasting rooms are enough for many tours you might want to fit one more in. Turn right out of the Martinelli parking lot towards Route 101 (about four miles away), and when you come to the light at Fulton Rd. turn left. In just over a mile you'll come to the entrance for Kendall Jackson on the left-hand side just before the overpass. Pay attention because it is not an impressive entranceway, especially compared to the building, which is beautiful and dramatic. The Kendall Jackson Winery always gets high marks from guests for their tours, grounds, building, staff and, of course, for their wines.

By itself this is a nice introductory tour of the Russian River Valley, and from Kendall Jackson, the entrance to Route 101 South off of River Rd. is very accessible. However, you could also take Route 101 North. In about twelve miles, or twelve minutes, you will find yourself in Healdsburg.

Dry Creek Valley

To visit the Dry Creek Valley go past the 'Healdsburg Avenue' and the 'Downtown Healdsburg' exits to the 'Dry Creek Road' exit. After the exit turn left. In about three miles you'll come to a stop sign with the Dry Creek Store on the right-hand side. That is the place to pick up sandwiches for a picnic. Turn left at that stop sign onto Lambert Bridge Road and in about half a mile you'll see the best place to picnic, and of course taste some wonderful wines, the Passalacqua Winery. This is a small production winery with beautiful grounds, a friendly staff and it sits right in the middle of Dry Creek Valley.

After Passalacqua turn right out of their parking lot and go over the Lambert Bridge. At the next stop sign turn left onto West Dry Creek Road. In just under two winding miles you'll see the Lambert Bridge Winery on the right-hand side. If you didn't picnic yet, this is another great place for that, with gorgeous grounds, a great staff and wines that compare with the best of Napa (See map page 59).

Now backtrack up West Dry Creek Road, back across the Lambert Bridge to Dry Creek Road. At the stop sign turn left and head up valley. In about eight miles you'll see the Ferrari-Carano Winery on the left-hand side. This is the 'Crown Jewel' of Dry Creek Valley; beautiful gardens, spectacular buildings, nice gift shop and great wines. There are two tasting rooms. The one upstairs overlooks the gardens and vineyards. Downstairs, next to the famous wine caves, is the Enoteca where they serve their small lot wines.

Now from here, turn right out of their driveway and head back down Dry Creek Road. If you want to go very informal, about five miles down the road, on the left-hand side you'll see signs for groups of wineries including Amphora and Papapietro. You'll go up this driveway and it will bring you to an older industrial park/wood yard where a bunch of local wineries have set up shop in older buildings. There is not a vine in sight, but they offer some wonderful wines. Amphora offers some remarkable wines together with some beautiful ceramics made by the owner/winemaker. Papapietro is well known for their wonderful Zinfandel.

Following Dry Creek Road South from there will bring you to the entrance to Route 101 South. Or, you can go a couple of more blocks to Healdsburg Avenue. Turning right there will bring you to the middle of town.

Alexander Valley

The Dry Creek Valley and the Alexander Valley are parallel to each other and it is remarkable, considering how close they are, that their environments are so different. As we mentioned before, the Alexander Valley can be easily reached from either Route 101 or from Napa on Route 128. To reach the center of the valley from downtown Healdsburg head North on Healdsburg Avenue to Alexander Valley Road where you'll turn right. In about three and a half miles you'll come to a stop sign. If you turn left onto Geyserville Road, Route 128 North, that road will bring you to two very interesting wineries, Stryker Sonoma (known for its award winning architecture) and Murphy Goode (known for its great wines and friendly staff). Just make sure you stay on Route 128 since it jigs and jags a bit. If instead, at the stop sign you go straight and then bear to the right and follow Route 128 South you come to Sausal on the left (a charming, small, family run winery with a great picnic area), White Oak Vineyards and Winery on the right (a very Californian building with authentic Alexander Valley wines), and further on, Hanna Winery up on a hill on the left (who pulls their grapes from various areas and produces a spectacular Cabernet Sauvignon). All of these wineries are relatively small, with beautiful locations and good wines.

The Alexander Valley shares some characteristics with the Napa Valley; a long valley, running Northwest to Southeast, far enough from the ocean influence to produce the hot, steady, low humidity days that the Bordeaux grapes like. Also, where Napa has the fogs off the bay to provide some night time coolness and humidity, Alexander Valley has the Russian River which tracks along its floor, bringing cold water down from the mountains of Mendocino.

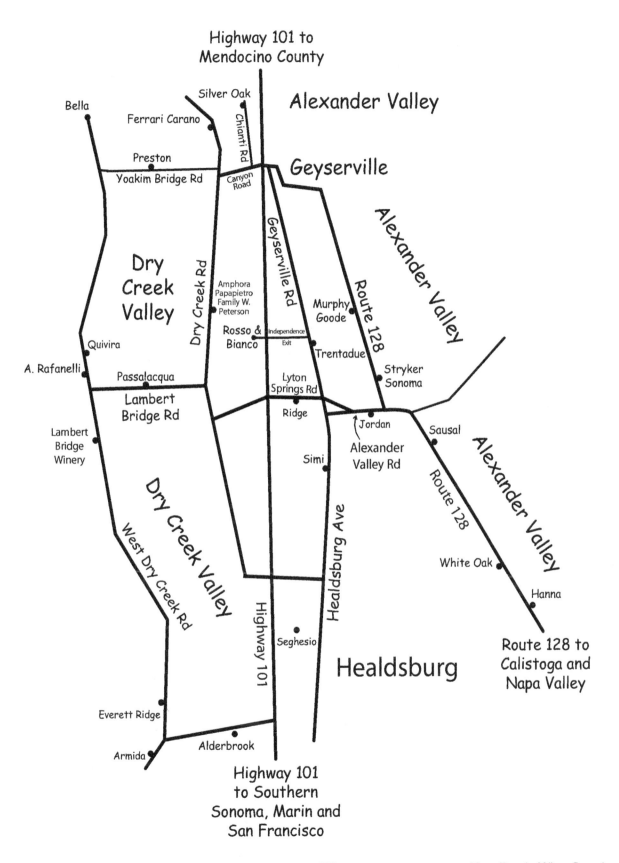

Two of the stars of Alexander Valley are Silver Oak and Jordan. The big Cabernet producer, Silver Oak of Napa has a second facility at the top of the Alexander Valley, only a few miles from Ferrari-Carano. If you would like to tie those together in a tour it is easy to do. When you leave Ferrari-Carano head South on Dry Creek Road, and in about three miles turn left onto Canyon Road. Take that for two miles to Chianti Road (just before the entrance to Route 101) and turn left. Follow that for about three miles and just before the road's end is Silver Oak on the left-hand side. Its remote location keeps it from being overwhelmed with visitors (See map on page 59).

The other star, Jordan Vineyard and Winery, is by appointment only, but it is worth the effort to plan ahead. They offer a tour and tasting that is delightful, and if you mistake the place for a chateau in France, you would not be the first person to do so. Like Silver Oak they make big reds, although while Silver Oak is the quintessential American winery, Jordan has a definite European style. Jordan is on Alexander Valley Road about a mile and a half from where it intersects Healdsburg Avenue. When you are coming from town, the driveway is on the right side of the road and while it is a wide entrance it has only a little sign, so take your time.

There are so many great wineries in these three areas that Healdsburg has become an important center for wine tourism. These three little tours just scratch the surface. When being driven by a professional guide, it is easy to visit all three valleys in the course of a day. If you were driving yourself, it would be difficult because increasing levels of wine-induced euphoria would make finding and navigating some of these little winding roads and driveways impossible.

Chapter Nine: Touring Napa Valley

Of course there's no way to talk about Wine Country tours without talking about Napa. We talked about Sonoma first because it is closer to the Golden Gate, but Napa county contains an amazing diversity of climates and soils and they've reached the point where all the land that is really suitable for vineyards is planted in vineyards. The rest of the county, other than houses, stores, hotels and restaurants is covered with trees, mostly oak, eucalyptus and redwoods. These trees do influence the flavors of the wine, and some of the most famous Oakville vineyards owe their spiciness to the large stands of eucalyptus trees nearby. Napa is America's most famous wine region and that's reflected in the number of wineries found there and the prices that they command for their wines.

The valley is thirty miles long by five miles wide, so you can travel the length and breadth of it in a day, but since many wineries are close together you could spend the entire day within a five-mile radius.

From Route 37 East you're going to follow Route 121/12 East to Route 29, where you have to turn left or right (See maps page 42). Turning left will bring you North up the Napa Valley, and that's where you want to go. You are going to pass the city of Napa, not really that obvious beyond the highway barriers. In a few miles and after a few traffic lights you'll be back out into the country. South of Oakville there are only a few wineries directly on the right side of the road. However, there are some very good wineries that are accessible on the side roads: Trefethen, Andretti, Laird, Havens, Noah, Bell, Jessup and, of course, Domaine Chandon.

For the sake of this tour though we're going to ask you to be patient, because just past the Oakville Grocery there are a profusion of world-class wineries on the right side of the road right in a row: *Opus One, Nickel and Nickel, Sequoia Grove, Turnbull, Cakebread, Sawyer, St. Supery and Peju.* These are all great wineries. Both Nickel and Nickel and Cakebread are by appointment only (it is not hard to get one unless it's last minute in the high season), but the others welcome visitors all day, seven days a week.

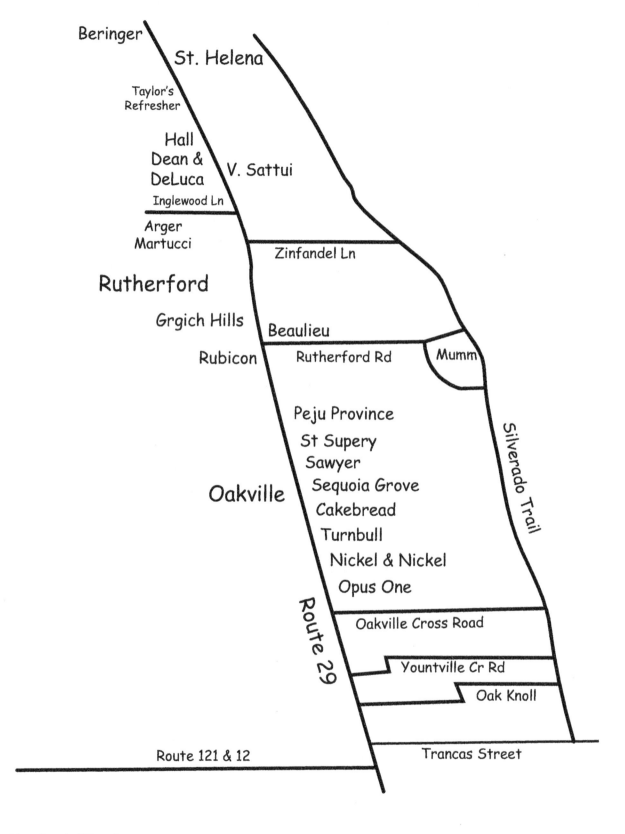

Beringer

St. Helena

Taylor's
Refresher

Hall
Dean &
DeLuca

V. Sattui

Inglewood Ln

Arger
Martucci

Zinfandel Ln

Rutherford

Grgich Hills

Beaulieu

Rubicon

Rutherford Rd

Mumm

Peju Province

St Supery

Sawyer

Sequoia Grove

Oakville

Cakebread

Turnbull

Nickel & Nickel

Opus One

Silverado Trail

Route 29

Oakville Cross Road

Yountville Cr Rd

Oak Knoll

Route 121 & 12

Trancas Street

For this tour, if you're not going to make an appointment, start off at Peju, one of the jewels of the Napa Valley, a good wine selection, beautiful gardens and buildings, original art and an entertaining and knowledgeable staff. Also, you're smart to visit them early, because they are so popular that in the afternoon it is not unusual to have to wait quite a while for a tasting slot (and unlike their neighbors they are open to six o'clock PM). They bring in their guests as groups, so that they'll receive a complete presentation. They do wine tasting as entertainment better than anybody.

Another option is to go North a short distance to Beaulieu Vineyards, known as BV. This is one of the grand old wineries that still produces a great product. They are just past Rutherford Road on the right side. They have two tasting rooms. To the right is the regular and to the left is the reserve. Both are good experiences, but for the wine aficionado, visit the reserve room with its marble tabletops and world-class vintages. Of course the tasting is more expensive, but you should share them. After all, the day is young and these are some heavy-duty reds. We're talking the BIG REDS that Rutherford and Oakville are famous for.

If you visit both of these wineries you'll need to get a bite to eat and here your choices depend on the season. If it's warm enough to eat outside then your best choices are all included in a small circle including: The winery/deli/picnic grounds of V. Sattui. They are very busy during the high season (a great deli), but even then, if you time it right this is a very convenient stop for food and wine.

Note: You cannot bring food or wine to V. Sattui. And, you cannot bring outside wine to drink on the grounds of any other winery as well due to Napa county regulations.

Right across the way from V. Sattui is Dean and DeLuca. It has a wonderful selection of picnic items and sandwiches. In fact, the market and wine shop is a gourmet's delight and is worth the visit by itself. There is a small outside 'wall' with an accompanying fountain where you can sit and enjoy your bite. You can also bring your food to a winery that permits picnicking. The best and most convenient locations for that are the Hall Winery and Arger Martucci.

They are family wineries with nice picnic areas and only a couple of minutes away. The Hall Winery is actually just next door to Dean & DeLuca and you can walk across the parking lot to reach it. They do a nice tasting that is not too heavy-handed. To reach Arger Martucci turn right out of the Dean & DeLuca parking lot and take the first right (it comes up immediately) on Inglewood. You'll see them on the left-hand side about three hundred yards down the road. This is a very small winery with excellent wines and a great staff. Another lunch option is to go North another mile to Taylor's Refresher. This is a well-known burger joint drive-in Napa Style with picnic tables all around. You may wait in line a while to order and pickup your food but it's worth the wait. Right across the street is the delightful and air conditioned Pizzaria Tra Vigne.

If the weather is too cool for picnic tables then continue North into St. Helena where you'll find a variety of restaurants both plain and fancy, but all good. After lunch, head North through downtown St. Helena. Within a half mile of the downtown you'll see the entrance to Beringer on the left side. Pay attention because it is an old entrance that was probably designed for grape wagons; tall stone gates, not very wide. Watch for

the blue and white historic marker sign on the right-hand side about 300 feet before the entrance. This is a good place to do the tour since they've been in continuous production since 1876. Besides, a tour will give you a chance to walk off some of that wine and food. They have two tasting areas; one is at the back of the property, above the parking lot, in the old winery. The other is the reserve tasting room that is located in the Rhine style mansion at the front of the property. The Beringer brothers constructed this as the replica of the house where they grew up in Germany. It is a beautiful building and it also houses a great gift shop (as does the other tasting room).

Now let's continue with our tour. Turn right as you come out of the Beringer driveway and head South back through St. Helena's downtown. At any time when you think that you've done enough tasting, feel free to just follow Route 29 South to home base. But, if you're still up for more wineries (you've clearly been temperate in your drinking or have a designated driver), there are a lot more to enjoy. All of those possibilities will be on the right-hand side as you go southbound.

If you didn't visit them picnic in hand, both Hall and Arger & Martucci are excellent choices, good wine and good people. Hall also has a great collection of sculpture. A little farther along is Whitehall Lane, this is easy to spot and both the staff and the wines are fun. Another option is a bit farther along and quite famous among wine aficionados, Grgich Hills Estate. Mike Grgich, originally from Croatia, is one of the grand old wine makers of the Napa Valley, and his relaxed style, slightly rustic, but roomy tasting room/barrel room is home to some very good Biodynamic wines.

If you still have some room for a tasting, or you're simply interested in a great tour, the next winery south from Grgich Hills, on the same side of the road is Rubicon, owned by Francis Ford Coppola, the moviemaker. It is an historic winery built originally by Captain Niebaum, a whaling captain who retired from the sea to the Wine Country of Napa in the late 1800's. It has changed hands many times over the years, but when 'Francis' purchased it he renovated it into a major tourist attraction. Besides some beautiful tasting rooms, it has one of the most elegant gift shops in Napa. Unfortunately, such success meant that they were swamped with business, so he changed the name from Niebaum Coppola to Rubicon, after his first wine, and upped the price per person to twenty-five dollars. That includes the tasting fees, the tour and access to the museum

that covers not only filmmaking but the family history, including some of his Oscars. It's not a cheap date, but it is elegant, gracious and a lot of fun, so well worth the price.

From here, if you want to stop for dinner you have a wealth of choices. Just about all of these would be a lot more convenient with a reservation. Just South, on the right side of Route 29 there is a pair of great restaurants with long, wonderful reputations, Mustards Grill and Brix. If you turn left at the traffic light, and then right onto Washington, that will take you down the main street of the food capitol of Wine Country, Yountville. The Napa Valley Grill, Bouchon, Hurley's, Bistro Jeanty, Ad Hoc, Redd, and of course The French Laundry (for which reservations made eight weeks previously are expected) line this street (See map on page 69). There is plenty of satisfaction to be found there. If you would like some more variety, then head farther south to the city of Napa, take the First Street Exit, bear left and follow it to the middle of town where you'll find a nice selection of restaurants for all price ranges. After dinner, when the traffic has calmed down, you can have a nice ride back to your hotel (See restaurant list page 134).

Your Day in Wine Country

Another Napa Tour

Because Napa is such a small county, half the size of Sonoma, many of its wineries are close together, and very accessible to visitors from San Francisco. Napa is also internationally famous so it attracts a lot of visitors. Based on popularity let's take another sample tour of the Valley that combines big wineries and little wineries, the famous and the local favorites.

Coming up from San Francisco you can pass up the group of wineries just North of the Route 37, Route 121 intersection (and the Racetrack) and continue on towards Napa, by turning right at that light just North of those first wineries. Instead of bearing left towards downtown Sonoma you'll continue straight on Route 121 through the rolling hills of Carneros.

A note about Carneros: This is the only part of either county where grape vines are planted carpet-like over the rolling hills. The term Carneros means 'sheep' or 'ram', because this was the area where the Spanish grazed their sheep. The Carneros winds that come in off the bay keep this area cool, encouraging a nice thick, woolly coat. Those winds are an important factor in creating the terroir of the region, producing grapes with good acidity and great structure. Carneros wines are always good food wines, since they cleanse the pallet. The area is planted in Chardonnay and Pinot Noir close to the bay, with some additional Syrah and Merlot in the foothills above.

At the next traffic light you'll see the Nicholson Ranch on the left-hand side. This is a small, family owned winery that sits on top of their caves. But continue straight to Napa. After that light, as you pass over the next hill, you're in Napa County and pretty soon you'll see Domaine Carneros on the right-hand side. This is owned by Taittinger Champagne from France, and the building is modeled on the family's ancestral home. At this point you're basically in Europe because French or Spanish Sparkling Wine producers own the vineyards on both sides of the road. If you'd like to add a sparkle to your day then stop at Domaine Carneros. Since it's early and there's a lot of wine to taste, we suggest that a couple share a flight rather than get one for each person. They'll bring you three small champagne flutes and a single flight amounts to quite a bit of wine. They are very elegant wines, but don't overdo it.

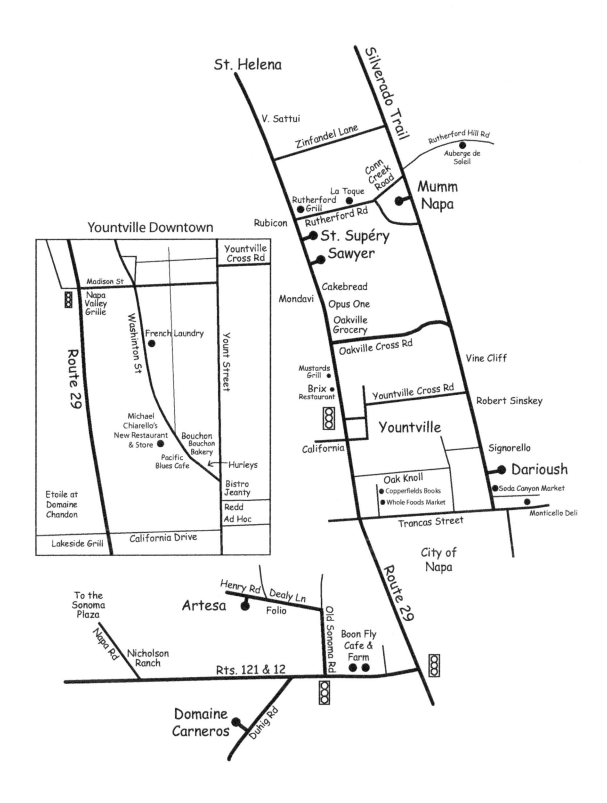

St. Helena

Silverado Trail

V. Sattui

Zinfandel Lane

Rutherford Hill Rd

Auberge de Soleil

Conn Creek Road

La Toque

Rutherford Grill

Mumm Napa

Rubicon

Rutherford Rd

St. Supéry

Sawyer

Cakebread

Mondavi

Opus One

Oakville Grocery

Oakville Cross Rd

Vine Cliff

Mustards Grill

Brix Restaurant

Yountville Cross Rd

Robert Sinskey

Yountville

California

Signorello

Oak Knoll

Darioush

Copperfields Books

Soda Canyon Market

Whole Foods Market

Monticello Deli

Trancas Street

City of Napa

Route 29

Yountville Downtown

Yountville Cross Rd

Madison St

Napa Valley Grille

Washinton St

French Laundry

Yount Street

Route 29

Michael Chiarello's New Restaurant & Store

Bouchon
Bouchon Bakery

Pacific Blues Cafe

Hurleys

Bistro Jeanty

Etoile at Domaine Chandon

Redd
Ad Hoc

Lakeside Grill

California Drive

To the Sonoma Plaza

Henry Rd

Dealy Ln

Artesa

Folio

Old Sonoma Rd

Boon Fly Cafe & Farm

Napa Rd

Nicholson Ranch

Rts. 121 & 12

Route 29

Domaine Carneros

Duhig Rd

Get back on the road and just past Domaine Carneros is a traffic light, and there you're going to turn left onto Old Sonoma Road. Then, in about a quarter of a mile you'll take the first left onto Dealy Rd. Just before the turn you'll see some small blue signs on the right side of the road pointing left towards the wineries. In most cases, in Napa, those small blue signs are the only helpful warning you'll get about a winery's location until you get to their driveway. Follow Dealy and at the next intersection bear left onto Henry Rd. It will seem like you're just going straight. This will bring you to two marvelous wineries. First you'll see the Folio Winemaker's Studio on the left side, owned by Michael Mondavi and featuring wines from several wineries, but keep going and you'll come to the entrance for Artesa.

Artesa sits on top of a hill and has the best views in Carneros. It was built by Codorniu of Spain. They took the top of the hill off and then constructed the caves and winery, finishing by putting the top of the hill back on again.

As a result it looks kind of like a bunker from the outside, but as you climb up the stairs and go inside it is a remarkable experience, elegant, modern, but with a lovely little museum that encompasses the 500 hundred years of their family's wine making experience. Artesa is a destination winery, so it tends to be better in the morning before the afternoon crowds make it hard to reach the tasting bar. That's why we've made it one of the first stops on the tour. Bring your camera, but if you forget one, they sell some in the gift shop.

After Artesa you'll return the way you came, back to the light and turn left. In just a couple of miles you'll come to Route 29. Turn left there and that will bring you past the city of Napa, and up into the famous Napa Valley.

If you've visited both Domaine Carneros and Artesa then you really need to eat so we suggest that you stop in at the food center of the western world, the little town of Yountville. If you want to stop at a restaurant there are plenty of choices: Bouchon, the Napa Valley Grill, Hurley's, Redd, and just North of town, on Route 29, Brix and Mustards. On the weekends or the middle of the season, a restaurant lunch can take a long time, so if you just want to pick up a sandwich quickly and get going, then our suggestion is the Bouchon Bakery. While they make great pastries and breads, they also have some wonderful sandwiches in their cases that are a favorite among the locals. They even have a nice little courtyard out front with tables and chairs.

If you want to go a little farther north you could stop at the Oakville Grocery. They make a wide variety of snacks and sandwiches, and they also have picnic tables. But be forewarned, on busy weekends if you arrive there at lunchtime there will be a crush of people who had the same great idea. If possible pick up your sandwiches early, before eleven o'clock and tuck them away with some cold water until you're hungry.

As we pass the Oakville Grocery we're coming into winery central, and the choices are astounding. You could visit Opus One or Mondavi, which are across the road from each other. You could visit Francis Ford Coppola's Rubicon Estate or call ahead for an appointment and visit Cakebread Cellars. Or, if you'd like a more intimate experience, just a short distance past Opus One and Cakebread is the Sawyer Cellars, a small, family-run winery that makes some great wines, most of which are grown just outside the door. In fact the owners, Charlie and Joanne Sawyer, live nearby. Their winemaker, Brad Warner, had been with Mondavi for thirty years before he retired, and started working with Charlie Sawyer. Here in the midst of these famous wineries, Sawyer's is one of those places where you're treated like just plain folks who dropped by to enjoy the wines, and that's what small wineries are all about (See map page 69).

Another option is just past Sawyer on the right side, St. Supéry. This is owned by a French family with wineries in Europe and it has a subtle elegance in its design that is reflected in its wines. The modern winery and tasting room sit behind a stately Victorian. The tasting room is sleek but relaxed, with a good gift shop and a knowledgeable staff. Upstairs they host gallery exhibits and have a wonderful self-guided tour overlooking the winery. They also offer guided tours, and on the weekends a special tasting of their best wines in their 'Divine Wine Room'. (See map page 69).

At this point if you visited Domaine Carneros, Artesa, had some lunch and then visited Sawyer and St. Supéry, then you've visited two big wineries and two small wineries and probably had enough wine to drink for the moment. Our suggestion is to go a little farther north and turn right on the Rutherford Road and take that over to the Silverado Trail. Even if you've drunk enough wine you should still see the Silverado Trail. When you get to the stop sign turn right on the trail and head South. In about a mile you'll see the sign for Mumm Napa Valley on the right-hand side. This was founded by another great French Champagne house. Late in the day the best thing to taste is Sparkling Wine. It's light, refreshing and the patio at Mumm's is a charming place to relax.

But even more importantly, it also has a great gift shop and a lovely and quite well known photography gallery. It includes a permanent Ansel Adams collection, and a visiting gallery that tends to feature nature themes. One exhibit that is always looked forward to is the annual photography show during the Mustard Festival. During the winter the vineyards cultivate wild mustard between the rows, as a way to restore nitrogen to the soil and control moisture and erosion. When the blooms burst into bright yellow stripes between the bare vines it makes a beautiful site for those passing by.

There's an interesting story about how wild mustard first came to the region. When the Franciscan fathers were first exploring the region, they would carry a bag of mustard seeds over their shoulders. In the bottom of the bag was a little hole to let seeds fall out marking their path. That way, the next spring when they would return from the south they would know where they had traveled before.

Since you're pointed South on the Silverado trail anyway, continue that way and enjoy an absolutely beautiful drive. There are many fine wineries that you could visit: Robert Sinskey, Vine Cliff (by appointment), Signorello, but the place that you really shouldn't miss is Darioush. The stone for the building was quarried in Iran, carved in Italy and shipped to Napa to be assembled. It is based on a Persian Temple and it is beautiful inside and out. The owners came from the Persian town of Syrah, Persia was one of the places where wine making began and Darioush celebrates that history in their architecture, their exquisite gift shop and artwork. From here you can travel farther South to turn right onto Trancas Street, which will bring you back to Route 29 South. This will take you to Route 121 West and back to San Francisco. Just follow the signs. Of course, that's not to say that there isn't more to Napa.

The Towns of Northern Napa

Because the Napa Valley is only thirty miles long, from San Francisco the northern sections are easily accessible for a day trip, as long as you make the northern-most towns your morning destination. Then you can spend the rest of the day working your way South. The largest town in northern Napa is St. Helena. This was the original center of the Napa Wine Country in the late 1800's and it is a charming, sophisticated town, surrounded on all sides by great wineries. For a touch of history drive through town and

Your Day in Wine Country

visit the Beringer Winery. Beringer has been in continuous production since 1876, making it through prohibition by making sacramental and medicinal wines. They have some great tours, beautiful grounds, including their centennial tree that has been there since 1776. Beringer has two tasting rooms. Their reserve tasting room is in the Mansion that was modeled after the two brothers' family home in Germany. In there they offer world-class wines, some of which are only sold at the winery. The main tasting room is in the old winery building. Their modern winery that produces over eight million cases of wine a year is hidden behind trees across the street.

Past St. Helena is the most northern town in Napa, Calistoga. This has a feeling of an old style western town and it is filled with hot spring spas and a fair share of tasting rooms. They even have an old faithful geyser that may not be as grand as Yellowstone's, but it is just as dependable.

There's a funny story about how Calistoga got its name. There was a land developer, Sam Brannan, who in the late 1800's entertained his investors with copious amounts of wine, touting the town's similarity to the mineral springs of Saratoga, New York. He was describing this little town as the Saratoga of California, and in his inebriated state it turned into the "Calistoga of Sarafornia", and of course the name stuck.

In the ten miles between St. Helena and Calistoga there are some very remarkable destination wineries; Sterling, Clo Pegase, Schramsberg, Beringer, and the Castello di Amorosa. There are also many smaller wineries that are well known for their remarkable wines; Rombauer, Frank Family, Benessere, Chateau Montelena (they're actually just North of Calistoga), Reverie, and Diamond Mountain. The northern parts of Napa, like the northern parts of Sonoma, may not be the first places you explore, but since you're going to come back, keep them in mind for those future trips. Check the directory for Northern Napa day trips on page 187.

Chapter Ten: Navigating the Main Roads

The BIG Roads

Both Sonoma and Napa counties are agricultural to the core. The residents defend their growing land fanatically and one of the ways they do that is by refusing to expand their roads. As a result most of the roads are two lanes, and many are one lane, and others, especially up in the mountains could be charitably called goat paths. This makes navigating a bit of a challenge and in fact, was part of the motivation for this book.

The two most important roads to know are the central routes that run the length of each valley. In Sonoma that road is Route 12. When it passes through various towns it's called many names but it is always clearly marked as Route 12. It spans the two counties, but the part we're most concerned with is where it travels through the Carneros district in the south, to the historic town of Sonoma, and then the Sonoma Valley, or Valley of the Moon, including the important grape-growing towns of Glen Ellen and Kenwood, through the county seat of Santa Rosa, ending at the lovely, classic North Bay town of Sebastopol, which is just minutes from the Russian River Valley wineries.

The Sonoma Valley is fairly narrow and heavily wooded compared to the Napa Valley, and in most of the valley Route 12 travels in lonely splendor, without a parallel road, except in the south. There Arnold Drive travels to the West of Route 12, North through the town of Glen Ellen, connecting to Route 12 about four miles South of Kenwood. Arnold is a smaller road than Route 12, with some areas that necessarily move slowly, but on the weekends, when traffic is creeping along Route 12 through downtown Sonoma, Boyes Hot Springs and Agua Caliente, this is a good alternative.

An Arnold Drive Hint: This is the road that takes you to downtown Glen Ellen, home to some wonderful wineries and great restaurants. If you're heading either direction this is a great place to pick up picnic supplies at the Glen Ellen Market. Also, just up the hill is the remarkable Benziger Winery, which along with great wines, and a great tour, has some excellent picnic areas.

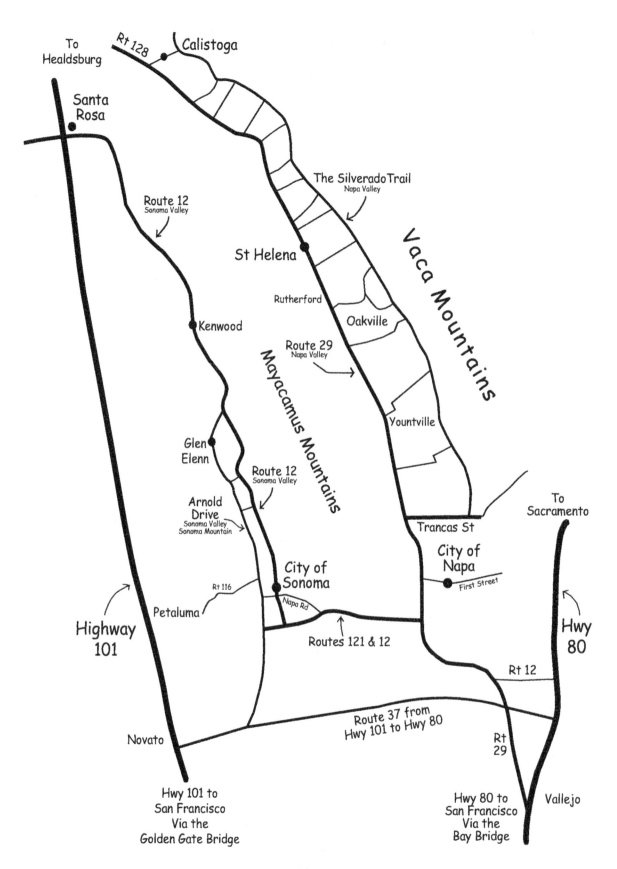

The Main Roads of Napa

Napa's main road is Route 29, known along certain parts as St. Helena Highway. The part we're most concerned with runs from Carneros in the south, past the city of Napa, all the way North to Calistoga. In the process it bisects the most valuable vineyard land in America, the Napa Valley. It also strings together all of the important towns: Napa, Yountville (of culinary fame), Oakville, Rutherford, St. Helena and Calistoga.

Just to the East of Route 29, hugging the feet of the Vaca Mountains is the Silverado Trail. It starts at the north end of the city of Napa and travels the entire length of the valley. It makes a beautiful alternative on busy traffic days, and it is home to many smaller wineries.

While there are many roads to cross over from Route 29 to the Silverado Trail, if you want to experience the full length of the Silverado where the wineries abound, then take the exit off Route 29 for Trancas Street and bear to the right after the exit. You'll pass through some shopping areas, but in a couple of miles just past the last of the stores you'll see the Silverado Trail on the left-hand side at a traffic light. Even though a small segment of it goes off to the right further on, all of the wineries are to the left up valley, so turn that way.

Taking a tour of the Napa Valley by traveling North and then South on Route 29 is simpler and potentially faster because the wineries along Route 29 are packed together pretty tightly in places. There are other wineries on the cross roads connecting Route 29 to the Silverado Trail.

The roads are arranged like a ladder, with Route 29 and the Silverado Trail as the uprights and roads like Yountville Crossroad, Oakville Crossroad and Rutherford Road as the rungs so it's hard to get lost.

Dry Creek
Valley

Alexander
Valley

Sonoma Valley
Valley of the Moon

Napa Valley

Sonoma
County

Napa
County

City of
Napa

Russian
River Valley

Hwy
101

City of
Sonoma

Pacific
Ocean

Marin
County

Carneros
District

Highway 80

Golden Gate Bridge

Chapter Eleven: Sonoma and Napa, Yin and Yang

There is both a city of Sonoma and a county of Sonoma. There is both a city of Napa and a county of Napa. Why anyone would name both the city and the county the same thing is beyond us, but they did, so there it is.

The town of Sonoma is a cute little village of about nine thousand people situated in the southeastern corner of the quite large and complex Sonoma County. The county borders San Pablo bay in the south (the northern extension of San Francisco Bay) and the Pacific Ocean in the Northwest. To the Southwest it borders Marin County, to the North, Mendocino County and to the East, its more famous, but much smaller cousin, Napa County. Sonoma is very varied in its American Viticultural Areas (AVAs) and produces a wide variety of produce besides excellent wine grapes.

The city of Napa is a much larger town of about seventy thousand people in the southern part of Napa County. At the county's center is the Napa Valley, which is only thirty miles long by five miles at its widest, where the primary business is growing fine grapes and making wine. Most of the population is concentrated in the city and towns and the rest of the county is pretty sparsely populated, except for wineries, farmhouses, mansions, hotels, spas and great restaurants.

Your Day in Wine Country

Both counties are longer than they are wide, and both border the bay in the south along the AVA called Carneros. From the cooler southern parts of the counties to the warmer northern parts of the valleys (such as Dry Creek in Sonoma and Calistoga in Napa) the temperature can span thirty degrees Fahrenheit at the same time.

When people refer to Sonoma or Napa they are usually referring to the counties. When local people mean the cities, they'll refer to them as downtown Sonoma or downtown Napa, or alternatively "the town of".

It's interesting to note that Sonoma and Napa are two of the only towns in the region with Native American names rather than Spanish or English names. It is actually possible that their origins come from Chinese colonies of shipwrecked sailors and their concubines, stranded during the voyages of the great Chinese treasure fleets in the early fourteen hundreds.

For example, rice was already being cultivated in the Sacramento region when the Spanish arrived, and it's still in widespread cultivation there today. The Spanish reported seeing Chinese Junks off the coast when they first explored the region, and remnants of an ancient Chinese ship made from teak wood was discovered buried in the silt of the Sacramento River, with rice still in her hull. It makes you think!

Sometimes it seems like the only things that people in Wine Country talk about are wine, food and the weather. If they talk about something else it's because of how it relates to the other three.

Some of the Differences Between Napa and Sonoma

In Sonoma people know that they're farmers and they're okay with that. In Napa sometimes they think that they're movie stars and sometimes they are. Napa is famous internationally due to their great wine and their even greater marketing. Sonoma is popular locally and among wine collectors. During the high tourist season, June through September, Napa Valley gets the lion's share of the visitors, although on the Summer weekends both counties can be swamped with tourists. That's because a large segment of the most loyal wine visitors live within driving distance of the wineries.

During November to May the tourist traffic is split equally between the two counties, because the visitors tend to be more knowledgeable, either locals or collectors. What do they know that you might want to? The wines in Sonoma are every bit as good as those from Napa, and they are often more reasonable, because they grow a wider variety of grapes. Napa wines are more expensive because the land is more expensive, and because they specialize in more expensive grapes. They also have the internationally famous 'Napa' name that they have worked hard to promote and marketing matters!

Does Napa's fame make the folks from Sonoma crazy? Not really! Traditionally there was never a lot of contact between the counties; the mass of the Mayacamas Mountains prevented that. Sonoma was always more connected to Marin County in the South and Mendocino County in the North. Napa is more connected to Solano and Lake Counties. Also Sonoma and Napa are quite different. Napa is a small county that primarily grows premium wine grapes. Sonoma county is twice as big, it borders the ocean, and it grows more grapes than Napa, but it also grows tons of other produce; apples, cherries, nuts, plus cows, goats, sheep, turkeys and on and on. So, Sonoma's identity isn't as completely tied to making wine. In Napa they make and pour wine, and everything else, all of the great restaurants, theaters, hotels and spas are there to support that.

It makes for a very different experience. Napa is fancier, Sonoma is more relaxed. Napa is stylish, while Sonoma is folksy. Napa has the famous labels but Sonoma has the history. Napa has the most glamorous architecture, while Sonoma is hidden and intimate. The Napa Valley is a broad sunny expanse that outshines all of its neighbors, while Sonoma shares its borders with trendy Marin and some gorgeous Pacific coastline. Napa gets more visitors, but Sonoma is more convenient to San Francisco via the Golden Gate, one of the most photographed bridges in the world, and is on the way to Napa. In Napa everything is pretty close, while Sonoma takes more time to navigate.

But even in the busiest season, in both counties there are plenty of small family-owned wineries that make excellent products and that will welcome visitors of all ages graciously. You just need to look for them beyond the main roads.

Here is a tour guide's trick:

The Wine Country is served by a number of good, local magazines that are primarily used as vehicles for advertising. The articles are of course about their advertisers, both big and small. Big wineries have big advertisements, medium wineries have medium-sized ads and small wineries have small ads. Very little wineries may not advertise at all, but instead depend upon word of mouth. A good source for them is the tasting room staff of other local wineries.

Most of the people pouring wine for you, when asked, will offer suggestions about where to go next. This is a mixed blessing. The winery they are suggesting probably is connected to the winery they are working at, or to a friend or family member. It's probably a good winery and more than likely one of the smaller ones that get less traffic.

But before you go gallivanting off to visit their suggestion you should ask two questions, which you can probably answer by consulting the maps and directory at the back of this book. First, is it convenient to get to, based on your proposed route that day? Second, is there something interesting about the wines, the location or the place that makes it stand out from the other wineries that you plan to visit?

What makes a winery stand out? When it comes to the wine, extraordinary reputation, unusual varietals, interesting blends, organic farming methods or Biodynamic farming and wine-making methods, unfiltered wines, the use of wild yeasts, or a particular talent for making a specific wine, like Schug's gift for Carneros style Pinot Noirs, or Bella's very Dry Creek style Zinfandel.

There are also things beyond the wine that make a great winery experience; great artwork like the unique collection found at Imagery, great architecture like Artesa's, an entertaining staff like Peju's, beautiful gardens like Ferrari-Carano's, or historic significance like Buena Vista or Beringer.

So ask for recommendations but remember
that the typical tasting staff doesn't visit many other
wineries, so take any recommendations with a grain of
salt, and don't twist your tour all out of shape trying to fit
one more winery into a day that's already well planned out.

Chapter Twelve: Using the Mapped Tours
A Fast Track Chapter

The tours are divided into five groups based on your starting point. The individual tour maps are focused on relatively small areas and at the beginning of each group is an overview map showing the routes into that area. The page number to the right of the winery name refer to the page in the directory where you will find more in-depth information about that winery.

The tour routes of the Maps are generally designed to allow you to make mostly right-hand turns. In an area that is primarily served by two-lane roads and very few traffic lights, that on weekends is often overwhelmed with traffic, this is both a time-saver and a safety factor. When you add in the fact that many drivers have had a bit of wine to drink, having an additional safety factor built in is desirable. The necessary left turns in the tours are generally at intersections with less traffic, better visibility, and when possible, a traffic light or other helpful aid.

Five Important Points:

One: Unless you have a designated driver, don't plan to visit all of the wineries on the list, its just too much wine to consume and still drive safely. Instead select three along the route that sound like the most interesting and take the time to enjoy them. We've built the tours, often times, so that the most interesting wineries are at the beginning. If you make a tour with just those two, or three or four, leaving the others out, you'll still have a great time.

Two: While planning the trip so that you are taking mostly right-hand turns is the best idea, some of the tours can be started from either end. A tour that starts at downtown Napa may also work wonderfully starting from downtown Calistoga. If they are a loop just travel them in the same circular direction. In Napa Valley it is sometimes safer to make right turn circuits between Route 29 and the Silverado to avoid left-hand turns.

Three: The information pages adjoining the maps include the mileage between the wineries. The time for each segment does not include time spent getting in and out of the car, which with a larger group can be time-consuming. Use the information. This is an agricultural area and signs are often less than obvious. For instance, Napa wineries are allowed only two relatively small white on blue signs as the sole warning and guidepost to their entranceways. When you are flying up the Silverado Trail at fifty miles an hour it is amazingly easy to miss them. Many other wineries have no signs at all until you are at their doorway. It is one of the reasons that people use professional guides, and every now and then even they miss driveways the first time.

Four: In Napa many crossroads are marked with signs about one hundred or more feet before the actual road. There often is no sign at all at the road itself. This is an aspect of agricultural roads that city and suburban dwellers may find odd. It is done that way because there are fewer roads and people are traveling fast. When you see the road sign start slowing down and watch the painted lines on the road as your indicators. They will tell you where to turn. This is especially helpful when the grass is high, or the vines are filled with leaves and encroaching on the edges of the roads.

Five: If you want to visit the full gamut of wineries and you don't want to have to spit out the wine, then hire a driver, or better yet, a qualified winery tour guide. If they know the area well, that's great. If they don't know the area, this book is filled with well-tested and proven tours. If the driver you hire is concerned about the practicality of the tours consider the information below.

An interesting note: Most of these tours were driven and developed in stretched limousines and larger vehicles, where driving, turning and stopping is all done with the greatest concern for safety, comfort and grace. It is one of the reasons that the tours work so well, even when you're not familiar with the area and you've had a little bit of wine to drink. The working title of this book was "The Limousine Driver's Winery Guide to Napa and Sonoma Counties". If we can fit a thirty-foot limousine safely along these routes, a convertible Mustang should have no problem.

The Tour Directory: Starting in Southern Sonoma

Tour One - Page 92

The Sonoma Plaza, Valley of the Moon and Carneros, A Good Introduction
to a Beautiful Region. A Good Wine Variety finishing with Sparklers.
Wineries: Castle, Kunde, Benziger, Gloria Ferrer (Sparkling)
Five hour tour locally, seven hour tour from SF
A good day trip from San Francisco. $$ Moderately Priced

Tour Two - Page 94

Carneros and the Sonoma Plaza, Beautiful Views, Great Gift Shops.
Wineries: Jacuzzi, Homewood, Sebastiani, Gloria Ferrer (Sparkling)
Five hour tour locally, Seven hour tour from SF
A good day trip from San Francisco. $$ Moderately Priced

Tour Three - Page 96

Friendly Wineries from Carneros up through the Valley of the Moon,
Wide Variety of Wines, Suitable for a Group, Great Art and Gift Shops.
Wineries: Jacuzzi, Gundlach Bundschu, Imagery, Chateau St. Jean, Loxton
Six hour tour locally, eight hour tour from SF
A good day trip from San Francisco. $$ Moderately Priced

Tour Four - Page 98

Great Red Wines in Sonoma Valley, Great Art and Gift Shops.
Wineries: Arrowood, Imagery, Chateau St. Jean, Wellington
Five hour tour locally, Seven hour tour from SF
A good day trip from San Francisco. $$ Moderately Priced

Tour Five - Page 100

Valley of the Moon, Glen Ellen and Carneros into Napa, Beautiful Views and Art Works.
A Nice variety of Wineries starting in Glen Ellen and Crossing into Napa.
Wineries: Imagery, Benziger, B.R. Cohn, Nicholson, Artesa
Five hour tour locally. $$ Moderately Priced

Tour Six - Page 102

Valley of the Moon from Bottom to Top, Great Art, Architecture and Gift Shops.

Wineries: Imagery, Benziger, Ledson, Loxton, B.R. Cohn

Six hour tour locally, eight hour tour from SF

A good day trip from San Francisco. $$ Moderately Priced

Tour Seven - Page 104

The Sonoma Plaza and the Valley of the Moon, Charming with Great Gift Shops.

Wineries: Charles Creek, Castle, Westwood (app) Imagery, Chateau St. Jean, Loxton

Six hour tour locally, eight hour tour from SF

A good day trip from San Francisco. $$ Moderately Priced

Tour Eight - Page 106

A Wide Variety of Wines in the Valley of the Moon.

Wineries: Arrowood, Kunde, Landmark, Kaz, St. Francis

Six hour tour locally, eight hour tour from SF

A good day trip from San Francisco. $$ Moderately Priced

Tour Nine - Page 108

A Cross-County Carneros Tour, Great for a Hot Day, **One Appontment**

Pinot Noir, Chardonnay, Sparklers, Good Gift Shops.

Wineries: Jacuzzi, Bouchaine, Ceja (App), Schug, Gloria Ferrer (Sparkling)

Six hour tour locally, eight hour tour from SF

A good day trip from San Francisco in hot weather. $$$ Moderately Expensive

Restaurants & Hotels of Southern Sonoma   Page 110

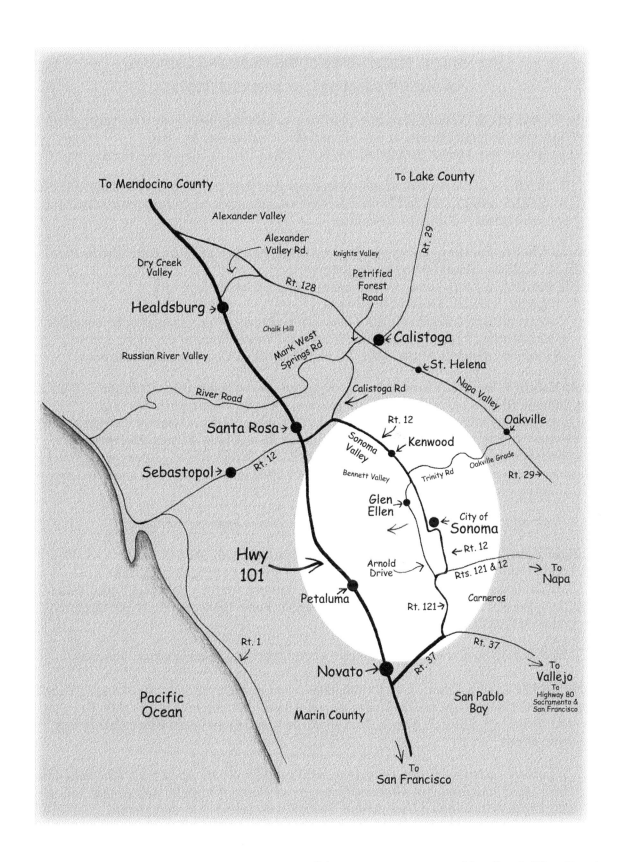

Tour One in Southern Sonoma:
The Sonoma Plaza, Valley of the Moon and Carneros,
A Good Introduction to a Beautiful Region

Castle Vineyards & Winery 707.996.1966 www.castlevineyards.com *On Plaza*   Page 217
122 W. Spain St. Sonoma Hours: 11 am - 6 pm daily Tasting Fee: $5 - $10
Wine List: Pinot Noir, Merlot, Zinfandel, Syrah, Viognier, Chardonnay, Rosé, Syrah Port

> *Turn left out of the front door of Castle, cross the street and the Sonoma Cheese Factory
> is ½ block away on the left hand side. Great sandwiches and other picnic supplies to
> eat later at either Kunde or Benziger.*

Sonoma Cheese Factory 800-535-2855 www.sonomacheesefactory.com *On the Plaza*
2 Spain St., Sonoma Hours: 8:30 am – 6 pm
The Fig Pantry 707.933.3000 www.thegirlandthefig.com/thefigpantry
1190 E. Napa St., Sonoma Hours: 7 am - 7 pm
> *Take Spain Street west to the light and turn right onto Route 12, up the Valley of the
> Moon, heading to the Kunde Estate Winery & Vineyards: total 9.8 miles, approx
> 18 minutes. Kunde is on the right side and looks like a Georgian style cow barn.*

Kunde Estate Winery & Vineyards 707.833.5501 www. kunde.com *Beautiful*   Page 238
10155 Sonoma Hwy., Kenwood Hours: 10:30 am – 4:30 pm Tasting Fee: $5 - $10
Wine List: Sauvignon Blanc, Chardonnay, Syrah, Zinfandel, Merlot, Cabernet Sauvignon, Primitivo, Sangiovese, Barbera, Gewürztraminer, Grenache Rosé, Claret, Blends, Zinfandel Port
  With two thousand acres in vines the Kunde family has provided grapes for wine makers
in the area for generations. In the early 1990's they started making their own wine, and they offer an amazing variety.

> *Heading to Benziger Family Winery: total 4.8 miles approx 7 minutes*

Benziger Family Winery 707.935.4500 www.benziger.com *Best Tours*   Page 214
1883 London Ranch Rd., Glen Ellen Hours: 10 am – 5 pm Tasting Fee: $5 - $10
Wine List: Zinfandel, Cabernet Sauvignon, Merlot, Barbera, Malbec, Cabernet Franc, Petite
Blanc, Sangiovese, Pinot Blanc, Chardonnay, Viognier, Fumé Blanc, Syrah, White Burgundy,
Claret, Muscat Canelli

> *Heading to Gloria Ferrer Champagne Caves: total 14.5 miles approx 26 minutes*

Gloria Ferrer Caves & Vineyards 707.996.7256 www.gloriaferrer.com *Sparkling*   Page 231
23555 Carneros Hwy 121, Sonoma Hours: 10 am – 5 pm Tasting Fee: by the glass $4 - $10
Wine List: Sparklers, Blanc de Blancs, Brut, Blanc de Noirs, Cuvee, Brut Rosé, Chardonnay,
Pinot Noir, Syrah

> *If you are returning to San Francisco, head south on Route 121 to the traffic light and
> bear right onto Route 37. That will bring you to Route 101 South. Follow that back to
> the city over the Golden Gate Bridge. From Gloria Ferrer it is about forty-
> five minutes to the city in regular traffic. In Rush hour traffic it is about one and
> a half to two hours. See the list of restaurants in southern Sonoma on page 108.*

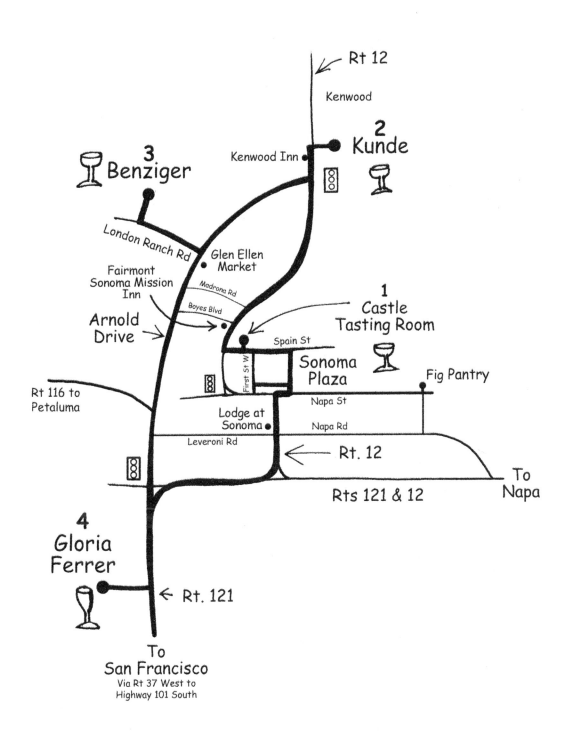

Rt 12

Kenwood

2
Kunde

Kenwood Inn

3.
Benziger

London Ranch Rd

Glen Ellen
Market

Fairmont
Sonoma Mission
Inn

Madrona Rd

Boyes Blvd

Arnold
Drive

1
Castle
Tasting Room

Spain St

Sonoma
Plaza

First St W

Fig Pantry

Rt 116 to
Petaluma

Napa St

Lodge at
Sonoma

Napa Rd

Leveroni Rd

Rt. 12

Rts 121 & 12

To
Napa

4
Gloria
Ferrer

← Rt. 121

To
San Francisco
Via Rt 37 West to
Highway 101 South

Tour Two in Southern Sonoma
Carneros and the Sonoma Plaza, Beautiful Views, Great Gift Shops

Jacuzzi Family Vineyards 707.931.7575 www.jacuzziwines.com *Beautiful*   Page 235
24724 Arnold Dr., Sonoma Hours: 10 am - 5:30 pm Tasting Fee: comp - $5
Wine List: Chardonnay, Pinot Noir, Barbera, Sangiovese, Arneis, Merlot, Nebbiolo, Primitivo,
Pinot Grigio, Moscato Blanc, Blends - This also the site of the **Olive Press Gift Shop**

*Head north on Route 121. At the light bear right, continuing on Route 121. Burndale Rd
and the Homewood Winery are on the right hand side: total 4.8 miles, 8 minutes*

Homewood Winery 707.996.6353 www.homewoodwinery.com *Small Winery*   Page 234
23120 Burndale Rd.,Vineburg Hours: 10 am - 4 pm daily Tasting Fee: Comp - $5
Wine List: Sauvignon Blanc, Chardonnay, Pinot Noir, Grenache, Merlot, Syrah, Zinfandel,
Blends

*Turn right from Burndale east on Rt 121. At the light turn left onto Napa Road. At
Broadway-Rt 12 turn right towards the Plaza: total 5.3 miles, approx 11 minutes*

There are many lunch options at the Plaza. See the restaurant list on page 110. If you would like
to picnic on the Plaza you can pick up lunch at:
The Sonoma Cheese Factory 800-535-2855 www.sonomacheesefactory.com
2 Spain St., Sonoma Hours: 8:30 am - 6 pm
A great place for lunch with an historic and charming enclosed patio is:
The Sunflower Cafe at 421 First St. West just down from Spain St. Map on pg 18.

*From the Plaza follow Spain Street East to 4th St. and the Sebastiani Vineyards:
total 0.6 miles, less than 2 minutes*

Sebastiani Vineyards and Winery 707.938.5532 www.sebastiani.com *History*   Page 259
389 – 4th St. E., Sonoma Hours: 10 am - 5 pm daily Tasting Fee: - $5 - $10 Great Gift Shop
Wine List: Chardonnay, Cabernet Sauvignon, Merlot, Barbera, Zinfandel, Pinot Noir
        Alternate: Follow the Signs to **Ravenswood Winery** for great Zins & Cabs   Page 251

*Follow Broadway south to Rt 121, bear right to the light. Turn left and the Gloria Ferrer
Champagne Caves will be on the right hand side: total 8.9 miles, approx 18 minutes*

Gloria Ferrer Caves & Vineyards 707.996.7256 www.gloriaferrer.com *Sparkling* Page 231
23555 Carneros Hwy 121, Sonoma Hours: 10 am - 5 pm daily Tasting Fee: $4-$10 per glass
Wine List: Sparklers, Blanc de Blancs, Brut, Blanc de Noirs, Cuvee, Brut Rosé, Chardonnay,
Pinot Noir, Syrah

*To return to San Francisco turn right out of the drive and follow Rt 121 to Rt 37. Turn
right and follow that to Hwy 101 South. In light traffic it is forty-five minutes to
San Francisco, in rush hour it takes an hour and a half. During the week consider having dinner in Sonoma and driving back to the city after the worst of the traffic is past.*

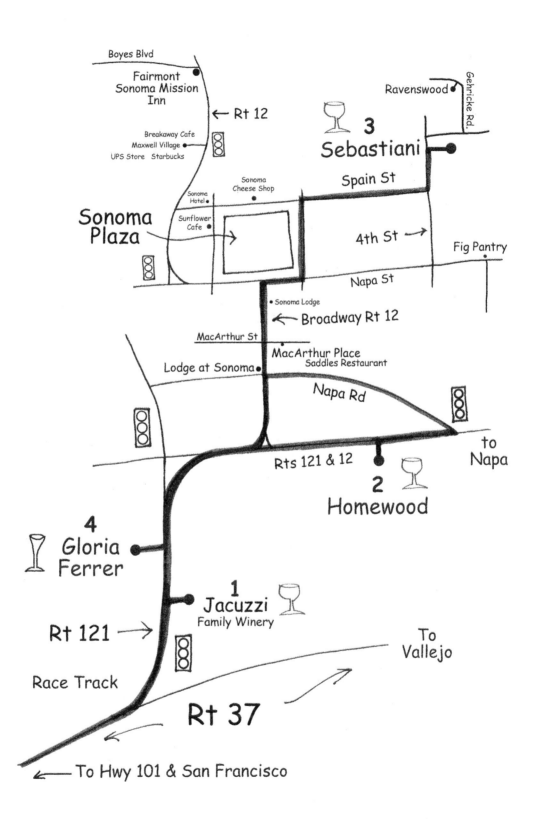

Tour Three in Southern Sonoma

Friendly Wineries from Carneros up through the Valley of the Moon

From the Golden Gate Bridge it is about thirty five minutes to Jacuzzi via Route 101 North, Route 37 East and Route 121 North.

Jacuzzi Family Vineyards 707.931.7575 www.jacuzziwines.com *Beautiful*   Page 235
24724 Arnold Dr., Sonoma   Hours: 10 am - 5:30 pm Tasting Fee: comp - $5
Wine List: Chardonnay, Pinot Noir, Barbera, Sangiovese, Arneis, Merlot, Nebbiolo, Primitivo, Pinot Grigio, Moscato Blanc, Blends - This also the site of the **Olive Press Gift Shop**
For Food: The Cornerstone Gardens just past Jacuzzi on the right. Cafe, Shops & Tasting Rooms, including Grange Sonoma (a Sonoma Collective), Roshambo and Carneros Family Wineries.

Heading to Gundlach-Bundschu: total 7.3 miles, approx 15 minutes

Gundlach Bundschu Winery 707.938.5277 www.gunbun.com *Five Generations* Page 231
2000 Denmark St., Sonoma   Hours: 11 am - 4:30 pm   Tasting Fee: $5-$10
Wine List: Zinfandel, Gewürztraminer, Chardonnay, Pinot Noir, N.V. Red Bearitage, Gamay Beaujolais, Cabernet Franc, Merlot, Cabernet Sauvignon, N.V. Sonoma Red

Heading to the fig pantry: total 1.7 miles, approx 5 minutes

Pick up picnic items to eat at Imagery's picnic tables later
Our Picnic Supply suggestions are: **Whole Food Market** on West Second Street, or the **Sonoma Cheese Shop** on Napa Street on the Plaza or **The Fig Pantry** at 1190 E. Napa St.

Heading to Imagery Estate Winery: total 8.1 miles, approx 20 minutes

Imagery Estate Winery 877.550.4278 www.imagerywinery.com *Wine Art*   Page 234
14335 Hwy 12, Glen Ellen   Hours: 10 am - 4:30 pm   Tasting Fee: $5-$10
Wine List: Cabernet Franc, Petite Sirah, Barbera, Sangiovese, Malbec, White Burgundy, Pinot Blanc, Viognier, Petite Sirah Port, Interlude: Chocolate Infused Port, Blends (WOW Red, WOW Oui)

Heading to Chateau St. Jean Winery: total 4.4 miles, approx 10 minutes

Chateau St. Jean Winery 707.833.4134 www.chateaustjean.com *Gardens*   Page 219
8555 Sonoma Hwy., Kenwood   Hours: 10 am - 5 pm Tasting Fee: $10 - $15 *Deli*
Wine List: Pinot Blanc, Chardonnay, Viognier, Pinot Noir, Merlot, Malbec, Cabernet Sauvignon

Heading to Loxton Cellars: total 2.7 miles approx 5 minutes

Loxton Cellars 707.935.7221 www.loxtoncellars.com *Small Charming Winery*   Page 241
11466 Dunbar Rd., Glen Ellen   Hours: 11 am - 5 pm daily by appt Tasting Fee: comp - $5
Wine List: Rosé Vin Gris of Syrah, Zinfandel, Syrah, Cabernet Sauvignon, Syrah Port, Chardonnay, Shiraz

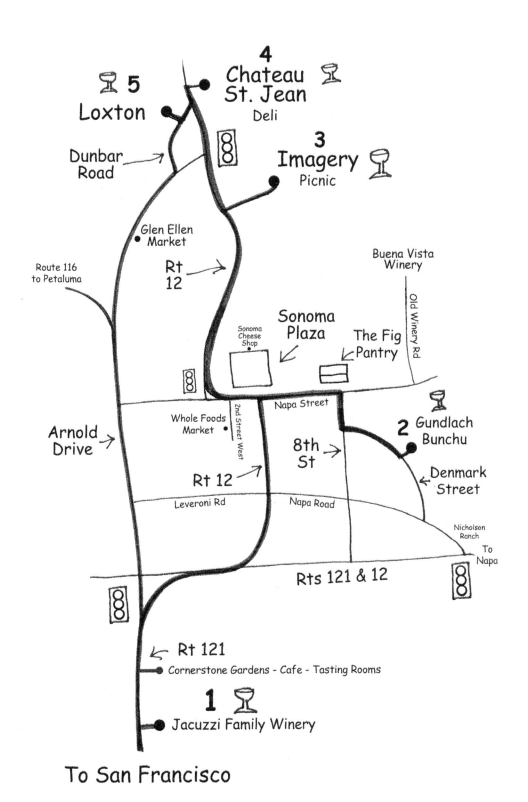

5 Loxton

4 Chateau St. Jean
Deli

3 Imagery
Picnic

Dunbar Road

Glen Ellen Market

Route 116 to Petaluma

Rt 12

Buena Vista Winery

Old Winery Rd

Sonoma Cheese Shop

Sonoma Plaza

The Fig Pantry

Arnold Drive

Whole Foods Market

2nd Street West

Napa Street

8th St

2 Gundlach Bunchu

Denmark Street

Rt 12

Leveroni Rd

Napa Road

Nicholson Ranch

To Napa

Rts 121 & 12

Rt 121

Cornerstone Gardens - Cafe - Tasting Rooms

1 Jacuzzi Family Winery

To San Francisco

Tour Four in Southern Sonoma
Great Red Wines in Sonoma Valley, Great Art and Gift Shops

Take Route 12 north from the Sonoma Plaza. The shared driveway for Arrowood and Imagery is six miles north of the Plaza on Route 12. It comes up quickly on the right side after a rising, right-turning curve. There are banners flying by the signs.

Arrowood Vineyards & Winery 707.938.2600 www.arrowoodswinery.com *Red* Page 211
14347 Sonoma Hwy., Glen Ellen Hours: 10 am - 4:30 pm Tasting Fee: $5
Wine List: Chardonnay, Pinot Blanc, Viognier, Gewürztraminer, Merlot, Cabernet Sauvignon, Syrah, Late Harvest Riesling, Blends
Well known for their wonderful red wines, great tasting room with nice vineyard views.

When you are in the Arrowood tasting room you can see Imagery across the way

Imagery Estate Winery 877.550.4278 www.imagerywinery.com *Gift Shop* Page 234
14335 Hwy 12, Glen Ellen Hours: 10 am - 4:30 pm Tasting Fee: $5-$10
Wine List: Cabernet Franc, Petite Sirah, Barbera, Sangiovese, Malbec, White Burgundy, Pinot Blanc, Viognier, Petite Sirah Port, Interlude: Chocolate Infused Port, Blends (WOW Oui)
Imagery has a wonderful gallery of art created for their labels over the past twenty years. The reserve tasting room is towards the back and a bit more private. Get a Benziger coupon.

Turn right on Route 12 and Head North to Chateau St. Jean : 4.4 miles, 5 minutes

Picnic items available at Chateau St. Jean's to eat at their picnic tables or patio

Chateau St. Jean Winery 707.833.4134 www.chateaustjean.com *Deli* Page 219
8555 Sonoma Hwy., Kenwood Hours: 10 am - 5 pm Tasting Fee: $5-$10 *Gift Shop*
Wine List: Pinot Blanc, Chardonnay, Viognier, Pinot Noir, Merlot, Malbec, Cabernet Sauvignon
This is one of the jewels of Sonoma Valley, gardens, architecture, great wine, wonderful gift shop and a friendly staff. The reserve tasting room is in the mansion. Worth the price.

Turn left on Route 12 Heading South to Wellington Vineyards. Bear right onto Dunbar Rd. which bears right at an angle: 2.9 miles, 4 minutes

Wellington Vineyards 707.939.0708 www.wellingtonvineyards.com *Unique* Page 270
11600 Dunbar Rd., Glen Ellen Hours: 11 am - 5 pm daily Tasting Fee: comp - $5
Wine List: Cabernet Sauvignon, Viognier, Merlot, Zinfandel, Syrah, Rousanne, Chardonnay
A little rustic, friendly and charming, with some unusual wines for you to enjoy.

Return to Rt 12 and follow that south to reach the Sonoma Plaza. Staying on Rt 12 through town will bring you to Rt 121 and then 37 and 101 back to the city. Follow the signs. All roads lead to San Francisco, or at least most of them.

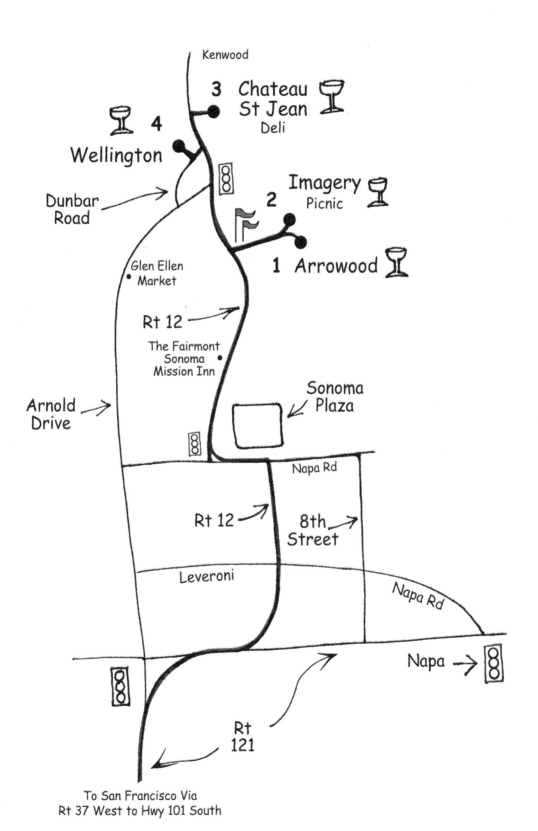

Kenwood

3 Chateau St Jean
Deli

4 Wellington

Dunbar Road

Imagery Picnic
2

1 Arrowood

Glen Ellen Market

Rt 12

The Fairmont Sonoma Mission Inn

Sonoma Plaza

Arnold Drive

Napa Rd

Rt 12
8th Street

Leveroni

Napa Rd

Napa →

Rt 121

To San Francisco Via
Rt 37 West to Hwy 101 South

Your Day in Wine Country

Tour Five in Southern Sonoma
Valley of the Moon, Glen Ellen and Carneros Into Napa
Beautiful Views and Art Works

Take Route 12 north from the Plaza. Arrowood & Imagery share a driveway 6 miles from the Plaza. It comes up on the right side after a right turning curve. Watch for banners flying.

Imagery Estate Winery 877.550.4278 www.imagerywinery.com *Great Art* Page 234
14335 Hwy 12, Glen Ellen Hours: 10 am - 4:30 pm Tasting Fee: $5 - $10
Wine List: Cabernet Franc, Petite Sirah, Barbera, Sangiovese, Malbec, White Burgundy, Pinot Blanc, Viognier, Petite Sirah Port, Interlude: Chocolate Infused Port, Blends (WOW Oui)
Imagery has a wonderful gallery of art created for their labels over the past twenty years. The reserve tasting room is towards the back and a bit more private. Get a Benziger coupon.
> *Turn right Heading North to the light, turn left on Arnold Drive to the Glen Ellen Market: total 2.0 miles, approx 8 minutes*

Pick up picnic items to eat at Benziger's picnic tables at the
Glen Ellen Market 707.996.3411 www.sonoma-glenellenmkt.com
13751 Arnold Dr., Glen Ellen Hours: 7 am - 8 pm
> *Turn right out of the parking lot and immediately left onto London Ranch Rd. up the hill to Benziger Family Winery: total 0.8 miles, approx 5 minutes*

Benziger Family Winery 707.935.4500 www.benziger.com *The Best Tours* Page 214
1883 London Ranch Rd., Glen Ellen Hours: 10 am - 5 pm daily Tasting Fee: $5 - $10
Wine List: Zinfandel, Cabernet Sauvignon, Merlot, Barbera, Malbec, Cabernet Franc, Petite Blanc, Sangiovese, Pinot Blanc, Chardonnay, Viognier, Fumé Blanc, Syrah, White Burgundy, Claret, Muscat Canelli
> *Head back to Arnold Drive, turn left to traffic light at Rt 12, turn right, the winery is 1.8 miles on the right-hand side. Total 3.5, approx ten minutes*

B.R. Cohn Winery 707.938.4064 www.brcohn.com Page 212
15000 Sonoma Hwy. Glen Ellen Hours: 10am - 5pm Tours by appt Tasting Fee: $10 (CWP)
Wine List: Cabernet Sauvignon, Zinfandel, Chardonnay, Merlot, Syrah Blend
> *Turn right (south) on Route 12, follow through town, turn left on Napa Rd (traffic light) towards Napa to Nicholson Ranch: total 10.4 miles, approx 20 minutes*

Nicholson Ranch 707.938.8822 www.nicholsonranch.com *Great Views* Page 246
4200 Napa Rd., Sonoma Hours: 10 am - 6 pm daily Tasting Fee: $10 - $15
Wine List: Chardonnay, Pinot Noir, Syrah, Merlot
> *Turn left out of drive, left at the light, left at Old Sonoma Rd and follow signs to Artesa Winery: total 4.9 miles, approx 10 minutes*

Artesa Winery 707.254.2140 www.artesawinery.com *Great Building & Views* Page 211
1345 Henry Rd., Napa Hours: 10 am - 5 pm daily Tasting Fee: $5 - $10 *Bar Like Scene*
Wine List: Cabernet Sauvignon, Chardonnay, Merlot, Pinot Noir, Tempranillo, Albarino, Garnacha Rosado, Late Harvest Gewürztraminer, Blends

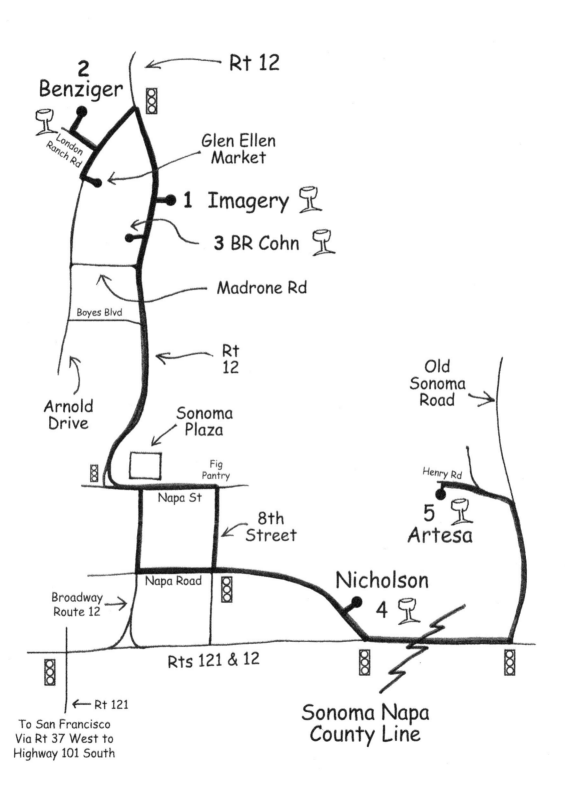

2 Benziger

Rt 12

London Ranch Rd

Glen Ellen Market

1 Imagery

3 BR Cohn

Madrone Rd

Boyes Blvd

Rt 12

Arnold Drive

Sonoma Plaza

Old Sonoma Road

Fig Pantry

Napa St

Henry Rd

8th Street

5 Artesa

Broadway Route 12

Napa Road

Nicholson

4

Rts 121 & 12

Sonoma Napa County Line

← Rt 121

To San Francisco Via Rt 37 West to Highway 101 South

Your Day in Wine Country

Tour Six in Southern Sonoma

Valley of the Moon from Bottom to Top, Great Art, Architecture and Gift Shops

Imagery Estate Winery 877.550.4278 www.imagerywinery.com *Great Art*   Page 234
14335 Hwy 12, Glen Ellen   Hours: 10 am - 4:30 pm   Tasting Fee: $5 - $10
Wine List: Cabernet Franc, Petite Sirah, Barbera, Sangiovese, Malbec, White Burgundy, Pinot Blanc, Viognier, Petite Sirah Port, Interlude: Chocolate Infused Port, Blends (WOW Oui)

Turn right Heading North to the light, turn left on Arnold Drive to the Glen Ellen Market: total 2.0 miles, approx 5 minutes

Pick up picnic items to eat at Benizger's picnic tables at
Glen Ellen Market 707.996.3411 www.sonoma-glenellenmkt.com
13751 Arnold Dr., Glen Ellen   Hours: 7 am - 8 pm

Turn right out of the parking lot and immediately left onto London Ranch Rd. up the hill to Benziger Family Winery: total 0.8 miles, approx 2 minutes

Benziger Family Winery 707.935.4500 www.benziger.com *The Best Tours*   Page 214
1883 London Ranch Rd., Glen Ellen   Hours: 10 am - 5 pm daily   Tasting Fee: $5 - $10
Wine List: Zinfandel, Cabernet Sauvignon, Merlot, Barbera, Malbec, Cabernet Franc, Petite Blanc, Sangiovese, Pinot Blanc, Chardonnay, Viognier, Fumé Blanc, Syrah, White Burgundy, Claret, Muscat Canelli

Head North on Arnold Drive, left at light to Ledson Winery & Vineyards: total 5.5 miles, approx 10 minutes

Ledson Winery & Vineyards 707.537.3810 www.ledson.com *Great Building*   Page 240
7335 Hwy 12, Santa Rosa   Hours: 10 am - 5 pm daily   Tasting Fee: $5 - $10 *Deli*
Wine List: Merlot, Pinot Noir, Sangiovese, Syrah, Petite Sirah, Zinfandel, Cabernet Sauvignon, Cabernet Franc, Malbec, Barbera, Mourvèdre, Primitivo, Grenache, Chardonnay, Sauvignon Blanc, Johannisberg Riesling, Rosé, Madera Port

Head South to Loxton Cellars bearing right at Dunbar, Loxton driveway comes up immediately on the right hand side: total 4.9 miles, approx 10 minutes

Loxton Cellars 707.935.7221 www.loxtoncellars.com *Small & Friendly*   Page 241
11466 Dunbar Rd., Glen Ellen   Hours: 11 am - 5 pm daily by appt   Tasting Fee: comp - $5
Wine List: Rosé Vin Gris of Syrah, Zinfandel, Syrah, Cabernet Sauvignon, Syrah Port, Chardonnay, Shiraz

Follow Route 12 South to B.R. Cohn Winery on the right side, 3.7 miles appr 5 mins

B.R. Cohn Winery 707.938.4064 www.brcohn.com   Page 212
15000 Sonoma Hwy. Glen Ellen   Hours: 10am - 5pm   Tours by appt   Tasting Fee: $10 (CWP)
Wine List: Cabernet Sauvignon, Zinfandel, Chardonnay, Merlot, Syrah Blend

Follow Route 12 South to the Sonoma Plaza for a great dinner, or continue on Rt 12 to Rt 121, bear right at the Light. Turn left to Rt 37, bear right to Hwy 101 & San Francisco.

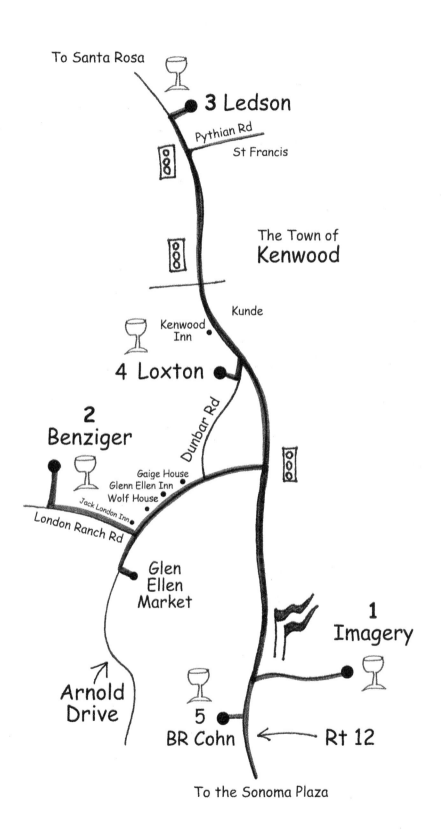

To Santa Rosa

3 Ledson

Pythian Rd

St Francis

The Town of
Kenwood

Kunde

Kenwood
Inn

4 Loxton

2 Benziger

Dunbar Rd

Gaige House
Glenn Ellen Inn
Wolf House
Jack London Inn

London Ranch Rd

Glen
Ellen
Market

1 Imagery

Arnold
Drive

5 BR Cohn

Rt 12

To the Sonoma Plaza

Your Day in Wine Country

Tour Seven in Southern Sonoma
The Sonoma Plaza & the Valley of the Moon, Charming with Great Gift Shops

Charles Creek Vineyard 707.935.3848 www.charlescreek.com *On the Plaza* Page 218
483 First St West, Sonoma Hours: 11 am - 6 pm daily Tasting Fee: $5 - $10 *See Pg. 18*
Wine List: Merlot, Cabernet Sauvignon, Syrah, Chardonnay, Grenache, Chocolate Dessert Wine, Blends, known for their great Chardonnay

> *Just walk up First Street West to the corner of Spain St, cross the street and turn left.*

Castle Vineyards & Winery 707.996.1966 www.castlevineyards.com *Plaza* Page 217
122 W. Spain St., Sonoma Hours: 11 am - 6 pm daily Tasting Fee: $5 - $10
Wine List: Pinot Noir, Merlot, Zinfandel, Syrah, Viognier, Chardonnay, Rosé, Syrah Port

> *Turn left and follow Spain St to the middle of the next block, Cheese shop is on the left.*

Pick up picnic items to eat at Imagery's picnic tables later
Sonoma Cheese Factory 800-535-2855 www.sonomacheesefactory.com
2 Spain St., Sonoma Hours: 8:30 am - 6 pm
Or visit a restaurant on the Plaza. A favorite of ours is
The Sunflower Cafe at 421 First St. West just below Spain Street. Restaurant List on page 110

Westwood Winery 707.480.2251 11 East Napa St. #3 *On the Plaza* Page 270
This is a small, very comfortable tasting room that is **by appointment**. John Kelly, the winemaker produces fantastic Pinot Noir and Syrah and pours it for you himself. Tasting Fee: $10

> *Follow Spain St to Rt 12, turn right, Imagery Estate Winery will be just after a rising curve in the road to the right, look for the banners: total 6.9 miles, approx 15 minutes*

Imagery Estate Winery 877.550.4278 www.imagerywinery.com *Great Art* Page 234
14335 Hwy 12, Glen Ellen Hours: 10 am - 4:30 pm Tasting Fee: $5 - $10
Wine List: Cabernet Franc, Petite Sirah, Barbera, Sangiovese, Malbec, White Burgundy, Pinot Blanc, Viognier, Petite Sirah Port, Interlude: Chocolate Infused Port, Blends (WOW Oui)

> *Turn right onto Rt 12 to Chateau St. Jean Winery: total 4.4 miles, approx 8 minutes*

Chateau St. Jean Winery 707.833.4134 www.chateaustjean.com *Deli-Gift* Page 219
8555 Sonoma Hwy., Kenwood Hours: 10 am - 5 pm Tasting Fee: $10 - $15
Wine List: Pinot Blanc, Chardonnay, Viognier, Pinot Noir, Merlot, Malbec, Cabernet Sauvignon

> *Turn left onto Rt 12 to Dunbar Rd. & Loxton Cellars: total 2.7 miles, approx 5 minutes*

Loxton Cellars 707.935.7221 www.loxtoncellars.com *Friendly Winery* Page 241
11466 Dunbar Rd., Glen Ellen Hours: 11 am - 5 pm daily Tasting Fee: comp - $5
Wine List: Rosé Vin Gris of Syrah, Zinfandel, Syrah, Cabernet Sauvignon, Syrah Port, Chardonnay, Shiraz

> *Follow Rt 12 South back to the Plaza, or continue on Rt 12 to Rt 121, bear right to the Light. Turn left to Rt 37, bear right to Hwy 101 and San Francisco.*

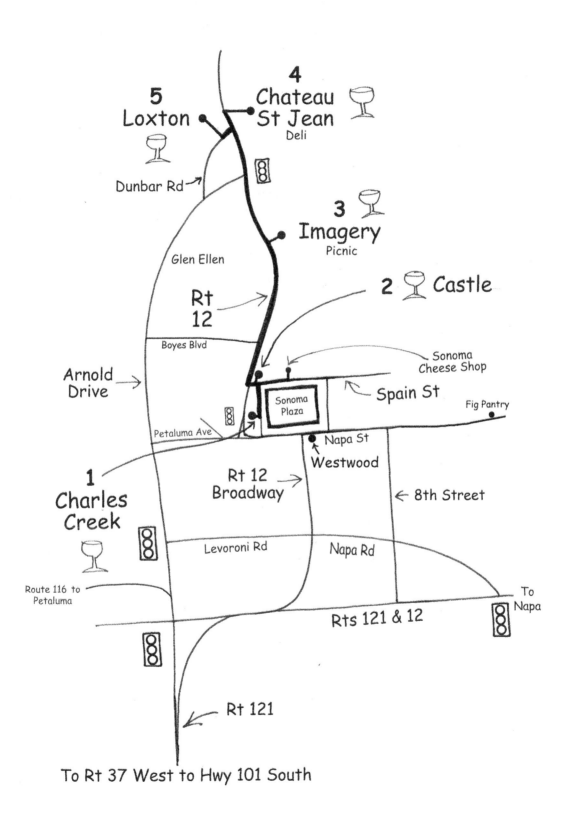

5
Loxton

Dunbar Rd

Glen Ellen

Rt
12

Boyes Blvd

Arnold
Drive

Petaluma Ave

4
Chateau
St Jean
Deli

3
Imagery
Picnic

2 Castle

Sonoma
Cheese Shop

Spain St

Fig Pantry

Sonoma
Plaza

Napa St
Westwood

1
Charles
Creek

Rt 12
Broadway

8th Street

Route 116 to
Petaluma

Levoroni Rd

Napa Rd

To
Napa

Rts 121 & 12

Rt 121

To Rt 37 West to Hwy 101 South

Your Day in Wine Country

Tour Eight in Southern Sonoma
A Wide Variety of Wines in the Valley of the Moon

Arrowood Vineyards & Winery 707.938.2600 www.arrowoodswinery.com *Red* Page 211
14347 Sonoma Hwy., Glen Ellen Hours: 10 am - 4:30 pm Tasting Fee: $5 - $10
Wine List: Chardonnay, Pinot Blanc, Viognier, Gewürztraminer, Merlot, Cabernet Sauvignon, Syrah, Late Harvest Riesling, Blends. Well known for their Cabernet Sauvignon blends

Heading to Kunde Estate Winery & Vineyards: total 4.1 miles, approx 5 minutes

Kunde Estate Winery & Vineyards 707.833.5501 www.kunde.com *Beautiful* Page 238
10155 Sonoma Hwy., Kenwood Hours: 10:30 am – 4:30 pm Tasting Fee: $5 - $10
Wines: Sauvignon Blanc, Chardonnay, Syrah, Zinfandel, Merlot, Cabernet Sauvignon, Primitivo, Meritage, Sangiovese, Barbera, Gewürztraminer, Grenache Rosé, Claret, Blends, Zinfandel Port

Turn right and Head to Café Citti on the left hand side: total 1.0 miles, approx 2 minutes

One lunch suggestion is:
Café Citti 707.833.2690
9049 Sonoma Hwy., Kenwood Hours: 11 am - 3:30 pm; 5 pm - 8:30 pm Friday till 9PM
There are picnic tables at Kunde & Landmark, or see restaurant list on page 110.

Turn left and Head to Adobe Canyon Rd and Landmark Winery on the right hand side, about 0.6 miles, approx 2 minutes

Landmark Winery 707.833.0053 www.landmarkwine.com *Unique Wines* *Picnic* Page 239
101 Adobe Canyon Rd., Kenwood Hours: 10 am - 4:30 pm Tasting Fee: $5 - $10
Wine List: Rhone Varietals, Chardonnay, Pinot Noir, Syrah

Continue on Adobe Canyon Rd to Kaz Vineyards & Winery: 0.1 miles, approx 1 minute

Kaz Vineyards & Winery 707.833.2536 www.kazwinery.com *Small* *Friendly* Page 237
233 Adobe Canyon Rd., Kenwood Hours: 11 am - 5 pm, Fri – Mon Tasting Fee: none listed
Wine List: Chardonnay, Sauvignon Blanc , Nebbiola Rosa (Rosé), Grenache, Sangiovese, Barbera, Zinfandel, Syrah, Cabernet Franc, Port, Blends including ZAM - (Zinfandel, Alicante Bouschet & Mourvèdre) also including Carignane, Malbec

Turn right on Rt. 12 and head to St. Francis Vineyard & Winery at the light on the right-hand side: total 1.7 miles, approx 5 minutes

St. Francis Vineyard & Winery 707.833.0242 www.stfranciswine.com *Views* Page 262
100 Pythian Rd., Santa Rosa Hours: 10 am - 5 pm Tasting Fee: $5 - $20
Wine List: Chardonnay, Cabernet Sauvignon, Merlot, Zinfandel, Syrah

Due to the traffic light, it is easy to head south again on Rt 12, despite traffic, to the Sonoma Plaza and on to Rt 121, 37 and 101 South to San Francisco.

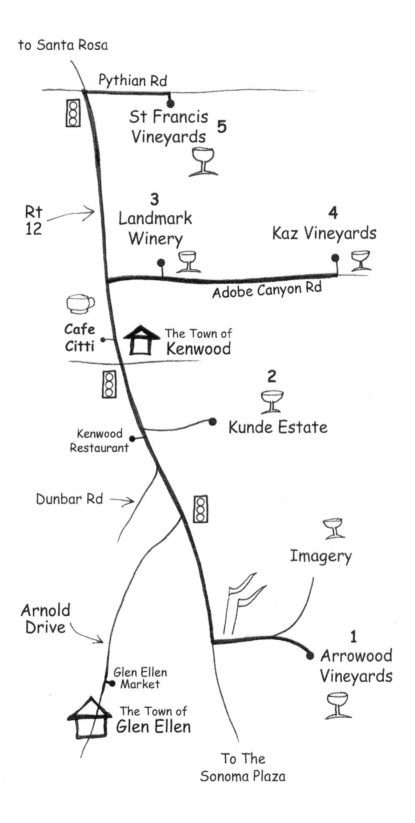

to Santa Rosa

Pythian Rd

St Francis Vineyards **5**

Rt 12

3
Landmark Winery

4
Kaz Vineyards

Adobe Canyon Rd

Cafe Citti

The Town of Kenwood

2
Kunde Estate

Kenwood Restaurant

Dunbar Rd

Imagery

Arnold Drive

1
Arrowood Vineyards

Glen Ellen Market

The Town of Glen Ellen

To The Sonoma Plaza

Tour Nine in Southern Sonoma
A Cross-County Carneros Tour, Great for a Hot Day, One Appointment

Jacuzzi Family Vineyards 707.931.7575 www.jacuzziwines.com *Beautiful*   Page 235
24724 Arnold Dr., Sonoma Hours: 10 am - 5:30 pm Tasting Fee: comp - $5
Wine List: Chardonnay, Pinot Noir, Barbera, Sangiovese, Arneis, Merlot, Nebbiolo, Primitivo, Pinot Grigio, Moscato Blanc, Blends - This also the site of the **Olive Press Gift Shop**

Turn right at the Cornerstone Gardens and Marketplace: 1.2 miles, 2 minutes

Pick up picnic items to eat at Bouchaine's picnic tables later
One picnic supply suggestion is:
The Café at Cornerstone Marketplace 707.935.1681 www.cornerstonegardens.com
23584 Arnold Dr., Sonoma Hours: 9 am-5 pm daily
The location of Grange Sonoma winery collective tasting room, Roshambo & Carneros Family Wineries.

Turn right to light, turn right to Duhig Rd. Look for Dominae Carneros, turn right and follow map to Bouchaine Vineyards: total 11.0 miles, approx 20 minutes

Bouchaine Vineyards 707.252.9065 www.bouchaine.com *Carneros Style*   Page 215
1075 Buchli Station Rd., Napa Hours: 10:30 am - 4 pm Tasting Fee: $5 - $10
Wine List: Chardonnay, Pinot Noir, Pinot Gris, Syrah, Pinot Meunier, Gewurtraminer

Heading to Ceja Vineyards: total 1.3 miles, approx 5 minutes

Ceja Vineyards 707.255.3954 www.cejavineyards.com *Appointment Charming*   Page 217
1016 Las Amigas Rd., Napa Hours: **appt only** Tasting Fee: $20
Wine List: Chardonnay, Merlot, Pinot Noir, Cabernet Sauvignon, Syrah, Blend

Follow Rt 121 to West where it turns south at the light, look for the market and gas station on the far left corner. To reach Schug Carneros Estate Winery go straight across the intersection to the end of the road: total 2.8 miles, approx 5 minutes

Schug Carneros Estate Winery 707.939.9363 www.schugwinery.com *Great Pinot* Page 258
602 Bonneau Rd., Sonoma Hours: 10 am - 5 pm daily Tasting Fee: $5, $10 for reserve
Wine List: Sauvignon Blanc, Chardonnay, Pinot Noir, Merlot, Cabernet Franc, Cabernet Sauvignon, Syrah, Blanc de Noirs Sparkling Pinot Noir

Head back to the light, turn right to Gloria Ferrer Champagne Caves, on the right hand side: total 1.1 miles approx 5 minutes

Gloria Ferrer Caves & Vineyards 707.996.7256 www.gloriaferrer.com *Sparkling*   Page 231
23555 Carneros Hwy 121, Sonoma Hours: 10 am – 5 pm Tasting Fee: by the glass $4 - $10
Wine List: Sparklers, Blanc de Blancs, Brut, Blanc de Noirs, Cuvee, Brut Rosé, Chardonnay, Pinot Noir, Syrah

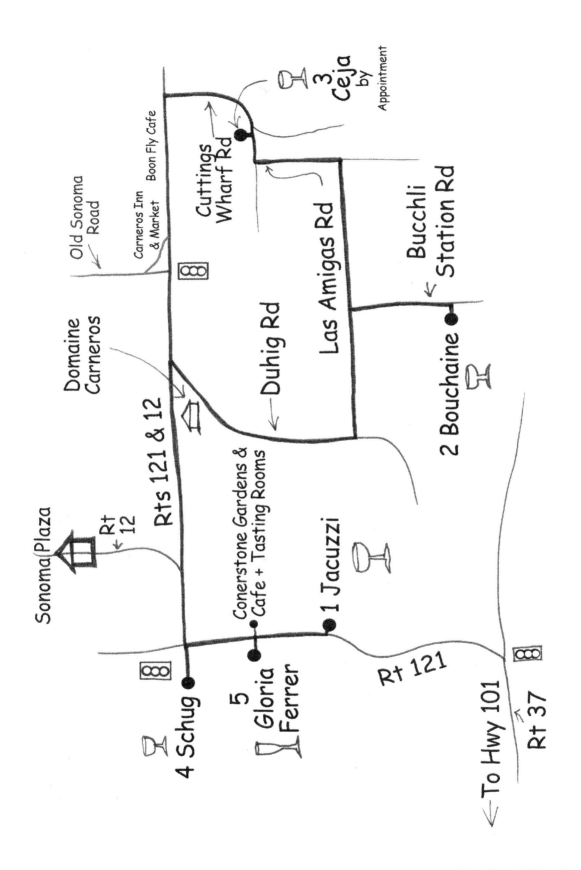

109

Restaurants & Lodgings in Southern Sonoma

Basque Boulangerie Café: 460 First St. E. Sonoma. 707.935.7687. Bakery & Sandwiches. Pg.18
Breakaway Café: 19101 Sonoma Hwy. Maxwell Village. Sonoma. 707.996.5949. Comfort. Pg.95
Café Citti: 9049 Sonoma Hwy. Kenwood. 707.833.2690. Italian Comfort. Pg. 107
Café La Haye: 140 E. Napa St. Sonoma. 707.935.5994. Fine Contemporary. Pg.18
Carneros Bistro & Wine Bar (at the Lodge at Sonoma): 1325 Broadway, Sonoma. 707.931.2402. Californian. Pg.18
Cornerstone Gardens Café: 23584 Arnold Dr. Sonoma. 704.935.1681. Market & Sandwiches Pg. 109
Della Santina: 133 E. Napa St. Sonoma. 707.935.0576. Italian. Pg.18
Deuce: 691 Broadway, Sonoma.707.933.3823. Fine Contemporary. Pg.18
El Dorado Kitchen: 405 First St. West, Sonoma. 707-996-3030. Fine Contemporary. Pg.18
Glen Ellen Market: 13751 Arnold Dr. Glen Ellen. 707.996.3411. Market. Pg. 103
Glen Ellen Inn Oyster Grill & Martini Bar: Located in the Glen Ellen Inn. See Below. Pg. 103
Il Pasticciere Fiorini: 248 W. Napa St. Sonoma. Italian Pastries & Lunch 707.996.6119. Pg. 18
Kenwood Restaurant: 9900 Sonoma Hwy. Kenwood. 707.833.6326. Fine Contemporary. Pg. 107
La Salette: 452 First Street East, Suite H. Sonoma, CA 95476. 707.938.1927. Mediterranean. Pg.18
Mary's Pizza Shack: 8 West Spain St. Sonoma. 707.938.8300. Italian. Pg.18
Maya Restaurant: 101 East Napa Street, Sonoma. 707.935.3500. Mexican. Pg.18
Murphy's Irish Pub: 464 First St. East, Sonoma. Irish. Pg.18
Red Grape Pizzeria: 529 First St. West, Sonoma. 707.996.4103. Italian. Pg.18
Rin's Thai Restaurant: 139 E. Napa St. Sonoma. 707.938.1462. Thai. Pg.18
Saddles Steakhouse: 29 E. MacArthur St. Sonoma. 707.938.2929. Best Steak. Pg.95
Sante': 707-938-9000 Located at the Fairmont Sonoma Mission Inn. See below. Fine Contempory. Pg. 93
Shiso: 522 Broadway, Sonoma. 707.933.9331. Japanese. Pg.18
Sonoma Cheese Factory: 2 Spain St. Sonoma. 800-535-2855. Market & Cheese Samples. Pg.18
Sonoma Market: 500 West Napa Street, Sonoma, 707.996.3411. Picnic Supplies. Pg.18
Sonoma-Meritage Martini Oyster Bar & Grill: 165 W. Napa St. Sonoma. 707.938.9430. Seafood.   Pg.18
Starbucks Coffee: 19239 Sonoma Hwy. Maxwell Village. Sonoma. 707.935.3187. Comfort. Pg.95
Sunflower Caffé: 421 First St. West, Sonoma. 707-996-6645. Sandwiches, Salads & Wine. Pg.18
Taste of the Himalayas: 464 First St. East, Sonoma. 707.996.1161. Nepalese. Pg.18
The Big 3: 707-938-9000 ext 2410. Located at the Fairmont Sonoma Mission Inn. See below. California Cuisine. Pg. 93
The Depot Hotel Cucina Rustica: 271 First St. West, Sonoma. 707.938.2980. Italian. Pg.18
the fig café & winebar: 13690 Arnold Dr. Glen Ellen. 707.938.2130. Californian. Pg.18
the fig pantry: 1190 E. Napa St. Sonoma. 707.933.3000. Market. Pg. 97
The General's Daughter: 400 W. Spain St. Sonoma. 707.938.4004. Contemporary Dining. Pg.18
the girl & the fig: 110 West Spain St. Sonoma. 707.938.3634. French Style Californian. Pg.18
The Swiss Hotel Bar & Restaurant: 18 West Spain St. Sonoma. 707.938.3298. Californian. Pg.18
Whole Foods Market: 201 West Napa St. Sonoma. 707.938.8500. Picnic Supplies. Pg.18
Wolf House: 13740 Arnold Dr. Glen Ellen. 707.996.4401. Californian. Pg. 103

Lodgings

Bed & Breakfast Association of Sonoma Valley: 800-969-4667 www.sonomabb.com
Cottage Inn & Spa: 302 First St. E. Sonoma. 800.944.1490 - 707.996.0719 www.cottageinnandspa.com Pg.18
El Dorado Hotel: 405 First St. W. Sonoma 707.996.3220 www.eldoradosonoma.com Pg.18
Fairmont Sonoma Mission Inn & Spa: 100 Boyes Blvd. Sonoma. 800.862.4945 www.fairmont.com/sonoma Pg.95
Gaige House Inn: 13540 Arnold Dr. Glen Ellen 800.935.0237 707.935.0237 www.gaigehouse.com Pg.103
Glen Ellen Inn: 13670 Arnold Dr. Glen Ellen 707.996.1174 www.glenelleninn.com Pg.103
Inn at Sonoma: 630 Broadway. Sonoma 888-568-9818 www.InnatSonoma.com Pg.95
Jack London Lodge: 13740 Arnold Dr. Glen Ellen 707.938.8510 Pg.103
Kenwood Inn and Spa: 10400 Sonoma Hwy Kenwood 800.353.6966 707.833.1293 Pg.93
MacArthur Place: Broadway & MacArthur St. Sonoma 800.722.1866 707.938.2929 www.macarthurplace.com Pg.95
Sheraton Sonoma County - Petaluma: 745 Baywood Dr. Petaluma 707.283.2888
Sonoma Hotel: 110 W. Spain St. Sonoma 800.468.6016 707.996.2996 www.sonomahotel.com Pg.18
The Lodge at Sonoma Resort & Spa: 1325 Broadway, Sonoma. 707.935.6600 www.thelodgeatsonoma.com Pg.93
The Swiss Hotel: 18 West Spain St. Sonoma. 707.938.3298. www.swisshotelsonoma.com Pg.18

Wine Shipping: UPS Store 19201 Sonoma Hwy (Maxwell Village) 707-935-3438 Pg.95

Tour Directory: Starting in Southern Napa

One - Page 114

The Judgment of Paris Tour, Three Great Wineries that Put Napa on the Map.

Wineries: Stag's Leap Cellars, Grgich Hills, Chateau Montelena

Four hour tour locally, seven hour tour from SF. $$ Moderately Priced

Two - Page 116

A Pleasant Mixed Tour, Big and Little Wineries, Something for Everyone,
Touring From Yountville to St. Helena.

Wineries: Goosecross, Plumpjack, Rutherford Hill, Beringer,
Domaine Chandon (Sparkling)

Six hour tour locally, eight hour tour from SF

A good day trip from San Francisco. $$ Moderately Priced

Three - Page 118

The Stag's Leap District, Big Reds, Great Tour for a Hot Day, Good Gift Shops.

Wineries: Darioush, Clo Du Val, Regusci, Stag's Leap Cellars, Robert Sinskey

Six hour tour locally, eight hour tour from SF

A good day trip from San Francisco. $$ Moderately Priced

Four - Page 120

Scenic Artesa Followed by Small Wineries on the Silverado Trail, Great Views,
Good Wine Variety, Great Introduction to the Silverado Trail.

Wineries: Artesa, Goosecross, Regusci, Signorella, Luna

Six hour tour locally, eight hour tour from SF

A good day trip from San Francisco. $$ Moderately Priced

Five - Page 122

Over Golden Gate, Carneros and Southern Napa, Beautiful Wineries,
Great Views, Good Tour for a Hot Day, Great Gift Shops.

Wineries: Jacuzzi, Artesa, Miner, Silverado, Darioush

Six hour tour locally, eight hour tour from SF

A good day trip from San Francisco. $$ Moderately Priced

Best with a Car and Driver

Six - Page 124

Sparkling Wines and Beautiful Wineries, Great Gift Shops, One Appointment.

Wineries: Domaine Carneros (Sparkling), V. Sattui, Schramsberg (Appointment for tours at specific times, Sparkling), Beringer, Artesa

Six hour tour locally, eight hour tour from SF. $$ Moderately Priced

Seven - Page 126

A Great First Tour from San Francisco, Show places, Great Gift Shops.

Wineries: Domaine Carneros (Sparkling), Artesa, Rubicon, Silverado, Darioush

Six hour tour locally, eight hour tour from SF

A good day trip from San Francisco. $$$ Moderately Expensive

Best with a Hired Car and Driver

Eight - Page 128

Around the Stag's Leap District Along the Silverado Trail, Big Reds, Tasting in a Cave, One Appointment.

Wineries: Frazier (App), Signorello, Regusci, Robert Sinskey, Cliff Lede

Six hour tour locally, eight hour tour from SF

A good day trip from San Francisco. $$$ Moderately Expensive

Best with a Hired Car and Driver

Nine - Page 130

The Southern Silverado Trail, Starting off Tasting in a Cave, One Appointment.

Wineries: Jarvis (App), Darioush, Regusci, Robert Sinskey

Six hour tour locally, eight hour tour from SF

A good day trip from San Francisco. $$$$ Expensive

Best with a Hired Car and Driver

Ten - Page 132

Big, Prestigious Red Wine Labels, One Appointment.

Wineries: Stag's Leap Cellars, Silver Oak, Opus One, Joseph Phelps (App)

Six hour tour locally, eight hour tour from SF. $$$$ Expensive

Best with a Hired Car and Driver

Restaurants & Hotels of Southern Napa   Page 134

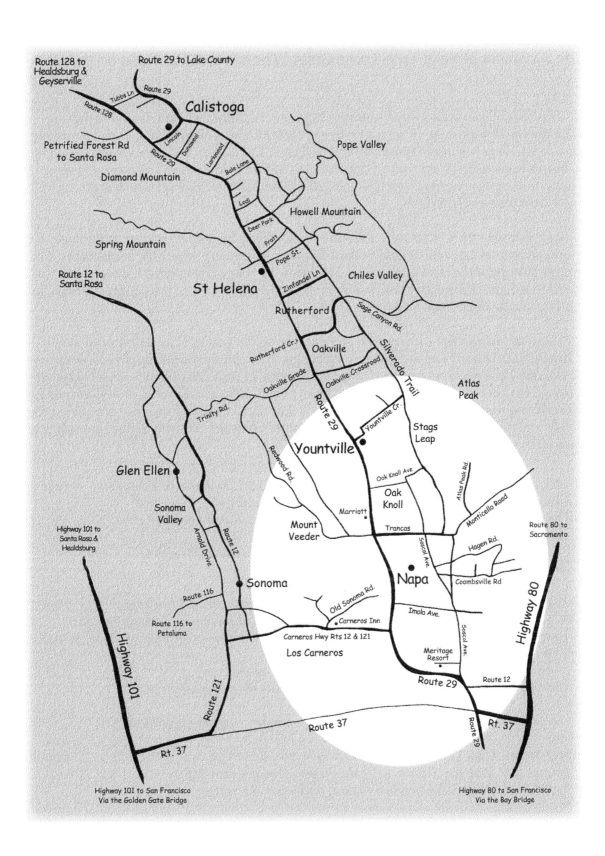

Your Day in Wine Country

Tour One in Southern Napa
The Judgment of Paris Tour, Three Great Wineries that Put Napa on the Map

This tour only contains three wineries, but they are three that contributed to putting Napa on the world wine map. In 1976 a tasting competition was organized in Paris comparing the best of the French wines to those of the Americans. The Judges were French wine makers and wine professionals. To everyone's surprise the California wines took top honors in some very important categories. Stag's Leap Wine Cellars won for the Cabernet Sauvignon, one of France's most treasured products.

As a side note the Cellars were sold this year by the original owner Warren Winarski for one hundred and seventy one million dollars. Chateau Montelena, where the wine maker was Mike Grgich, won for the top Chardonnay. The following year Mike opened his own winery in partnership with the Hills coffee family, Grgich Hills. To get a sense of the quality of wines they have produced, do their reserve tastings.

The tour has another nice quality. It encompasses the entire Napa Valley from Stag's Leap through Rutherford and St Helena to Calistoga. We recommend eating in St. Helena unless it is a very busy weekend because the traffic heading north to St Helena will be backed up to V. Sattui. In that case head south on Rt 29 from Grgich Hills and turn left on Rutherford Rd. which will bring you to the Silverado Trail. Follow that north to Deer Park and turn left. At Rt 29 turn right and follow that to Lincoln, the main street of Calistoga. Turning right there will bring you to a number of nice places to have lunch.

Stag's Leap Wine Cellars   707.261.6441   www.cask23.com   *Reserve Tasting*   Page 263
5766 Silverado Trail, Napa   Hours: 10 am - 4:30 pm   Tasting Fee: $10 - $30
Wine List: Riesling, Sauvignon Blanc, Chardonnay, Merlot, Cabernet Sauvignon

North to Oakville Cross Rd, turn left to Rt 29, turn right to Grgich Hills Cellar: total 9.7 miles, approx 15 minutes

Grgich Hills Cellar   707.963.2784   www.grgich.com   *Friendly & Traditional*   Page 231
1829 St. Helena Hwy S., Rutherford   Hours: 9:30 am - 4:30 pm daily   Tasting Fee: $10
Wine List: Chardonnay, Fumé Blanc, Violetta (botrytis dessert wine), Cabernet Sauvignon, Zinfandel, Merlot

See notes above about Route. See restaurant lists on pages 186 & 208.

Heading to Chateau Montelena: approx 16.4 miles, approx 30 minutes

Chateau Montelena Winery   707.942.5105   www.montelena.com   *Great Site*   Page 219
1429 Tubbs Ln., Calistoga   Hours: 9:30 am - 4 pm   Tasting Fee: $15
Wine List: Chardonnay, Cabernet Sauvignon, Zinfandel, Riesling

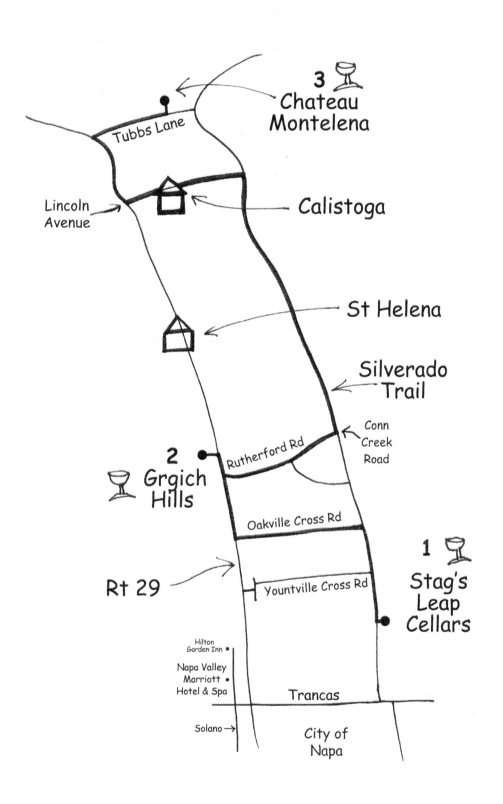

3 🍷 Chateau Montelena

Tubbs Lane

Lincoln Avenue

Calistoga

St Helena

Silverado Trail

Conn Creek Road

2 🍷 Grgich Hills

Rutherford Rd

Oakville Cross Rd

Rt 29

Yountville Cross Rd

1 🍷 Stag's Leap Cellars

Hilton Garden Inn •

Napa Valley Marriott Hotel & Spa •

Trancas

Solano →

City of Napa

115

Tour Two in Southern Napa
A Pleasant Mixed Tour, Big and Little Wineries, Something for Everyone

Goosecross Cellars 707.944.1986 www.goosecross.com *Small Winery*   Page 231
1119 State Ln., Yountville   Hours: 10 am-4:30 pm   Tasting Fee: $5   *Friendly*
Wine List: Viognier, Chenin Blanc, Sauvignon Blanc, Chardonnay, Sparkling Rosé, Cabernet
Sauvignon, Zinfandel, Merlot, Pinot Noir, Syrah, Blends

Follow Yountville Cr. Rd to Rt 29 & turn right, to Oakville Cr. Rd, turn right to Plump-jack Winery. The sign is before the hill on the left: total 3.6 miles, approx 10 minutes

Plumpjack Winery 707.945.1220 www.plumpjack.com *Charming*   Page 250
620 Oakville Cross Rd., Oakville   Hours: 10 am – 4 pm   Tasting Fee: $10-$20
Wine List: Cabernet Sauvignon, Chardonnay, Merlot

Backtrack to Oakville Grocery: total 2.1 miles, approx 5 minutes

Pick up picnic items to eat at Rutherford Hill Winery's picnic tables later at
Oakville Grocery 707.944.8802   7856 St. Helena Hwy, Oakville   Hours: 7 am – 6 pm

Head north & turn right at Rutherford Rd., follow to the Silverado Trail, turn left and then a quick right onto Rutherford Hill Rd. Look for the large boulder-sign at the intersection, follow to the top of the hill to Rutherford Hill Winery: total 5.3 miles, approx 10 minutes

Rutherford Hill Winery 707.963.7194 www. rutherfordhill.com *Picnic-Views*   Page 257
200 Rutherford Hill Rd., Rutherford   Hours: 10 am – 5 pm   Tasting Fee: $5 - $10
Wine List: Zinfandel Port, Merlot, Cabernet Sauvignon, Sangiovese, Blends, Petite Verdot, Char-donnay, Syrah, Malbec, Sauvignon Blanc

North on Silverado, left on Pratt, right on Rt 29 to Beringer Vineyards immediately on left: total 5.3 miles approx 11 minutes

Beringer Vineyards 707.967.4412 www.beringer.com *Great Tours*   Page 214
2000 Main St., St. Helena   Hours: 10 am – 5 pm   Tasting Fee: $5 - $10
Wine List: Chardonnay, Sauvignon Blanc, Pinot Noir, Merlot, Cabernet Sauvignon, Riesling, Viognier, White Zinfandel, White Merlot, Chenin Blanc, Gewürztraminer, Pinot Grigio, Shiraz

Rt 29 south to Yountville exit, California Dr, bear right to Domaine Chandon: total 8.7 miles approx 12 minutes

Domaine Chandon 707.944.2280 www.domainechandon.com *Sparkling*   Page 224
1 California Dr., Yountville   Hours: 10 am - 6 pm   Tasting Fee: $10 & by the glass
Wine List: Brut, Blanc de Noirs, Rosé, Sparkling Chardonnay, Blanc de Blancs, Pinot Noir, Pinot
Meunier, Chardonnay, Unoaked Pinot Noir Rosé, Unoaked Chardonnay

After 6 pm Domain Chandon offers wine by the glass as a bar. This is due to being the only winery in Napa with a Restaurant attached to it, Etoile, the Star.

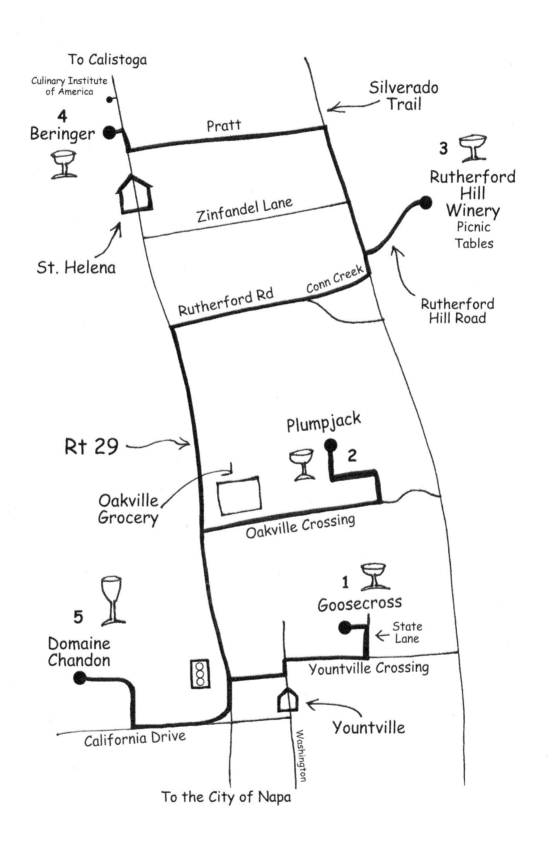

To Calistoga

Culinary Institute of America

4
Beringer

Silverado Trail

Pratt

3
Rutherford Hill Winery
Picnic Tables

St. Helena

Zinfandel Lane

Rutherford Rd

Conn Creek

Rutherford Hill Road

Plumpjack

Rt 29

2

Oakville Grocery

Oakville Crossing

1
Goosecross

State Lane

5
Domaine Chandon

Yountville Crossing

Washington

California Drive

Yountville

To the City of Napa

Tour Three in Southern Napa
The Stag's Leap District, Big Reds, Great Tour for a Hot Day, Good Gift Shops

Pick up picnic items to eat at Regusci Winery's picnic tables later at
Soda Canyon Market   707.252.0285
4006 Silverado Trail, Napa Hours: 8 am – 6 pm
Or eat lunch in Yountville, see restaurant list on page 134

North on Silverado Trail to Darioush: total 0.5 miles, approx 2 minutes

Darioush 707.257.2345 www.darioush.com *Gorgeous*   Page 222
4240 Silverado Trail, Napa Hours: 10:30 am - 5 pm Tasting Fee: $20
Wine List: Cabernet Sauvignon, Shiraz, Chardonnay, Merlot, Semillon, Sauvignon, Blanc, Pinot Noir, Viognier

North on Silverado Trail to Clos du Val: total 1.6 miles, approx 2 minutes

Clos Du Val 707.261.5225 www.closduval.com *French Style*   Page 220
5330 Silverado Tr., Napa Hours: 10 am - 5 pm Tasting Fee: $10 - $20 (waived w/purchase)
Wine List: Cabernet Sauvignon, Chardonnay, Merlot, Pinot Noir, Blend

North on Silverado Trail to Regusci Winery: total 0.8 miles, approx 2 minutes

Regusci Winery 707.254.0403 www.regusciwinery.com *Picnic-Family*   Page 252
5584 Silverado Trail, Napa Hours: 10 am - 4 pm Tasting Fee: $5 - $10
Wine List: Cabernet Sauvignon, Merlot, Zinfandel, and Chardonnay (Chardonnay is from Far Niente's grapes)

North on Silverado Trail to Stag's Leap Cellars: total 0.6 miles approx 2 minutes

Stag's Leap Wine Cellars 707.261.6441 www.cask23.com *Famous Reds*   Page 263
5766 Silverado Trail, Napa Hours: 10 am - 4:30 pm Tasting Fee: $10 - $30
Wine List: Riesling, Sauvignon Blanc, Chardonnay, Merlot, Cabernet Sauvignon

North on Silverado Trail to Robert Sinskey Vineyards: total 4.7 miles approx 5 minutes

Robert Sinskey Vineyards 707.944.9090 www.robertsinskey.com *Fun-Tasty*   Page 254
6320 Silverado Trail, Napa Hours: 10 am - 4:30 pm daily Tasting Fee: $10 - $20
Wine List: Pinot Blanc, Rosé of Pinot Noir, Pinot Gris, Vin Gris of Pinot Noir, Pinot Noir, Merlot, Cabernet Franc, Cabernet Sauvignon, Blends, Late Harvest Zinfandel

Yountville Cross Rd to Washinton & Bouchon Bakery: total 2.7 miles approx 6 minutes

Bouchon Bakery for coffee and snacks 707.944.8037 www.bouchonbakery.com
6534 Washington St., Yountville Hours: 7 am – 7 pm

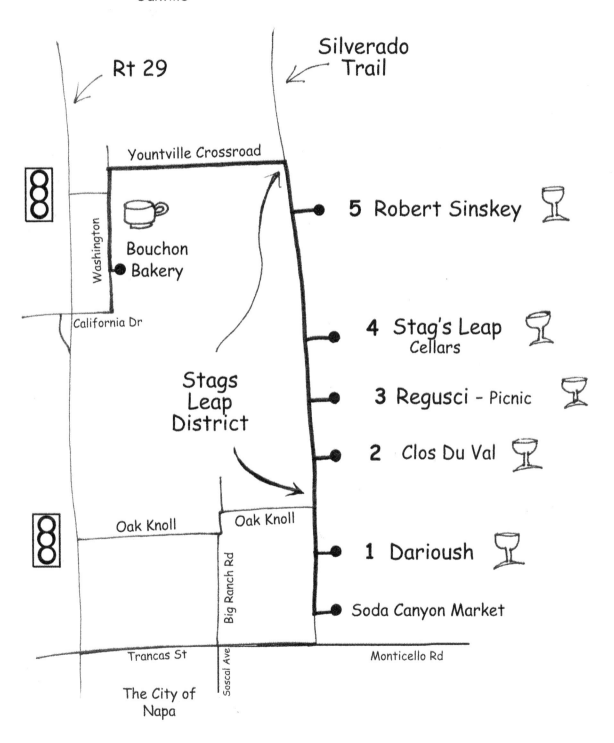

Oakville

Rt 29

Silverado
Trail

Yountville Crossroad

Washington

Bouchon
Bakery

California Dr

Stags
Leap
District

Oak Knoll

Oak Knoll

Big Ranch Rd

Soscal Ave

Trancas St

Monticello Rd

The City of
Napa

5 Robert Sinskey

4 Stag's Leap
Cellars

3 Regusci - Picnic

2 Clos Du Val

1 Darioush

Soda Canyon Market

Tour Four in Southern Napa
Scenic Artesa Followed by Small Wineries on the Silverado Trail, Great Views

Artesa Winery 707.254.2140 www.artesawinery.com *Great Views* Page 211
1345 Henry Rd., Napa Hours: 10 am - 5 pm daily Tasting Fee: $5 - $10
Wine List: Cabernet Sauvignon, Chardonnay, Merlot, Pinot Noir, Tempranillo, Albarino, Garnacha Rosado, Late Harvest Gewürztraminer, Blends

> *Rt 121 East to Rt 29, turn left. At the Yountville exit bear right to Washinton, turn left to Bouchon Bakery on right hand side: total 14.9 miles, approx 25 minutes*

Pick up picnic items to eat at Goosecross or Regusci's picnic tables later at
Bouchon Bakery 707.944.8037 www.bouchonbakery.com
6534 Washington St., Yountville Hours: 7 am - 7 pm

> *Take Yountville Cross Rd to State Ln, turn left, then left again into Goosecross Cellars: total 2.2 miles, approx 6 minutes*

Goosecross Cellars 707.944.1986 www.goosecross.com **S**mall Fun Winery Page 231
1119 State Ln., Yountville Hours: 10 am- 4:30 pm daily Tasting Fee: $5 - $10
Wine List: Viognier, Chenin Blanc, Sauvignon Blanc, Chardonnay, Sparkling Rosé, Cabernet Sauvignon, Zinfandel, Merlot, Pinot Noir, Syrah, Blends

> *Take Yountville Cross Rd to Silverado Trail, turn right to Regusci Winery, on left-hand side: total 3.5 miles, approx 5 minutes*

Regusci Winery 707.254.0403 www.regusciwinery.com *Great Picnic Area* Page 252
5584 Silverado Trail, Napa Hours: 10 am - 4 pm Tasting Fee: $5 - $10
Wine List: Cabernet Sauvignon, Merlot, Zinfandel, and Chardonnay (Chardonnay is from Far Niente's grapes)

> *Turn left onto Silverado Trail to Signorello Vineyards, left side: 2.3 miles, 2 minutes*

Signorello Vineyards 707.255.5990 www.signorellovineyards.com *Views* Page 260
4500 Silverado Trail, Napa Hours: 10:30 am - 5 pm Tasting Fee: $5 - $10 *Small Winery*
Wine List: Cabernet Sauvignon, Zinfandel, Pinot Noir, Syrah Seta: Italian for ""silk"" is a Sauvignon-Semillon Blend

> *Turn left onto Silverado Trail to Luna Vineyards, right side: 1.7 miles 2 minutes*

Luna Vineyards 707.255.2474 www.lunavineyards.com *Italian Varietals* Page 241
2921 Silverado Trail, Napa Hours: 10 am - 5 pm daily Tasting Fee: $5 - $10
Wine List: Sangiovese, Merlot, Petite Sirah, Pinot Grigio, Tocai Fiulano, Chardonnay, Cabernet Sauvignon, Blends (Freakout)

> *Follow Silverado Trail south to Trancas (coffee and fuel), turn right to Rt 29 entrances*

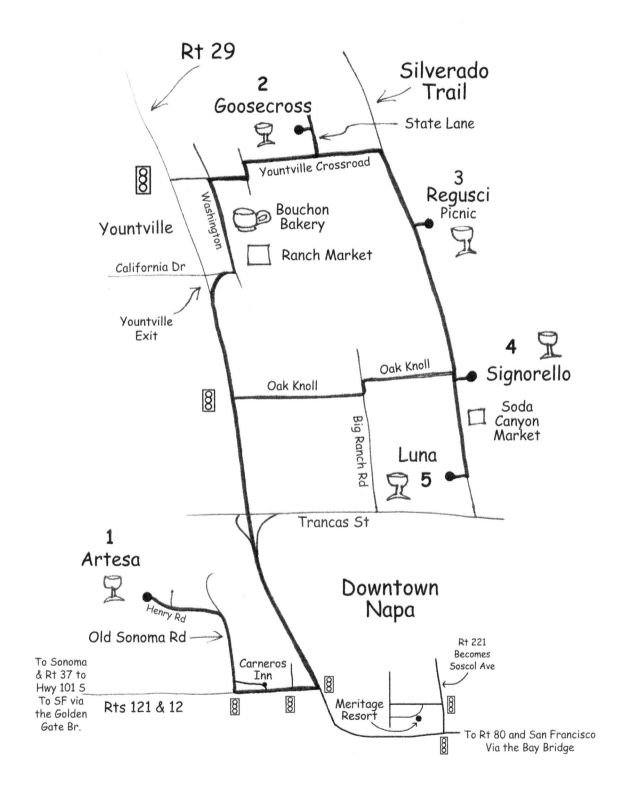

Rt 29

2
Goosecross

Silverado Trail

State Lane

Yountville Crossroad

Washington

Yountville

Bouchon Bakery

Ranch Market

3
Regusci
Picnic

California Dr

Yountville Exit

Oak Knoll

Oak Knoll

4
Signorello

Soda Canyon Market

Big Ranch Rd

Luna
5

Trancas St

1
Artesa

Henry Rd

Old Sonoma Rd

Downtown Napa

To Sonoma & Rt 37 to Hwy 101 S To SF via the Golden Gate Br.

Carneros Inn

Rts 121 & 12

Meritage Resort

Rt 221 Becomes Soscol Ave

To Rt 80 and San Francisco Via the Bay Bridge

Your Day in Wine Country

Tour Five in Southern Napa
Over the Golden Gate, Carneros and Southern Napa, Beautiful Wineries

Jacuzzi Family Vineyards 707.931.7575 www.jacuzziwines.com *Beautiful*   Page 235
24724 Arnold Dr., Sonoma   Hours: 10 am - 5:30 pm Tasting Fee: comp - $5
Wine List: Chardonnay, Pinot Noir, Barbera, Sangiovese, Arneis, Merlot, Nebbiolo, Primitivo,
Pinot Grigio, Moscato Blanc, Blends - This also the site of the **Olive Press Gift Shop**

For Food: The Blue Tree Cafe at the Conerstone Gardens and Market

Follow Rt 121 to Old Sonoma Rd. traffic light, turn left and then left again at Henry to
Artesa Winery, it is clearly marked: total 11.2 miles, approx 20 minutes

Artesa Winery 707.254.2140 www.artesawinery.com *Great Views*   Page 211
1345 Henry Rd., Napa   Hours: 10 am - 5 pm daily   Tasting Fee: $5 - $10
Wine List: Cabernet Sauvignon, Chardonnay, Merlot, Pinot Noir, Tempranillo, Albarino,
Garnacha Rosado, Late Harvest Gewürztraminer, Blends

Return Rt 121, turn left to Rt 29, turn left and go to the Oakville Cross Rd. Stop at the
Oakville Market for picnic supplies. If the traffic is heavy, go north on Rt 29 and
immediately turn right into Opus One's driveway, then bear right at the building and
take the drive out to the right. The gate will open as you approach. Turn left on Oakville
Cross Rd. to the Silverado Trail, turn left and the Miner Family Vineyards will
be on the right: total from Artesa 20.6 miles, approx 30 minutes

Miner Family Vineyards 707.944.9500 www.minerwines.com *Picnic-Views*   Page 244
7850 Silverado Trail, Oakville   Hours: 11 am - 5 pm   Tasting Fee: $5 - $10
Wine List: Chardonnay, Viognier, Sauvignon Blanc, Cabernet Sauvignon, Pinot Noir, Merlot,
Syrah, Petite Sirah, Zinfandel, Sangiovese, Rosato, Blends

Turn Left Heading to Silverado Vineyards: total 3.7 miles, approx 5 minutes

Silverado Vineyards 707.257.1770 www.silveradovineyards.com *Great Views*   Page 261
6121 Silverado Trail, Napa   Hours: 10:30 am - 4:30 pm   Tasting Fee: $10 - $20
Wine List: Sauvignon Blanc, Chardonnay, Merlot, Sangiovese, Cabernet Sauvignon

Turn Right Heading to Darioush: total 4.2 miles, approx 5 minutes

Darioush 707.257.2345 www.darioush.com *Gorgeous Building & Grounds*   Page 222
4240 Silverado Trail, Napa   Hours: 10:30 am - 5 pm   Tasting Fee: $20
Wine List: Cabernet Sauvignon, Shiraz, Chardonnay, Merlot, Semillon, Sauvignon, Blanc, Pinot
Noir, Viognier

Follow Silverado Trail south to Trancas (coffee and fuel), turn right to Rt 29 entrances

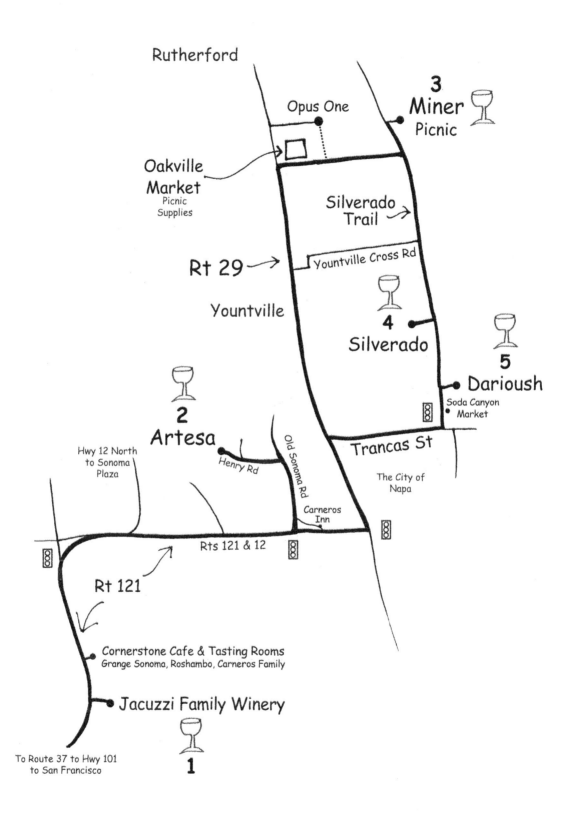

Rutherford

3
Miner
Picnic

Opus One

Oakville
Market
Picnic
Supplies

Silverado
Trail

Rt 29 →
Yountville Cross Rd

Yountville

4
Silverado

5
Darioush

Soda Canyon
Market

2
Artesa

Hwy 12 North
to Sonoma
Plaza

Henry Rd

Old Sonoma Rd

Trancas St

The City of
Napa

Carneros
Inn

Rts 121 & 12

Rt 121

Cornerstone Cafe & Tasting Rooms
Grange Sonoma, Roshambo, Carneros Family

Jacuzzi Family Winery

1

To Route 37 to Hwy 101
to San Francisco

Tour Six in Southern Napa
Sparkling Wines and Beautiful Wineries, Great Gift Shops, One Appointment

This Tour works well even if you leave out the appointment at Schramsberg, but if you can fit them in you're going to visit some of the oldest winery caves in Napa. The appointment includes a tour so plan to be early because the drive up the mountain is winding, even though the road is freshly paved and improved. This tour covers the entire length of the Napa Valley in a day.

Domaine Carneros 707.257.0101 www.domainecarneros.com *Sparkling*   Page 224
1240 Duhig Rd., Napa   Hours: 10 am - 6 pm daily   Tasting Fee: table service by the glass
Wine List: Brut Cuvee, Brut Rosé, Le Reve Blanc de Blancs, Pinot Noir

> *Follow Rt 121 East to Rt 29 North, turn left to V. Sattui Winery on the right-hand side: total 21.8 miles, approx 25 minutes*

> *V. Sattui Winery has a great deli & picnic area to buy lunch. You can not bring food on to their property but considering how good the deli is you really don't want to.*

V. Sattui Winery 707.963.7774 www.vsattui.com *Deli Picnic-Gift Shop*   Page 268
1111 White Ln., St. Helena   Hours: 9 am - 6 pm   Tasting Fee: complimentary
Wine List: Sparklers, Sauvignon Blanc, Semillon, Chardonnay, Riesling, Gamay Rouge, White Zinfandel, Rosato, Gewürztraminer, Pinot Noir, Merlot, Zinfandel, Cabernet Sauvignon, Sangiovese, Grappa, Port, Madeira, Muscat, Petite Sirah, Syrah, Blends

> *Turn right through St Helena to Schramsberg Vineyards. Watch the odometer because their road is hard to spot. It is just past Larkmead Lane on the left hand side: total 7.0 miles, approx 11 minutes. Their tours are done at specific times. Call them.*

Schramsberg Vineyards 707.942.2414 www.schramsberg.com *Appointment*   Page 258
1400 Schramsberg Rd., Calistoga Hrs: 10 am - 4 pm   Tours at Specific Times with Tasting: $25
Wine List: Sparkling wine; Brut Rosé, Cremant, Blanc de Noirs, Blanc de Blanc, Mirabelle

> Turn right (south) *to Beringer Vineyards: total 4.7 miles, approx 8 minutes*

Beringer Vineyards 707.967.4412 www.beringer.com *Great Tours*   Page 214
2000 Main St., St. Helena   Hours: 10 am - 5 pm   Tasting Fee: $5 - $10
Wine List: Chardonnay, Dessert Wines, Sauvignon Blanc, Pinot Noir, Merlot, Cabernet Sauvignon, Riesling, Viognier, White Zinfandel, White Merlot, Chenin Blanc, Gewürztraminer, Pinot Grigio, Shiraz

> Turn right (south) *to Rt. 121, turn right, at Old Sonoma Rd turn right, take first left onto Henry Rd. & Artesa Winery, clearly marked: total 24.8 miles, approx 40 minutes*

Artesa Winery 707.254.2140 www.artesawinery.com *Great Views*   Page 211
1345 Henry Rd., Napa   Hours: 10 am - 5 pm daily   Tasting Fee: $5 - $10
Wine List: Cabernet Sauvignon, Chardonnay, Merlot, Pinot Noir, Tempranillo, Albarino, Garnacha Rosado, Late Harvest Gewürztraminer, Blends

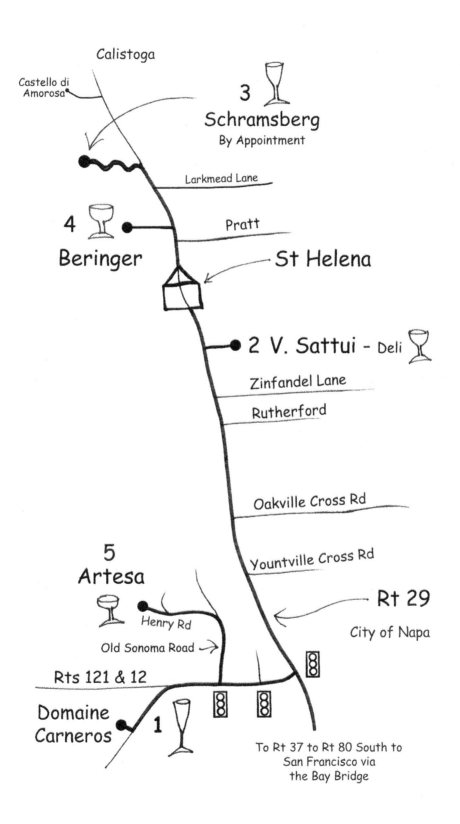

Calistoga

Castello di
Amorosa

3 Schramsberg
By Appointment

Larkmead Lane

4 Beringer

Pratt

St Helena

2 V. Sattui - Deli

Zinfandel Lane

Rutherford

Oakville Cross Rd

Yountville Cross Rd

5 Artesa

Rt 29

Henry Rd

City of Napa

Old Sonoma Road

Rts 121 & 12

Domaine Carneros

1

To Rt 37 to Rt 80 South to
San Francisco via
the Bay Bridge

Tour Seven in Southern Napa
A Great First Tour from San Francisco, Show places, Great Gift Shops

Domaine Carneros 707.257.0101 www.domainecarneros.com *Sparkling*   Page 224
1240 Duhig Rd., Napa   Hours: 10 am - 6 pm daily   Tasting Fee: table service by the glass
Wine List: Brut Cuvee, Brut Rosé, Le Reve Blanc de Blancs, Pinot Noir

East to light, left and then left again to Artesa Winery: total 2.7 miles, approx 7 minutes

Artesa Winery 707.254.2140 www.artesawinery.com *Views*   Page 211
1345 Henry Rd., Napa   Hours: 10 am - 5 pm daily   Tasting Fee: $5 - $10
Wine List: Cabernet Sauvignon, Chardonnay, Merlot, Pinot Noir, Tempranillo, Albarino, Garnacha Rosado, Late Harvest Gewürztraminer, Blends

Backtrack to light, left to Rt 29, left again to Oakville Grocery: 18.2 miles, 26 minutes

Pick up picnic items to eat at Oakville Grocery's picnic tables
Oakville Grocery 707.944.8802 www.oakvillegrocery.com
7856 St. Helena Hwy., Oakville   Hours: 9 am - 6 pm espresso bar from 7 am

North to Rubicon on the left-hand side opposite Rutherford Rd: 0.1 miles, 2 minutes

Rubicon Estate 707.968.1100 www.rubiconestate.com *Great Estate*   Page 256
1991 St. Helena Hwy., Rutherford   Hours: 10 am - 5 pm   Tasting & Tour Fee: $25
Wine List: Cabernet Sauvignon, Merlot, Cabernet Franc, Syrah, Blends
The most expensive fee on the tour but worth the price. Owned by Francis Ford Coppola.

*South to Oakville Cross Rd, turn left to Silverado Trail, turn right (south) to the
Silverado Vineyards: 5.9 miles 10 minutes*

Silverado Vineyards 707.257.1770 www.silveradovineyards.com *Views*   Page 261
6121 Silverado Trail, Napa   Hours: 10:30 am - 4:30 pm   Tasting Fee: $10 - $20
Wine List: Sauvignon Blanc, Chardonnay, Merlot, Sangiovese, Cabernet Sauvignon

Turn right (south) on the Silverado Trail to Darioush: total 4.2 miles approx 4 minutes

Darioush 707.257.2345 www.darioush.com *Gorgeous Building & Grounds*   Page 222
4240 Silverado Trail, Napa   Hours: 10:30 am - 5 pm   Tasting Fee: $20
Wine List: Cabernet Sauvignon, Shiraz, Chardonnay, Merlot, Semillon, Sauvignon Blanc, Pinot Noir, Viognier

*To Return to San Francisco continue south (left) on Silverado to traffic light, Trancas,
turn right (coffee shops and fuel) and follow that to Rt 29 south entrance.*

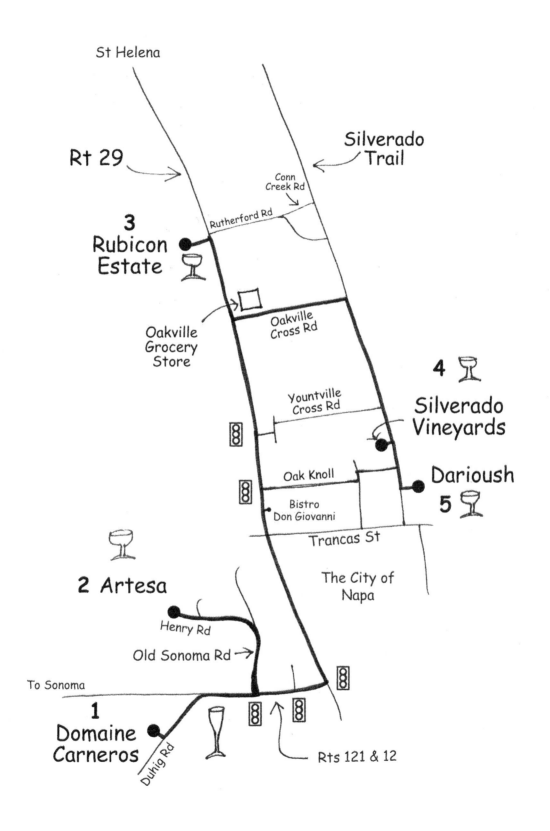

St Helena

Rt 29

Silverado Trail

Conn Creek Rd

Rutherford Rd

3
Rubicon
Estate

Oakville Grocery Store

Oakville Cross Rd

4
Silverado Vineyards

Yountville Cross Rd

Oak Knoll

Darioush
5

Bistro Don Giovanni

Trancas St

The City of Napa

2 Artesa

Henry Rd

Old Sonoma Rd

To Sonoma

1
Domaine Carneros

Duhig Rd

Rts 121 & 12

Your Day in Wine Country

Tour Eight in Southern Napa
Around the Stag's Leap District Along the Silverado Trail, Big Reds

The Frazier Winery cave is on the east side of the city of Napa in a beautiful, if out of the way area. From the south the easiest way to reach them is to go north on Rt 29, exit at Imola, bear right to Soscal. Turn left and then bear right onto the Silverado Trail. At Coombsville Rd turn right, and then left on Second Ave. The road will lead you to Rapp Ln. Go through the gate and bear right following the winery sign, to the end. You'll see the cave entrance. Watch out for flying golf balls.

Frazier Winery 707.255.3444 www.frazierwinery.com *Appointment Caves*   Page 229
70 Rapp Ln., Napa   Hours: 10 am - 4 pm Mon - Sat appt only   Tasting Fee: $20 - $25
Wine List: Cabernet Sauvignon, Merlot, Blend

Follow map to Soda Canyon Market: total 6.1 miles, approx 13 minutes

Pick up picnic items to eat at Regusci Winery's picnic tables later at
Soda Canyon Market 707.252.0285
4006 Silverado Trail, Napa   Hours: 8 am – 6 pm

North on Silverado to Signorello (Just past Darioush): total 0.5 miles approx 3 minutes

Signorello Vineyards 707-255-5990 *Charming Small Family Winery*   Page 260
4500 Silverado Trail   Hours: 10 am - 5 pm   Tasting Fee: $5-$10
Wine List: Semillon, Sauvignon Blanc, Pinot Noir, Cabernet Sauvignon, Merlot

North on Silverado to Regusci Winery: total 16.6 miles, approx 24 minutes

Regusci Winery 707.254.0403 www.regusciwinery.com *Picnic-Old Style Napa*   Page 252
5584 Silverado Trail, Napa   Hours: 10 am - 4 pm   Tasting Fee: $5 - $10
Wine List: Cabernet Sauvignon, Merlot, Zinfandel, and Chardonnay (Chardonnay is from Far Niente's grapes)

North on Silverado to Robert Sinskey Vineyards: total 2.4 miles, approx 2 minutes

Robert Sinskey Vineyards 707.944.9090 www.robertsinskey.com *Fun & Tasty*   Page 254
6320 Silverado Trail, Napa   Hours: 10 am - 4:30 pm daily   Tasting Fee: $10 - $20
Wine List: Pinot Blanc, Rosé of Pinot Noir, Pinot Gris, Vin Gris of Pinot Noir, Pinot Noir, Merlot, Cabernet Franc, Cabernet Sauvignon, Blends, Late Harvest Zinfandel

North on Silverado, almost immediately turn left onto Yountville Cross Rd to Cliff Lede Vineyards on left hand side: total 0.4 miles, approx 2 minutes

Cliff Lede Vineyards 707.944.8642 www.CliffLedeVineyards.com *Charming*   Page 220
1473 Yountville Cross Rd., Yountville   Hours: 10 am - 5 pm   Tasting Fee: $15-$20
Wine List: Cabernet Sauvignon, Merlot, Claret,

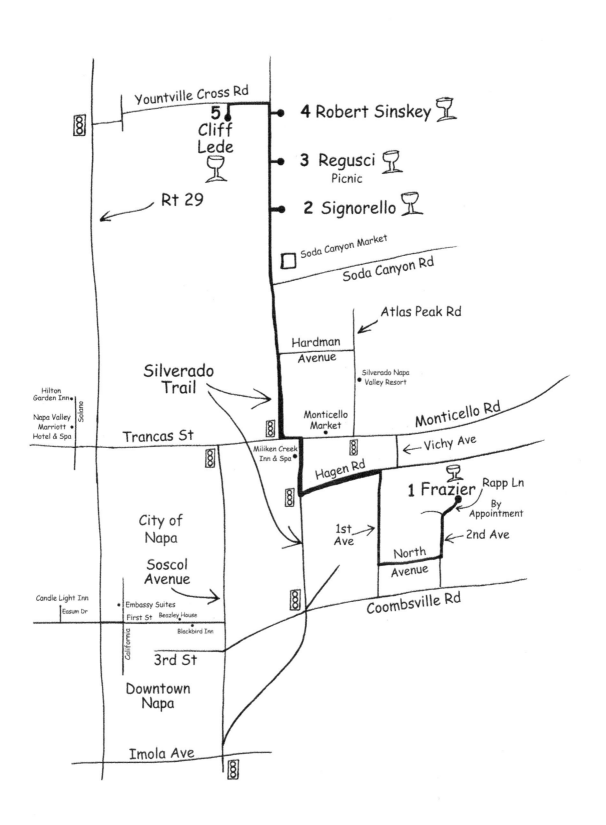

Yountville Cross Rd

5
Cliff
Lede

4 Robert Sinskey

3 Regusci
Picnic

Rt 29

2 Signorello

Soda Canyon Market

Soda Canyon Rd

Atlas Peak Rd

Hardman
Avenue

Silverado
Napa
Valley Resort

Silverado
Trail

Hilton
Garden Inn

Monticello Rd

Napa Valley
Marriott
Hotel & Spa

Solano

Monticello
Market

Trancas St

Vichy Ave

Miliken Creek
Inn & Spa

Hagen Rd

Rapp Ln
1 Frazier

By
Appointment

City of
Napa

1st
Ave

2nd Ave

Soscol
Avenue

North
Avenue

Candle Light Inn

Easum Dr

Embassy Suites

First St   Beazley House

California

Blackbird Inn

Coombsville Rd

3rd St

Downtown
Napa

Imola Ave

Your Day in Wine Country

Tour Nine in Southern Napa

The Southern Silverado Trail, Starting off in a Cave, One Appointment

Jarvis is off the beaten path. From Rt. 29 take the Trancas St. Exit East. That will turn into Monticello and take you up into the hills. After you see the 'old man' rock formation complete with smoking pipe, Jarvis will be a little ways up on the left-hand side, (watch the mailbox numbers). It is a big electronic gate and the keypad/intercom is on the left-hand side. Once inside bear to the right and follow the signs. Plan on two hours at
Jarvis and keep in mind they have a strict cancellation policy.

Jarvis Vineyards 800.255.5280 www.jarviswines.com *Appointment-Caves*   Page 235
2970 Monticello Rd., Napa   Hours: 11 am - 4 pm by appt   Tasting Fee: $20 - $30
Wine List: Chardonnay, Cabernet Sauvignon, Malbec, Merlot, Petit Verdot, Cabernet Franc, Blends

Go back to the Silverado Trail, turn right to the Soda Canyon Market: total 6.6 miles, approx 9 minutes

Pick up picnic items to eat at Regusci Winery's picnic tables later at either the
Monticello Deli & Market
Monticello Rd. between Silverado Trail and Atlas Peak Rd., or
Soda Canyon Market   707.252.0285
4006 Silverado Trail, Napa   Hours: 8 am – 6 pm

Continue north to Darioush: total 0.5 miles, approx 2 minutes

Darioush 707.257.2345 www.darioush.com *Beautiful Building & Grounds*   Page 222
4240 Silverado Trail, Napa   Hours: 10:30 am - 5 PM   Tasting Fee: $20
Wine List: Cabernet Sauvignon, Shiraz, Chardonnay, Merlot, Semillon, Sauvignon, Blanc, Pinot Noir, Viognier

Turn right (north) to Regusci Winery: total 2.5 miles, approx 2 minutes

Regusci Winery 707.254.0403 www.regusciwinery.com *Picnic*   Page 252
5584 Silverado Trail, Napa   Hours: 10 am - 4 pm   Tasting Fee: $5 - $10
Wine List: Cabernet Sauvignon, Merlot, Zinfandel, and Chardonnay (Chardonnay is from Far Niente's grapes)

Turn right (north) to Robert Sinskey Vineyards: total 2.4 miles, approx 2 minutes

Robert Sinskey Vineyards 707.944.9090 www.robertsinskey.com *Fun*   Page 254
6320 Silverado Trail, Napa   Hours: 10 am - 4:30 pm daily   Tasting Fee: $10 - $20
Wine List: Pinot Blanc, Rosé of Pinot Noir, Pinot Gris, Vin Gris of Pinot Noir, Pinot Noir, Merlot, Cabernet Franc, Cabernet Sauvignon, Blends, Late Harvest Zinfandel

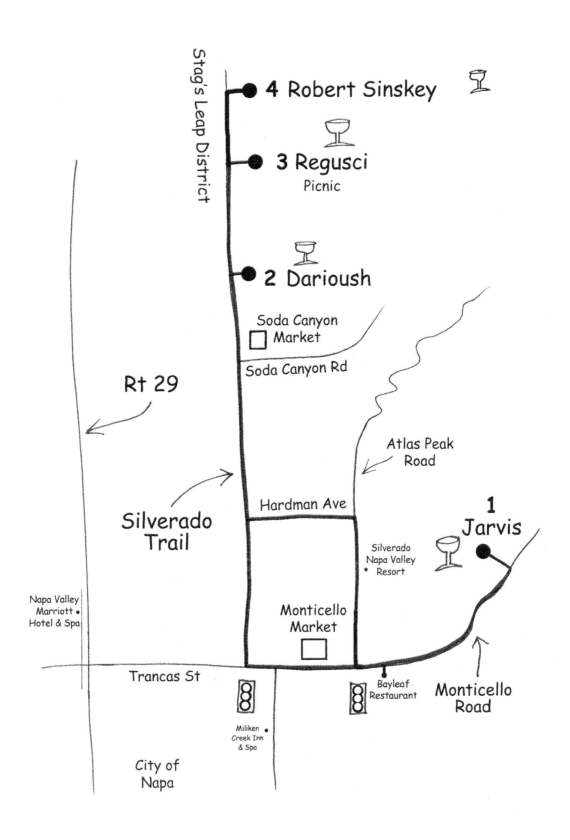

4 Robert Sinskey

Stag's Leap District

3 Regusci

Picnic

2 Darioush

Soda Canyon Market

Soda Canyon Rd

Rt 29

Atlas Peak Road

Hardman Ave

1 Jarvis

Silverado Trail

Silverado Napa Valley Resort

Napa Valley Marriott Hotel & Spa

Monticello Market

Trancas St

Bayleaf Restaurant

Monticello Road

Miliken Creek Inn & Spa

City of Napa

Tour Ten in Southern Napa
Big, Prestigious Red Wine Labels, One Appointment

These are all wineries that are famous for their big red Cabernet Sauvignon & Merlot based Bordeaux style wines. Since Cab is king in Napa they are in the right place at the right time growing the right grapes. Stag's Leap Cellars is famous for its win at the 1976 Judgement of Paris comparison of French and American wines. Silver Oak is a favorite with many new red wine drinkers because of their use of the warm flavored American oak barrels and the willingness to not release the wine until after extensive aging both in the barrels and in the bottle, resulting in a wine that is ready to drink the day it is sold. Opus One, the cooperative venture of the Mondavi and Von Rothchild families is a long time standard of what Napa is capable of and it's architecture continues to impress. Joseph Phelps has the highest reputation among serious big red fans for their wonderful, serious wines that continue to please. Drink lots of water on this tour, because these are high alcohol wines with huge, dehydrating tannins.

Stags Leap Wine Cellars 707.261.6441 www.cask23.com *Judgment of Paris*   Page 263
5766 Silverado Trail, Napa   Hours: 10 am-4:30 pm   Tasting Fee: $10-$30
Wine List: Riesling, Sauvignon Blanc, Chardonnay, Merlot, Cabernet Sauvignon

   North to Oakville Cross Rd, turn left to Silver Oak which will be on the left-hand side: total 5.9 miles, approx 8 minutes

Silver Oak Cellars 707.944.8808 www.silveroak.com *Popular Big Reds*   Page 260
915 Oakville Cross Rd., Oakville   Hours: 9 am-4 pm Closed Sundays   Tasting Fee: $10
Wine List: Cabernet Sauvignon blends from Napa and Alexander Valley, Sonoma

   Continue on Oakville to Rt 29, turn right and the Oakville Grocery is immediately on the right-hand side, pull into parking lot and shop for picnic lunch: 1.1 miles approx 3 minutes

One lunch suggestion is:
Oakville Grocery 707.944.8802 www.oakvillegrocery.com
7856 St. Helena Hwy., Oakville   Hours: 9 am-6 pm daily   espresso bar from 7 am

   Turn right (north) on Rt 29 and immediately turn right into the drive for Opus One: total 312 feet, approx 1 minute

Opus One 707.944.9442 www.opusonewinery.com *A World Standard*   Page 247
7900 St. Helena Hwy, Oakville   Hours: 10 am-4 pm daily   Tasting Fee: $25
Wine List: Blends of: Cabernet Sauvignon, Cabernet Franc, Merlot. Recent vintages add Malbec and/or Petit Verdot

   North on Rt 29, right on Zinfandel, left on Silverado to Taplin: 5.7 miles 11 minutes

Joseph Phelps Vineyards 707.967.3720 www.jpvwines.com *Appointment-Elegant*   Page 236
200 Taplin Rd., St. Helena   Hours: 9 am-5 pm Mon-Sat; 10 am-4 pm Sun   appt only
Tasting Fee: $20+ They also offer a variety of wine seminars.
Wine List: Cabernet Sauvignon, Chardonnay, Merlot, Pastiche, Sauvignon Blanc, Syrah, Viognier

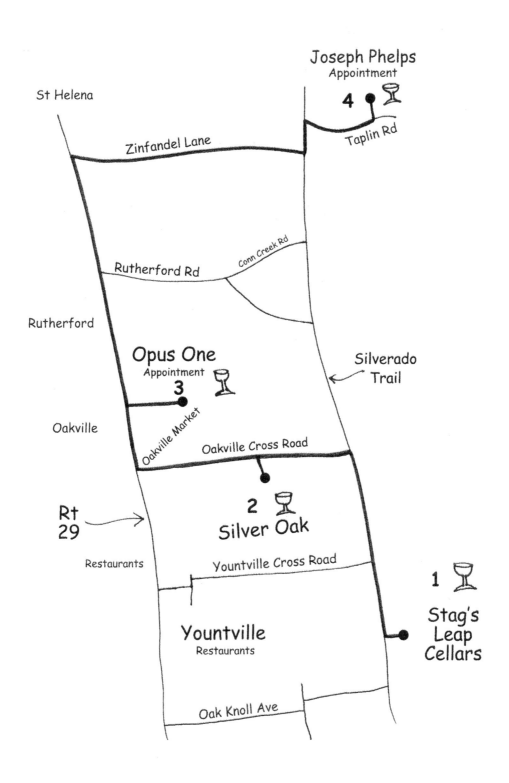

St Helena

Zinfandel Lane

Joseph Phelps
Appointment
4 ● 🍷
Taplin Rd

Conn Creek Rd

Rutherford Rd

Rutherford

Opus One
Appointment
3 ● 🍷

Silverado
Trail

Oakville

Oakville Market

Oakville Cross Road

Rt
29

2 🍷
Silver Oak

Restaurants

Yountville Cross Road

1 🍷
Stag's
Leap
Cellars

Yountville
Restaurants

Oak Knoll Ave

Restaurants & Lodgings in Southern Napa & Carneros

Angele: 540 Main St. Napa. 707.252.8115. French Downtown Napa

Bayleaf Restaurant: 2025 Monticello, Napa 707.257.9720. Californian. Pg. 131

Bistro Don Giovanni: 4110 Howard Ln. (Just off Rt 29) Napa. 707.224.3300. Italian. Pg. 127

Boon Fly Café: 4048 Sonoma Hwy (Just off Rt121, Carneros Hwy in the Carneros Inn Complex) Napa. 707.299.4872. Comfort. Pg. 69 & Pg. 109

Caffe Cicero: 1245 1st Street, Napa. 707.252.3636. American Downtown Napa

Celadon: 500 Main St. Napa. 707.254.9690. Californian Downtown Napa

Cole's Chop House: 1122 Main St. Napa. 707.224.6328. Dinner Only. Steak Downtown Napa

Farm: 4048 Sonoma Hwy (Just off Rt. 121, Carneros Hwy in the Carneros Inn Complex) Napa. 707.299.4880. Californian. Pg. 69

Fume' Bistro: 4050 Byway East (Just off Rt 29 north) Napa. 707.257.1999. Californian

Gillwoods Café: 1320 Napa Town Center, Napa. 707.253.0409. Comfort Downtown Napa

Grill at Silverado Resort: 1600 Altas Peak Rd. Napa. 707.257.5400. Country Club. Pg. 131

Julia's Kitchen at Copia: 500 1st Street, Napa. 707.265.5700. Californian Downtown Napa

Monticello Deli: 1810 Monticello Rd. Napa. Between Silverado and Atlas Peak. Pg 69

Siena Restaurant: At the Meritage Resort (see below). Fine Italian. Pg 121

Soda Canyon Store: 4006 Silverado Trail (At the corner of Soda Canyon Rd) Napa, Market. Pg 69

The Meritage Bar: At the Meritage Resort (see below). Casual Californian. Pg 121

Whole Foods Market: 3682 Bel Aire Plaza, Napa. 707.224.6300. (Just off Trancas St. East of Rt 101) picnic supplies. Pg. 69

Zuzu: 829 Main St. Napa 707.224.8555. Small Plates Downtown Napa

Lodgings

Beazley House: 1910 First St. Napa 800.559.1649 707.257.1649 www.beazleyhouse.com Pg. 129

Blackbird Inn: 1755 First St. Napa 707-226-2450 www.blackbirdinnnapa.com

Candlelight Inn: 1045 Easum Dr. Napa 800.624.0395 707.257.3717 www.candlelightinn.com Pg. 129

Embassy Suites Hotel N.V: 1075 California Blvd. Napa. 800.EMBASSY - 707.253.9450 Pg. 129

Gaia Napa Valley Hotel: 3600 Broadway, Hwy 29 American Canyon 888.798.3777 707.674.2100 www.gaiahotelnapavalley.com

Hilton Garden Inn 3585 Solano Ave. Napa 707.252.0444 www.hiltongardeninn.com Pg. 129

Milliken Creek Inn & Spa 1815 Silverado Tr. Napa 800.835.6112 707.255.1197 www.millikencreekinn.com Pg. 129

Napa River Inn 500 Main St. Napa 877.251.8500 707.251.8500 www.napariverinn.com

Napa Valley Marriott Hotel & Spa 3425 Solano Ave. Napa 707.253.8600 www.napavalleymarriott.com Pg. 129

Silverado Napa Valley Resort 1600 Atlas Peak Rd. Napa 800.532.0500 707.257.0200 www.silveradoresort.com Pg. 129

The Carneros Inn 4048 Sonoma Hwy Napa 707.299.4900 www.TheCarnerosInn.com Pg. 121

The Meritage Resort at Napa 875 Bordeaux Way Napa 866.370.NAPA 707.251.1900 www.themeritageresort.com Pg. 121

The Napa Inn & Spa 1137 Warren St. Napa 800.435.1144 707.257.1444 www.napainn.com

Wine Shipping: Buffalo's Shipping Post 2417 Solano Ave. Napa 94558 707-226-7942

Tour Directory: Starting in Central Napa
An Hour and a Half from San Francisco

One - Page 140
Very Small, Fun Wineries from Yountville, North to Calistoga with a Wide Variety of Wines.
Wineries: Goosecross, Sequoia Grove, Benessere, Frank Family
Six hour tour locally. $$ Moderately Priced

Two - Page 142
Start with Great Art and Add an Interesting Variety of Wines.
Wineries: Hess Collection, Elizabeth Spencer, Corison, Grgich Hills
Five hour tour locally, seven hour tour from SF. $$ Moderately Priced

Three - Page 144
A Charming Tour of Smaller Wineries, a Great Variety of Wines including Bordeaux, Sparkling and Italian Varietals.
Wineries: Sequoia Grove, Arger Martucci, Mumm Napa (Sparkling), Pine Ridge, Luna
Six hour tour locally, eight hour tour from SF
A good day trip from San Francisco. $$ Moderately Priced
Best with a Hired Car and Driver

Four - Page 146
Great Napa Reds, Mondavi followed by Small Premium Wineries.
Wineries: Mondavi, Plumpjack, Rutherford Hill, Corison, Whitehall
Six hour tour locally, eight hour tour from SF. $$ Moderately Priced

Five - Page 148
A Great Party Tour for a Group along Route 29, Great Gift Shops.
Wineries: Peju, Frank Family, Grgich Hills, Cosentino, Domaine Chandon (Sparkling)
Six hour tour locally, eight hour tour from SF
A good day trip from San Francisco. $$ Moderately Priced
Best with a Hired Car and Driver

Six - Page 150

A Mix of Small, Medium and Big Wineries with a Good Variety of Wines
from Rutherford North to Calistoga, Charming, Great Gift Shops.
Wineries: Turnbull, Romabauer, Benessere, St. Clement, Beringer
Six hour tour locally. $$ Moderately Priced

Seven - Page 152

An Afternoon Tour of Big and Small Gorgeous Wineries from St. Helena to Carneros,
Good for a Group, Wonderful Views, Great Gift Shops.
Wineries: Hall, Beringer, Mumm Napa (Sparkling), Regusci, Artesa
Six hour tour locally, eight hour tour from SF. $$ Moderately Priced

Eight - Page 154

An Easy Tour for a Large Group Along Rt. 29 to Wineries with Big Histories
and Large Tasting Rooms. The Rubicon Tour and Tasting is Expensive, but Worth it!
Wineries: Beaulieu, Louis M. Martini, Trinchero, Beringer, Sutter Home, Rubicon ($$$)
Six hour tour locally, eight hour tour from SF. $$ Moderately Priced

Nine - Page 156

Charming, Small, Family Wineries Combined with some Famous Places
to End the Day, Great Red Wines, Two Appointments, Great Gift Shops.
Wineries: Sawyer, Kelham (App), Vine Cliff (App), Stag's Leap, Darioush
Six hour tour locally, eight hour tour from SF
A good tour from San Francisco. $$$ Moderately Expensive
Best with a Hired Car and Driver

Ten - Page 158

Beautiful Wineries, Great Art, a Wide Variety of Wines, Bring a Camera
for the Views, Two Appointments, Great Gift Shops.
Wineries: St. Supéry, Hall, Kelham (App), Mumm Napa (Sparkling),
Vine Cliff (App), Silverado, Darioush
Seven hour tour locally, nine hour tour from SF
A good day trip from San Francisco. $$$ Moderately Expensive
Best with a Hired Car and Driver

Eleven - Page 160

Oakville and Rutherford, Big and Small, Beautiful Buildings and Art,
Great Tours, One Appointment Starting with a Tour, Great Gift Shops.
Wineries: Nickel and Nickel (App) for tour, Beaulieu, Arger Martucci, Rubicon.
Six hour tour locally, eight hour tour from SF. $$$ Moderately Expensive

Twelve - Page 162

Prestigious Wineries with Beautiful Locations, Sparkling Wines,
Big Reds, Chardonnay, Two Appointments.
Wineries: Cakebread (App), Duckhorn (App), Hall,
Domaine Carneros (Sparkling), Artesa.
Six hour tour locally, eight hour tour from SF.
A good day trip from San Francisco. $$$ Moderately Expensive.

Thirteen - Page 164

Very Big Reds, Famous Labels Starting with One Appointment.
Wineries: Cardinale (App), Opus One (likes appointments but not always necessary),
Rubicon, Mondavi's 'To Kalon' Reserve Room
Six hour tour locally, eight hour tour from SF.
A good day trip from San Francisco. $$$$ Expensive.
Best with a Hired Car and Driver.

Fourteen - Page 166

Big Reds, Cabernet, Two appointments, Great Tours,
Make the Appointments far in Advance.
Wineries: Far Niente (App) for tour, Vine Cliff (App), Plumpjack, Silver Oak
Six hour tour locally, eight hour tour from SF.
A good day trip from San Francisco. $$$$ Expensive tours and tastings.
Best with a Hired Car and Driver.

Restaurants & Hotels of Central Napa Page 168

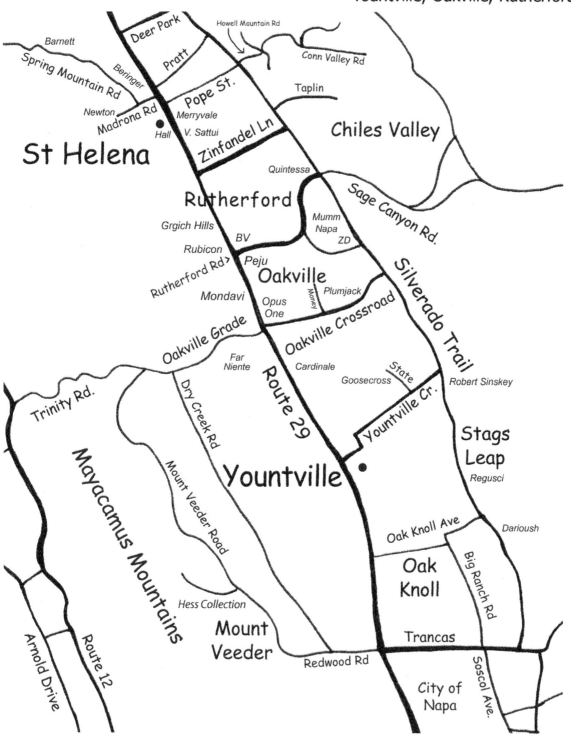

A Close-Up of Wine Central
Yountville, Oakville, Rutherford

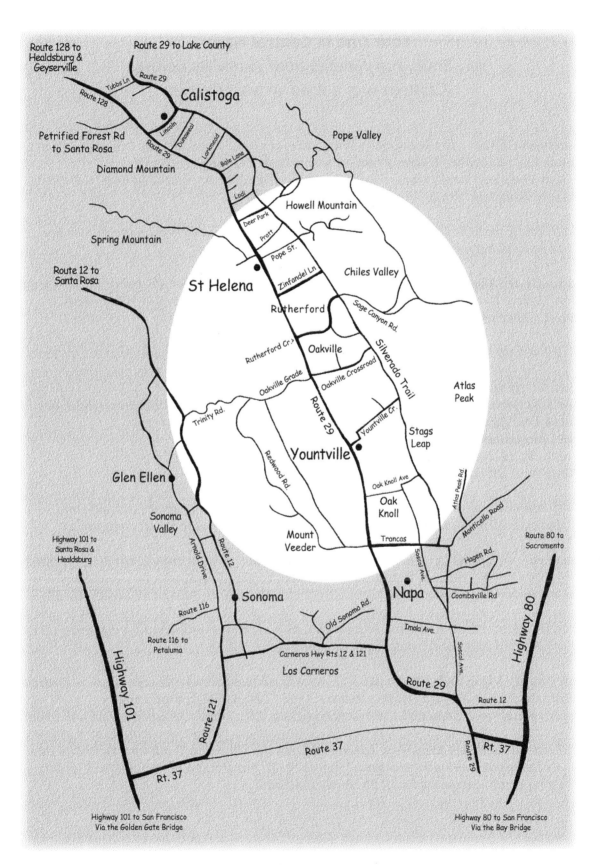

Tour One in Central Napa
Very Small, Fun Wineries from Yountville, North to Calistoga with a Wide Variety of Wines

Goosecross Cellars 707.944.1986 www.goosecross.com *Small Family Winery* Page 231
1119 State Ln., Yountville Hours: 10 am - 4:30 pm daily Tasting Fee: $5
Wine List: Viognier, Chenin Blanc, Sauvignon Blanc, Chardonnay, Sparkling Rosé, Cabernet Sauvignon, Zinfandel, Merlot, Pinot Noir, Syrah, Blends

> *Follow Yountville Cross Rd to Rt 29, turn right to Sequoia Grove, on the right-hand side: total 6.2 miles, approx 11 minutes*

Sequoia Grove Vineyards 707.944.2945 www.sequoiagrove.com *Friendly* Page 259
8338 St. Helena Hwy. S. Rutherford Hours: 10:30am - 5pm Tasting Fee: $10 - $20
Wine List: Cabernet Sauvignon, Chardonnay, Syrah

> *Turn right (north) to downtown St. Helena for lunch: total 4.7 miles approx 15 minutes*

Two lunch suggestions are:
Taylor's Refresher A famous drive-in on the left-hand side across from Merryvale Winery
Pizzaria Tra Vigne across the street from Taylor's and opposite Merryvale
Market (Restaurant) 707.963.3799 www.marketsthelena.com
1347 Main St., St. Helena Hours: 11:30 am – 10 pm daily
See Restaurant list on page 168

> *Continue north on Rt 29 to Big Tree Rd (past Lodi Ln) on the right-hand side and Benessere, at the end of the road bear left: total 4.2 miles approx 10 minutes*

Benessere 707.963.5853 www.benesserevineyards.com *Italian Style Charm* Page 213
1010 Big Tree Rd., St. Helena Hours: 10 am – 5 pm Tasting Fee: $10
Wine List: Pinot Grigio, Sangiovese, Syrah, Zinfandel, Pinot Noir, Muscat di Canelli, Blends

> *Continue north on Rt 29 to Larkmead Ln, turn right to Frank Family Vineyards, on the right hand side: total 2 miles approx 4 minutes*

Frank Family Vineyards 707.942.0859 www.frankfamilyvineyards.com *Fun* Page 229
1091 Larkmead Ln., Calistoga Hours: 10 am – 5 pm Tasting Fee: complimentary
Wine List: Sangiovese, Zinfandel, Cabernet Sauvignon, Chardonnay, Sparklers, Zinfandel Port

> *To head south you can follow Larkmead Ln to the Silverado Trail, turn right and this will take you south all the way to Trancas St. To reach Rt 29 turn right there and it will bring you to entrances for Rt 29 North and South.*

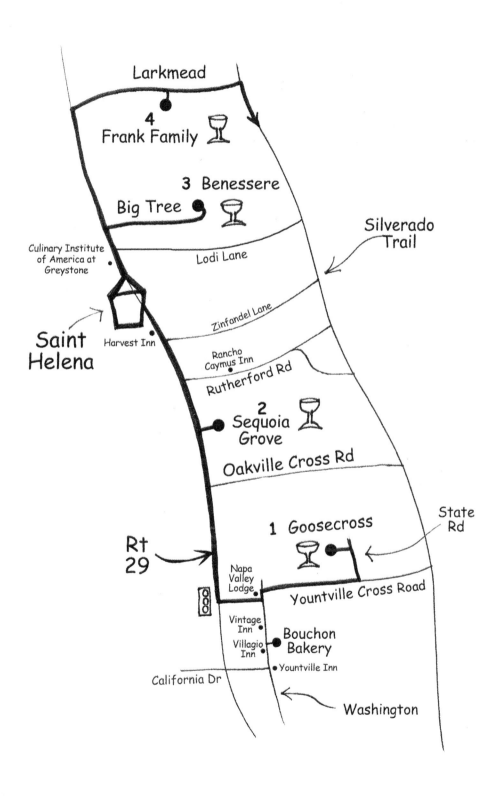

Larkmead

4 Frank Family

3 Benessere

Big Tree

Culinary Institute of America at Greystone

Lodi Lane

Silverado Trail

Saint Helena

Harvest Inn

Zinfandel Lane

Rancho Caymus Inn

Rutherford Rd

2 Sequoia Grove

Oakville Cross Rd

State Rd

1 Goosecross

Rt 29

Napa Valley Lodge

Yountville Cross Road

Vintage Inn

Bouchon Bakery

Villagio Inn

Yountville Inn

California Dr

Washington

Your Day in Wine Country

Tour Two in Central Napa
Start with Great Art and Add an Interesting Variety of Wines

The Exit for Redwood Road and Trancas Street are at the northern edge of the city of Napa. Trancas goes East while Redwood goes West. The road to the Hess Collection is winding. From the exit it is about seven miles. Watch for their signs. The ride should take about ten to fifteen minutes. Redwood starts off as a four lane residential road. But it narrows to a two lane country road. The Dry Creek Road will veer off to the right, but stay on Redwood. At a certain point Redwood makes a left and the road straight ahead becomes Mount Veeder Road. This turn comes up just after a sharp curve with a green house on the left-hand side. The winery is a short distance up the mountain on the left side. The winery was originally used by the Christian Brothers Winery, and you'll pass their complex just before Hess on the left. Now the two stone barns include the Hess Art collection, well worth the visit, and the winery, tasting room and gift shop. This is a destination winery that makes going out the way worth your time.

Hess Collection Winery 707.255.8584   www.hesscollection.com Art Gallery   Page 233
4411 Redwood Rd. Napa   Hours: 10am - 5pm daily Tasting Fee: $10
Wine List: Cabernet Sauvignon, Sauvignon Blanc, Chardonnay, Syrah, Late Harvest Riesling, Malbec, Cabernet Franc, Syrah Rosé, Petite Sirah, Zinfandel, Sauvignon Blanc, Viognier, Semillon, Shiraz,

Back to Rt 29, north to the Oakville Grocery: total 14.7 miles, approx 30 minutes

Pick up picnic items to eat at Oakville Grocery's own picnic tables:
Oakville Grocery 707.944.8802 www.oakvillegrocery.com
7856 St. Helena Hwy., Oakville   Hours: 9 am-6 pm daily espresso bar from 7 am

Turn right (north) to Rutherford Rd. Turn right and the Elizabeth Spencer tasting room is immediately on the right hand side: total 2.0 miles, approx 5 minutes

Elizabeth Spencer Wines 707.963.6067 www.elizabethspencerwines.com   Page 226
1165 Rutherford Rd., Rutherford Hours: 10 am - 6 pm Tasting Fee: $5 *Charming*
Wine List: Chardonnay, Pinot Noir, Syrah, Cabernet Sauvignon

North on Rt 29 to Corison Wines on left hand side: total 2.4 miles, approx 4 minutes

Corison Wines 707.963.0826 www.corison.com *Great Reds Rustic*   Page 221
987 St. Helena Hwy S., St. Helena Hours: 10 am - 5 PM by appt Tasting Fee: $10
Wine List: Cabernet Sauvignon, Gewürztraminer

Turn right (south) to Grgich Hills Cellar on right hand side: 1.5 miles, approx 3 minutes

Grgich Hills Cellar 707.963.2784 www.grgich.com *Friendly and Traditional*   Page 231
1829 St. Helena Hwy S., Rutherford Hours: 9:30 am - 4:30 pm daily Tasting Fee: $10
Wine List: Chardonnay, Fumé Blanc, Violetta (botrytis dessert wine), Cabernet Sauvignon, Zinfandel, Merlot

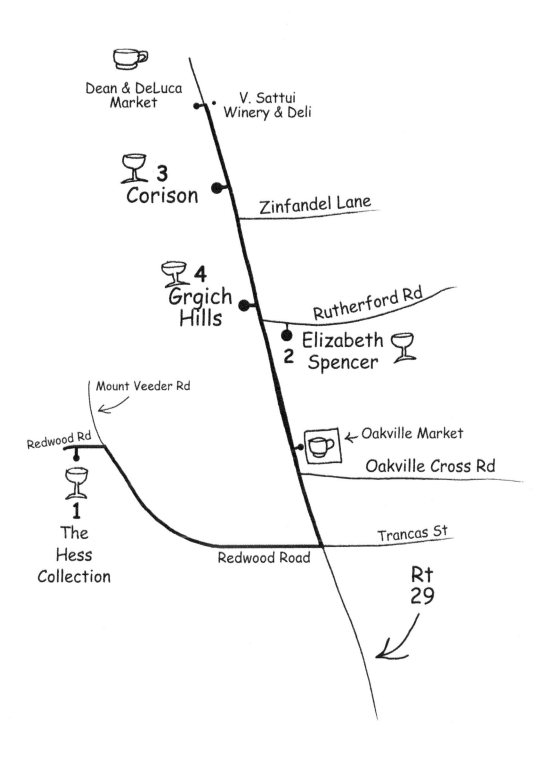

Dean & DeLuca
Market

V. Sattui
Winery & Deli

3
Corison

Zinfandel Lane

4
**Grgich
Hills**

Rutherford Rd

2 Elizabeth
Spencer

Mount Veeder Rd

Redwood Rd

Oakville Market

Oakville Cross Rd

1
**The
Hess
Collection**

Trancas St

Redwood Road

Rt
29

Your Day in Wine Country

Tour Three in Central Napa
A Charming Tour of Smaller Wineries, a Great Variety of Wines. Big Reds, Sparkling, and Italian Varietals

Sequoia Grove Vineyards 707.944.2945 www.sequoiagrove.com *Friendly*   Page 259
8338 St. Helena Hwy. S. Rutherford Hours: 10:30am - 5pm   Tasting Fee: $10 - $20
Wine List: Cabernet Sauvignon, Chardonnay, Syrah

Turn right (north) to Dean & DeLuca on left side: total 3.1 miles, approx 8 minutes

Pick up picnic items to eat at Arger-Martucci Vineyards' picnic tables later at
Dean & DeLuca 707.967.9980 www.deandeluca.com
607 S. St. Helena Hwy, St. Helena Hours: 7 am – 8 pm

Turn right (south) and turn right at the first corner, Inglewood. Arger-Martucci Vineyards is a short distance down the street on the left-hand side, look for the winery tanks. The tasting room is the building in the back behind the tanks, just follow the signs: total less than 1 mile, approx 2 minutes

Arger Martucci Vineyards 707.963.4334 www.arger-martucciwine.com *Picnic*   Page 211
1455 Inglewood Ave., St. Helena Hours: 10 am - 4 pm daily Tasting Fee: $10 - $20
Wine List: Chardonnay, Viognier, Pinot Noir, Syrah, Cabernet Sauvignon, Blends (French)

Turn right (south) to Zinfandel Lane, turn left, go to the Silverado Trail, turn right to Mumm Napa Valley, just past Rutherford Rd: total 4.3 miles approx 8 minutes

Mumm Napa Valley 707.967.7700 www.mummnapa.com ***Sparkling-Fun***   Page 245
8445 Silverado Trail, Rutherford Hours: 10 am-5 pm Tasting Fee: $5-$15 by glass/flight
Wine List: Pinot Noir, Chardonnay, Santana, DVX, Demi Sec, Sparkling Pinot Noir, Cuvee M Red, Blanc de Blanc, Brut Prestige, Blanc de Noirs, Cuvee M

Turn right (south) to Pine Ridge: total 6.3 miles approx 10 minutes

Pine Ridge Winery 707.944.8111 www.pineridgewinery.com   Page 250
5901 Silverado Trail Napa Hours: 10:30am - 4:30pm   Tasting Fee: $10 - $20
Wine List: Chenin Blanc-Viognier, Rosé, Merlot, Cabernet Franc, Malbec, Cabernet Sauvignon

Turn right (south) to Luna: total 5 miles approx 7 minutes

Luna Vineyards 707.255.2474 www.lunavineyards.com *Italian Varietals*   Page 241
2921 Silverado Trail, Napa Hours: 10 am - 5 pm daily Tasting Fee: $10 - $20
Wine List: Sangiovese, Merlot, Petite Sirah, Pinot Grigio, Tocai Fiulano, Chardonnay, Cabernet Sauvignon, Blends (Freakout)

Turn right (south) to Trancas, then right again to Route 29, fuel, coffee & snacks.

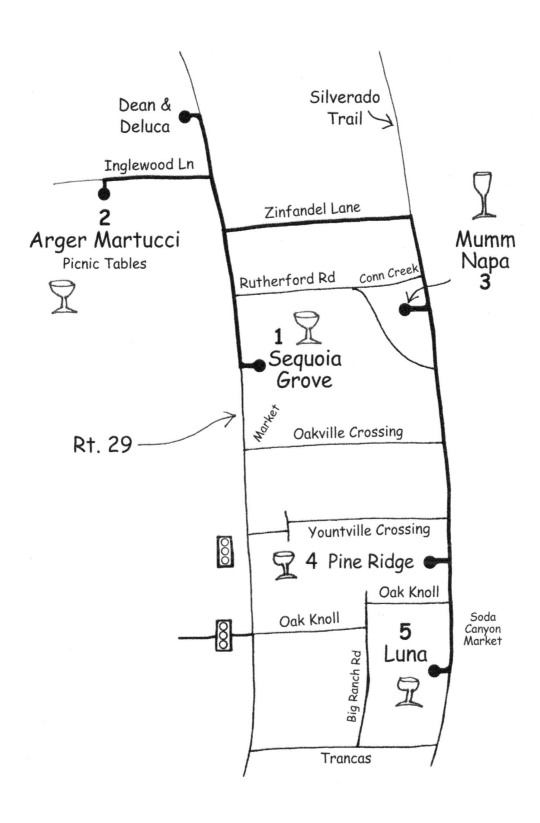

Dean & Deluca

Silverado Trail

Inglewood Ln

2
Arger Martucci
Picnic Tables

Zinfandel Lane

Mumm Napa
3

Rutherford Rd   Conn Creek

1 Sequoia Grove

Market

Rt. 29

Oakville Crossing

Yountville Crossing

4 Pine Ridge

Oak Knoll

Oak Knoll

5 Luna

Soda Canyon Market

Big Ranch Rd

Trancas

Tour Four in Central Napa
Great Napa Reds, Mondavi followed by Small Premium Wineries

On this tour you can either picnic at the Rutherford Hill Winery, or if you would prefer a restaurant there is a great option on the way, The **Auberge du Soleil** hotel. There is both a bar and restaurant and for lunch the bar is great. It is first come first served and the seats on the patio have a million dollar view of the valley. We highly recommend it.

Robert Mondavi Winery 707.226.1395 www.robertmondaviwinery.com *Big*   Page 253
7801 St. Helena Hwy., Oakville   Hours: 10 am - 5 pm   Tasting Fee: $5 - $50+
Wine List: Fumé Blanc, Chardonnay, Pinot Noir, Merlot, Cabernet Sauvignon, Moscato d'Oro, Sauvignon Blanc, Zinfandel, Dry Rosé   The reserve tasting is in the To Kalon Room $20

Turn right (south) to Oakville Grocery on left-hand side: 0.2 miles, approx 2 minutes

If you would like to picnic at Rutherford Hill's picnic area under the olive trees drop by
Oakville Grocery 707.944.8802 www.oakvillegrocery.com
7856 St. Helena Hwy., Oakville   Hours: 9 am - 6 pm espresso bar from 7AM
From Oakville Grocery turn right onto Rt 29 and right again into Opus One Winery, at the winery bear right and take the drive out to Oakville Cross Road. The gate will open as you approach. Turn left to Plumpjack Winery on left hand side: total 2.1 miles, approx 4 minutes

Plumpjack Winery 707.945.1220 www.plumpjack.com *Charming Small Winery* Page 250
620 Oakville Cross Rd., Oakville   Hours: 10 am - 4 pm   Tasting Fee: $10
Wine List: Cabernet Sauvignon, Chardonnay, Merlot

Continue to Silverado Trail, turn left to Rutherford Hill Rd. Turn right to top of hill. Auberge is on the way, Winery is at the top: total 4.3 miles, approx 10 minutes

Rutherford Hill Winery 707.963.7194 www.rutherfordhill.com *Picnic-Views*   Page 257
200 Rutherford Hill Rd., Rutherford   Hours: 10 am - 5 pm   Tasting Fee: $10
Wine List: Zinfandel Port, Merlot, Cabernet Sauvignon, Sangiovese, Blends, Petite Verdot, Chardonnay, Syrah, Malbec, Sauvignon Blanc

Go north and turn left on Zinfandel Ln. then turn right on Rt 29 to Corison Wines, on the left-hand side: total 3.3 miles, approx 10 minutes

Corison Wines 707.963.0826 www.corison.com *Great Wines-Rustic*   Page 221
987 St. Helena Hwy S., St. Helena   Hours: 10 am - 5 pm by instant appt   Tasting Fee: $10
Wine List: Cabernet Sauvignon, Gewürztraminer

Turn right (south) to Whitehall Lane Winery: total 0.8 miles approx 3 minutes

Whitehall Lane Winery 707.963.7035 www.whitehalllane.com *Fun-Stylish*   Page 270
1563 St. Helena Hwy S., St. Helena   Hours: 11 am - 5:45 pm   Tasting Fee: $10
Wine List: Cabernet Sauvignon, Merlot, Chardonnay, Belmuscato Dessert Wine

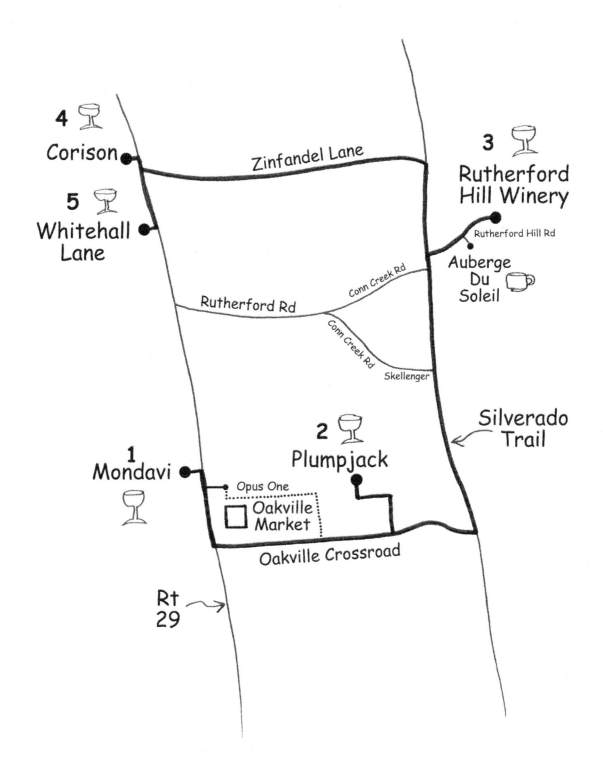

Tour Five in Central Napa
A Great Party Tour for a Group along Route 29, Great Gift Shops

This tour is based on passing through downtown St. Helena before traffic builds up.

Peju Province Winery   707.963.3600   www.peju.com   *Gorgeous-Fun*   Page 249
8466 St. Helena Hwy., Rutherford   Hours: 10 am - 6 pm   Tasting Fee: $5 - $10
Wine List: Sauvignon Blanc, Chardonnay, French Colombard, Syrah, Merlot, Cabernet Franc, Zinfandel, Cabernet Sauvignon, Blends

Turn right (north) to Sunshine Foods on left side: total 3.9 miles, approx 10 minutes

Pick up picnic items to eat at Frank Family's picnic tables later at
Sunshine Foods Market   707.963.7070   www.sunshinefoodsmarket.com
1115 Main St., St. Helena   Hours: 7 am - 8 pm   See restaurant maps on pages 168 & 208

North to Larkmead, turn right to Frank Family Vineyards: 5.7 miles, approx 8 minutes

Frank Family Vineyards   707.942.0859   www.frankfamilyvineyards.com   *Fun*   Page 229
1091 Larkmead Ln., Calistoga   Hours: 10 am - 4 pm   Tasting Fee: Complimentary   *Picnic*
Wine List: Sangiovese, Zinfandel, Cabernet Sauvignon, Chardonnay, Sparklers, Zinfandel Port

Head South to Grgich Hills (Past Provenance) right side: 8.7 miles, approx 14 minutes

Grgich Hills Cellar   707.963.2784   www.grgich.com   *Old Style Friendly*   Page 231
1829 St. Helena Hwy S., Rutherford   Hours: 9:30 am - 4:30 pm daily   Tasting Fee: $10
Wine List: Chardonnay, Fumé Blanc, Violetta (botrytis dessert wine), Cabernet Sauvignon, Zinfandel, Merlot

Turn right (south) to Cosentino Winery, right side: total 4.3 miles, approx 6 minutes

Cosentino Winery   707.944.1220   www.cosentinowinery.com   *Fun*   Page 221
7415 St. Helena Hwy., Yountville   Hours: 10 am - 5 pm   Tasting Fee: $15 - $20
Wine List: Bianco, Chardonnay, Gewürztraminer, Semillon, Sangiovese, Dolcetto, Tempranillo, Petite Sirah, Pinot Noir, Merlot, Cabernet Franc, Cabernet Sauvignon, Zinfandel, Meritage, Late Harvest Viognier, Botrytis Semillon, Blends

Turn right (south) to the Yountville Exit, bear right onto California Drive to Domaine Chandon on the right-hand side: total 2.1 miles approx 3 minutes

Domaine Chandon   707.944.2280   www.domainechandon.com   *Sparkling*   Page 224
1 California Dr., Yountville   Hours: 10 am - 6 pm daily   Tasting Fee: $10 & by the glass
Wine List: Brut, Blanc de Noirs, Rosé, Sparkling Chardonnay, Blanc de Blancs, Pinot Noir, Pinot Meunier, Chardonnay, Unoaked Pinot Noir Rosé, Unoaked Chardonnay
        Because Domaine Chandon includes a restaurant after six o'clock they are able to offer wine by the glass and snacks on their very spacious patio. A very nice place to end the day.

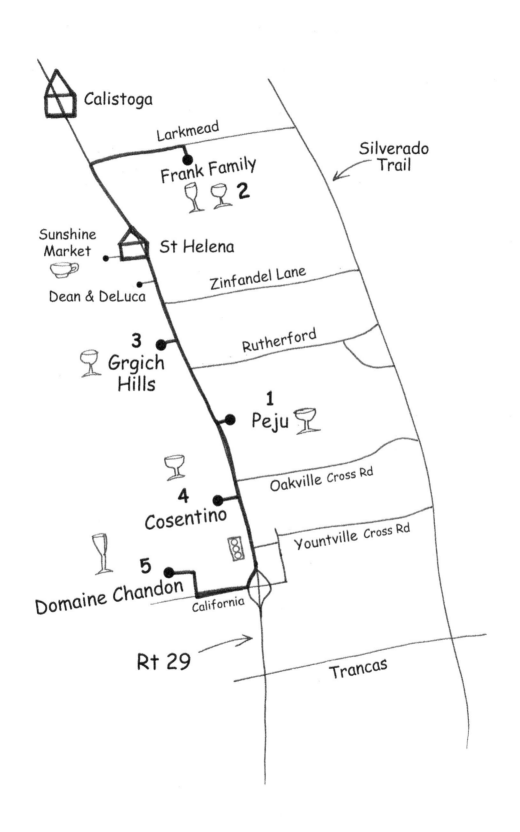

Calistoga

Larkmead

Frank Family
2

Sunshine
Market

St Helena

Zinfandel Lane

Dean & DeLuca

3
Grgich
Hills

Rutherford

1
Peju

Silverado
Trail

Oakville Cross Rd

4
Cosentino

Yountville Cross Rd

5
Domaine Chandon

California

Rt 29

Trancas

Tour Six in Central Napa
A Mix of Small, Medium and Big Wineries with a Good Variety of Wines

Turnbull Wine Cellars 8210 St. Helena Hwy. Oakville *Photo Gallery* Page 267
707.963.5839 info@turnbullwines.com www.turnbullwines.com
Hours: 10am - 4:30pm daily Tasting Fee: $10 - $20
Wine List: Sauvignon Blanc, Old Bull Red, Viognier, Toroso, Cabernet Sauvignon, Merlot, Barbera, Syrah

Turn left (south) to Oakville Grocery: total 1.2 miles, approx 2 minutes

Pick up picnic items to eat at Rombauer's picnic tables later
Oakville Grocery 707.944.8802 www.oakvillegrocery.com
7856 St. Helena Hwy., Oakville Hours: 9 am - 6 pm espresso bar from 7AM
See restaurant lists on pages 168 & 208. If you pick lunch up early and put it in a cooler you can avoid the lunchtime rush at Oakville, and having to make a left-hand turn from Turnbull.

Turn right (north) to Rutherford Rd., turn right and follow to Silverado Trail, turn left to Rombauer Vineyards on the left hand side: total 9.9 miles, approx 17 minutes

Rombauer Vineyards 707.963.5170 www.rombauervineyards.com *Picnic-Views* Page 255
3522 Silverado Trail N., St. Helena Hours: 10 am - 5 pm Tasting Fee: $10
Wine List: Cabernet Sauvignon, Merlot, Chardonnay, Zinfandel, Port, Blend

Turn right (south) to Lodi, right to Rt. 29, turn right to Big Tree Rd to Benesserre, at the end of the road bear left: total 2.4 miles, approx 6 minutes

Benessere 707.963.5853 www.benesserevineyards.com *Small-Italian Varietals* Page 213
1010 Big Tree Rd., St. Helena Hours: 10 am - 5 pm Tasting Fee: $10
Wine List: Pinot Grigio, Sangiovese, Syrah, Zinfandel, Pinot Noir, Muscat di Canelli, Blends

Left on Rt 29 (south) to St. Clement Vineyards, on a hill on the right-hand side: total 2.5 miles, approx 8 minutes

St. Clement Vineyards 800.331.8266 www.stclement.com **Charming-Views** Page 262
2867 N. St. Helena Hwy., St. Helena Hours: 10 am - 4 pm Tasting Fee: $10 - $25 *Gifts*
Wine List: Cabernet Sauvignon, Merlot, Sauvignon Blanc, Chardonnay, Syrah

Heading to Beringer Vineyards: total 1.0 miles approx 2 minutes

Beringer Vineyards 707.967.4412 www.beringer.com *Grand Estate-Tours* Page 214
2000 Main St., St. Helena Hours: 10 am - 5 pm Tasting Fee: $5 - $10 *Gift Shop*
Wine List: Chardonnay, Dessert Wines, Sauvignon Blanc, Pinot Noir, Merlot, Cabernet Sauvignon, Riesling, Viognier, White Zinfandel, White Merlot, Chenin Blanc, Gewürztraminer, Pinot Grigio, Shiraz

Follow Rt 29 south (right) through St. Helena and all points south

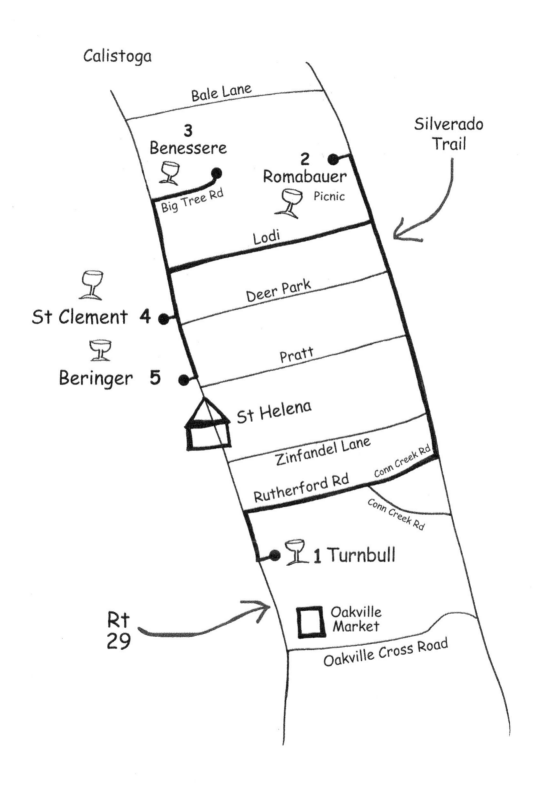

Calistoga

Bale Lane

3
Benessere

2
Romabauer   Picnic

Big Tree Rd

Silverado
Trail

Lodi

Deer Park

St Clement **4**

Pratt

Beringer **5**

St Helena

Zinfandel Lane

Conn Creek Rd

Rutherford Rd

Conn Creek Rd

1 Turnbull

Rt
29

Oakville
Market

Oakville Cross Road

Tour Seven in Central Napa

An Afternoon Tour of Big & Small Gorgeous Wineries from St. Helena to Carneros

If you are starting the tour later in the day pick up picnic items to eat at Hall's picnic tables at
Dean & DeLuca 707.967.9980 www.deandeluca.com
607 S. St. Helena Hwy., St. Helena Hours: 7 am - 8 pm M-Sun
Otherwise consult the restaurant list on page 168

Dean & DeLuca is the next driveway south of Hall. You can walk across the lot.

Hall 707.967.2620 www.hallwines.com *Great Art-Picnic*   Page 232
401 St. Helena Hwy S., St. Helena Hours: 10 am - 5:30 pm Tasting Fee: $10
Wine List: Cabernet Sauvignon, Merlot, Sauvignon Blanc *-See note in directory-*

Turn left (north) to Beringer Vineyards: total 2.1 miles, approx 4 minutes

Beringer Vineyards 707.967.4412 www.beringer.com *Grand Estate-Tours*   Page 214
2000 Main St., St. Helena Hours: 10 am - 5 pm Tasting Fee: $5 - $10
Wine List: Chardonnay, Dessert Wines, Sauvignon Blanc, Pinot Noir, Merlot, Cabernet Sauvignon, Riesling, Viognier, White Zinfandel, White Merlot, Chenin Blanc, Gewürztraminer, Pinot Grigio, Shiraz

Turn right (south) and immediately left onto Pratt. At Silverado Trail turn right (south) to Mumm Napa Valley, past Rutherford Rd on right: 5.9 miles, 11 minutes

Mumm Napa Valley 707.967.7700 www.mummnapa.com *Sparkling-Fun*   Page 245
8445 Silverado Trail, Rutherford Hours: 10 am - 5 pm Tasting Fee: $5 - $15 glass/flight
Wine List: Pinot Noir, Chardonnay, Santana, DVX, Demi Sec, Sparkling Pinot Noir, Cuvee M Red, Blanc de Blanc, Brut Prestige, Blanc de Noirs, Cuvee M

Turn right (south) to Regusci Winery on left side past Yountville Cross Rd. : total 7.3 miles, approx 8 minutes

Regusci Winery 707.254.0403 www.regusciwinery.com *Old style Napa*   Page 252
5584 Silverado Trail, Napa Hours: 10 am - 4 pm Tasting Fee: $5 - $10
Wine List: Cabernet Sauvignon, Merlot, Zinfandel, and Chardonnay (Chardonnay is from Far Niente's grapes)

Turn left (south) to Trancas, turn right to Rt 29 south entrance, at Rt 121 traffic light turn right to Old Sonoma Rd traffic light, turn right to first left, follow to Artesa Winery: total 15.1 miles, approx 25 minutes. Artesa is a good stop on the way back to the City.

Artesa Winery 707.254.2140 www.artesawinery.com *Great Views*   Page 211
1345 Henry Rd., Napa Hours: 10 am - 5 pm daily Tasting Fee: $5 - $10
Wine List: Cabernet Sauvignon, Chardonnay, Merlot, Pinot Noir, Tempranillo, Albarino, Garnacha Rosado, Late Harvest Gewürztraminer, Blends

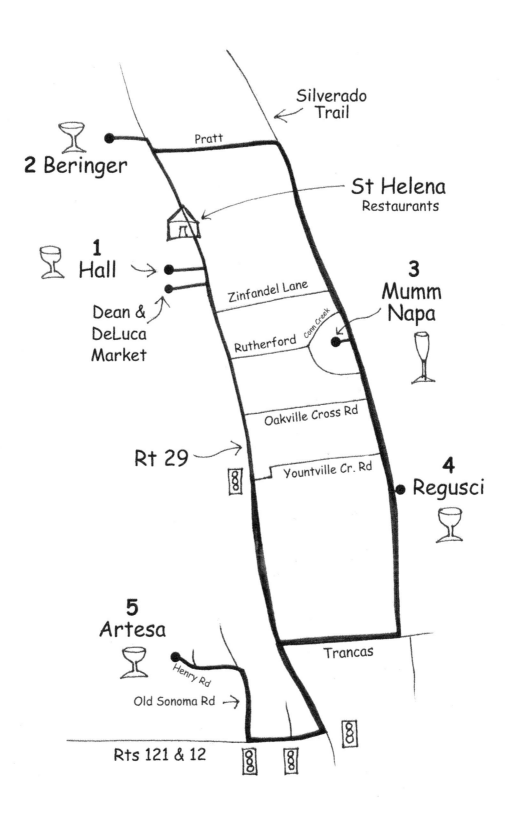

Silverado Trail

Pratt

2 Beringer

St Helena
Restaurants

1 Hall

Dean & DeLuca Market

Zinfandel Lane

3 Mumm Napa

Conn Creek

Rutherford

Oakville Cross Rd

Rt 29

Yountville Cr. Rd

4 Regusci

5 Artesa

Henry Rd

Old Sonoma Rd

Trancas

Rts 121 & 12

Your Day in Wine Country

Tour Eight in Central Napa
An Easy Tour for a Large Group Along Rt. 29 to Wineries with Big Histories
Select the Wineries that Appeal to You - Or Hire a Driver

Beaulieu Vineyard 707.967.5230 www.bvwines.com *Great Reds-Reserve Room* Page 213
1960 St. Helena Hwy., Rutherford Hours: 10 am - 5 pm Tasting Fee: $5 - $20
Wine List: Cabernet Sauvignon, Chardonnay, Pinot Noir, Merlot, Zinfandel, Syrah, Sauvignon Blanc, Shiraz, Sangiovese, Viognier, Port, Blends
Turn right (north) to Louis Martini Winery on the right side: 2.0 miles, 3 minutes

Louis M Martini Winery 707.963.2736 www.louismartini.com *Great Reds-Fun* Page 241
254 St. Helena Hwy. S., St. Helena Hours: 10 am - 6 pm Tasting Fee: $5
Wine List: Cabernet Sauvignon, Zinfandel
*Turn right (north) to **Taylor's Refresher** on the left-hand side: 1.0 mile, 5 minutes*

One lunch suggestion is the popular drive-in and burger joint, including Ahi Tuna burgers:
Taylor's Refresher 707.963.3486 www.taylorsrefresher.com
933 Main St., St. Helena Hours: 11 am - 7 pm
Or consult the restaurant list on pg 168, there are plenty of restaurants in St Helena
Turn left (north) to Trinchero Family Winery, right side after Lodi: 2.5 miles, 10 minutes

Trinchero Family Winery 707.963.3104 3070 St. Helena Hwy N. St. Helena Page 267
Hours: 10 am - 5 pm Tasting Fee: $5 - $20. *Classic with a Great Education Center*
Wine List: Cabernet Sauvignon, Chardonnay, Pinot Noir, Merlot, Sauvignon Blanc, Meritage.
One of the great old families of Napa.
Turn left (south) to Beringer Vineyards on the right-hand side: 1.5 miles, 5 minutes

Beringer Vineyards 707.967.4412 www.beringer.com *Grand Estate-Tours* Page 214
2000 Main St., St. Helena Hours: 10 am - 5 pm Tasting Fee: $5 - $10
Wine List: Chardonnay, Dessert Wines, Sauvignon Blanc, Pinot Noir, Merlot, Cabernet Sauvignon, Riesling, Viognier, White Zinfandel, White Merlot, Chenin Blanc, Gewürztraminer, Pinot Grigio, Shiraz
Turn right (south) to Sutter Home Winery, on the right-hand side across from Louis M Martini: total 2.0 miles, approx 10 minutes

Sutter Home Winery 707.963.3104 www.sutterhome.com *Famous* Page 265
277 St. Helena Hwy. S., St. Helena Hours: 10 am - 5 pm Tasting Fee: Complimentary
Wine List: White Zinfandel, Moscato, Chardonnay, Pinot Grigio, Cabernet Sauvignon, Merlot, Sauvignon Blanc, Chenin Blanc, Merlot, White Cabernet Sauvignon, Pinot Noir, Zinfandel, Gewürztraminer. Owned by the Trichero family.
Turn right (south) to Rubicon Estate on the right side: total 2.0 miles, approx 3 minutes

Rubicon Estate 707.968.1100 www.rubiconestate.com *Grand Estate-Espresso* Page 256
1991 St. Helena Hwy., Rutherford Hours: 10 am - 5 pm Tasting & Tour Fee: $20
Wine List: Cabernet Sauvignon, Merlot, Cabernet Franc, Syrah, Blends
Owned by Francis Ford Coppola

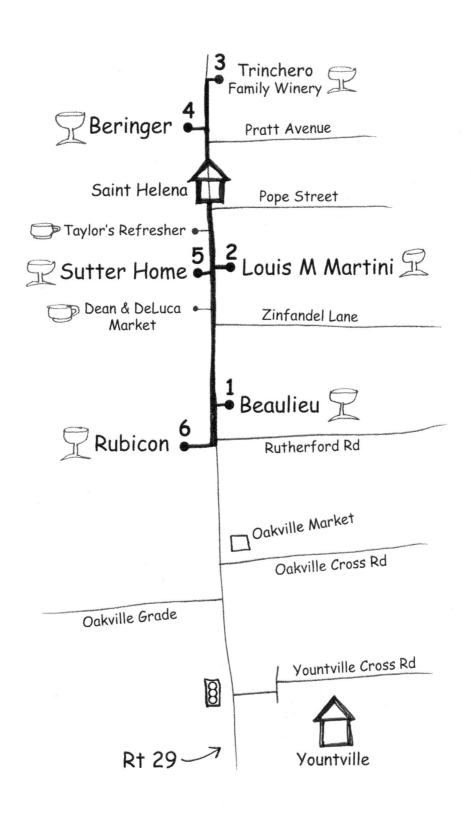

3 Trinchero Family Winery

4 Beringer

Pratt Avenue

Saint Helena

Pope Street

Taylor's Refresher

5 Sutter Home   **2** Louis M Martini

Dean & DeLuca Market

Zinfandel Lane

1 Beaulieu

6 Rubicon

Rutherford Rd

Oakville Market

Oakville Cross Rd

Oakville Grade

Yountville Cross Rd

Rt 29

Yountville

Tour Nine in Central Napa
Charming, Small, Family Wineries Combined with
Some Famous Places to End the Day, Two Appointments

Sawyer Cellars 707.963.1980 www.sawyercellars.com *Small and Friendly*   Page 258
8350 St. Helena Hwy., Rutherford   Hours: 10 am - 5 pm daily by appt   Tasting Fee: $7.50 - $15
Wine List: Cabernet Sauvignon, Merlot, Sauvignon Blanc, Meritage, Blend

North to Dean & DeLuca on the left-hand side: total 3.3 miles, approx 5 minutes

Pick up picnic items to eat at Dean & DeLuca's side patio or picnic at **V. Sattui Winery**
1111 White Ln., St. Helena   Hours: 9 am - 6 pm Deli & Picnic Tables (You can not bring in food)
Dean & DeLuca 707.967.9980 www.deandeluca.com
607 S. St. Helena Hwy., St. Helena   Hours: 7 am - 8 pm M-Sun
    This is a destination market, and in fact the hardest thing about going there is getting
everyone to leave again for the next stop on the tour. If you are in hurry and the line at the sandwich bar is too long look in the refrigerator case next to it. The pre-made sandwiches are great
and they always have an array of salads as well. Otherwise consult restaurant list on pg. 168

South to Zinfandel Ln, turn left to Kelham Vineyards: total 1.3 miles, approx 2 minutes

Kelham Winery 707.963.2000 www.kelhamvineyards.com *Appointment*   Page 237
360 Zinfandel Ln., St. Helena   Hours: **appt only**   Tasting Fee:$20+
Wine List: Cabernet Sauvignon, Sauvignon Blanc, Merlot

Turn left to Silverado, right to Vine Cliff Winery: total 5.6 miles, approx 8 minutes

Vine Cliff Winery 707.944.1364 www.vinecliff.com *Appointment-Caves-Tour*   Page 269
7400 Silverado Trail, Yountville   Hours: 10 am - 5 pm daily by appt   Tasting Fee: $25
Wine List: Cabernet Sauvignon, Chardonnay, Merlot
    Continue south on Silverado to Stag's Leap Cellars: total 3.9 miles, approx 4 minutes

Stag's Leap Wine Cellars 707.261.6441 www.cask23.com *Respected Red Wines* Page 263
5766 Silverado Trail, Napa   Hours: 10 am - 4:30 pm   Tasting Fee: $10 - $30
Wine List: Riesling, Sauvignon Blanc, Chardonnay, Merlot, Cabernet Sauvignon

Continue south on Silverado to Darioush: total 3.1 miles, approx 3 minutes

Darioush 707.257.2345 www.darioush.com *Gorgeous-Fun-Gift Shop*   Page 222
4240 Silverado Trail, Napa   Hours: 10:30 am - 4:30 pm   Tasting Fee: $20
Wine List: Cabernet Sauvignon, Shiraz, Chardonnay, Merlot, Semillon, Sauvignon, Blanc, Pinot
Noir, Viognier
    This is a good last stop for the day if your hotel is towards the south. It has a great gift
shop, beautiful bathrooms and while it gets busy late in the day it is fun. It's gates sometimes
close at 4:30PM so if you are running late stop at the Regusci winery instead, on the same side of
the road just south of Stag's Leap Cellars.

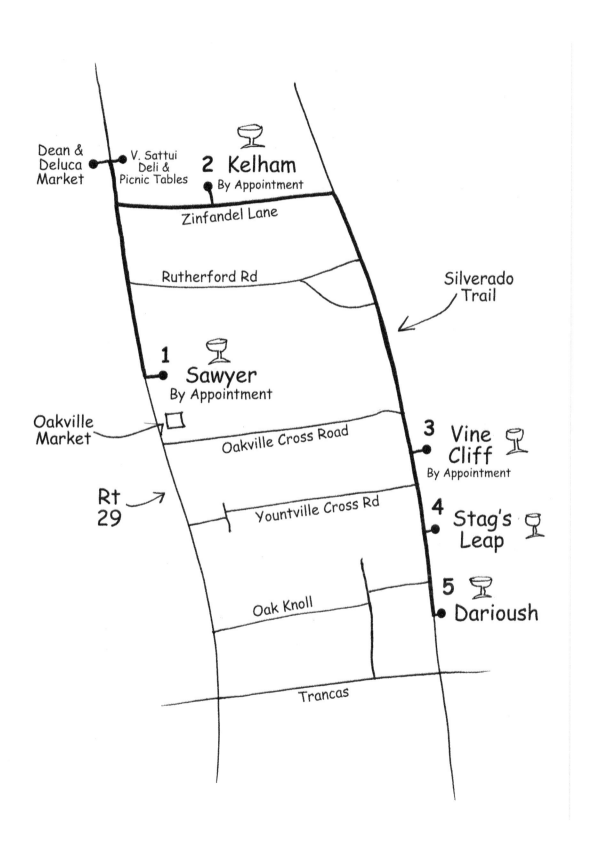

Your Day in Wine Country

Tour Ten in Central Napa
Beautiful Wineries, Great Art, a Wide Variety of Wines,
Bring a Camera for the Views, Two Appointments, Great Gift Shops

St. Supéry Vineyards & Winery 707.963.4507 www.stsupery.com *Elegant*   Page 262
8440 St. Helena Hwy., Rutherford   Hours: 10 am - 5:30 pm   Tasting Fee: $10 - $15
Wine List: Sauvignon Blanc, Cabernet Sauvignon, Merlot, Chardonnay, Unoaked Chardonnay, Syrah, Cabernet Franc   *Limousines need to call ahead!*
Turn right to Dean & DeLuca (Across from V Sattui): 3 miles, 10 minutes

Pick up picnic items to eat at Hall's:
Dean & DeLuca 707.967.9980 www.deandeluca.com
607 S. St. Helena Hwy., St. Helena   Hours: 7 am - 8 pm M-Sun
Hall is next door to Dean & DeLuca. Walk across the parking lot rather than drive.

Hall 707.967.2620 www.hallwines.com *Great Art Picnic*   Page 232
401 St. Helena Hwy S., St. Helena   Hours: 10 am - 5:30 pm   Tasting Fee: $10
Wine List: Cabernet Sauvignon, Merlot, Sauvignon Blanc *-See note in directory-*
South to Zinfandel, left to Kelham Vineyards & Winery: 1.5 miles, 5 minutes

Kelham Winery 707.963.2000 www.kelhamvineyards.com *Appoint-Gracious*   Page 237
360 Zinfandel Ln., St. Helena   Hours: **appt only**   Tasting Fee: $20+
Wine List: Cabernet Sauvignon, Sauvignon Blanc, Merlot
Turn left to Silverado & then right to Mumm Napa Valley: 2.8 miles, 8 minutes

Mumm Napa Valley 707.967.7700 www.mummnapa.com *Sparkling-Fun*   Page 245
8445 Silverado Trail, Rutherford   Hours: 10 am - 5 pm   Tasting Fee: $5 - $15 glass/flight
Wine List: Pinot Noir, Chardonnay, Santana, DVX, Demi Sec, Sparkling Pinot Noir, Cuvee M Red, Blanc de Blanc, Brut Prestige, Blanc de Noirs, Brut Reserve
Turn right & go South to Vine Cliff Winery: total 2.8 miles, approx 5 minutes

Vine Cliff Winery 707.944.1364 www.vinecliff.com *Appointment-Caves-Tour*   Page 269
7400 Silverado Trail, Yountville Hours: 10 am - 5 pm daily **by appt** Tasting Fee: $25
Wine List: Cabernet Sauvignon, Chardonnay, Merlot
Turn left & go South to Silverado Vineyards: total 2.7 miles, approx 5 minutes

Silverado Vineyards 707.257.1770 www.silveradovineyards.com *Great Views* Page 261
6121 Silverado Trail, Napa   Hours: 10:30 am - 5 pm   Tasting Fee: $10 - $20
Wine List: Sauvignon Blanc, Chardonnay, Merlot, Sangiovese, Cabernet Sauvignon
Turn right & go South to Darioush: total 4.2 miles, approx 4 minutes

Darioush 707.257.2345 www.darioush.com *Gorgeous-Gift Shop-Fun*   Page 222
4240 Silverado Trail, Napa   Hours: 10:30 am - 5 pm   Tasting Fee: $20
Wine List: Cabernet Sauvignon, Shiraz, Chardonnay, Merlot, Semillon, Sauvignon Blanc, Pinot Noir, Viognier
Darioush is a great place to finish a tour, gorgeous, great gift shop and social scene.

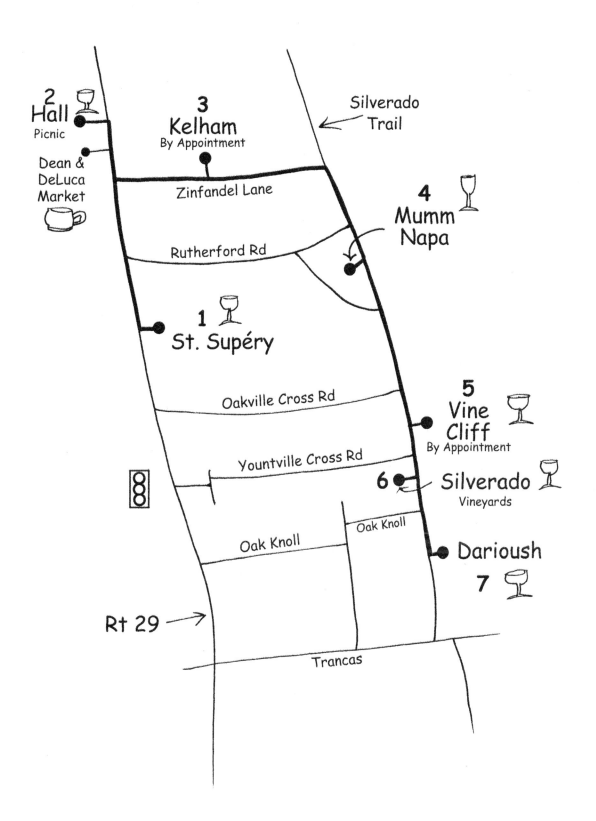

2
Hall
Picnic

Dean &
DeLuca
Market

3
Kelham
By Appointment

Silverado
Trail

Zinfandel Lane

Rutherford Rd

4
**Mumm
Napa**

1
St. Supéry

Oakville Cross Rd

5
**Vine
Cliff**
By Appointment

Yountville Cross Rd

6
Silverado
Vineyards

Oak Knoll

Oak Knoll

Darioush

7

Rt 29

Trancas

Tour Eleven in Central Napa
Oakville and Rutherford, Big and Small, Beautiful Buildings and Art, Great Tours, One Appointment Starting with a Tour

Nickel and Nickel is easy to find. It is on the right hand side just north of the Oakville Cross Rd and the Oakville Market, just past Opus One and across the street from Robert Mondavi. It is quite a neighborhood. It is open by appointment and the gate is electronic. Beautiful grounds and quite a good tour. The wines of course are very good. They are associated with the Far Niente winery.

Nickel & Nickel 707.967.9600 www.nickelandnickel.com *Appointment-Tour*   Page 246
8164 St. Helena Hwy, Oakville   Hours: 10 am - 3 pm   **appt** Tour & Tasting Fee: $40
Wine List: Chardonnay, Cabernet Sauvignon, Merlot, Syrah, Zinfandel

Turn right (north) to Beaulieu Vineyard on the right side: 1.9 miles, 3 minutes

Beaulieu Vineyard 707.967.5230 www.bvwines.com *Great Reds-Reserve Room*   Page 213
1960 St. Helena Hwy., Rutherford   Hours: 10 am - 5 pm   Tasting Fee: $5 - $20
Wine List: Cabernet Sauvignon, Chardonnay, Pinot Noir, Merlot, Zinfandel, Syrah, Sauvignon Blanc, Shiraz, Sangiovese, Viognier, Port, Blends

Turn right (north) to Dean & DeLuca, left-hand side : total 2.1 miles,approx 4 minutes

Pick up picnic items to eat at Arger-Martucci's picnic tables later
Dean & DeLuca 707.967.9980 www.deandeluca.com 607 S. St. Helena Hwy., St. Helena
Hours: 7 am - 8 pm M-Sun, or **Sunshine Foods** 1115 Main St. (Rt. 29) St Helena.

Turn right (south) and take first right, Inglewood Ave. Arger-Martucci Vineyards is a short distance down on the left-hand side: total 4.4 miles, approx 9 minutes

Arger-Martucci Vineyards 707.963.4334 www.arger-martucciwine.com *Friendly* Page 211
1455 Inglewood Ave., St. Helena   Hours: 10 am - 4 pm daily Tasting Fee: $10 *Picnic*
Wine List: Chardonnay, Viognier, Pinot Noir, Syrah, Cabernet Sauvignon, Blends

Turn right (south) to Rubicon on the right-hand side: 2.8 miles, approx 5 minutes

Rubicon Estate 707.968.1100 www.rubiconestate.com *Great Estate-Espresso*   Page 256
1991 St. Helena Hwy., Rutherford   Hours: 10 am - 5 pm   Tour & Tasting Fee: $25
Wine List: Cabernet Sauvignon, Merlot, Cabernet Franc, Syrah, Blends

This tour is made up of very unique wineries. Some serious, others very light-hearted. Arger Martucci is a very small winery and can get quite busy on the weekends, but they always seem to find room for everyone.

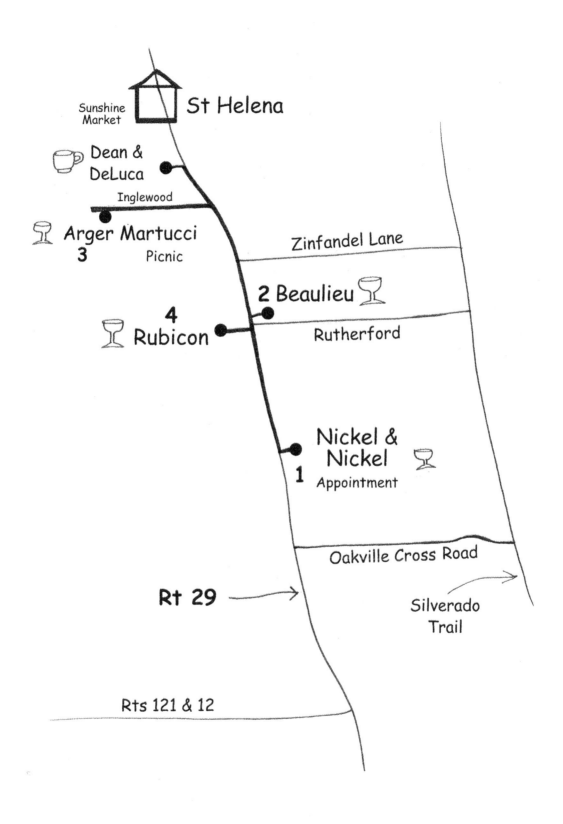

Sunshine Market

St Helena

Dean & DeLuca

Inglewood

Arger Martucci
3
Picnic

Zinfandel Lane

2 Beaulieu

4
Rubicon

Rutherford

Nickel & Nickel
1
Appointment

Oakville Cross Road

Rt 29

Silverado Trail

Rts 121 & 12

Tour Twelve in Central Napa
Prestigious Wineries with Beautiful Locations, Sparkling Wines, Big Reds, Chardonnay, Two Appointments

Finding Cakebread is easy except for one thing, their sign is not very obvious. They are north of the Oakville Cross Rd on the right hand side. They are the next winery past Turnbull, and if you reach Sequoia Grove (both good wineries) you've gone too far. Slow down and look for their mail box which has their name on it prominently. They are by appointment and it is important to arrive at least five minutes early.

Cakebread Cellars 707.963.5221 www.cakebread.com *Appointment* Page 216
8300 Saint Helena Hwy., Rutherford Hours: 10 am - 4 pm daily **by appt** Tasting Fee: $10
Wine List: Sauvignon Blanc, Chardonnay, Pinot Noir, Merlot, Syrah, Zinfandel, Cabernet Sauvignon, Rubaiyat (blend of Pinot Noir, Syrah & Zinfandel) Allow 1 & 1/2 hours for appointment.

Rutherford Rd. to Duckhorn Vineyards, entrance on Lodi: 7.6 miles, approx 20 minutes

Duckhorn Vineyards 707.963.7108 www.duckhorn.com *Appointment-Charming* Pg 225
3027 Silverado Trail N., St. Helena Hours: 10 am - 4 pm **by appt** Tasting Fee: $10 - $25
Wine List: Sauvignon Blanc, Merlot, Cabernet Sauvignon,

Two wineries equals lunch. One suggestion is Taylors' Refresher. Lodi to Rt 29 south: Total 2.9 miles, approx 12 minutes. You can also pick up picnic supplies at Sunshine Foods or Dean & DeLuca to eat at Hall's, or consult the restaurant list on page 168

Taylor's Refresher 707.963.3486 www.taylorsrefresher.com
933 Main St., St. Helena Hours: 11 am - 7 pm

Turn right (south) to Hall: total 1.1 miles, approx 2 minutes

Hall 707.967.2620 www.hallwines.com *Picnic-Beautiful Art* Page 232
401 St. Helena Hwy S., St. Helena Hours: 10 am - 5:30 pm Tasting Fee: $10
Wine List: Cabernet Sauvignon, Merlot, Sauvignon Blanc *-See note in directory-*

Turn right (south) to the Yountville exit & Domaine Carneros: 21.8 miles, 29 minutes

Domaine Carneros 707.257.0101 www.domainecarneros.com *Sparkling-Fun* Page 224
1240 Duhig Rd., Napa Hours: 10 am - 6 pm daily Tasting Fee: table service by the glass
Wine List: Brut Cuvee, Brut Rosé, Le Reve Blanc de Blancs, Pinot Noir

If you are returning to the city, go to Artesa Winery: total 2.7 miles approx 7 minutes

Artesa Winery 707.254.2140 www.artesawinery.com *Great Views-Bar Feel* Page 211
1345 Henry Rd., Napa Hours: 10 am - 5 pm daily Tasting Fee: $5 - $10
Wine List: Cabernet Sauvignon, Chardonnay, Merlot, Pinot Noir, Tempranillo, Albarino, Garnacha Rosado, Late Harvest Gewürztraminer, Blends

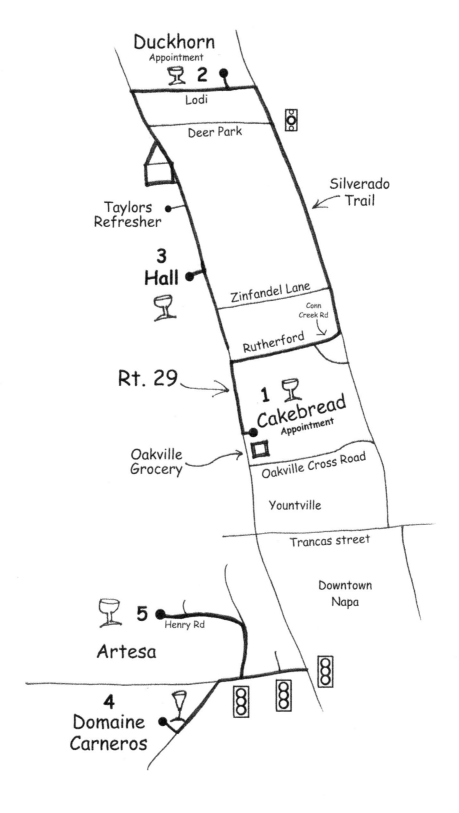

Tour Thirteen in Central Napa
Very Big Reds, Famous Labels Starting with One Appointment

This tour is made up of wineries that do the big, red wines and have the big, dramatic buildings to go with them. Cardinale schedules tastings at specific times so it can be a challenge to fit them in with other appointments. Opus One likes when people make an appointment, but unless they are slammed with business they will not turn customers away. Drink lots of water!!!

Cardinale Estate 707.948.2643 www.cardinale.com *Scheduled Appointment* Page 216
7600 St. Helena Hwy., Oakville Hours: 10:30 am - 5 pm daily Tasting Fee: $35 - $150
Wine List: single vintage Cabernet Sauvignon-based blend
This building was originally the Joseph Pepi winery and is now owned by Kendall Jackson. It is a beautiful location and home to serious wines.
> *Turn right (north) to Opus One, it is the gate just past the Oakville Market. The sign is small but the building is very dramatic: total 0.9 miles, approx 2 minutes*

Opus One 707.944.9442 www.opusonewinery.com *Architecture* Page 247
7900 St. Helena Hwy., Oakville Hours: 10 am-4 pm daily *Likes Appointments* Tasting Fee: $25
Wine List: Blends of: Cabernet Sauvignon, Cabernet Franc, Merlot. Recent vintages add Malbec and/or Petit Verdot. They offer one large sample for $25.
They do a wonderful tour but it requires an appointment well in advance. They were started as a joint venture of the Mondavi family and the Von Rothchild family.
> *For lunch either head up to the Rutherford Grill, or if you just want a quick bite, go out the exit that leads to Oakville Cross Rd. The gate will open as you approach. Turn right back towards the market.*

One lunch suggestion is:
Oakville Grocery 707.944.8802 7856 St. Helena Hwy., Oakville Hours: 9 am-6 pm daily
Another lunch suggestion is the **Rutherford Grill** at the corner of Rt 29 and Rutherford Rd or consult the restaurant directory on page 168. Auberge du Soleil is also convenient.
> *Head north from Oakville Grocery to Rubicon Estate, the entrance is just across from Rutherford Rd: total 2.6 miles, approx 3 minutes. Or consult the restaurant list on page 168.*

Rubicon Estate 707.968.1100 www.rubiconestate.com *Grand Estate-Tours* Page 256
1991 St. Helena Hwy., Rutherford Hours: 10 am - 5 pm Tasting Fee: $25
Wine List: Cabernet Sauvignon, Merlot, Cabernet Franc, Syrah, Blends
Started by Captain Neibaum, later famous as Inglenook and now owned by Francis Ford Coppola who originally called it Neibaum Coppola, but has since renamed it Rubicon, after his premier wine. A very gracious place to spend an afternoon.
> *Turn right (south) to Robert Mondavi Winery: total 2.1 miles, approx 3 minutes*

Robert Mondavi Winery 707.226.1395 www.robertmondaviwinery.com *Big* Page 253
7801 St. Helena Hwy., Oakville Hours: 10 am - 5 pm Tasting Fee: $5 - $50+
Wine List: Fumé Blanc, Chardonnay, Pinot Noir, Merlot, Cabernet Sauvignon, Moscato d'Oro, Sauvignon Blanc, Zinfandel, Dry Rosé
For their best wines go back to the To Kalon Reserve room and share a tasting, $25.

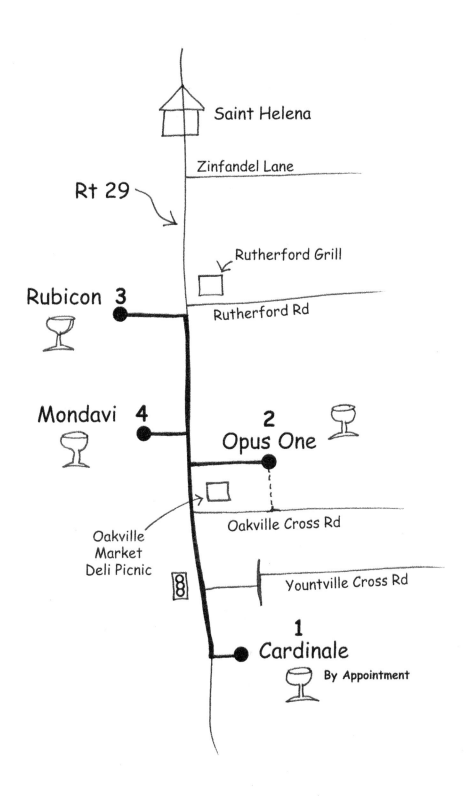

Saint Helena

Zinfandel Lane

Rt 29

Rutherford Grill

Rubicon **3**

Rutherford Rd

Mondavi **4**

2
Opus One

Oakville
Market
Deli Picnic

Oakville Cross Rd

Yountville Cross Rd

1
Cardinale

By Appointment

Tour Fourteen in Central Napa
Big Reds, Cabernet, Two Appointments, Great Tours,
Make the Appointments far in Advance

When you are driving from Rt 29 over Oakville Grade Far Niente's very long, straight driveway is on the left-hand side. There is a very small metal sign on the right side of the gate. The sign is not easy to spot, so look for the very impressive driveway. **Be Early for your Appointment!** They work with groups so they will not wait for you. They have been known to turn people away for being late. Great gardens and building, tour is 1 & 1/2 hours minimum.

Far Niente 707.944.2861 www.farniente.com *Appointment Required*   Page 227
1350 Acacia Dr., Oakville Hours: 10 am - 4 pm Mon - Sat **appt only** Tour & Tasting Fee: $75
Wine List: Cabernet Sauvignon, Chardonnay
> Go back to Route 29, turn right and the restaurants will be on the right hand side.
> *To Mustards and Brix: total 3.0 miles, approx 7 minutes*

Our lunch suggestions are: (*or consult the restaurant list on page 168*)
Brix Restaurant & Wine Shop of Napa Valley 707.944.2749 www.brix.com
7377 St. Helena Hwy., Yountville Hours: Sun-Thu 11:30 am-9 pm Fri-Sat 11:30 am-10 pm

Mustard's Grill 707-944-2424 *A small restaurant, make a reservation.*
7399 St. Helena Hwy., Yountville Hours: Mon-Thu 11:30 am-9 pm Fri 11:30 am-10 pm
Sat 11:00 am-10 pm Sun 11:00 am-9 pm
> *Turn right to light, cross over the Yountville Cross Rd to the Silverado Trail and turn*
> *left to Vine Cliff Winery:total 4.8 miles, approx 8 minutes*

Vine Cliff Winery 707-944-1364 www.vinecliff.com *Appointment-Caves-Tour*   Page 269
7400 Silverado Trail, Yountville Hours: 10 am - 5 pm daily **by appt** Tasting Fee: $25
Wine List: Cabernet Sauvignon, Chardonnay, Merlot
Family run, fantastic wines, wonderful, intimate tour.
> *Turn right on Silverado, left on Oakville, at the bottom of a curving turn Plumpjack*
> *Winery sign is on the right side: total 1.0 miles approx 2 minutes*

Plumpjack Winery 707.945.1220 www.plumpjack.com *Small-Charming*   Page 250
620 Oakville Cross Rd., Oakville Hours: 10 am - 4 pm Tasting Fee: $5 - $10
Wine List: Cabernet Sauvignon, Chardonnay, Merlot
Charming, small tasting room, nice gift shop.
> *Turn right onto Oakville Cross Rd (towards Rt 29) and the Silver Oak Cellars sign is on*
> *the left hand side: total 1.0 miles approx 2 minutes*

Silver Oak Cellars 707.944.8808 www.silveroak.com *Popular Cab Blend*   Page 260
915 Oakville Cross Rd., Oakville Hours: 9 am - 4 pm Closed Sun. Tasting Fee: $10
Wine List: Cabernet Sauvignon from Napa Valley and Sonoma's Alexander Valley
They taste two wines made in the popular Silver Oak style.   See note in directory

> *To head south take the Silverado Trail, less traffic and easier turns.*

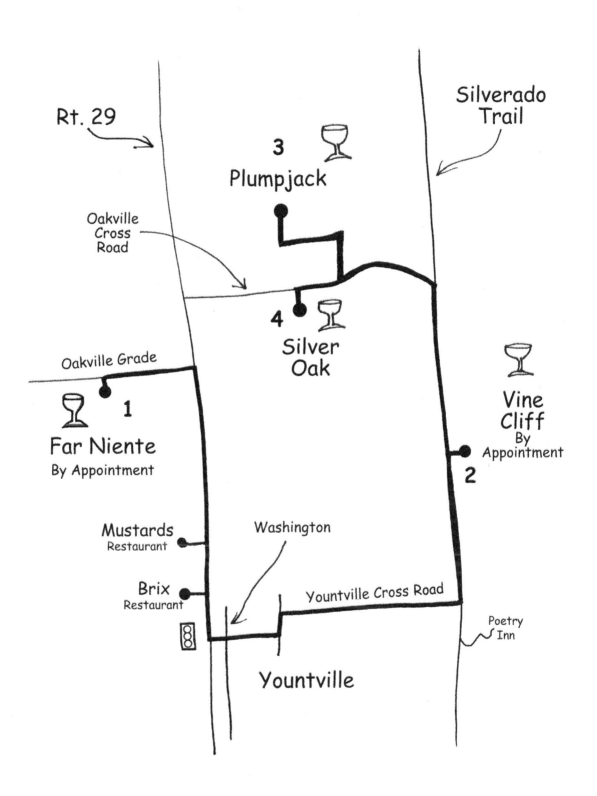

Rt. 29

Silverado Trail

3
Plumpjack

Oakville Cross Road

4
Silver Oak

Oakville Grade

1
Far Niente
By Appointment

Vine Cliff
By Appointment
2

Mustards
Restaurant

Washington

Brix
Restaurant

Yountville Cross Road

Poetry Inn

Yountville

Restaurants in Central Napa

Refer to Map on Page 69
For St. Helena Restaurants See List on Page 208

Yountville

Ad Hoc: 6476 Washington St. Yountville. 707.944.2487. Dinner Only, Comfort
Bistro Jeanty: 6510 Washinton St. Yountville. 707.944.0103. French
Bouchon: 6534 Washinton St. Yountville. 707.944.8037. Bistro French
Bouchon Bakery: 6528 Washinton St. Yountville. 707.944.2253. Bakery and Sandwiches
Brix: 7377 St. Helena Hwy (Rt. 29) Yountville. 707.944.2749. Californian
Etoile at Domaine Chandon: 1 California Dr. Yountville. 707.204.7529. French
Hurley's: 6518 Washington St. Yountville. 707.944.2345. American
Michael Chiarello's 'unnamed' Napa Style Restaurant, V Marketplace Yountville. Opening 2008
Mustards Grill: 7399 St Helena Hwy (Rt. 29) Yountville. 707.944.2424. Californian
Napa Valley Grille:6795 Washington St. (The Corner of Rt. 29 and Madison) Yountville. 707.944.8686. Californian
Pacific Blues Café: 6525 Washington St. Yountville. 707.944.4455. Burgers
Redd: 6480 Washington St. Yountville. 707.944.2222. Fine Contemporary
The French Laundry: 6640 Washington St. Yountville. 707.944.2380. Extraordinary Dining

Oakville

Oakville Grocery: 7856 St Helena Hwy (Rt. 29) Oakville. 707.944.8802. Market

Rutherford

Auberge De Soleil: 180 Rutherford Hill Rd. Rutherford. 707.963.1211. French
La Toque: 1140 Rutherford Rd. Rutherford. 707.963.9770. Dinner Only. Fine Contemporary
Rutherford Grill: 1180 Rutherford Rd (At the Corner of Rt. 29 Northbound) Rutherford. 707.963.1792. American

Lodgings

Auberge du Soleil: 180 Rutherford Hill Rd. Rutherford   800.348.5406   707.963.1211 www.aubergedusoleil.com Pg. 147
Lavender Inn: 2020 Webber Ave. Yountville 800.522.4140 www.lavendernapa.com
Maison Fleurie: 6529 Yount St. Yountville 800.788.0369 707.944.2056 www.maisonfleurienapa.com
Napa Valley Lodge: 2230 Madison St. Yountville. 888-455-2468 Pg. 141
Poetry Inn: 6380 Silverado Trail. Napa 707.944.0646 www.poetryinn.com Pg.167
Rancho Caymus Inn: 1140 Rutherford Rd. Rutherford. 707.963.1777 www.ranchocaymus.com Pg. 141
Villagio Inn and Spa: 6481 Washington St. Yountville   800.351.1133   707.944.1112 www.Villagio.com Pg. 141
Vintage Inn: 6541 Washington St. Yountville 800.351.1133 707.944.1112 www.vintageinn.com Pg. 141
Yountville Inn: 6462 Washington St. Yountville 888.366.8166 707.944.5600 www.yountvilleinn.com   Pg. 141

Your Day in Wine Country   168

Tour Directory: Starting in Northern Sonoma

One - Page 172

Combining Alexander Valley, Dry Creek and Russian River, One Appointment, Beautiful Wineries, Cabernet, Zinfandel, Pinot and Chardonnay, Sparkling.

Wineries: Jordan (App), Passalacqua, Lambert Bridge, Rodney Strong, J Vineyard.

Five hour tour locally, nine hour tour from SF

A good day trip from San Francisco. $$ Moderately Priced

Best with a Car and Professional Driver

Two - Page 174

Valley of the Moon and Glen Ellen, Great Wine Variety, Charming and Educational Tours, Biodynamic Vineyards, Great Views, Good Gift Shops.

Wineries: St. Francis, Loxton, Benziger, Chateau St, Jean

Six hour tour locally, eight hour tour from SF

A good day trip from San Francisco. $$ Moderately Priced

Best with a Car and Professional Driver

Three - Page 176

Russian River and Dry Creek, Great Views and Buildings, Unique and Authentic, Sparkling, Pinot Noir, Chardonnay and Big Reds, Good Gift Shops.

Wineries: Deloach, Iron Horse, Hop Kiln, Lambert Bridge, Bella, Ferrari Carano

Seven hour tour locally, ten hours done from San Francisco

A good day trip from San Francisco. $$ Moderately Priced

Best with a Car and Professional Driver

Four - Page 178

Dry Creek Valley Top to Bottom, Beautiful Wineries and Gardens, Great Views, World Class Zinfandel, Pinot Noir and Chardonnay, Good Gift Shops.

Wineries: Ferrari Carano, Dry Creek, Quivira, Alderbrook

Five hour tour locally, nine hour tour from SF. $$ Moderately Priced

Five - Page 180

Alexander Valley and Dry Creek, Beautiful Wineries and Views,
One Appointment, World Class Reds, Chardonnay and Zinfandel.
Wineries: Hanna, Jordan (App), Passalacqua, Lambert Bridge
Five hour tour accessible to Napa. $$ Moderately Priced

Six - Page 182

A Short Dry Creek Valley Sampler Tour, Beauty, Charm and Great Wines,
Big Reds, Chardonnay and Zinfandel, Good Gift Shops.
Wineries: Ferrari Carano, Passalacqua, Lambert Bridge
Four hour tour locally. $$ Moderately Priced

Seven - Page 184

The Western Russian River Valley with History and Redwoods,
Sparkling, Pinot Noir, Chardonnay, Zinfandel, Good Tours and Gift Shops.
Wineries: Kendall Jackson, Korbel (Sparkling), Hartford Family, Martinelli
Six hour tour locally. $$ Moderately Priced

Restaurants & Hotels of Northern Sonoma   Page 186

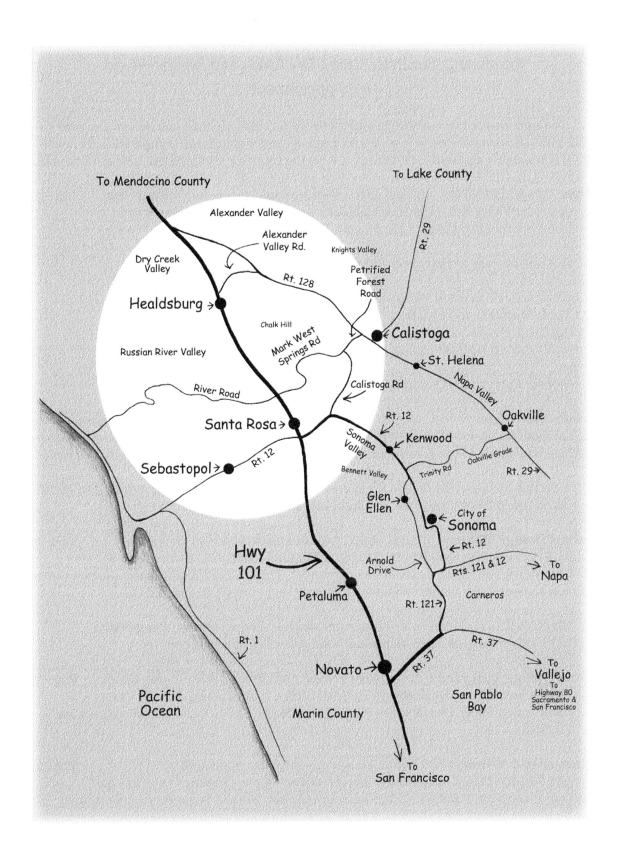

Tour One in Northern Sonoma
Combining Alexander Valley, Dry Creek and Russian River,
One Appointment

The sign for Jordan is not large and there are no signs warning you before you arrive at the driveway, however the drive is wide and gracious and it stands out compared to its neighbors. If you are coming from Healdsburg, it is on the right-hand side. Go to the top of the hill.

Jordan Vineyard & Winery 707.431.5250 www.jordanwinery.com *Appointment* Page 236
1474 Alexander Valley Rd., Healdsburg Hours: **Appt Only** Tasting Fee: $20
Wine List: Cabernet Sauvignon, Chardonnay, Dessert Wine, Olive Oil

Follow the map to Dry Creek Market: total 5.1 miles, approx 15 minutes

Pick up picnic items to eat at Passalaqua's picnic tables later
Dry Creek Market 707.433.4171
3495 Dry Creek Rd., Healdsburg,
or eat in downtown Healdsburg, see the restaurant list on page 186

Follow the map to Passalacqua Winery: total 0.4 miles, approx 2 minutes

Passalacqua Winery 707.433.5550 www. passalacquawinery.com *Picnic* Page 248
3805 Lambert Bridge Rd., Healdsburg Hours: 11 am – 5 pm Tasting Fee: Comp - $5 - $10
Wine List: Sauvignon Blanc, Chardonnay, Zinfandel, Merlot, Cabernet Sauvignon-*Charming!*

Continue on Lambert Bridge Rd to end, turn left to Lambert Bridge Winery, on right-hand side of West Dry Creek Rd: total 0.9 miles approx 2 minutes

Lambert Bridge Winery 707.431.9600 www.lambertbridge.com *Great Reds* Page 239
4085 W. Dry Creek Rd., Healdsburg Hours: 10:30 am – 4:30 pm Tasting Fee: $5 - $10
Wine List: Sauvignon Blanc, Chardonnay, Zinfandel, Syrah, Cuvee, Petite Sirah, Merlot, Cabernet Franc, Cabernet, Sauvignon, Vinegar, Mustard, Mayonnaise, Grapeseed Oil

Backtrack to Healdsburg Ave and head south to Rodney Strong Vineyards & J Vineyards, on the same driveway: total 9.0 miles approx 20 minutes

Rodney Strong Vineyards 707.433.6511 www.rodneystrong.com *Great Building* Page 255
11455 Old Redwood Hwy, Healdsburg Hours: 10 am – 5 pm Tasting Fee: $5 - $10
Wines: Sauvignon Blanc, Chardonnay, Pinot Noir, Merlot, Syrah, Cabernet Sauvignon, Meritage, Zinfandel, Port

J Vineyards & Winery 707.431.5430 www.jwine.com *Sparkling* Page 235
11447 Old Redwood Hwy, Healdsburg Hours: 11 am – 5 pm Tasting Fee: $10 - $20
Wine List: Pinot Noir, Pinot Gris, Chardonnay, Vin Gris, Dessert Wine Pear Liqueur, Rosé

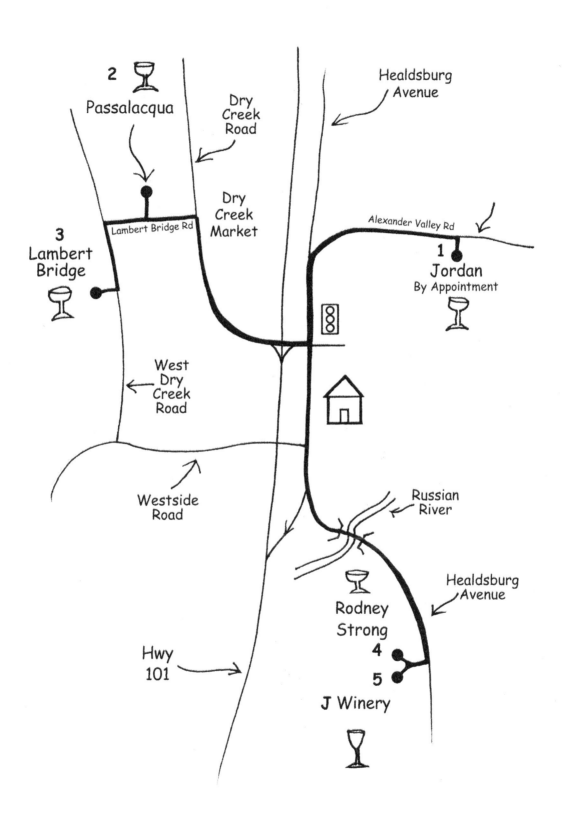

2 Passalacqua

Dry Creek Road

Healdsburg Avenue

Dry Creek Market

Lambert Bridge Rd

3 Lambert Bridge

Alexander Valley Rd

1 Jordan
By Appointment

West Dry Creek Road

Westside Road

Russian River

Rodney Strong

4

Healdsburg Avenue

Hwy 101

5 J Winery

Tour Two in Northern Sonoma

Valley of the Moon and Glen Ellen, Great Wine Variety, Charming and Educational Tours, Biodynamic Vineyards, Great Views, Good Gift Shops

This is a good tour to make from Santa Rosa traveling south into the Valley of the Moon. It also works well if you are staying in Glen Ellen or Kenwood. It combines one of the largest wineries, Chateau St. Jean Winery, with one of the smallest, Loxton.

St. Francis is at a traffic light and easy to find on Rt 12 south of Santa Rosa.

St. Francis Vineyard & Winery   707.833.0242   www.stfranciswine.com   *Views*   Page 262
100 Pythian Rd., Santa Rosa   Hours: 10 am - 5 pm   Tasting Fee: $5 - $20
Wine List: Chardonnay, Cabernet Sauvignon, Merlot, Zinfandel, Syrah

Turn left (south) to Dunbar Rd., bear right and Loxton Cellars comes up quickly on the right hand side, watch out for kangaroos: total 4.3 miles, approx 6 minutes

Loxton Cellars   707.935.7221   www.loxtoncellars.com   *Small-Friendly*   Page 241
11466 Dunbar Rd., Glen Ellen   Hours: 11 am - 5 pm daily   Tasting Fee: $5
Wine List: Rosé Vin Gris of Syrah, Zinfandel, Syrah, Cabernet Sauvignon, Syrah Port, Chardonnay, Shiraz

Follow Rt 12 south to the next light and turn right. This will bring you into Glen Ellen, the Market will be on the left-hand side: total 2.4 miles, approx 5 minutes

Pick up picnic items to eat at Benziger Family Winery's picnic tables later at
Glen Ellen Market   707.996.3411   www.sonoma-glenellenmkt.com
13751 Arnold Dr., Glen Ellen   Hours: 7 am - 8 pm

Turn right out of the lot and take the first left onto London Ranch Rd. Benziger Family Winery will be up the hill on the right-hand side: total 0.8 miles, approx 5 minutes

Benziger Family Winery   707.935.4500   www.benziger.com   *Best Tours-Gifts*   Page 214
1883 London Ranch Rd., Glen Ellen   Hours: 10 am - 5 pm daily   Tasting Fee: $5 - $10
Wine List: Zinfandel, Cabernet Sauvignon, Merlot, Barbera, Malbec, Cabernet Franc, Petite Blanc, Sangiovese, Pinot Blanc, Chardonnay, Viognier, Fumé Blanc, Syrah, White Burgundy, Claret, Muscat Canelli

Back track to Rt 12, at the light turn left (north), Chateau St. Jean Winery will be on the right-hand side past the Kenwood traffic light: total 6.2 miles approx 10 minutes

Chateau St. Jean Winery   707.833.4134   www.chateaustjean.com   *Beautiful-Gifts*   Page 219
8555 Sonoma Hwy., Kenwood   Hours: 10 am - 5 pm   Tasting Fee: $10 - $15
Wine List: Pinot Blanc, Chardonnay, Viognier, Pinot Noir, Merlot, Malbec, Cabernet Sauvignon, Pinot Blanc, Chardonnay, Viognier, Pinot Noir, Merlot, Malbec

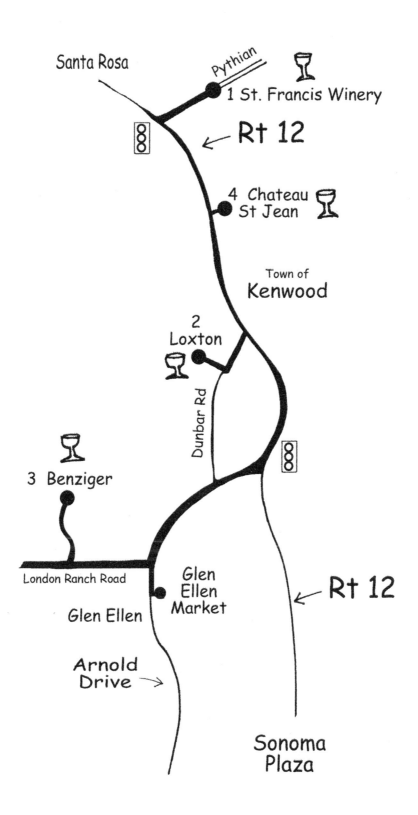

Your Day in Wine Country

Tour Three in Northern Sonoma
Russian River and Dry Creek, Great Views and Buildings, Unique and Authentic

The southern Russian River Valley is a good place to start when coming from San Francisco. The Guerneville Rd. exit that brings you to DeLoach is off of Hwy 101 is just north of Santa Rosa.

De Loach Vineyards 707.526.9111 www.deloachvineyards.com *Friendly*   Page 223
1791 Olivet Rd., Santa Rosa Hours: 10 am - 4:30 pm daily Tasting Fee: $5 - $10
Wine List: Sauvignon Blanc, Chardonnay, Pinot Noir, Zinfandel
    Follow the map to Iron Horse Vineyards: total 5.5 miles, approx 10 minutes

Iron Horse Vineyards 707.887.1507 www.ironhorsevineyards.com *Views*   Page 235
9786 Ross Station Rd., Sebastopol Hours: 11 am - 3:30 pm Tasting Fee: $10
Wine List: Chardonnay, Pinot Noir, Viognier, Sangiovese, Merlot, Cabernet Sauvignon, Sparklers, Cuvee, Blanc de Blanc, Brut, Blanc de Noir *Sparkling Wines*
    Follow the map to the La Rosa Market: total 2.0 miles, approx 4 minutes

Pick up picnic items to eat at Hop Kiln Winery's picnic tables later, one suggestion is:
Aioli, a Gormet Deli 707.887.2476, 6536 Front St., Forestville Hrs: 8am–6pm Closed Sun or backtrack to the town of Graton where there are several nice restaurants including the very good **Underwood of Graton**. It is a small town and the restaurants are easy to find.
    Follow map from downtown Forestville to Hop Kiln Winery: 7.5 miles, 12 minutes

Hop Kiln Winery 707.433.6491 hopkilnwinery.com *Architecture-Gifts-Picnic*   Page 234
6050 Westside Rd., Healdsburg Hours: 10 am - 5 pm Tasting Fee: $5 - $10
Wine List: Cabernet Sauvignon, Chardonnay, Riesling, Zinfandel, A Thousand Flowers, Marty Griffin's Big Red, Primitivo Vineyard Zinfandel, Rosa Bellissima, Old Windmill Vineyard
    Continue on Westside, turn left on West Dry Creek to Lambert Bridge Winery on the
    left-hand side: 9.4 miles, 20 minutes

Lambert Bridge Winery 707.431.9600 www.lambertbridge.com *Great Wines*   Page 239
4085 W. Dry Creek Rd., Healdsburg Hours: 10:30 am – 4:30 pm Tasting Fee: $5 - $10
Wine List: Sauvignon, Blanc, Chardonnay, Zinfandel, Syrah, Cuvee, Petite Sirah, Merlot, Cabernet Franc, Cabernet, Sauvignon, Vinegar, Mustard, Mayonnaise, Grapeseed Oil
    Continue on West Dry Creek to Bella Vineyards: total 5.6 miles, approx 14 minutes

Bella *Vineyards & Wine Caves* 707.473.9171 www.BellaWinery.com *Cave Tasting*   Page 213
9711 W. Dry Creek Rd., Healdsburg Hours: 11 am - 4:30 pm daily appt Tasting Fee: $5
Wine List: Zinfandel, Syrah
    Back track to Yoakim Bridge Rd, turn left & left again on Dry Creek Rd. to Ferrari-
    Carano Vineyards & Winery on the left-hand side: total 1.0 miles, approx 5 minutes

Ferrari-Carano Vineyards & Winery 800.831.0381 www.ferrari-carano.com   Page 228
8761 Dry Creek Rd., Healdsburg Hours: 10 am - 5 pm Tasting Fee: $5 *Gorgeous*
Wine List: Grenache Rosé, Chardonnay, Sangiovese, Syrah, Cabernet Sauvignon, Fumé Blanc, Zinfandel, Merlot, Blends

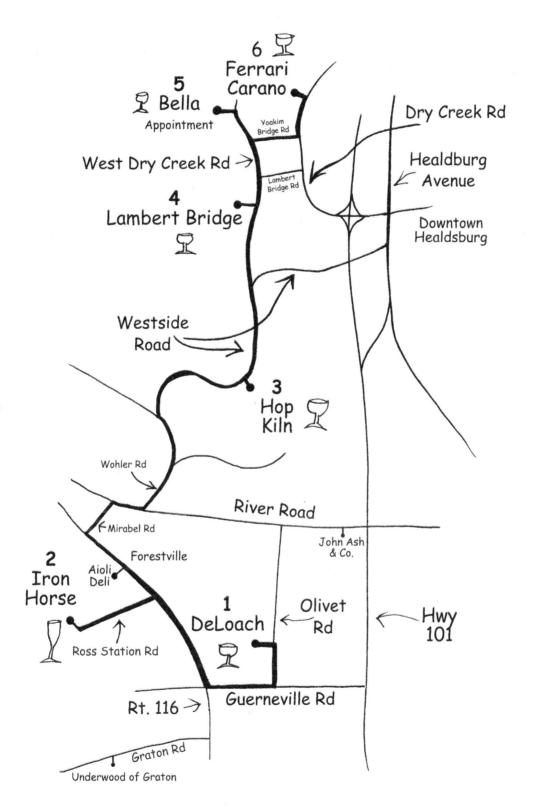

6 🍷
Ferrari
Carano

5 🍷 Bella
Appointment

Dry Creek Rd

Healdburg
Avenue

Yoakim
Bridge Rd

West Dry Creek Rd →

Lambert
Bridge Rd

Downtown
Healdsburg

4
Lambert Bridge
🍷

Westside
Road

3
Hop
Kiln 🍷

Wohler Rd

River Road

← Mirabel Rd

John Ash
& Co.

Forestville

2
Iron
Horse

Aioli
Deli

1
DeLoach
🍷

Olivet
Rd

← Hwy
101

🥂

Ross Station Rd

Guerneville Rd

Rt. 116 →

Graton Rd

Underwood of Graton

Your Day in Wine Country

Tour Four in Northern Sonoma

Dry Creek Valley Top to Bottom, Beautiful Wineries and Gardens, Great Views, World Class Zinfandel, Pinot Noir and Chardonnay, Good Gift Shops

This tour works well from the south because you end up, at the end of the day, closer to your starting point. The only hard part is that Ferrari Carano is so beautiful that it is a hard act to follow, however the others make up for that with some very good wines and a fun gift shop at the end of the day at Alderbrook.

Ferrari-Carano Vineyards & Winery 800.831.0381 www.ferrari-carano.com   Page 228
8761 Dry Creek Rd., Healdsburg Hours: 10 am - 5 pm Tasting Fee: $5 - $10   *Gorgeous*
Wine List: Grenache Rosé, Chardonnay, Sangiovese, Syrah, Cabernet Sauvignon, Fumé Blanc, Zinfandel, Merlot, Blends

> *Right (south) onto Dry Creek Rd, the Dry Creek General Store is on the left-hand side: total 5.5 miles, approx 7 minutes*

Pick up picnic items to eat at Dry Creek Vineyard's picnic tables later at
Dry Creek General Store 707.433.4171 www.dcgstore.com
3495 Dry Creek Rd., Healdsburg Hours: 6 am - 6 pm Mo-Th; Fr-Sa till 7PM
Or consult the restaurant list on page 186 and drive into nearby Healdsburg

> *From the Dry Creek Store head across the road to the Dry Creek Vineyard. You can see it from the store: 2 minutes*

Dry Creek Vineyard 707.433.1000 www.drycreekvineyard.com *Picnic*   Page 225
3770 Lambert Bridge Rd., Healdsburg Hours: 10:30 am - 4:30 pm Tasting Fee: $5-$10
Wine List: Dry Chenin Blanc, Fumé Blanc, Zinfandel, Merlot, Cabernet Sauvignon, Meritage, Dessert Wines, Blends

> *Continue on Lambert Bridge Rd to end, turn right to Quivira Vineyards, on the right-hand side: total 0.8 miles, approx 5 minutes*

Quivira Vineyards 707.431.8333 www.quivirawine.com *Biodynamic*   Page 251
4900 W. Dry Creek Rd., Healdsburg Hours: 11 am - 5 pm daily Tasting Fee: $5-$10
Wine List: Zinfandel, Sauvignon Blanc, Syrah, Petite Sirah, Grenache, Rhone blends
> *Turn left (south) to Westside Rd, turn left, Alderbrook Winery will be on the right-hand side: total 5.2 miles, approx 9 minutes*

Alderbrook Winery 707.433.5987 www.alderbrook.com *Great Gift Shop*   Page 209
2306 Magnolia Dr., Healdsburg Hours: 10 am - 5 pm Tasting Fee: Complimentary
Wine List: Pinot Noir, Sauvignon Blanc, Chardonnay, Cabernet Sauvignon, Merlot, Syrah, Viognier, Zinfandel, Gewürztraminer
> *Turn right on Westside Rd, this will bring you into Healdsburg as well to an entrance for Hwy 101 south.*

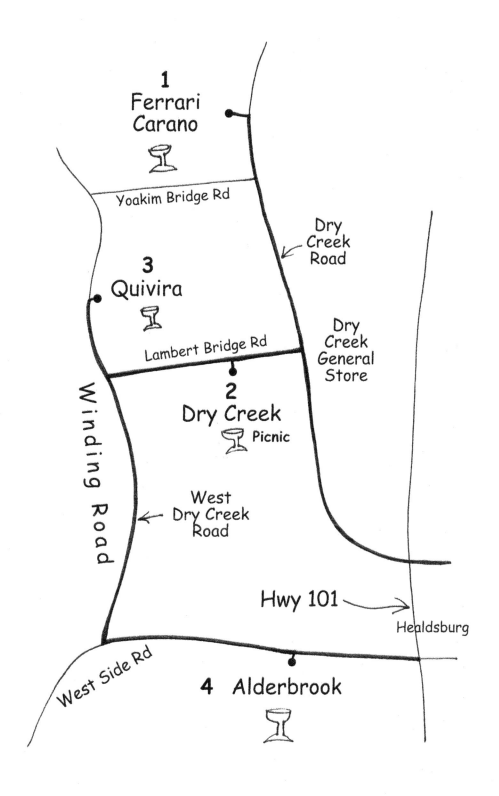

1
Ferrari
Carano
🍷

Yoakim Bridge Rd

Dry
Creek
Road

3
Quivira
🍷

Lambert Bridge Rd

Dry
Creek
General
Store

2
Dry Creek
🍷 Picnic

West
Dry Creek
Road

Winding Road

Hwy 101 →

Healdsburg

West Side Rd

4 Alderbrook
🍷

179

Your Day in Wine Country

Tour Five in Northern Sonoma
Alexander Valley and Dry Creek, Beautiful Wineries and Views,
One Appointment, A Great Tour from the Napa Valley

From Napa you can follow Rt 128 north from Calistoga through Knight's Valley into the Alexander Valley. Hanna is one of the first wineries that you come to on the right-hand side.

Hanna Winery & Vineyards 707.575.3371 www.hannawinery.com *Views*   Page 232
9280 Hwy. 128, Healdsburg   Hours: 10 am - 4 pm   Tasting Fee: $10 - $20
Wine List: Merlot, Zinfandel, Pinot Noir, Cabernet Sauvignon, Sauvignon Blanc, Syrah, Blends, Cabernet Franc, Rosé

> *Continue north on Rt 128 but when it turns north follow Alexander Valley Road towards Healdsburg. Jordan Vineyard & Winery will be on the left-hand side. The sign is small but the driveway entrance is wide and gracious: total 4.6 miles, approx 10 minutes*

Jordan Vineyard & Winery 707.431.5250 www.jordanwinery.com *Appointment*   Page 236
1474 Alexander Valley Rd., Healdsburg   Hours: **appt only** Mon-Sat   Tasting Fee: $20
Wine List: Cabernet Sauvignon (style: Bordeaux), Chardonnay (style: white burgundy), Dessert Wine, Olive Oil

> *Continue on Alexander Valley Rd to the end, turn left onto Healdsburg Ave. Turn right on Dry Creek Rd. The Dry Creek Store is on the right-hand side: 5.1 miles, 11 minutes*

Pick up picnic items to eat at Passalacqua's picnic tables
Some suggestions are:
Dry Creek General Store 707.433.4171 www.dcgstore.com
3495 Dry Creek Rd., Healdsburg   Hours: 6 am - 6 pm Mo-Th; Fr-Sa till 7PM
Another is **The Oakville Market** on the corner of Matheson & Center Streets on the southeast corner of the Plaza in the center of town. You can also eat at any of the wonderful restaurants that Healdsburg has to offer, see the restaurant list on page 186.

> *From the Dry Creek Store head across the road towards Lambert Bridge to Passalacqua Winery. You can see it from the store: total 0.4 miles, less than 2 minutes*

Passalacqua Winery 707.433.5550 www.passalacquawinery.com *Picnic*   Page 248
3805 Lambert Bridge Rd., Healdsburg   Hours: 11 am - 5 pm   Tasting Fee: $5 - $10
Wine List: Sauvignon Blanc, Chardonnay, Zinfandel, Merlot, Cabernet Sauvignon

> *Continue on Lambert Bridge Rd. to the end, turn left onto West Dry Creek Rd. Lambert Bridge Winery is on the right hand side: total 0.9 miles, approx 2 minutes*

Lambert Bridge Winery 707.431.9600 www.lambertbridge.com *Great Wines*   Page 239
4085 W. Dry Creek Rd., Healdsburg   Hours: 10:30 am - 4:30 pm   Tasting Fee: $5 - $10
Wine List: Sauvignon Blanc, Chardonnay, Zinfandel, Syrah, Cuvee, Petite Sirah, Merlot, Cabernet Franc, Cabernet, Sauvignon, Vinegar, Mustard, Mayonnaise, Grapeseed Oil

> *To leave the area, back track past Passalacqua to Dry Creek Rd. Turn right there and it will bring you to Hwy 101 and Healdsburg. The alternate route south on West Dry Creek is a very narrow winding road and not easy to do late in the day.*

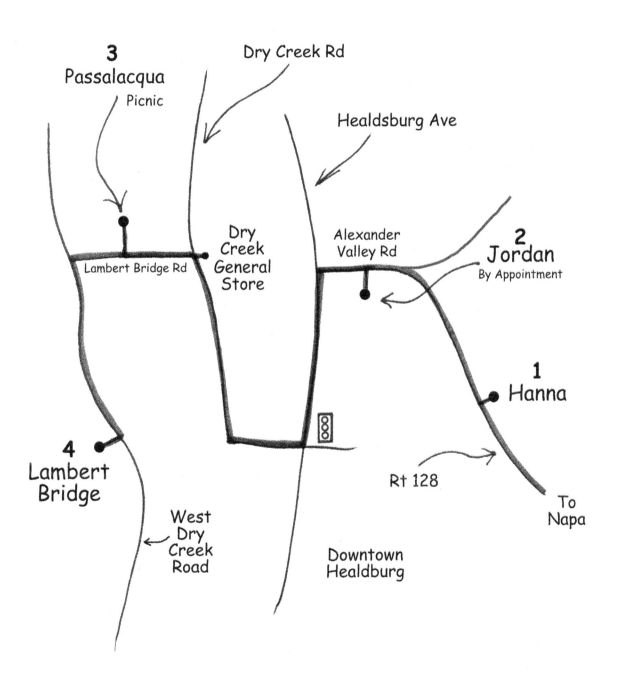

3
Passalacqua
Picnic

Dry Creek Rd

Healdsburg Ave

Dry
Creek
General
Store

Lambert Bridge Rd

Alexander
Valley Rd

2
Jordan
By Appointment

1
Hanna

4
Lambert
Bridge

West
Dry
Creek
Road

Rt 128

To
Napa

Downtown
Healdburg

Your Day in Wine Country

Tour Six in Northern Sonoma
A Short Dry Creek Valley Sampler Tour, Beauty, Charm and Great Wines

Sometimes you don't have that much time to tour. You might have driven up from San Francisco, which could be one and a half to two hours, depending on traffic, and you need to get back that evening. So here is a short tour including three excellent wineries. If you don't feel like having a picnic, or the weather is not cooperating, then drive into the town of Healdsburg and consult the restaurant map on page 186.

Among tour guides, the Dry Creek Valley is a favorite destination. The wineries are all small, family run and charming. The wines are good, the Zinfandel has become the standard everyone else is measured against. The tradition of grape growing and wine making extends back generations here to the early Italian immigrants who first made this area home. Because the valley is small and tucked away from both ocean and bay, it produces a steady warmth that is pleasing to both people and grapes.

Ferrari-Carano Vineyards & Winery 800.831.0381 www.ferrari-carano.com Page 228
8761 Dry Creek Rd., Healdsburg Hours: 10 am - 5 pm Tasting Fee: $5 - $10 *Gorgeous*
Wine List: Grenache Rosé, Chardonnay, Sangiovese, Syrah, Cabernet Sauvignon, Fumé Blanc, Zinfandel, Merlot, Blends

Turn right (south) on Dry Creek Rd to the Dry Creek Store: 5.5 miles, 7 minutes

Pick up picnic items to eat at Passalacqua's picnic tables later
Dry Creek General Store 707.433.4171 www.dcgstore.com
3495 Dry Creek Rd., Healdsburg Hours: 6 am - 6 pm Mo-Th; Fr-Sa till 7PM

*From the Dry Creek Store head across the road towards Lambert Bridge to
Passalacqua Winery. You can see it from the store: total 0.4 miles, less than 2 minutes*

Passalacqua Winery 707.433.5550 www.passalacquawinery.com *Picnic* Page 248
3805 Lambert Bridge Rd., Healdsburg Hours: 11 am - 5 pm Tasting Fee: $5 - $10
Wine List: Sauvignon Blanc, Chardonnay, Zinfandel, Merlot, Cabernet Sauvignon

*Continue on Lambert Bridge Rd to the end, turn left onto West Dry Creek Rd, Lambert
Bridge Winery is on the right-hand side: total 0.9 miles, approx 2 minutes*

Lambert Bridge Winery 707.431.9600 www.lambertbridge.com *Great Wines* Page 239
4085 W. Dry Creek Rd., Healdsburg Hours: 10:30 am - 4:30 pm Tasting Fee: $5 - $10
Wine List: Sauvignon, Blanc, Chardonnay, Zinfandel, Syrah, Cuvee, Petite Sirah, Merlot, Cabernet Franc, Cabernet, Sauvignon, Vinegar, Mustard, Mayonnaise, Grapeseed Oil

*To leave the area, back track past Passalacqua to Dry Creek Rd. Turn right there and
it will bring you to Hwy 101 and Healdsburg. The alternate route south on West
Dry Creek is a very, very narrow winding road and not easy to drive late in the day.*

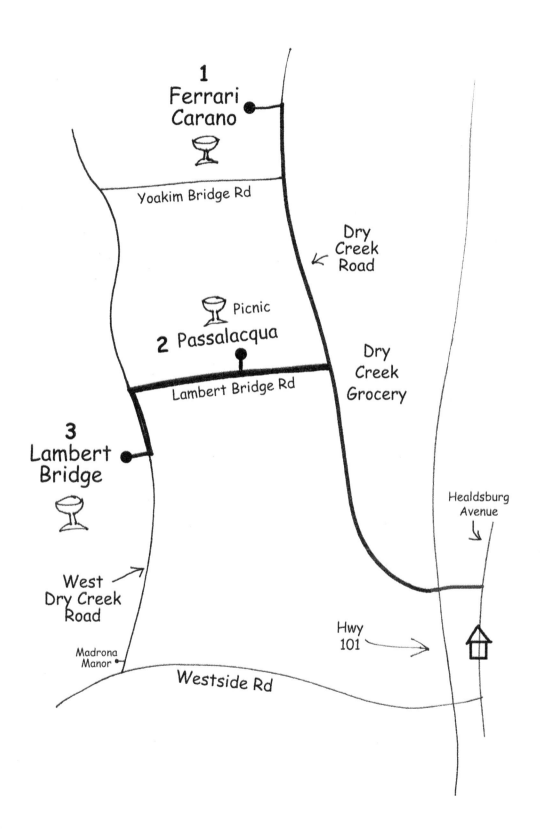

1
Ferrari Carano

Yoakim Bridge Rd

Dry Creek Road

Picnic
2 Passalacqua

Lambert Bridge Rd

Dry Creek Grocery

3
Lambert Bridge

Healdsburg Avenue

West Dry Creek Road

Madrona Manor

Hwy 101

Westside Rd

Your Day in Wine Country

Tour Seven in Northern Sonoma
The Western Russian River Valley with History, Redwoods & Great Wines

This is a completely Russian River Tour, although Kendall Jackson like many larger wineries pulls their grapes from many areas. We start off at Kendall because it is very convenient to Hwy 101. The River Rd. exit is north of Santa Rosa. Follow it to the first light, Fulton Rd. Turn right and the suprisingly unimpressive entrance to Kendall Jackson is on the left-hand side before the overpass. The building, the wines and the friendly staff make up for it. They also offer some wonderful tours. **The majority of the tasting rooms on this tour have gift shops.**

Kendall-Jackson 707.433.7102 www.kj.com *Beautiful Building-Tours* Page 237
5007 Fulton Rd., Fulton Hours: 10 am - 5 pm daily Tasting Fee: $5 - $15
Wine List: Cabernet Sauvignon, Merlot, Syrah, Chardonnay, Pinot Noir, Riesling, Sauvignon Blanc

Turn right (south) on Fulton Rd. At the light turn right onto River Rd. Korbel Champagne Cellars is on the right side: 12.1 miles, 20 minutes

Korbel Champagne Cellars has a great deli and picnic tables, or drive a little farther into Guerneville where there are a number of restaurants

Korbel Champagne Cellars 707.824.7000 www.korbel.com *Sparkling-Tours* Page 238
13250 River Rd., Guerneville Hours: 9 am - 5 pm Tasting Fee: Comp - $10
Wine List: Sparklers, Blanc de Noirs, Chardonnay Champagne, Moscato Frizzante, Merlot Champagne, Brut Rosé, Pinot Grigio Sparkler

Back track on River Rd to Martinelli Rd. Turn right. The Hartford Family Wines is on the left-hand side: total 5.8 miles, approx 15 minutes. Winding but pretty.

Hartford Family Wines 707.887.8010 www.hartfordwines.com *Great Wines* Page 232
8075 Martinelli Rd., Forestville Hours: 10 am - 4:30 pm daily Tasting Fee: Comp - $10
Wine List: Pinot Noir (8 or 9 different versions), Chardonnay, Old Vine Zinfandel

Back track to River Rd, turn right to Martinelli Vineyards & Winery, on the right-hand side: total 7.7 miles, approx 12 minutes

Martinelli Vineyards & Winery 707.525.0570 www.martinelliwinery.com Page 243
3360 River Rd., Windsor Hours: 10 am - 5 pm daily Tasting Fee: Comp - $5 *Great Wines*
Wine List: Chardonnay, Pinot Noir, Syrah, Zinfandel, Gewürztraminer, Muscat Alexandria, Sauvignon Blanc.

From Martinelli turn right (east). You are only minutes from the entrance to Hwy 101.

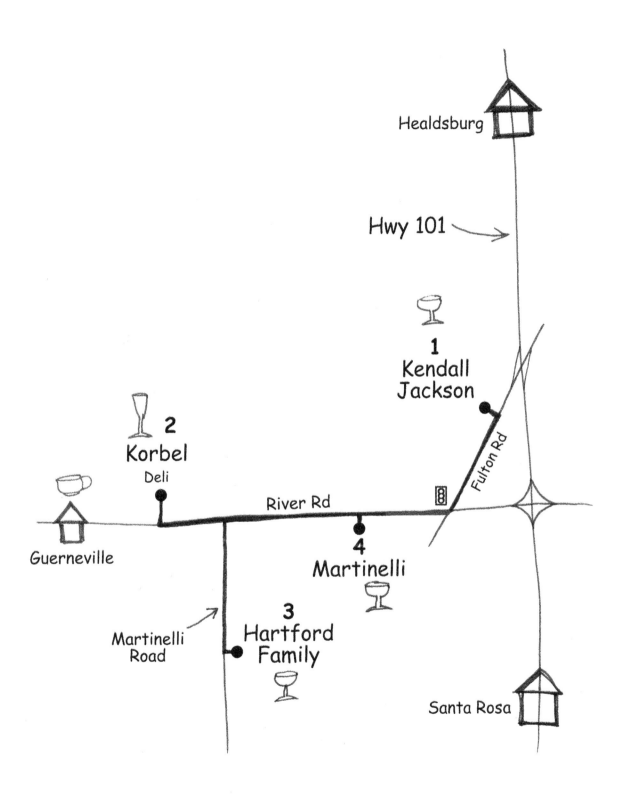

Healdsburg

Hwy 101 →

1
Kendall
Jackson

2
Korbel
Deli

River Rd

Fulton Rd

Guerneville

4
Martinelli

Martinelli
Road

3
Hartford
Family

Santa Rosa

Restaurants in Northern Sonoma

Bear Republic Brewing: 345 Healdsburg Ave. 707-433-2337. Family Restaurant. Map Below
Bistro Ralph: 109 Plaza St. Healdsburg. 707.433.1380. Contemporary Dining. Map Below
Cyrus: 29 North St. Healdsburg. 707.433.3311. Contemporary Dining. Map Below
Dry Creek Kitchen: 317 Healdsburg Ave. 707.431.0330. Californian. Map Below
Dry Creek Store: 3495 Dry Creek Rd. Healdsburg. 707.433.4171. Market   page 179
Flavor Bistro: 96 Old Court House Square, Santa Rosa. 707.573.9600. Californian.
John Ash & Co: River Rd. E. Santa Rosa. 707.527.7687. Contemporary Dining   page 177
la Rosa Market: 6555 Front St. Forestville. 707.887.8375. Market   page 177
Madrona Manor: 1001 Westside Rd. Healdsburg. 707.433.4231. Contemp Dining   page 183
Oakville Grocery: 124 Matheson St. Healdsburg. 707.433.3200. Market. Map Below
Underwood Bar and Bistro: 9113 Graton Rd. Graton. 707.823.7023. Euro Bistro   page 177
Zin Restaurant & Wine Bar: 344 Center St. Healdsburg: 707.473.0946. Regional. Map Below

Lodgings
DoubleTree Sonoma Wine Country: One DoubleTree Dr. Rohnert Park   707.584.5466
 www.dtsonoma.com
Fountaingrove Inn Hotel & Conference Ctr: 101 Fountaingrove Pkwy. Santa Rosa   800.222.6101
707.578.6101 www.fountaingroveinn.com
Healdsburg Inn on the Plaza: 112 Matheson St. Healdsburg   800.431.8663   707.433.6991
www.healdsburginn.com   See map below
Hilton Sonoma Wine Country: 3555 Round Barn Blvd. Santa Rosa 800.445.8667   707.523.7555
www.winecountryhilton.com
Hotel Healdsburg: 25 Matheson St. Healdsburg   800.889.7188   707.431.2800
www.hotelhealdsburg.com   See map below
Hyatt Vineyard Creek : 170 Railroad St. Santa Rosa   707.284.1234 vineyardcreek.hyatt.com
Les Mars Hôtel : 27 North St. Healdsburg 877.431.1700 707.433.4211 www.lesmarshotel.com
Madrona Manor: 1001 Westside Rd. Healdsburg 800.258.4003 707.433.4231
www.madronamanor.com Pg. 183

Tour Directory: Starting in Northern Napa

One - Page 190

Great White Wines from Napa Valley.

Wineries: Chateau Montelena, Rombauer, Grgich Hills, St. Supery

Five hour tour locally. $$ Moderately Priced

Two - Page 192

Wineries in Sight of Calistoga, Great Art, Buildings and Views.

Wineries: Clos Pegase, Chateau Montelena, Rombauer, Benessere

Five hour tour locally. $$ Moderately Priced

Three - Page 194

Not Just Bordeaux Reds from Napa, Pinot Noir, Chardonnay and Sparkling. One Appointment, a Festive Day Trip.

Wineries: Failla (App), Rombauer, ZD, Goosecross, Domaine Chandon (Sparkling)

Six hour tour locally. $$ Moderately Priced

Four - Page 196

Beautiful Tour of Smaller Wineries for a Group, a Wide Variety, Great Gift Shops.

Wineries: Hall, Whitehall Lane, Rutherford Hill, Mumm Napa (Sparkling),
Goosecross, Signorello, Darioush

Eight hour tour locally, ten hour tour from SF, $$ Moderately Priced

Best with a Hired Car and Driver

Five - Page 198

The Castles of Calistoga, Dramatic Buildings with Fun, Family Wineries,
Good for a Group, Great Gift Shops, One Appointment.

Wineries: Castello di Amorosa for Tour (Appointment Recommended),
Clos Pegase, Cuvaison, Frank Family, Beringer

Seven hour tour locally. $$$ Moderately Expensive

Your Day in Wine Country

Six - Page 200

Distinctive Wineries and Big Reds, Entertaining People, From Calistoga
South to Oakville, One Appointment.
Wineries: Frank Family, Duckhorn (App), Arger Martucci, Silver Oak
Six hour tour locally. $$$ Moderately Expensive

Seven - Page 202

Riding the Cable Cars and Drinking Wine Between Calistoga and
St. Helena, Great Views, Good Gift Shops, One Appointment.
Wineries: Sterling, Frank Family, Rombauer, Duckhorn (App)
Six hour tour locally. $$$ Moderately Expensive

Eight - Page 204

Spring Mountain Tour, All by Appointment Wineries, Great Views and Tours.
Wineries: Barnett, Pride Mountain, Schweiger, Spring Mountain
Six hour tour locally, eight hour tour from SF. $$$$ Expensive
Best with a Hired Car and Driver

Nine - Page 206

From Spring Mountain south to Oakville and Oak Knoll, Prestigious, Expensive Red
Wines, All by Appointment Wineries, Gorgeous Wineries, Great Views, Plan in Advance.
Wineries: Newton, Barnett, Joseph Phelps, Rudd, Darioush (No appointment required)
Six hour tour locally, eight hour tour from SF. $$$$ Expensive
Best with a Hired Car and Driver

**Restaurants & Hotels of Northern Napa Including the
Towns of St. Helena and Calistoga Page 208**

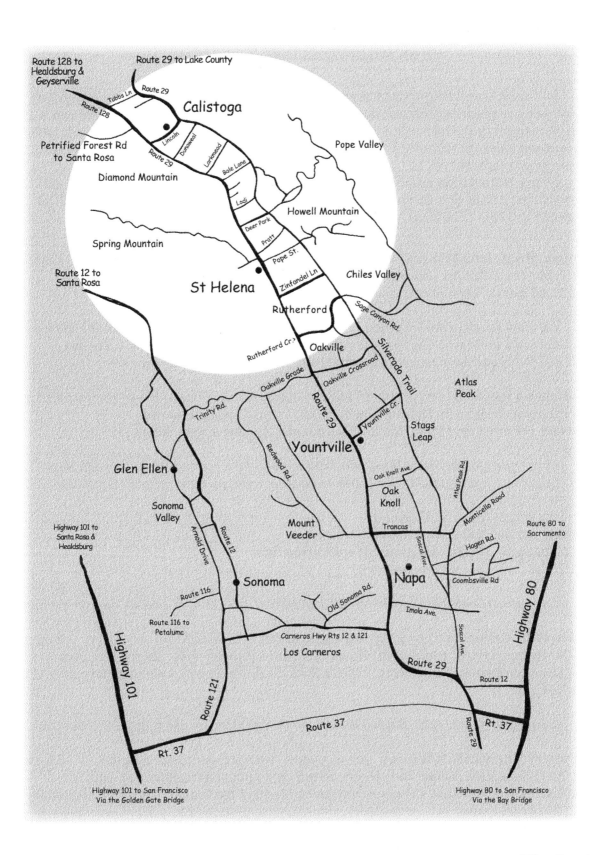

189

Tour One in Northern Napa
Great White Wines from Napa Valley

In Napa it is well known that Cabernet Sauvignon is King. However some people don't like red wines as much as white, so what do you do? Pick wineries that do great white wines. For lunch you can eat in St. Helena or if you pick up sandwiches, Rombauer has great picnic tables. In downtown Calistoga there are some good stores, the **Cal Mart** market, 1491 Lincoln Ave., makes a great sandwich.

To reach Montelena you can travel north on Rt 29. At Calistoga it will turn right and go through the middle of town and Rt 121 will continue north towards Healdsburg. You'll go straight on Rt 121 to Tubbs lane, turn right and the entrance will be on the left-hand side.

Chateau Montelena Winery 707.942.5105 www.montelena.com *Gardens*   Page 219
1429 Tubbs Ln., Calistoga   Hours: 9:30 am - 4 pm   Tasting Fee: $10 - $15
Wine List: Chardonnay, Cabernet Sauvignon, Zinfandel, Riesling

Turn left (east) to the Silverado Trail, turn right to Rombauer Vineyards, it will be on the right-hand side. The road curves to the right and the winery is on a wooded hill so the entrance comes up quickly: total 8.2 miles, approx 15 minutes

Rombauer Vineyards 707.963.5170 www.rombauervineyards.com *Views-Picnic*   Page 255
3522 Silverado Trail N., St. Helena   Hours: 10 am - 5 pm Tasting Fee: $10
Wine List: Cabernet Sauvignon, Merlot, Chardonnay, Zinfandel, Port, Blend

Turn right (south) on the Silverado Trail to Lodi, turn right to Rt 29, turn left into St Helena, heading to Market on the right side: total 4.0 miles, approx 8 minutes

One lunch suggestion in St. Helena is:
Market 707.963.3799 www.marketsthelena.com
1347 Main St., St. Helena   Hours: 11:30 am - 10 pm daily
Consult the restaurant list on page 208.

Go south to Grgich Hills Cellar on the right-hand side: total 3.3 miles, approx 5 minutes

Grgich Hills Cellar 707.963.2784 www.grgich.com *Old Style Napa*   Page 231
1829 St. Helena Hwy. S., Rutherford   Hours: 9:30 am - 4:30 pm daily   Tasting Fee: $10
Wine List: Chardonnay, Fumé Blanc, Violetta (botrytis dessert wine), Cabernet Sauvignon, Zinfandel, Merlot

Turn right (south) to St. Supéry Winery on the left side: 1.3 miles, approx 3 minutes

St. Supéry Vineyards & Winery 707.963.4507 www.stsupery.com *Elegant*   Page 262
8440 St. Helena Hwy., Rutherford   Hours: 10 am - 5:30 pm   Tasting Fee: $10 - $15
Wine List: Sauvignon Blanc, Cabernet Sauvignon, Merlot, Chardonnay, Unoaked Chardonnay, Syrah, Cabernet Franc
Only open to limousines with an appointment. Call ahead!

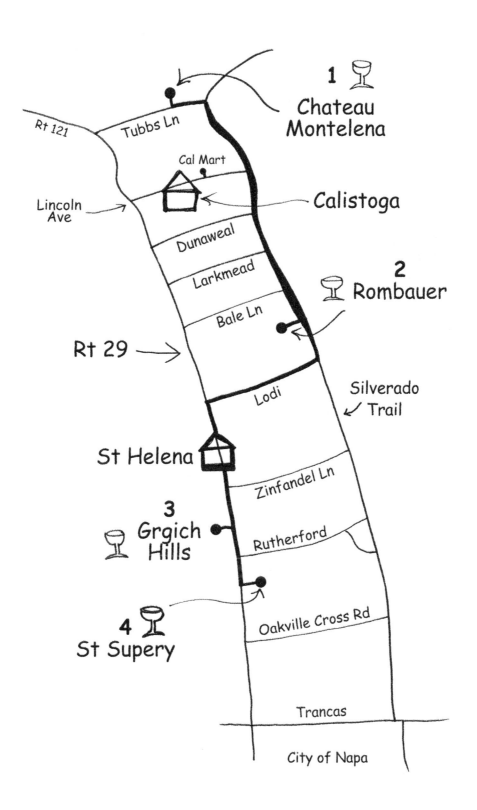

1 🍷
Chateau
Montelena

Rt 121

Tubbs Ln

Cal Mart

Lincoln
Ave

Calistoga

Dunaweal

Larkmead

2 🍷 Rombauer

Bale Ln

Rt 29 →

Lodi

Silverado
↙ Trail

St Helena

Zinfandel Ln

3 🍷
Grgich
Hills

Rutherford

4 🍷
St Supery

Oakville Cross Rd

Trancas

City of Napa

Tour Two in Northern Napa
Wineries in Sight of Calistoga, Great Art, Buildings and Views

To get to Clos Pegase is simple, head north on Rt 29 and turn right on Dunaweal Lane. It is on the left-hand side. You can't miss it, designed by Michael Graves with monumental sculptures dotting the grounds, it is just a preview for the art collection it contains.

Clos Pegase Winery 707.942.4981 www.clospegase.com *Great Art & Building* Page 220
1060 Dunaweal Ln., Calistoga Hours: 10:30 am - 5 pm Tasting Fee: $10 - $20
Wine List: Chardonnay, Sauvignon Blanc, Pinot Noir, Merlot, Cabernet Sauvignon

Back track to Rt 29 and turn right (north). Continue straight on Rt 121 when Rt 29 turns right throught downtown Calistoga. At Tubbs Ln turn right. Chateau Montelena Winery is on the left: 3.6 miles, 9 minutes

Chateau Montelena Winery 707.942.5105 www.montelena.com *Building-Gardens* Page 219
1429 Tubbs Ln., Calistoga Hours: 9:30 am - 4 pm Tasting Fee: $10 - $15
Wine List: Chardonnay, Cabernet Sauvignon, Zinfandel, Riesling

Back track to Lincoln Ave, turn left to Cal Mart on the left side: 2.5 miles, 5 minutes

Pick up picnic items to eat at Rombauer's picnic tables later at
Cal Mart 707.942.6271
1491 Lincoln Ave., Calistoga Hours: 7 am - 8 pm

Head south on Rt 29 to Bale Lane, turn left to Silverado Trail, turn right and Rombauer Vineyards will be on the right-hand side: total 6.1 miles, approx 11 minutes

Rombauer Vineyards 707.963.5170 www.rombauervineyards.com *Views-Picnic* Page 255
3522 Silverado Trail N., St. Helena Hours: 10 am - 5 pm Tasting Fee: $10
Wine List: Cabernet Sauvignon, Merlot, Chardonnay, Zinfandel, Port, Blend

Turn right (south) to Lodi Ln and turn right again. At Rt 29 turn right (north) to Big Tree Rd. Turn right. At the end of the road bear left and follow the signs to Benessere: total 2.4 miles approx 6 minutes

Benessere 707.963.5853 www.benesserevineyards.com *Charming & Small* Page 213
1010 Big Tree Rd., St. Helena Hours: 10 am – 5 pm Tasting Fee: $10
Wine List: Pinot Grigio, Sangiovese, Syrah, Zinfandel, Pinot Noir, Muscat di Canelli, Blends

From Benessere to head south you can follow Rt 29 into St Helena. If it is the weekend and you would like to avoid the traffic cross over to Silverado Trail either at Bale or Lodi and turn right (south) which will avoid the traffic through St Helena and Oakville.

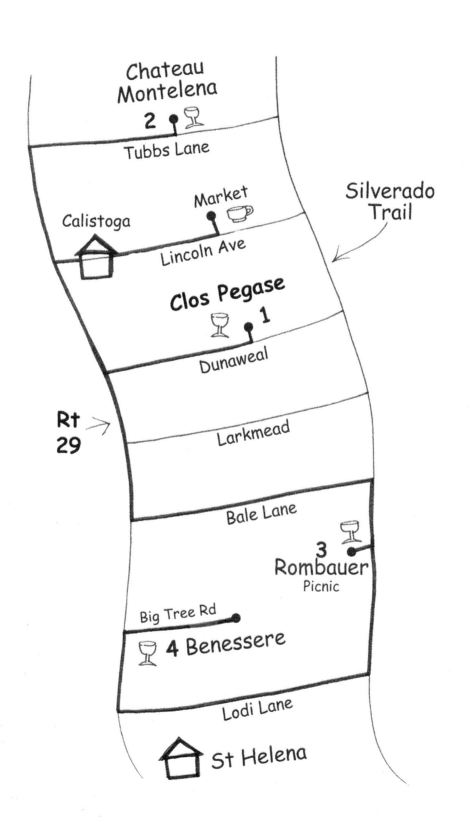

Chateau
Montelena

2

Tubbs Lane

Market

Calistoga

Lincoln Ave

Clos Pegase

1

Dunaweal

Silverado
Trail

Rt
29

Larkmead

Bale Lane

3
Rombauer
Picnic

Big Tree Rd

4 Benessere

Lodi Lane

St Helena

Tour Three in Northern Napa
Not Just Bordeaux Reds from Napa, Pinot Noir, Chardonnay and Sparkling.
One Appointment, a Festive Day Trip

Visit Dean & DeLuca, Sunshine Foods or Cal Mart in Calistoga for Picnic Supplies. From Dean and DeLuca, if the north bound traffic is heavy, which is typical on the weekends, head south to Zinfandel Lane and cross over to the Silverado Trail and head north to Failla. The driveway for Failla is directly across from the Rombauer entrance.

Failla 707.963.0530 www.faillawines.com *Very Small-Charming-Appointment* Page 227
3530 Silverado Trail, St. Helena Hours: 11 am - 4 pm by appt Tasting Fee: varies
Wine List: Pinot Noir, Viognier, Syrah, Chardonnay

Heading across Silverado Tr. to Rombauer Vineyards: total 121 feet, approx 1 minute

Rombauer Vineyards 707.963.5170 www.rombauervineyards.com *Views-Picnic* Page 255
3522 Silverado Trail N., St. Helena Hours: 10 am - 5 pm Tasting Fee: $10
Wine List: Cabernet Sauvignon, Merlot, Chardonnay, Zinfandel, Port, Blend

Turn right (south) to ZD, just past Mumm Napa on the right side: 9.1 miles, 15 minutes

ZD Wines 707.963.5188 www.zdwines.com *Friendly* Page 271
8380 Silverado Trail, Napa Hours: 10 am - 4:30 pm Tasting Fee: $10 - $15
Wine List: Chardonnay, Pinot Noir, Cabernet Sauvignon, Blends

Turn right (south) to Yountville Cross Rd, turn right to State Ln, turn right and Goosecross Cellars is on the left-hand side: total 5.2 miles, approx 7 minutes

Goosecross Cellars 707.944.1986 www.goosecross.com *Small Family Winery* Page 231
1119 State Ln., Yountville Hours: 10 am-4:30 pm Tasting Fee: $5
Wine List: Viognier, Chenin Blanc, Sauvignon Blanc, Chardonnay, Sparkling Rosé, Cabernet Sauvignon, Zinfandel, Merlot, Pinot Noir, Syrah, Blends

Continue across Yountville Cross Rd. At Washington turn left and go through Yount ville. At California Dr. turn right, go under the highway and Domaine Chandon is on the right-hand side, clearly marked: total 2.6 miles, approx 10 minutes

Domaine Chandon 707.944.2280 www.domainechandon.com *Sparkling* Page 224
1 California Dr., Yountville Hours: 10 am - 6 pm Tasting Fee: none listed
Wine List: Brut, Blanc de Noirs, Rosé, Sparkling Chardonnay, Blanc de Blancs, Pinot Noir, Pinot Meunier, Chardonnay, Unoaked Pinot Noir Rosé, Unoaked Chardonnay

If you want to have a great dinner nearby there are a host of great restaurants across the way in downtown Yountville. Just follow California Ave. under the Rt 29 overpass and turn left on Washington Street. See the restaurant lists on pages 134 & 168 & map on page 69.

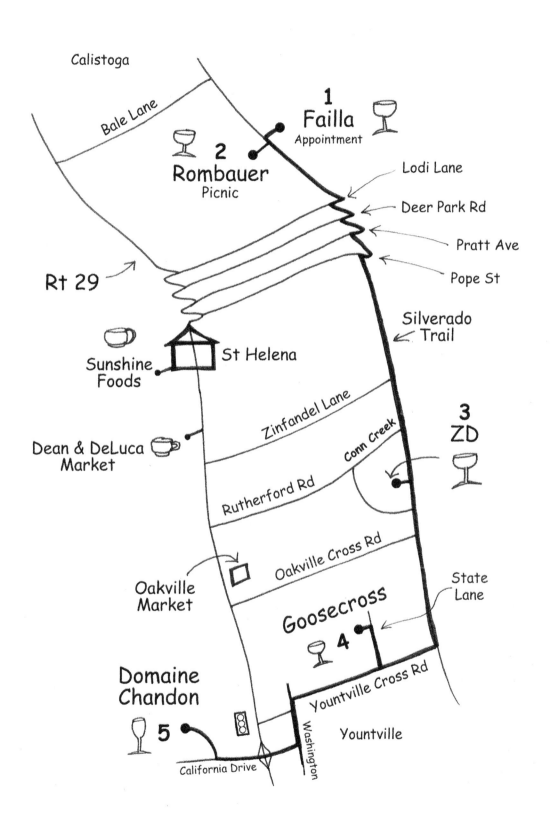

Calistoga

Bale Lane

1 Failla Appointment

2 Rombauer Picnic

Lodi Lane

Deer Park Rd

Pratt Ave

Pope St

Rt 29

Silverado Trail

Sunshine Foods

St Helena

Zinfandel Lane

Dean & DeLuca Market

Conn Creek

3 ZD

Rutherford Rd

Oakville Cross Rd

State Lane

Oakville Market

Goosecross 4

Domaine Chandon

Yountville Cross Rd

Washington

Yountville

5

California Drive

Tour Four in Northern Napa
Beautiful Smaller Wineries for a Group, Great Gift Shops, Professional Driver Tour

Hall 707.967.2620 www.hallwines.com *Great Art*   Page 232
401 St. Helena Hwy., St. Helena   Hours: 10 am – 5:30 pm   Tasting Fee: $5-$10
Wine List: Cabernet Sauvignon, Merlot, Sauvignon Blanc   *- see note in directory-*
    Turn right to Dean & DeLuca (Next Driveway): total 0.25 miles, approx 1 minute

Pick up picnic items to eat at Rutherford Hill Winery's picnic tables at
Dean & DeLuca 707.967.9980 www.deandeluca.com
607 S. St. Helena Hwy., St., Helena   Hours: 7 am - 8 pm M-Sun
    Turn right (south) to Whitehall Lane Winery: total 1.1 miles, approx 2 minutes

Whitehall Lane Winery 707.963.7035 www.whitehalllane.com *Very Cool*   Page 270
1563 St. Helena Hwy., St. Helena,   Hours: 11 am - 5:45 pm   Tasting Fee: $10
Wine List: Cabernet Sauvignon, Merlot, Chardonnay, Belmuscato Dessert Wine
    South to Rutherford Rd, north on Silverado, right on Rutherford Hill: 3.5 miles 8 mins

Rutherford Hill Winery 707.963.7194 www.rutherfordhill.com *Views-Picnic*   Page 257
200 Rutherford Hill Rd., Rutherford   Hours: 10 am - 5 pm   Tasting Fee: $5 - $10
Wine List: Zinfandel Port, Merlot, Cabernet Sauvignon, Sangiovese, Blends, Petite Verdot, Chardonnay, Syrah, Malbec, Sauvignon Blanc,
    South on Silverado to Mumm Napa Valley, right side: total 1.6 miles approx 3 minutes

Mumm Napa Valley 707.967.7700 www.mummnapa.com *Sparkling-Fun*   Page 245
8445 Silverado Trail, Rutherford,   Hours: 10 am - 5 pm   Tasting Fee: $5 - $15
Wine List: Pinot Noir, Chardonnay, Santana, DVX, Demi Sec, Sparkling Pinot Noir, Cuvee M Red, Blanc de Blanc, Brut Prestige, Blanc de Noirs, Cuvee M
    South to Yountville Cr Rd to State & Goosecross Cellars: 5.4 miles approx 8 minutes

Goosecross Cellars 707.944.1986 www.goosecross.com *Small Family Winery*   Page 231
1119 State Ln. Yountville   Hours: 10 am - 4:30 pm daily   Tasting Fee: $5
Wine List: Viognier, Chenin Blanc, Sauvignon Blanc, Chardonnay, Sparkling Rosé, Cabernet Sauvignon, Zinfandel, Merlot, Pinot Noir, Syrah, Blends
    Backtrack to Silverado, turn right to Signorello Vineyards, left side: 5.8 miles 8 minutes

Signorello Vineyards 707.255.5990 www.signorellovineyards.com *Charming*   Page 260
4500 Silverado Trail, Napa,   Hours: 10:30 am - 5 pm   Tasting Fee: $5 - $10
Wine List: Cabernet Sauvignon, Zinfandel, Pinot Noir, Syrah, Sauvignon-Semillon Blend
    Turn left (south) to Darioush on the left-hand side: total 0.2 miles approx 2 minutes

Darioush 707.257.2345 www.darioush.com *Gorgeous & Fun*   Page 222
4240 Silverado Trail, Napa,   Hours: 10:30 am - 5 pm   Tasting Fee: $20
Wine List: Cabernet Sauvignon, Shiraz, Chardonnay, Merlot, Semillon, Sauvignon, Blanc, Pinot Noir, Viognier

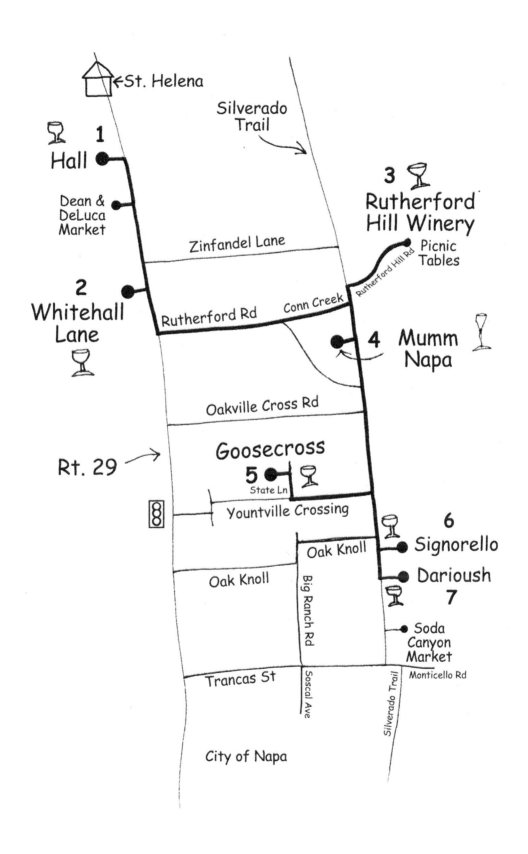

←St. Helena

Silverado Trail

1
Hall

Dean & DeLuca Market

3
Rutherford Hill Winery

Picnic Tables

Zinfandel Lane

2
Whitehall Lane

Rutherford Rd   Conn Creek   Rutherford Hill Rd

4 Mumm Napa

Oakville Cross Rd

Rt. 29 →

Goosecross

5
State Ln

Yountville Crossing

6 Signorello

Oak Knoll

Oak Knoll   Big Ranch Rd

Darioush
7

Soda Canyon Market

Trancas St   Soscal Ave   Monticello Rd

Silverado Trail

City of Napa

197   Your Day in Wine Country

Tour Five in Northern Napa
The Castles of Calistoga, Dramatic Buildings with Fun, Family Wineries, Good for a Group, Great Gift Shops, One Appointment

As you travel north on Rt 29 the entrance to Castello di Amorosa is on the left side past Larkmead Ln. and before Dunaweal Ln. It has a wide driveway and a good-sized sign.

Castello di Amorosa 707.286.7273 www.castellodiamorosa.com *Architecture-Tour*   Page 216
4045 N. St. Helena Hwy., Calistoga   Hours: 9:30 am - 4:30 pm weekdays   Tasting Fee: $10-20
Wine List: Chardonnay, Pinot Grigio, Pinot Bianco, Gewurtraminer, Rosato d'Sangiovese, Merlot, Sangiovese, Cabernet Sauvignon, Super Tuscan, Muscato, Blends
We recommend making an **appointment** for the tour, which takes about 1 & 1/2 hours.
Turn left (north) to Dunaweal & turn right to Clos Pegase: 5.0 miles, approx 10 minutes

Clos Pegase Winery 707.942.4981 www.clospegase.com *Great Building-Art*   Page 220
1060 Dunaweal Ln., Calistoga   Hours: 10:30 am - 5 pm   Tasting Fee: $10 - $20
Wine List: Chardonnay, Sauvignon Blanc, Pinot Noir, Merlot, Cabernet Sauvignon
Back track to Rt 29, turn right (north) to Lincoln, turn right and Cal Mart is on the left side in the middle of Calistoga: total 2.5 miles, approx 5 minutes

Pick up picnic items to eat at Cuvaison's picnic tables at
Cal Mart 707.942.6271   Good Sandwiches
1491 Lincoln Ave., Calistoga   Hours: 7 am - 8 pm
Continue on Lincoln to Silverado Trail, turn right (south) to Cuvaison Estate Wines on the left-hand side past Dunaweal Ln: total 2.2 miles, approx 5 minutes

Cuvaison Estate Wines 707.942.2468 www.cuvaison.com *Picnic*   Page 222
4550 Silverado Trail N., Calistoga   Hours: 10 am - 5 pm   Tasting Fee: $8 - $10
Wine List: Pinot Noir, Cabernet Sauvignon, Chardonnay, Merlot, Syrah, Zinfandel, Port
Turn left (south) to Larkmead Ln, turn right to Frank Family Vineyards, on the left-hand side: total 2.8 miles approx 5 minutes

Frank Family Vineyards 707.942.0859 www.frankfamilyvineyards.com *Fun*   Page 229
1091 Larkmead Ln., Calistoga   Hours: 10 am – 5 pm   Tasting Fee: Comp
Wine List: Sangiovese, Zinfandel, Cabernet Sauvignon, Chardonnay, Sparklers, Zinfandel Port
Turn left to Rt 29, turn left (south) to Beringer Vineyards on the right-hand side just past Greystone, the Culinary Institute of America: total 4.8 miles approx 10 minutes

Beringer Vineyards 707.967.4412 www.beringer.com *Great Estate*   Page 214
2000 Main St., St. Helena   Hours: 10 am – 5 pm   Tasting Fee: $5 - $10   *Reserve Tasting*
Wine List: Chardonnay, Dessert Wines, Sauvignon Blanc, Pinot Noir, Merlot, Cabernet Sauvignon, Riesling, Viognier, White Zinfandel, White Merlot, Chenin Blanc, Gewürztraminer, Pinot Grigio, Shiraz'
From Beringer turning right (south) will bring you into the center of St Helena in a few minutes. There are great places for dinner. Consult the restaurant list on page 168

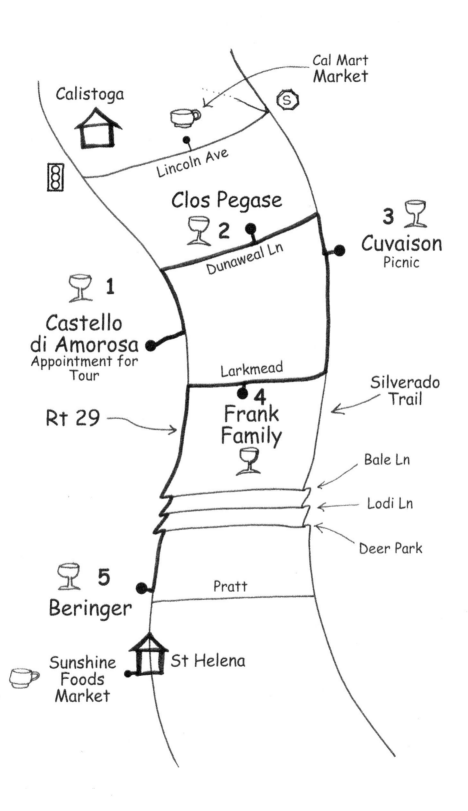

Cal Mart
Market

Calistoga

Lincoln Ave

Clos Pegase

2

Dunaweal Ln

3

Cuvaison
Picnic

1

Castello
di Amorosa
Appointment for
Tour

Larkmead

4

Frank
Family

Silverado
Trail

Rt 29

Bale Ln

Lodi Ln

Deer Park

5

Beringer

Pratt

Sunshine
Foods
Market

St Helena

Tour Six in Northern Napa
Distinctive Wineries and Big Reds, Entertaining People,
From Calistoga South to Oakville, One Appointment

You can reach Frank Family from either Rt 29 or the Silverado Trail. If it is a busy weekend Rt 29 into St Helena will be jammed with traffic so take the Silverado Trail north. It is a little curvy north of Zinfandel Lane but it will save you time and aggravation. During the week a couple can sometimes arrive at Duckhorn without an appointment and sit down for a tasting, but on the weekends or in high season, or with a larger group call ahead. It is a lovely place.

Frank Family Vineyards 707.942.0859 www.frankfamilyvineyards.com *Fun* Page 229
1091 Larkmead Ln., Calistoga Hours: 10 am - 4 pm Tasting Fee: complimentary
Wine List: Sangiovese, Zinfandel, Cabernet Sauvignon, Chardonnay, Sparklers, Zinfandel Port

Turn right to Silverado Trail, and turn right (south) to Lodi Ln. Turn right and Duckhorn Vineyards is immediately on the right hand side: 4.1 miles, 10 minutes

Duckhorn Vineyards 707.963.7108 www.duckhorn.com *Appointment-Elegant* Page 225
3027 Silverado Trail N., St. Helena Hours: 10 am - 4 pm by appt Tasting Fee: $25
Wine List: Sauvignon Blanc, Merlot, Cabernet Sauvignon

Continue on Lodi to Rt 29, turn left (south) through St Helena (less traffic this way) to Dean & DeLuca on the right hand side: total 6.2 miles, approx 15 minutes

Pick up picnic items to eat at Arger-Martucci's picnic tables at
Dean & DeLuca 707.967.9980 www.deandeluca.com *A Destination Market*
607 S. St. Helena Hwy., St. Helena Hours: 7 am - 8 pm M-Sun
Or consult restaurant list on page 168

Turn right (south) and take the first right turn onto Inglewood Ave. Arger-Martucci Vineyards is on the left-hand side: total less than 1 mile, approx 2 minutes

Arger-Martucci Vineyards 707.963.4334 www.arger-martucciwine.com *Picnic* Page 211
1455 Inglewood Ave., St. Helena Hours: 10 am - 4 pm daily Tasting Fee: $10
Wine List: Chardonnay, Viognier, Pinot Noir, Syrah, Cabernet Sauvignon, Blends

Turn right (south) on Rt 29 to the Oakville Cross Rd. Look for the Oakville market. Turn left and Silver Oak Cellars is on the right-hand side: 5.6 miles, 15 minutes

Silver Oak Cellars 707.944.8808 www.silveroak.com *Popular Reds* Page 260
915 Oakville Cross Rd., Oakville Hours: 9 am - 4 pm Tasting Fee: $10
Wine List: Cabernet Sauvignon

Returning via Silverado is the best way to head to your hotel due to turns and traffic

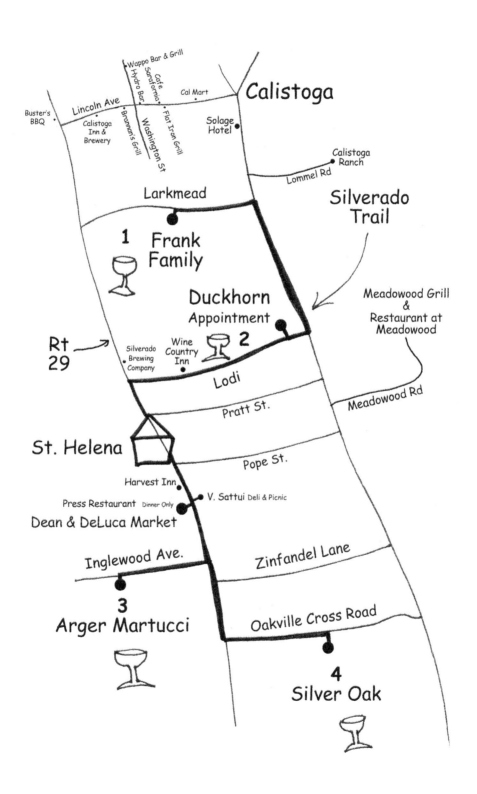

Wappo Bar & Grill

Café Sarafornia

Hydro Bar

Cal Mart

Calistoga

Buster's BBQ

Lincoln Ave

Solage Hotel

Calistoga Inn & Brewery

Brannan's Grill

Flat Iron Grill

Washington St

Calistoga Ranch

Lommel Rd

Larkmead

Silverado Trail

1

Frank Family

Duckhorn

Appointment

Meadowood Grill & Restaurant at Meadowood

Rt 29

Silverado Brewing Company

Wine Country Inn

2

Lodi

Meadowood Rd

Pratt St.

St. Helena

Pope St.

Harvest Inn

Press Restaurant *Dinner Only*

V. Sattui Deli & Picnic

Dean & DeLuca Market

Inglewood Ave.

Zinfandel Lane

3

Arger Martucci

Oakville Cross Road

4

Silver Oak

Your Day in Wine Country

Tour Seven in Northern Napa
Riding the Cable Cars and Drinking Wine Between Calistoga and St. Helena, Great Views, Good Gift Shops, One Appointment

Pick up picnic items to eat at Rombauer's picnic tables at
Cal Mart   707.942.6271   Great Sandwiches
1491 Lincoln Ave., Calistoga   Hours: 7 am - 8 pm

Take Lincoln to Rt 29, turn left to Dunaweal Ln and turn left, Sterling Vineyards is on the right-hand side: total 2.1 miles, approx 5 minutes. Allow two hours for Sterling

Sterling Vineyards   707.942.3344   www.sterlingvineyards.com   *Tramway-Gifts*   Page 263
1111 Dunaweal Ln., Calistoga   Hours: 10 am - 4:30 pm   Tasting Fee: $20
Wine List: Cabernet Sauvignon, Merlot, Chardonnay, Pinot Noir, Shiraz, Sauvignon Blanc
Since you take the tramway to the winery on top of the hill, you should plan on two hours to enjoy Sterling. It is at the beginning of the day since that is when the lines are the shortest.

Turn right to the Silverado Trail, turn right to Larkmead, turn right to Frank Family Vineyards, on the left hand side: total 3.3 miles, approx 10 minutes

Frank Family Vineyards   707.942.0859   www.frankfamilyvineyards.com   *Fun*   Page 229
1091 Larkmead Ln., Calistoga   Hours: 10 am - 4 pm   Tasting Fee: comp
Wine List: Sangiovese, Zinfandel, Cabernet Sauvignon, Chardonnay, Sparklers, Zinfandel Port

Backtrack to Silverado and turn right, Rombauer Vineyards is on the right-hand side past Bale Ln and Crystal Springs Rd: total 2.8 miles, approx 5 minutes

Rombauer Vineyards   707.963.5170   www.rombauervineyards.com   *Views-Picnic*   Page 255
3522 Silverado Trail N., St. Helena   Hours: 10 am - 5 pm   Tasting Fee: $10
Wine List: Cabernet Sauvignon, Merlot, Chardonnay, Zinfandel, Port, Blend

Turn right to Lodi Ln, turn right and Duckhorn Vineyards is immediately on the right hand side: total 1.4 miles, approx 5 minutes

Duckhorn Vineyards   707.963.7108   www.duckhorn.com *Appointment*   Page 225
3027 Silverado Trail N., St. Helena   Hours: 10 am - 4 pm by appt   Tasting Fee: $10 - $25
Wine List: Sauvignon Blanc, Merlot, Cabernet Sauvignon

For heading south you can travel either by Rt 29 or the Silverado Trail. If the traffic is heavy take the Trail. It will save you time and aggravation.

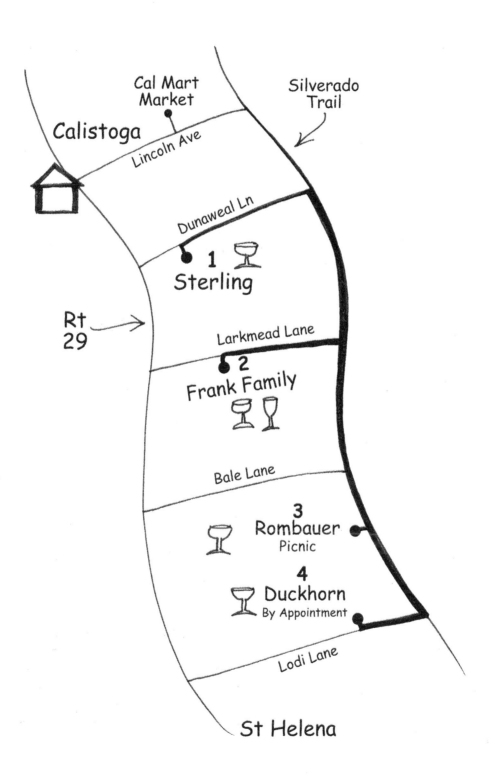

Cal Mart
Market

Silverado
Trail

Calistoga

Lincoln Ave

Dunaweal Ln

1 Sterling

Rt
29

Larkmead Lane

2
Frank Family

Bale Lane

3
Rombauer
Picnic

4
Duckhorn
By Appointment

Lodi Lane

St Helena

203

Tour Eight in Northern Napa
Spring Mountain Tour, All by Appointment Wineries,
Great Views and Tours

Every winery on Spring Mountain is by appointment and some are harder to get than others. Of these four, Schweiger is the most open to last minute appointments. Not because they are less interesting, they just are more recent to winemaking, although they have grown grapes for many years. If you think that you are going to be pressed for time, leave them out of the original plan, and then slip them back in if the time allows.

There are no places to pick up lunch on Spring Mountain and once you are up there you don't want to come down just to pick up sandwiches.

Pick up picnic items to eat at **Pride Mountain Vineyards**' picnic tables at
Sunshine Foods Market 707.963.7070 www.sunshinefoodsmarket.com
1115 Main St., St. Helena

Turn left (north) on Rt 29 to Madrona Ave. Turn left to Spring Mountain Rd., turn right and head up the mountain. At the top look for a gravel road to the right with a large collection of mail boxes. Follow the signs to Barnett Vineyard: 5.8 miles, 20 minutes

Barnett Vineyards 707.963.7075 www.barnettvineyards.com *Appointment*   Page 212
4070 Spring Mountain Rd., St. Helena Hours: 10 am - 4 pm by appt Tasting Fee: $20
Wine List: Cabernet Sauvignon, Pinot Noir, Chardonnay

Turn right to Pride Mountain Vineyards on the right hand side: 0.1 miles, 2 minutes

Pride Mountain Vineyards 707.963.4949 www.pridewines.com *Appointment*   Page 251
4026 Spring Mountain Rd., St. Helena Hours: appt only Tasting Fee: $10 - $20
Wine List: Merlot, Cabernet Sauvignon, Cabernet Franc, Viognier, Chardonnay
They have fantastic **picnic** areas

Turn left to Schweiger Vineyards: about 3 minutes

Schweiger Vineyards 707.963.4882 www.schweigervineyards.com *Appointment* Page 258
4015 Spring Mountain Rd., St. Helena Hours: 11 am - 4 pm by appt Tasting Fee: $10
Wine List: Sauvignon Blanc, Chardonnay, Merlot, Cabernet Sauvignon, Dedication™, Petite Sirah, Port, Estate Red Wine

Turn left to Spring Mountain Vineyards at the bottom of the mountain: total 4.0 miles approx 15 minutes

Spring Mountain Winery 707.967.4188 www.springmtn.com *Appointment-Tour*   Page 261
2805 Spring Mountain Rd., St. Helena Hours: 10 am - 5 pm by appt Tour & Tasting Fee: $25
Wine List: Syrah, Cabernet Sauvignon, Sauvignon Blanc, Blend
Allow 1 & 1/2 hours for the tour and tasting.

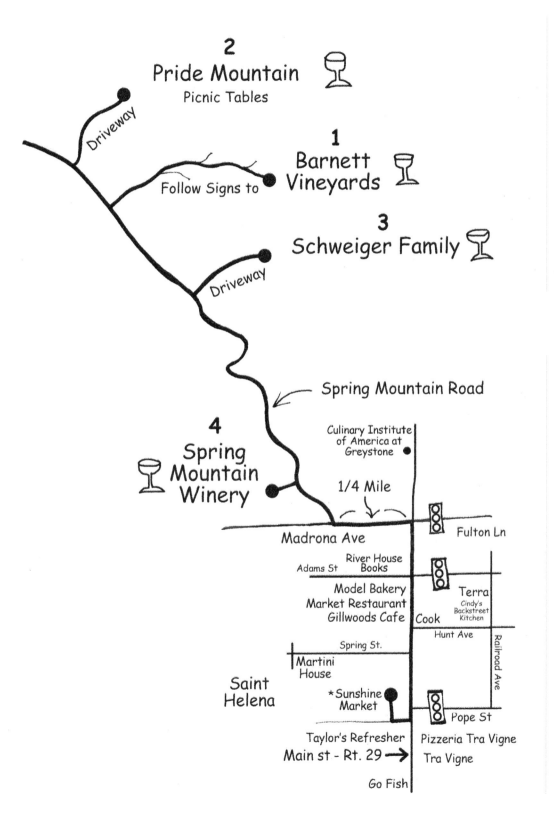

2
Pride Mountain
Picnic Tables

Driveway

Follow Signs to

1
Barnett Vineyards

3
Schweiger Family

Driveway

Spring Mountain Road

4
Spring Mountain Winery

Culinary Institute of America at Greystone

1/4 Mile

Madrona Ave

Fulton Ln

River House Books

Adams St

Model Bakery
Market Restaurant
Gillwoods Cafe

Terra
Cindy's Backstreet Kitchen

Cook

Hunt Ave

Spring St.

Railroad Ave

Martini House

Saint Helena

★Sunshine Market

Pope St

Taylor's Refresher
Main st - Rt. 29 →

Pizzeria Tra Vigne
Tra Vigne

Go Fish

Your Day in Wine Country

Tour Nine in Northern Napa

From Spring Mountain South to Oakville and Oak Knoll, Prestigious, Expensive Red Wines, All by Appointment Wineries, Gorgeous Wineries, Great Views, Plan in Advance

Reach Newton by following Madrona Rd. to the end. Turn right and head up the hill, go through the gates and keep climbing, Newton is at the top of the road.

Newton Vineyard 707.963.9000 www.newtonvineyard.com *Timed Appointment* Page 246
2555 Madrona Ave., St. Helena Hours: 1 to 2 tours daily, Call for times! Tasting Fee: $30
Wine List: Chardonnay, Merlot, Cabernet Sauvignon, Cabernet Franc, Petit Verdot, Blends

Take Madrona back to Spring Mountain Rd., on the left-hand side. Head up the mountain. At the top look for a gravel road to the right with a large collection of mail boxes. Follow the signs to Barnett Vineyards: total 5.9 miles, approx 20 minutes

Barnett Vineyards 707.963.7075 www.barnettvineyards.com *Appointment-Picnic* Page 212
4070 Spring Mountain Rd., St. Helena Hours: 10 am - 4 pm daily Tasting Fee: $20
Wine List: Cabernet Sauvignon, Pinot Noir, Chardonnay

Spring Mountain to Madrona to Rt 29, turn right to Market (restaurant on the right-hand side mid-block): total 5.6 miles, approx 20 minutes

You can picnic at Barnett or eat in St. Helena. One lunch suggestion is:
Market 707.963.3799 www.marketsthelena.com
1347 Main St., St. Helena Hours: 11:30 am - 10 pm daily Restaurant lists on pages 186 & 208

Either go north to Pratt or right to Zinfandel (depending on traffic) to Joseph Phelps Vineyards: total 2.6 miles, approx 10 minutes

Joseph Phelps Vineyards 707.967.3720 www.jpvwines.com *Appointment* Page 236
200 Taplin Rd., St. Helena Hours: 9 am - 5 pm Mon - Sat: 10 am - 4 pm Tasting Fee: $20+
Wine List: Cabernet Sauvignon, Chardonnay, Merlot, Pastiche, Sauvignon Blanc, Viognier

South on Silverado Tr. to Oakville Cr. Rd, turn right to Rudd: 4.9 miles, 10 minutes

Rudd 707.944.8577 www.ruddwines.com *Appointment-Exclusive* Page 256
500 Oakville Cross Rd., Oakville Hours: appt only, Closed Sun-Mon Tasting Fee: $35 - $60
Wine List: Cabernet Sauvignon, Chardonnay, Sauvignon, Blanc, Blends

Darioush makes a good stop if your hotel is in the south: 7.5 miles, approx 10 minutes

Darioush 707.257.2345 www.darioush.com *Gorgeous No Appointment Req* Page 222
4240 Silverado Trail, Napa Hours: 10:30 am - 5 PM Tasting Fee: $20
Wine List: Cabernet Sauvignon, Shiraz, Chardonnay, Merlot, Semillon, Sauvignon, Blanc, Pinot Noir, Viognier

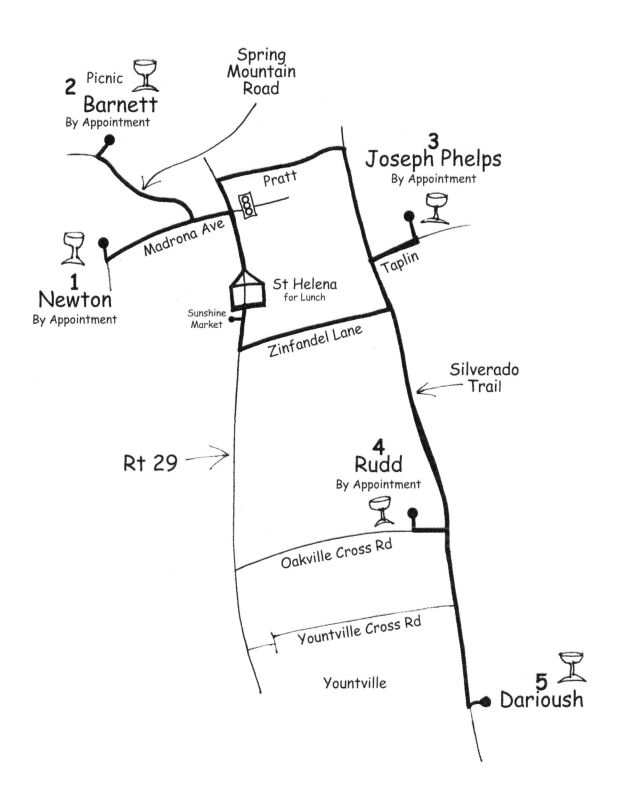

2 Picnic
Barnett
By Appointment

Spring Mountain Road

3
Joseph Phelps
By Appointment

Pratt

Taplin

Madrona Ave

St Helena
for Lunch

Sunshine Market

1
Newton
By Appointment

Zinfandel Lane

Silverado Trail

Rt 29

4
Rudd
By Appointment

Oakville Cross Rd

Yountville Cross Rd

Yountville

5
Darioush

207

Restaurants in Northern Napa

Dean & DeLuca: 607 S. St. Helena Hwy St. Helena. 707.967.9780. Market Pg. 201
Cindy's Back Street Kitchen: 1327 Railroad Ave. St. Helena. 707.963.1200. Californian Pg. 205
Cook St. Helena: 1310 Main St. (Rt. 29) St. Helena. 707.963.7088. Californian Pg. 205
Culinary Institute of America at Greystone: 2555 Main St. St. Helena. 707.967.1010.
One of America's finest cooking schools in one of Napa's most historic buildings. They offer
seminars, cooking supplies, books and a cafe plus the **Wine Spectator Restaurant**. This is a
destination for anyone who is serious about the enjoyment of food & wine. Fine Dining Pg. 205
Gillwoods Cafe: 1313 Main St. (Rt. 29) St. Helena. 707.963.1788. Comfort Pg. 205
Go Fish: 641 Main St. (Rt. 29) St. Helena. 707.963.0700. Seafood Pg. 205
Market: 1347 Main St. (Rt. 29) St. Helena. 707.963.3799. Californian Pg. 205
Martini House: 1245 Spring St. St. Helena. 707.963.2233. Californian Pg. 205
Meadowood Grill: 900 Meadowood Ln. St. Helena. 707.963.3646. Country Club Pg. 201
Model Bakery: 1357 Main St. St. Helena. 707.963.8192. Bakery & Sandwiches Pg. 205
Pizzeria Tra Vigne: 1016 Main St. (Facing Merryvale Winery) St. Helena. 707.967.9999.
Italian Pg. 205
Press: 587 St. Helena Hwy. St. Helena. 707.967.0550. Dinner only. Fine Contemporary Pg. 201
Restaurant at Meadowood: 900 Meadowood Ln. St. Helena. 707.967.1205. Dinner.
Fine Contemporary Pg. 201
Sunshine Foods 1115 Main St. (Rt. 29) St Helena. Market Pg. 205
Taylor's Refresher: 933 Main St. (Rt. 29) St. Helena. 707.963.3486. Great Burgers Pg. 205
Terra: 1345 Railroad Ave. St. Helena. 707.963.8931. Dinner Only. Fine Contemporary Pg. 205
Tra Vigne: 1050 Charter Oak (Just off Rt. 29), St. Helena. 707.963.4444. Italian Pg. 205

Calistoga

Brannan's: 1374 Lincoln Ave. Calistoga. 707.942.2233. Californian Pg. 201
Buster's: 1207 Foothill Blvd. Calistoga. 707.942.5605. BBQ Pg. 201
Café Sarafornia: 1413 Lincoln Ave. Calistoga. 707.942.0555. Comfort Pg. 201
Cal Mart: 1491 Lincoln Ave. Calistoga. Market Pg. 201
FlatIron Grill: 1440 Lincoln Ave. Calistoga. 707.942.1220. Steak Pg. 201
Hydro Bar & Grill: 1403 Lincoln Ave. Calistoga. 707.942.9777. American Pg. 201
Wappo Bar & Bistro: 1226 Washington St. Calistoga. 707.942.4712. Californian Pg. 201

Lodging See map on page 201

Calistoga Ranch 580 Lommel Rd. Calistoga 707.254.2800 www.calistogaranch.com
Harvest Inn One Main St. St. Helena 800.950.8466 www.harvestinn.com
Meadowood Napa Valley 900 Meadowood Ln. St. Helena 800.458.8080 707.963.3646
www.meadowood.com
EuroSpa & Inn 1202 Pine St. Calistoga 707.942.6829 www.eurospa.com
Solage Calistoga 755 Silverado Tr. Calistoga 707.226.0803   www.solagecalistoga.com
Wine Country Inn 1152 Lodi Ln. St. Helena 888.465.4608 707.963.7077
www.winecountryinn.

Directory of Wineries in Napa and Sonoma Counties

Abbreviations Key:
CWP – Complimentary with purchase   PIE – Purchase is expected (customary at small wineries)
pp – per person   TF – Tasting Fee   TR – Tasting Room

A. Rafanelli Winery 4685 W. Dry Creek Rd. Healdsburg (Northern Sonoma)
707.433.1385   www.arafanelliwinery.com
Hours: by appt only   Tasting Fee: $5 (parties over 6) cash/check only
Wine List: Cabernet Sauvignon, Merlot, Zinfandel
Notes: They enjoy tremendous loyalty from their customers and during the annual Passport Weekend, they are always swamped with purchasers who trail in a line down the driveway.
Part of Tour on page: 59

Acacia Winery 2750 Los Amigas Rd. Napa   (Carneros)
707.226.9991 acacia.info@acaciavineyard.com www.acaciawinery.com
Hours: 12pm - 4pm by appt only M-Sa   Tasting Fee: $10
Wine List: Pinot Noir, Chardonnay

Acorn Winery 12040 Old Redwood Hwy. Healdsburg (Northern Sonoma)
707.433.6440 nachbaur@acornwinery.com www.acornwinery.com
Hours: by appt only Appt required by permit Tasting Fee: $5 (CWP)
Wine List: Sangiovese, Dolcetto, Cabernet Franc, Zinfandel, Syrah, Blends

Adobe Road Winery 1995 S. McDowell Blvd. Ext. Petaluma
707.939.7967 www.adoberoadwines.com
Hours: by appt only Winery open to public on Fridays 4:30pm-8:30pm Tasting Fee: $5 (CWP)
Wine List: Petite Sirah, Syrah, Sauvignon Blanc, Pinot Noir, Cabernet Sauvignon, Zinfandel, Zinfandel Port
Added Highlights: Car Collection, Gift Shop
Notes: Owned by a famous sports car racer. Make an appt to see the car collection.

Aetna Springs Cellars 7227 Pope Valley Rd. Pope Valley
707.965.2675 kimsey@aetnaspringscellars.com www.aetnaspringscellars.com
Hours: by appt only   Tasting Fee: PIE
Wine List: Cabernet Sauvignon, Cabernet Franc, and Syrah

Alderbrook Winery 2306 Magnolia Dr. Healdsburg (Northern Sonoma)
707.433.5987 www.alderbrook.com
Hours: 10am - 5pm Closed major holidays. Tours by appt Tasting Fee: Complimentary
Wine List: Pinot Noir, Sauvignon Blanc, Chardonnay, Cabernet Sauvignon, Merlot, Syrah, Viognier, Zinfandel, Gewürztraminer
Added Highlights: Gift Shop, Picnic Area, Tours
Notes: A cute winery in a convenient location. Great lawn and gift shop and well made wines. Friendly staff who knows the area well.
Part of Tour on pages: 59, 179

Alexander Valley Vineyards 8644 Highway 128 Healdsburg (Northern Sonoma)
707.433.7209 www.avvwine.com
Hours: 10am - 5pm Closed major holidays. Tours of wine caves by appt. Tasting Fee: $0 - $10
Wine List: Gewürztraminer, Chardonnay, Viognier, Pinot Noir, Sangiovese, Zinfandel, Merlot, Cabernet Sauvignon Added Highlights: Gift Shop, Tours

Allora Vineyards 3244 Ehlers Ln.   St. Helena
707.963.6071 info@alloravineyards.com www.alloravineyards.com
Hours: by appt only   Tasting Fee: PIE
Wine List: Cabernet Sauvignon, Petite Sirah, Blends
Added Highlights: Architecture, Bocce Court, Gardens. The sell a line of glasses of their own design that greatly enhances the wines aroma. You are tasting in the cellar under the owner's home.

Alpha Omega 1155 Mee Ln.   St. Helena
707.963.9999 www.aowinery.com
Hours: 10am - 6pm   Tours on the hour. Tasting Fee: $10 (CWP)
Wine List: Cabernet Sauvignon, Chardonnay, Rosé, Blend
Added Highlights: Gardens, Tours
Notes: Also tasted here: Moss Creek, Harrison Vineyards & Voss

Altamura Winery 1700 Wooden Valley Rd.   Napa
707.253.2000 www.altamura.com
Hours: by appt only several weeks in advance   Tasting Fee: PIE
Wine List: Cabernet Sauvignon, Sangiovese

Amphora Winery 4791 Dry Creek Rd. Bldg. 6 Healdsburg (Northern Sonoma)
707.431.7767 info@amphorawines.com www.amphorawines.com
Hours: 11am - 4:30pm Fri & Sat, Mon - Thu by appt. (8 or larger by appt) Tasting Fee: $5
Wine List: Petite Sirah, Zinfandel, Merlot, Cabernet Sauvignon, Syrah
Added Highlights: Art Gallery
Notes: Tucked away along with Papapietro and Family wineries, Amphora takes it name from the ceramic vessels that the owner/wine maker has made for many years. Wonderful wines in an informal but lovely tasting room.   The winery is just through the door from the tasting room. If you arrive there during crush, any women in the group may have the opportunity to crush some grapes with their feet, Lucy style. A fun winery to visit and taste. A good value as well.
Part of Tour on page: 59

Anderson's Conn Valley Vineyards (Eagle's Trace) 680 Rossi Rd. St. Helena
707.963.8600 www.connvalleyvineyards.com
Hours: same day appts Tasting Fee: complimentary
Wine List: Cabernet Sauvignon, Pinot Noir, Blends: Éloge, Éloge Gold, Bordeaux style: Right Bank, Chardonnay
Added Highlights: Picnic Area, Tours
Notes: Picnic area available so bring a lunch. Bring a sweater for the cave tour. Tour lasts from 2-4 hours.

Andretti Winery 4162 Big Ranch Rd. Napa
707.259.6777 info@andrettiwinery.com www.andrettiwinery.com
Hours: 10am - 5pm Tours by appt Tasting Fee: $10-$20
Wine List: Chardonnay, Merlot, Cabernet Sauvignon
Added Highlights: Architecture, Gardens, Gift Shop, Tours
Notes: A must for racing buffs, Mario Andretti's winery is a charming, Italian inspired Winery.

Archipel 4611 Thomas Rd. Healdsburg (Northern Sonoma)
707.433.9000 www.archipelwines.com
Hours: 10am - 5pm Mon - Sat (Closed Sun) Tasting Fee: none listed
Wine List: Only one wine per vintage: 2002 was a blend of 49% Cabernet Sauvignon, 33% Merlot & 18% Cabernet Franc
Notes: Tasting at Vérité tasting room.

Arger-Martucci Vineyards 1455 Inglewood Ave. St. Helena
707.963.4334 www.arger-martucciwine.com
Hours: 10am - 4pm daily   Tasting Fee: $10
Wine List: Chardonnay, Viognier, Pinot Noir, Syrah, Cabernet Sauvignon, Blends
Added Highlights: Gardens, Gift Shop, Picnic Area
Notes: Kosta Arger, the winemaker, started off helping his father and uncles to make wine when he was a child. A physician by profession, he produces wonderful wines. This small winery is conveniently located but gets busy on the weekends. The staff is fantastic, Lonnie who manages the tasting room grew up in Healdsburg and was a tour guide for many years and is very knowledgeable about all aspects of Wine Country. With tables around the pool, this is a great place to bring a picnic lunch. The winery is located just steps from the tasting room. This is authentic Napa and a place you will revisit again and again.
Part of Tour on page: 62, 145, 161, 201

Arista Winery 7015 Westside Rd. Healdsburg (Northern Sonoma)
707.473.0606 info@aristawinery.com www.aristawinery.com
Hours: 11am - 5pm daily   Tasting Fee: $5
Wine List: Pinot Noir, Zinfandel, Gewürztraminer, Sauvignon Blanc
Added Highlights: Gardens, Pet Friendly, Picnic Area
Notes: Tasting room is surrounded by a Japanese Garden.

Armida Winery 2201 Westside Rd. Healdsburg (Northern Sonoma)
707.433.2222 info@armida.com www.armidawinery.com
Hours: 11am - 5pm   Tasting Fee: Complimentary
Wine List: Rosé, Pinot Noir, Chardonnay, Zinfandel, Gewürztraminer, Sauvignon Blanc, Cabernet Sauvignon
Added Highlights: Architecture, Bocce Court, Gardens, Picnic Area
Notes: Neat building and great views on the western hillsides of the Dry Creek Valley.
Part of Tour on page: 59

Arrowood Vineyards & Winery 14347 Sonoma Hwy. Glen Ellen
707.938.2600 hospitality@arrowoodvineyards.com www.arrowoodswinery.com
Hours: 10am - 4:30pm Tours by appt, $30 winery & cellar; $20 winery Tasting Fee: $5
Wine List: Chardonnay, Pinot Blanc, Viognier, Gewürztraminer, Merlot, Cabernet Sauvignon, Syrah, Late Harvest Riesling, Blends
Added Highlights: Gift Shop, Tours
Notes: For people who love great red wines in the classic style, Arrowood is a must visit in the Sonoma Valley. A beautiful location with great views from the tasting room, the staff is Sonoma Casual and it is just across the way from the Imagery Winery.
Part of Tour on page: 48, 99, 107

Artesa Winery 1345 Henry Rd. Napa (Carneros)
707.254.2140 TR info@artesawinery.com www.artesawinery.com
Hours: 10am - 5pm daily   Tasting Fee: $5 - $10
Wine List: Cabernet Sauvignon, Chardonnay, Merlot, Pinot Noir, Tempranillo, Albariño, Garnacha Rosado, Late Harvest Gewürztraminer, Blends
Added Highlights: Architecture, Art Gallery, Gift Shop, Views
Notes: A destination winery & quite a bar scene on the weekends. Spectacular location & views, the best in Carneros, bring a camera. Very convenient to San Francisco. Well made wines in the crisp, clean Carneros style. Great museum, good gift shop. Also tasted at Cornerstone, a collective tasting room. In high season they restrict limousines on the weekend, and even sometimes during the week.
Part of Tour on page: 69, 101, 121, 123, 127, 153, 163

Audelssa Estate Winery 13647 Arnold Dr. Glen Ellen
707.933.8514 info@audelssa.com www.audelssa.com
Hours: 11am - 5pm daily   Tasting Fee: $5
Wine List: Bordeaux Blend, Rhone Blend, Riesling, Chardonnay, Cabernet Sauvignon, Syrah
Added Highlights: Tours
Notes: The winery is located at 2992 Cavedale Rd. in Glen Ellen and can be visited by appointment, including amazing views of the bay and San Francisco. The address on Arnold drive is their very cozy tasting room in downtown Glen Ellen just across from the Fig Cafe. They make excellent wines done in the grand style that truly express the remarkable site where they are grown.
Tasting Room is Part of Tour on page: 48

August Briggs Wines 333 Silverado Trail Calistoga
707.942.4912 beth@augustbriggswines.com www.augustbriggswines.com
Hours: 10:30am - 4:30pm Appt req for parties of 4 or more Tasting Fee: Complimentary
Wine List: Pinot Meunier, Zinfandel, Pinot Noir, Chardonnay, Syrah, Petite Sirah, Cabernet Sauvignon
Added Highlights: Architecture, a very social tasting room.

B.R. Cohn Winery 15000 Sonoma Hwy. Glen Ellen
707.938.4064   www.brcohn.com
Hours: 10am - 5pm daily Tours by appt Tasting Fee: $10 (CWP)
Wine List: Cabernet Sauvignon, Zinfandel, Chardonnay, Merlot, Syrah Blend
Added Highlights: Doobie Brothers Gold Records, Gift Shop, Picnic Area, Tours all surrounded by vineyards and groves of olive trees.
Notes: The owner, Bruce Cohn, is the manager of the Doobie Brothers. Gold Records, Concerts, estate bottled olive oil plus a great gift shop add to the experience.
Part of Tour on page: 48, 101, 103

Baldacci Vineyards 6236 Silverado Trail Napa
707.944.9261 www.baldaccivineyards.com
Hours: by appt only   Tasting Fee: $5 (CWP)
Wine List: Limited production Estate grown Cabernet Sauvignon
Added Highlights: Caves. A wonderful family winery.

Ballentine Vineyards 2820 St. Helena Hwy. N. St. Helena
707.963.7919 info@ballentinevineyards.com www.ballentinevineyards.com
Hours: 10am - 5pm daily by appt   Tasting Fee: $5 (CWP)
Wine List: Cabernet Sauvignon, Chenin Blanc, Zinfandel, Merlot, Cabernet Franc, Syrah, Petite Sirah, Petit Verdot

Balletto Vineyards 5700 Occidental Rd. Santa Rosa (Northern Sonoma)
707.568.2455 info@ballettovineyards.com www.ballettovineyards.com
Hours: 10am - 4pm daily Tasting Fee: none listed
Wine List: Chardonnay, Pinot Grigio, Pinot Gris, Pinot Noir, Rosé of Pinot Noir, Syrah, Gewürztraminer, Zinfandel. Dutton Goldfield: Pinot Noir, Chardonnay, Zinfandel

Barnett Vineyards 4070 Spring Mountain Rd. St. Helena
707.963.7075 appt winecellar@barnettvineyards.com www.barnettvineyards.com
Hours: 10am - 4pm daily by appt Tasting Fee: $20
Wine List: Cabernet Sauvignon, Pinot Noir, Chardonnay
Added Highlights: Picnic Area, Tours
Notes: A charming little winery clinging to the side of Spring Mountain that produces spectacular wines. Incredible views and an excellent staff that loves what they do. Great place for a picnic. Make your appointment early so you don't miss out.   Part of Tour on page: 205, 207

Bartholomew Park Winery 1000 Vineyard Ln. Sonoma
707.935.9511 info@bartpark.com www.bartpark.com
Hours: 11am - 4:30pm daily   Tasting Fee: $5 and up
Wine List: Sauvignon Blanc, Merlot, Syrah, Zinfandel, Cabernet Sauvignon
Added Highlights: Art Gallery, Picnic Area, Museum, Resident Ghost or Two

Battaglini Estate Winery 2948 Piner Rd. Santa Rosa (Northern Sonoma)
707.578.4091 www.battagliniwines.com
Hours: by appt only   Tasting Fee: CWP
Wine List: Zinfandel, Chardonnay, Petite Sirah

Beaulieu Vineyard 1960 St. Helena Hwy. Rutherford
707.967.5230 www.bvwines.com
Hours: 10am - 5pm   Tasting Fee: $5 - $25
Wine List: Cabernet Sauvignon, Chardonnay, Pinot Noir, Merlot, Zinfandel, Syrah, Sauvignon Blanc,
Shiraz, Sangiovese, Viognier, Port, Blends
Notes: Gift Shop, One of the grand old wine houses of Napa. They have both a main tasting room and a
reserve room. Back in the old days, this was the site of major experimentation and innovation led by the
revered winemaker Andre Tchelistcheff. Now under corporate ownership, they still produce top quality
wines. For a special treat, do the expensive tasting in the reserve room with the white marble counter
tops and the big Rutherford Reds.
Part of Tour on page: 62, 161, 155

Behrens & Hitchcock Winery 4078 Spring Mountain Rd. St. Helena
Email only: info@behrensandhitchcock.com www.behrensandhitchcock.com
Hours: by appt only   Tasting Fee: none listed
Wine List: Merlot, Red Table Wine

Bella Vineyards & Wine Caves 9711 W. Dry Creek Rd. Healdsburg (Northern Sonoma)
707.473.9171 info@bellawinery.com www.BellaWinery.com
Hours: 11am - 4:30pm daily   Closed Major Holidays   Tasting Fee: $5
Wine List: Zinfandel, Syrah
Added Highlights: Architecture, Caves, Pet Friendly
Notes: A charming family winery at the top of the Dry Creek Valley specializing in Zinfandel, which they
do very well. The tastings are offered in the caves that burrow underneath the hillside vineyards. Beauti-
ful location reached by a very narrow road.
Part of Tour on page: 59, 177

Belvedere Vineyards and Winerie 4035 Westside Rd. Healdsburg (Northern Sonoma)
707.431.4442   Hours: 11am - 4pm   Tasting Fee: $5
Wine List: Chardonnay, Syrah, Merlot, Sangiovese, Riesling, Gewürztraminer
Added Highlights: Architecture, Gardens

Benessere 1010 Big Tree Rd. St. Helena
707.963.5853 info@benesserevineyards.com www.benesserevineyards.com
Hours: 10am - 5pm by appt only   Tasting Fee: $10
Wine List: Pinot Grigio, Sangiovese, Syrah, Zinfandel, Pinot Noir, Muscat di Canelli, Blends
Added Highlights: Gardens, Picnic Area
Notes: A real jewel just minutes off of Route 29. Built by a couple in love with Italy and Italian style
wines, they do them very well. Tiny tasting room, great staff, big friendly dog. Great to visit during crush
for an informal tour of the process. Romantic!
Part of Tour on page: 141, 151, 193

Bennett Lane Winery 3340 Highway 128 Calistoga
707.942.6684 www.bennettlane.com
Hours: 10am - 5pm   Tasting Fee: $7
Wine List: Chardonnay, Cabernet Sauvignon
Added Highlights: Picnic Area, Tours, Race Cars

Benovia Winery 3339 Hartman Rd. Santa Rosa (Northern Sonoma)
707.526.4441 bob@benoviawinery.com www.benoviawinery.com
Hours: 9am - 5pm Mon - Fri by appt & Sometimes Saturday   Tasting Fee: none listed
Wine List: Pinot Noir, Chardonnay, Zinfandel

Benziger Family Winery 1883 London Ranch Rd. Glen Ellen
707.935.4500 greatwine@benziger.com www.benziger.com
Hours: 10am - 5pm daily Tram tour $10.00 Closed Major Holidays Tasting Fee: $10 - $15 - Tour $15
Wine List: Zinfandel, Cabernet Sauvignon, Merlot, Barbera, Malbec, Cabernet Franc, Petite Blanc, Sangiovese, Pinot Blanc, Chardonnay, Viognier, Fumé Blanc, Syrah, White Burgundy, Claret, Muscat Canelli
Added Highlights: Biodynamic/Organic, Caves, Gardens, Gift Shop, Picnic Area, Special Partners Tour $45
Notes: Not only great wines in a great location, but also the best tours in Sonoma. A tractor pulls the trams up into the Biodynamic Vineyards. Tours are on the half hour, except 12:30pm, until 3pm. If you come to Sonoma, you need to visit Benziger. The very large Benziger clan originally made the Glen Ellen brand, selling it off to buy their property just below the old Jack London Ranch. They have become powerful advocates for Biodynamic Agriculture and they are well respected in the area.
Part of Tour on page: 48, 93, 101, 103, 175

Beringer Vineyards 2000 Main St. St. Helena
707.967.4412 www.beringer.com, worldwideestates.com
Hours: 10am - 5pm Closed Major Holidays Tour includes tasting. Tasting Fee: $5 - $10
Wine List: Chardonnay, Dessert Wines, Sauvignon Blanc, Pinot Noir, Merlot, Cabernet Sauvignon, Riesling, Viognier, White Zinfandel, White Merlot, Chenin Blanc, Gewürztraminer, Pinot Grigio, Shiraz
Added Highlights: Architecture, Caves, Gardens, Gardens, Gift Shop, Tours
Notes: Continuously in operation since 1876, right through Prohibition, Beringer is a major destination winery. Beringer offers an amazing variety of tours throughout the day. Don't be fooled by the large amount of consumer quality wine they produce. Visit their reserve tasting in the mansion to be impressed. If you are a serious wine geek, call ahead and arrange a sit down tasting upstairs in the Beringer Mansion. A little pricey but a fantastic experience with world class wines.
Part of Tour on page: 62, 117, 125, 151, 153, 155, 199

Berthoud Vineyards & Winery 20 Maldonado Ave. Sonoma
707.938.1482 bear2s@berthoudwinery.com www.berthoudwinery.com
Hours: by appt only   Tasting Fee: none listed
Wine List: Merlot, Cabernet Sauvignon, Syrah
Notes: Wines are only available at the winery

Blackstone Winery 8450 Sonoma Hwy. Kenwood
707.833.1999 www.blackstonewinery.com
Hours: 10:30am - 4:30pm daily   Tasting Fee: $5
Wine List: Merlot, Cabernet Sauvignon, Syrah, Zinfandel, Sauvignon Blanc, Chardonnay, Pinot Noir, Riesling, Gewürztraminer, Viognier
Added Highlights: Gardens
Notes: A well-known name with a surprisingly intimate and relaxed tasting room. They source their grapes from all over California and therefore offer some delightful variety. Great location that fits in well with multiple tours.   Part of Tour on page: 48

Bouchaine Vineyards 1075 Buchli Station Rd. Napa   (Carneros)
707.252.9065 www.bouchaine.com
Hours: 10:30am - 4pm   Tasting Fee: $5 - $10
Wine List: Chardonnay, Pinot Noir, Pinot Gris, Syrah, Pinot Meunier, Gewürztraminer
Added Highlights: Gardens, Picnic Area
Notes: Out in the rolling hills of Carneros, Bouchaine is a gorgeous winery with a first class product. The outdoor seating area is a great place to bring a bite to eat and, if you are filling your wine seller, this is a great value. Wonderfully friendly staff and great breezes on a hot day.
Part of Tour on page: 109

Bremer Family Winery 975 Deer Park Rd. St. Helena (Howell Mountain)
707.963.5411 www.bremerfamilywinery.com
Hours: 10am - 5pm daily by appt (max party of 6 in Winter) Tasting Fee: Complimentary
Wine List: Cabernet Sauvignon, Merlot, Zinfandel, Cabernet Franc, Claret, Petite Sirah, Port, White Port, Blend
Notes: Tastings are outdoors as their tasting room is quite small.

Buehler Vineyards 820 Greenfield Rd. St. Helena
707.963.2155 appt   www.buehlervineyards.com
Hours: 10am - 4pm by appt only Mon - Fri   Tasting Fee: none listed
Wine List: Cabernet Sauvignon, Chardonnay, Zinfandel

Buena Vista Winery 18000 Old Winery Rd. Sonoma   (Carneros)
707.938.1266 www.buenavistacarneros.com; buenavistawinery.com
Hours: 10am - 5pm   Tasting Fee: $5 - $20
Wine List: Sauvignon Blanc, Chardonnay, Merlot, Cabernet Sauvignon, Zinfandel, Pinot Noir
Added Highlights: Gift Shop, Picnic Area, Tours
Notes: Historic winery in the old town Sonoma. See the huge old style barrels and enjoy a picnic among the Eucalyptus trees. Map on page 97

Burgess Cellars 1108 Deer Park Rd. St. Helena (Howell Mountain)
707.963.4766 wines@burgesscellars.com www.burgesscellars.com
Hours: 10am - 4pm daily Tastings by appt. Retail sales hours listed. Tasting Fee: none listed
Wine List: Cabernet Sauvignon, Merlot, Syrah

Bush-Field Estate Vineyards & Winery 3200 Sonoma Mountain Rd. Petaluma
707.665.9762 www.bush-field.com
Hours: by appt only   Tasting Fee: none listed
Wine List: Pinot Noir

Cafaro Cellars 1591 Dean York Ln. St. Helena
707.963.7181
Hours: by appt only   Tasting Fee: none listed
Wine List: Bordeaux varietals

Cain Vineyard & Winery 3800 Langtry Rd. St. Helena (Spring Mountain)
707.963.1616 winery@cainfive.com www.cainfive.com
Hours: by appt only Fri-Sat mornings Tasting Fee: Complimentary
Wine List: Cabernet Sauvignon, Cabernet Franc, Merlot, Malbec, Petit Verdot, and a small amount of Syrah. They mainly make three Cabernet Blends, Cain Cuveé, Cain Concept, signature blend, Cain Five
Added Highlights: Tours, Views, they are down a long windy road half-way up Spring Mountain

Cakebread Cellars 8300 St. Helena Hwy.   Rutherford
707.963.5221 cindy@cakebread.com www.cakebread.com
Hours: 10am - 4pm daily by appt   Tasting Fee: $10
Wine List: Sauvignon Blanc, Chardonnay, Pinot Noir, Merlot, Syrah, Zinfandel, Cabernet Sauvignon, Rubaiyat (blend of Pinot Noir, Syrah & Zinfandel)
Added Highlights: Architecture, Gardens, Tours
Notes: A very busy, by appointment only winery in the center of Napa's busiest stretch of Route 29. Very busy on the weekends but the experience and the wines are first class. Be at least 10 minutes early for the appointment or you will get bumped. Tastings take 30-35 min; if you include the tour, allow 90 minutes.
Part of Tour on page: 62, 69, 163

Calafia Cellars 629 Fulton Ln. St. Helena
707.963.114 www.calafiacellars.com
Hours: by appt only Closed in January Tasting Fee: none listed
Wine List: Blends of Cabernet Sauvignon, Malbec, Petit Verdot & Merlot

Calistoga Cellars 1371 Lincoln Ave. Calistoga
707.942.7422 www.calistogacellars.com
Hours: 12pm - 5pm Fri - Sun by instant appt   Tasting Fee: $5
Wine List: Chardonnay, Sauvignon Blanc, Zinfandel, Merlot, Cabernet Sauvignon, Cabernet Port

Camellia Cellars 57 Front St. Healdsburg (Northern Sonoma)
707.433.1290 www.camelliacellars.com
Hours: 11am - 6pm daily Tasting Fee: $0 - $10 (CWP)
Wine List: Zinfandel, Sangiovese, Cabernet Sauvignon, Blends
Notes: Tastings are at Front Street Wineries, a collective tasting room.

Cardinale Estate 7600 St. Helena Hwy. Oakville
707.948.2643 info@cardinale.com www.cardinale.com
Hours: 10:30am - 5pm daily Tasting Fee: $35 - $150
Wine List: single vintage Cabernet Sauvignon-based blend
Added Highlights: Architecture
Notes: Most tastings are paired with cheeses or other foods. A gorgeous building and location, they make serious, big red wines. Check their schedule since tastings are done by appointment at very specific times, a very exclusive feeling with a very nice staff, owned by Kendall Jackson.
Part of Tour on page: 165

Casa Nuestra Winery & Vineyards 3451 Silverado Trail N. St. Helena
707.963.5783 info@casanuestra.com www.casanuestra.com
Hours: 10am - 5pm by appt only Mon - Sat (Closed Sun) Tasting Fee: $5 (CWP)
Wine List: French Colombard (botrytized), Chenin Blanc, Rosado, Tinto Classico, Cabernet Sauvignon, Merlot, Meritage, Cabernet Franc, Riesling, Blends
Added Highlights: Picnic Area, Rustic, Sixties and Seventies Memorabilia

Castello di Amorosa 4045 N. St. Helena Hwy. Calistoga
707.942.8200 reservations info@castellodiamorosa.com www.castellodiamorosa.com
Hours: 9:30am - 4:30pm weekdays, 5pm weekends & holidays. Tasting Fee: $10 up to 5 wines
Wine List: Chardonnay, Pinot Grigio, Pinot Bianco, Gewürztraminer, Rosato d'Sangiovese, Merlot, Sangiovese, Cabernet Sauvignon, Super Tuscan, Muscato, Blends
Added Highlights: Architecture, Gift Shop, Tours, Views
Notes: Northern Napa's new destination winery. Built to be an authentic European style Castle, besides being a winery it also rents its 110 rooms out for events, movie sets etc. Complete with a dungeon. In the

slow season, you can just walk in and get the next appointment, but if the season is at all busy, make an appointment in advance. Being a castle it is a little bit cool in the winter so dress accordingly, however it is great in the Summer. Great tasting room and a place not to be missed. Nicely made wines and friendly staff. Tour with tasting by appointment, $25 weekdays, $30 Sat, Sun & Holidays. Reserve Wines $35 weekdays & $40 Sat, Sun & Holidays.
Part of Tour on page: 199

Castle Vineyards & Winery 122 W. Spain St.   Sonoma
707.996.1966 x 101   www.castlevineyards.com
Hours: 11am - 6pm daily   Closed Major Holidays   Tasting Fee: $5 - $10
Wine List: Pinot Noir, Merlot, Zinfandel, Syrah, Viognier, Chardonnay, Rosé, Syrah Port
Added Highlights: Gardens, Gift Shop. Convenient to the Plaza
Notes: Located in downtown Sonoma, just off the Plaza, in a restored Craftsman Style Bungalow previously owned by the Sebastiani family. Crisp, clean Carneros style wines, pretty location, tremendously convenient, casual friendly staff. Wines are priced lower than their quality merits.
Part of Tour on page: 18, 93, 105

Catacula Lake Winery 4105 Chiles Pope Valley Rd.   St. Helena   (Chiles Valley)
707.965.1104 www.cataculalake.com
Hours: by appt only   Tasting Fee: none listed
Wine List: Cabernet Sauvignon, Sauvignon Blanc, Zinfandel, Cuvee (Merlot/Cab Blend)
Added Highlights: Picnic Area

Caymus Vineyards 8700 Conn Creek Rd.   Rutherford
707.963.3010 TR   www.caymus.com
Hours: by appt only   Arrive early or you will not be admitted   Tasting Fee: Complimentary
Wine List: Cabernet Sauvignon
Notes: Premium wine maker. Oenophiles will appreciate this nice sit down tasting. Don't be late or your appt will not be honored.

Ceja Vineyards 1016 Las Amigas Rd.   Napa   (Carneros)
707.255.3954 wine@cejavineyards.com www.cejavineyards.com
Hours: by appt only   Tasting Fee: $20   They have also opened a tasting room in downtown Napa
Wine List: Chardonnay, Merlot, Pinot Noir, Cabernet Sauvignon, Syrah, Blend
Added Highlights: Bocce Court, Gardens
Notes: A wonderful family winery in Carneros, beautiful building and location, great wines, wonderful people and a good story about a migrant Mexican family that has become important Napa winemakers. Gracious is the correct word. They are also opening a tasting room in Napa's downtown.
Part of Tour on page: 109

Cellar Door (at the Lodge at Sonoma) 1395 Broadway   Sonoma
707.938.4466 www.sonomacellardoor.com
Hours: 11am - 6pm Thu - Mon   Tue/Wed 4pm - 6pm   Tasting Fee: Complimentary
Wine List: Various wines from multiple wineries
Notes: They are a Collective tasting room located in The Lodge at Sonoma. You can currently taste wines from Chandelle, Sunset, Mayo Family & Richardson Wines. The Lodge is a lovely, convenient place.

Chalk Hill Estate Vineyards & Winery 10300 Chalk Hill Rd.   Healdsburg   (Northern Sonoma)
707.838.4306 concierge@chalkhill.com www.chalkhill.com
Hours: 10am - 3pm by appt Mon - Fri   Tasting Fee: $10 Tour: $15 (1.5 hours). Culinary tours $75 Wine List: Chardonnay, Sauvignon Blanc, Pinot Gris, Cabernet Sauvignon, Merlot, Semillon, Blends
Added Highlights: Architecture, Gardens, Gift Shop, Restaurant, Tours

Chanticleer 4 Vineyard View Dr.   Yountville
707.945.0566   info@chaticleerwine.com   www.chanticleerwine.com
Hours: by appt only   Tasting Fee: no tasting fee but purchases are customary
Wine List: Cabernet Sauvignon, Sangiovese
Added Highlights: Architecture, Gardens, tasting at the owners home

Chappellet Winery & Vineyard 1581 Sage Canyon Rd.   St. Helena
707.963.7136, 707-963-3262 winery@chappellet.com www.chappellet.com
Hours: by appt only 10:30am & 2pm M-F, Sat add a 12:30pm Tasting Fee: $15 - $25
Wine List: Cabernet Sauvignon, Merlot, Cabernet Franc, Chardonnay, Chenin Blanc, Cuvee
Added Highlights: Picnic Area, Views
Notes: It is a long, twisty ride up into the mountains. Be sure to get clear directions, as there are few
signs that are not very helpful. Worth the effort.

Charbay Winery & Distillery 4001 Spring Mountain Rd.   St. Helena
707.963.9327 info@charbay.com www.charbay.com
Hours: by appt only closed Sun   Tour Fee: $20   Tasting Fee: none listed
Wine List: Flavored Vodkas, (Blood Orange, Meyer Lemon, Green Tea, Grapefruit, Key Lime, Raspberry)
Ports, Pastis, Rum, Whiskey, Grappa, Black Walnut Liquor
Added Highlights: Tours

Charles Creek Vineyard 483 First St. W.   Sonoma   (On the Plaza)
707.935.3848 tastewine@charlescreek.com www.charlescreek.com
Hours: 11am - 6pm daily   Tasting Fee: $5 - $10
Wine List: Merlot, Cabernet Sauvignon, Syrah, Chardonnay, Grenache, Chocolate Dessert Wine, Blends
Added Highlights: Gift Shop
Notes: Located on the Sonoma Plaza. If you like warm buttery Chardonnay then this is the place for you.
A very cute tasting room with a good gift shop that looks out on the Plaza. Friendly, knowledgeable staff.
Look for the Cow sculpture made from corks, bottle caps and other wine related items.
Part of Tour on page: 18, 105

Charles Krug Winery 2800 St. Helena Hwy. N St. Helena
707.967.2229 TR   www.charleskrug.com
Hours: 10:30am - 5pm Closed Major Holidays Tasting Fee: $10 -$20
Wine List: Cabernet Sauvignon, Merlot, Sauvignon Blanc, Chardonnay, Pinot Noir, Zinfandel, Cabernet
Franc, Syrah
Added Highlights: Gift Shop
Notes: One of the oldest operating wineries in Napa, it is owned by the Peter Mondavi Family. They are
currently restoring their oldest winery buildings and when completed they will be a beautiful addition.

Chase Cellars 2252 Sulpher Spring Ave.   St. Helena
707.963.1284   www.chasecellars.com
Hours: 10am - 5pm by appt only   Tasting Fee: $15 (CWP except group of 8 or more)
Wine List: Zinfandel, Petite Sirah
Added Highlights: Architecture

Chateau Boswell 3468 Silverado Trail N.   St. Helena
707.963.5472 josh@chateauboswellwinery.com www.chateauboswellwinery.com
Hours: by appt only   Tasting Fee: $25
Wine List: Chardonnay, Cabernet Sauvignon
Added Highlights: Architecture

Chateau Felice   223 Center St.   Healdsburg   (Northern Sonoma)
707.443.9010 TR   www.chateaufelice.com
Hours: 11am - 6pm except Wed   (Wed by appt)   Tasting Fee: none listed
Wine List: Bordeaux Blend, Chardonnay, Cabernet Sauvignon, Cabernet Franc, Zinfandel, Merlot, Syrah
Added Highlights: Tours
Notes: Tasting room is not at the winery. Private winery tour by appt. 10603 Chalk Hill Rd.

Chateau Montelena Winery   1429 Tubbs Ln.   Calistoga
707.942.5105 www.montelena.com
Hours: 9:30am - 4pm   Tasting Fee: $15 - 25
Wine List: Chardonnay, Cabernet Sauvignon, Zinfandel, Riesling
Added Highlights: Architecture, Bocce Court, Gardens, Picnic Area, Tours
Notes: A winner in the famous Judgment of Paris wine tasting in 1976 that put Napa wines on the map, it was their Chardonnay that took some of the top honors. An historical building and wonderful grounds including Jade Lake and bocce courts. Friendly staff. Tour takes 1 ½ - 2 hours.
Part of Tour on page: 115, 191, 193

Chateau Potelle Winery   3875 Mount Veeder Rd.   Napa   Property sold as of Winter 2008
707.255.9440 x 18   info@chateaupotelle.com   www.chateaupotelle.com
Hours: 11am - 5pm Thu - Mon   Closed Tues & Wed   Tasting Fee: $5 - $10
Wine List: Chardonnay, Cabernet Sauvignon, Zinfandel, Sauvignon Blanc, Syrah, Blends
Added Highlights: Picnic Area
Notes: European style wines made by French winemakers who came to Napa in 1970's exploring for the French government, and then chose to stay. Wonderful wines, beautiful mountain location, rustic tasting room, great staff. Bring a picnic. The route is up over the Oakville Grade so it is winding but fun.
Note: The property was purchased by Kendall Jackson, but not the Ch. Potelle label. Call before visiting.

Chateau St. Jean Winery   8555 Sonoma Hwy.   Kenwood
707.833.4134 www.chateaustjean.com
Hours: 10am - 5pm   Tasting Fee: $10 - $15
Wine List: Pinot Blanc, Chardonnay, Viognier, Pinot Noir, Merlot, Malbec, Cabernet Sauvignon,
Added Highlights: Architecture, Art Gallery, Gardens, Gift Shop, Picnic Area, Restaurant/Market, Tours
Notes: One of the crown jewels of the Sonoma Valley. Great wines offered in two tasting rooms, the basic and the reserve in the mansion. Beautiful grounds, good deli with lovely patio tables and a picnic area. Best gift shop. If you truly love wines, call ahead for a reserve tasting, sitting outside on the patio at the mansion. Complimentary historical tours at 11am & 3pm. (45 min) Private tour & tasting can be arranged for $25 pp (1 1/2 hours)
Part of Tour on page: 48, 97, 99, 105, 175

Chimney Rock Winery   5350 Silverado Trail Napa
707.257.2641 x 3206   www.chimneyrock.com
Hours: 10am - 5pm daily   Tasting Fee: $20 - $30
Wine List: Cabernet Sauvignon, Fumé Blanc, Rosé of Cabernet Franc, Blends
Added Highlights: Architecture
Notes: The building is in the South African Dutch style on the former site of a Golf Course of the same name. A growing reputation for big reds right in the midst of the Stags Leap District.

Christopher Creek Winery   641 Limerick Ln.   Healdsburg (Northern Sonoma)
707.433.2001 TR   info@christophercreek.com   www.christophercreek.com
Hours: 11am - 5pm daily by appt only   Capacity 9-10 people   Tasting Fee: Complimentary
Wine List: Zinfandel, Syrah, Viognier, Syrah, Cabernet Sauvignon, Chardonnay, Petite Sirah, Port
Added Highlights: Picnic Area

Your Day in Wine Country

Cliff Lede Vineyards 1473 Yountville Cross Rd. Yountville
707.944.8642 info@CliffLedeVineyards.com www.CliffLedeVineyards.com
Hours: 10am - 5pm   Tasting Fees: $15-$20
Wine List: Cabernet Sauvignon, Merlot, Claret
Added Highlights: Art Gallery, Gardens, Gift Shop
Notes: Pronounced LAY-dee, this winery is on the northern edge of the Stag's Leap District. They offer good wines in a charming tasting room that spreads out into a lovely garden with an array of comfortable seating, and an art gallery. Very convenient to downtown Yountville, it is a nice way to end the day.
Part of Tour on page: 129

Cline Cellars 24737 Arnold Dr. Sonoma   (Carneros)
707.940.4000 www.clinecellars.com
Hours: 10am - 6pm Tours at 11AM, 1PM & 3PM Tasting Fee: Complimentary - $6
Wine List: Mourvèdre, Carignane, Syrah, Muscat Canelli, about a dozen Zinfandels, Viognier, Vin Gris, Vin Blanc, Vin Rouge, Marsanne, Blends
Added Highlights: Gardens, Tours
Notes: This is a great location, wonderful grounds, bird collection, animals and their model museum of the twenty-one historic Franciscan Missions just add to an amazing collection of wines. Site of the original San Francisco Solano mission. One of the great family wineries of Carneros, not to be missed.
Part of Tour on page: 41

Clos Du Bois Wines 19410 Geyserville Ave. Geyserville (Northern Sonoma)
707.857.3100 tastingroom@closdubois.com www.closdubois.com
Hours: 10am - 4:30pm daily Tasting Fee: $0 - $5 (inc logo glass)
Wine List: Cabernet Sauvignon, Chardonnay, Merlot, Pinot Grigio, Pinot Noir, Sauvignon Blanc, Shiraz, Zinfandel, Tempranillo, Fumé Blanc, Blends
Added Highlights: Gift Shop, Picnic Area, Tours
Notes: Complimentary tasting of 2 wines. Reserve tasting is $5 pp for 7 wines Print a coupon from their website for a free tasting & glass for 2 persons. They also have a great wine dictionary on website and "How To"s, such as "How to taste wines like a Pro", and more.

Clos Du Val 5330 Silverado Trail Napa
707.261.5225 www.closduval.com
Hours: 10am - 5pm Reserve Tasting: $20. (inc logo glass) Tasting Fee: $10 - $20 (CWP)
Wine List: Cabernet Sauvignon, Chardonnay, Merlot, Pinot Noir, Blend
Added Highlights: Bocce Court, Gift Shop, Picnic Area, Tours
Notes: Very much a French style winery in the heart of the Stag's Leap District. Good wines, friendly spacious tasting room, good place for a picnic on a hot day. Fun during crush because the sorters are handy to the tasting room. Lots of parking.
Part of Tour on page: 119

Clos Pegase Winery 1060 Dunaweal Ln. Calistoga
707.942.4981 x 213   www.clospegase.com
Hours: 10:30am - 5pm daily Tasting Fee: $10 - $20
Wine List: Chardonnay, Sauvignon Blanc, Pinot Noir, Merlot, Cabernet Sauvignon
Added Highlights: Architecture, Art Gallery, Gift Shop, Picnic Area, Tours
Notes: Winery as Gallery. A small eccentric tasting room with a good staff. The art collection, combined with the incredible building, makes this a destination winery. Just across the road from Sterling and minutes from Castello di Amorosa, it is worth the visit. Guided tours of the winery & grounds at 11am & 2pm, free of charge. No reservations necessary. For large groups, tours must be scheduled in advance.
Part of Tour on page: 193, 199

Colin Lee Vineyards & Winery 1189 Lawndale Rd. Kenwood
707.833.5433
Hours: by appt only   Tasting Fee: Purchase is Customary
Wine List: Cab Sauvignon, Petite Sirah, Syrah, Viognier
Notes: This is a very small winery where the tastings are done in the family's charming outdoor kitchen next to the winery. Guy, the owner/winemaker will pour the wines for you, which are very good so visit prepared to ship some home.

Collier Falls 4791 Dry Creek Rd. Healdsburg (Northern Sonoma)
707.433.0100 TR wine@collierfalls.com www.collierfalls.com
Hours: 10:30am - 4:30pm daily   Tasting Fee: $5 glass purchase
Wine List: Cabernet Franc, Cabernet Sauvignon, Petite Sirah, Petite Verdot, Zinfandel
Added Highlights: Gardens
Notes: Tastings are held at Family Wineries, a collective tasting room.

Conn Creek Winery 8711 Silverado Trail S. St. Helena
707.963.9100 www.conncreek.com
Hours: 10am - 4pm   Tours by appt (Winter hours: 11-4)   Tasting Fee: $10 - $25
Wine List: Cabernet Sauvignon, Cabernet Franc, Merlot
Added Highlights: Gift Shop, Tours. The land was so rocky that they had to use dynamite to plant.

Corison Wines 987 St. Helena Hwy. S. St. Helena
707.963.0826 bob@corison.com www.corison.com
Hours: 10am - 5pm daily by appt   Library tastings on Fri $25.   Tasting Fee: $10 - $25 (CWP)
Wine List: Cabernet Sauvignon, Gewürztraminer
Added Highlights: Gift Shop, Picnic Area
Notes: A small but very conveniently located winery, owned by a well respected winemaker. The wines are fantastic, the tasting room is the barrel room, and for the serious wine collector, this is a gem not to be missed. A diamond in the rough.
Part of Tour on page: 143, 147

Cornerstone Place (Grange Sonoma) 23564 Arnold Dr. Sonoma (A Collective)
707.933.8980 info@grangesonoma.com www.grangesonoma.com,www.cornerstoneplace.com
Hours: 10am - 5pm   Tasting Fee: none listed
Wine List: Albariño, Blends, Cabernet Franc, Cabernet Sauvignon, Chardonnay, Gewürztraminer, Meritage, Merlot, Petite Sirah, Pinot Noir, Rosé, Sauvignon Blanc, Tempranillo, Zinfandel
Added Highlights: Gardens, Gift Shop, Pet Friendly, Restaurant/Market
Notes: A collective tasting room for Artesa, Larson Family, Roshambo, Ridgeline Vineyards. Cornerstone also has shops, gardens & a Restaurant Market area. It makes a great place for a relaxing stop before heading back to San Francisco.
Part of Tour on page: 41, 109

Cosentino Winery 7415 St. Helena Hwy. Yountville
707.944.1220 www.cosentinowinery.com
Hours: 10am - 5pm   Tasting Fee: $15 - $20
Wine List: Bianco, Chardonnay, Gewürztraminer, Semillon, Sangiovese, Dolcetto, Tempranillo, Petite Sirah, Pinot Noir, Merlot, Cabernet Franc, Cabernet Sauvignon, Zinfandel, Meritage, Late Harvest Viognier, Botrytis Semillon, Blends
Added Highlights: Gift Shop
Notes: A busy, high energy place that offers well made wines. Late in the day, this is a great place to visit. Right next door the restaurant Mustard's Grill.
Part of Tour on page: 149

Coturri & Sons Winery 6725 Enterprise Rd.   Glen Ellen
707.525.9126 www.coturri.com
Hours: by appt only   Tasting Fee: none listed
Wine List: Blend, Cabernet Sauvignon, Carignane, Merlot, Pinot Noir, Sangiovese, Syrah, Zinfandel
Added Highlights: Very private, Biodynamic/Organic

Cuvaison Estate Wines 4550 Silverado Trail N.   Calistoga 707.942.2468
Tasting room at the Vineyards: 1221 Duhig Rd.   Napa 707.942.2455   (Carneros)
Hours: 10am - 5pm   Tasting Fee: $8 - $10; $15 w/tour
Wine List: Pinot Noir, Cabernet Sauvignon, Chardonnay, Merlot, Syrah, Zinfandel, Port
Added Highlights: Gift Shop, Picnic Area, Tours
Notes: Although it is placed at the top of the valley, the grapes and the wine are true Carneros; crisp, clean, and good with food. A small fun tasting room, a good staff, and a wonderfully convenient picnic area. Nice gift shop. The Carneros tasting room is across Duhig Rd. from Domaine Carneros.
Part of Northern Napa Tour on page: 199

D'Argenzio Winery 1301 Cleveland Ave. Ste A Santa Rosa (Northern Sonoma)
707.546.2466 inquiries@dargenziowine.com www.dargenziowine.com
Hours: by appt only   Tasting Fee: none listed
Wine List: Chardonnay, Pinot Noir, Zinfandel, Tocai Friulano, Merlot, Cabernet Sauvignon, Petite Sirah

Darioush 4240 Silverado Trail Napa
707.257.2345 x 130 concierge@darioush.com www.darioush.com
Hours: 10:30am - 5pm Appt for 6 or more in party Tasting Fee: $20
Wine List: Cabernet Sauvignon, Shiraz, Chardonnay, Merlot, Sauvignon, Blanc, Pinot Noir, Viognier
Added Highlights: Architecture, Gardens, Gift Shop, Pet Friendly
Notes: A Persian dream come to Napa. Done in the style of a Persian temple it is a joy to visit. One of the three best gift shops in the valley, and wines that get better and better every year. Not Stag's Leap by district but Stag's Leap by style. A Destination Winery. The owner's are from the Iranian town of Syrah and their winery is a celebration of the ancient Persian winery traditions. The stone was quarried in Iran, milled and carved in Italy and assembled in Napa at a cost of thirty million dollars. If Napa is the land of grand wineries, and it is, then Darioush is a natural addition.
Part of Tour on page: 69, 119, 123, 127, 131, 157, 159, 197, 207

Dashe Cellars 4791 Dry Creek Rd. Healdsburg (Northern Sonoma)
707.433.0100 TR   www.dashecellars.com
Hours: 10:30am - 4:30pm daily Tasting Fee: $5 glass purchase
Wine List: Riesling, Zinfandel, Merlot, Cabernet Sauvignon
Notes: Tastings are held at Family Wineries, a collective tasting room.

David Arthur Vineyards 1521 Sage Canyon Rd. St. Helena
707.963.5190 tours@davidarthur.com www.davidarthur.com
Hours: by appt only   Tasting Fee: none listed
Wine List: Sauvignon Blanc, Chardonnay, Merlot, Cabernet Sauvignon, Blends
Added Highlights: Gardens

David Coffaro Vineyard & Winery 7485 Dry Creek Rd. Geyserville (Northern Sonoma)
707.433.9715 www.coffaro.com
Hours: 11am - 4pm daily Tours by appt Fri 11am and 1pm Tasting Fee: none listed
Wine List: Pinot Noir, Cabernet Sauvignon, Petite Sirah, Carignane, Zinfandel, Estate Cuvee
Added Highlights: Tours

Davis Family Vineyards 52 Front St. Healdsburg (Northern Sonoma)
707.569.0171 sales@daviswines.com www.davisfamilyvineyards.com
Hours: 11am - 6pm daily Tasting Fee: none listed
Wine List: Chardonnay, Syrah, Zinfandel, Cabernet Sauvignon, Pinot Noir, Apple Brandy, Olive Oil
Added Highlights: Bocce Court
Notes: Tastings at Front Street Wineries, a collective tasting room.

De La Montanya Winery & Vineyards 999 Foreman Ln. Healdsburg (Northern Sonoma)
707.433.3711 appt dennis@dlmwine.com www.dlmwine.com
Hours: 11am - 4:30pm weekends or call for appt   Tasting Fee: $5 (CWP)
Wine List: Fumé Blanc, Viognier, Chardonnay, Rosé, Pinot Meunier, Pinot Noir, Zinfandel, Primitivo,
Petite Sirah, Syrah, Tempranillo, Cabernet Sauvignon, Blends
Added Highlights: Bocce Court, a newer winery with a fun approach

De Loach Vineyards 1791 Olivet Rd. Santa Rosa (Northern Sonoma)
707.526.9111 winestore@deloachvineyards.com www.deloachvineyards.com
Hours: 10am - 4:30pm daily   Tasting Fee: $5 - $10 (CWP)
Wine List: Sauvignon Blanc, Chardonnay, Pinot Noir, Zinfandel
Added Highlights: Biodynamic/Organic, Picnic Area, Tours, Vegetable Garden
Notes: The big winery in the Olivet area. Friendly, with a Sonoma casual staff, great wines in an intimate
setting. Biodynamic commitment and it shows in the quality. A nice location and convenient to the rest
of the Russian River Valley. Tours include barrel tasting at 10, 12 and 2pm daily. Also special OFS Re-
serve tasting with food pairing at 11, 1 and 3pm daily.
Part of Tour on page: 55, 177

de Lorimier Winery 2001 Hwy. 128 Geyserville (Northern Sonoma)
707.857.2000 discover@delorimierwinery.com www.delorimierwinery.com
Hours: 10am - 4:30pm   Tasting Fee: $5 - $10 (CWP)
Wine List: Sauvignon Blanc, Chardonnay, Meritage, Merlot, Blends, Botrytised dessert wine called Lace.
Under Mosaic label: Hand crafted, small lot vineyard designate Cabernet, Zinfandel, Malbec, Sangio-
vese, Sauvignon Blanc, Chardonnay, Merlot and Meritage
De Natale Vineyards   11020 Eastside Rd.   Healdsburg
707.431.8460 ronsandy@denatalevineyards.com www.denatalevineyards.com
Hours: by appt only   Tasting Fee: none listed
Wine List: Pinot Noir, Sangiovese, Petite Sirah, Syrah, Cabernet Sauvignon

Deerfield Ranch Winery 1310 Warm Springs Rd. Glen Ellen
707.833.5215 www.deerfieldranch.com
Hours: by appt only   Tasting Fee: $25
Wine List: Blends, Meritage, Cabernet, Chardonnay, Dessert Wine, Merlot, Pinot Noir, Sangiovese, Sau-
vignon Blanc, Syrah, Zinfandel, Grapeseed Oil
Added Highlights: Biodynamic/Organic, very high quality wines poured in their stunning caves

Del Dotto Estate Winery & Caves 1445 St. Helena Hwy. St. Helena
707.256.3332 mail@deldottvineyards.com www.deldottvineyards.com
Hours: 11am - 5pm daily Tasting Fee: $20 and up $30 bar tastings, $50 cave experience
Wine List: Cabernet Sauvignon, Merlot, Cabernet Franc, Sangiovese along with Pinot Noir from the So-
noma Coast and will soon be making Chardonnay
Added Highlights: Architecture, Caves, Gardens, Gift Shop, Tours
Notes: New facility for Del Dotto with imported marble everywhere! Look for the large amphora at the
entrance drive.

Del Dotto Vineyards 1055 Atlas Peak Rd. Napa
707.256.3332 TR-tours mail@DelDottoVineyards.com www.DelDottoVineyards.com
Hours: 11am - 5pm daily by appt only Tasting Fee: $20 and up Barrel tasting: $40 pp (1 to 1 1/12 hours)
Wine List: Cabernet Sauvignon, Cabernet Franc, Merlot, Sangiovese, Petit Sirah, Zinfandel
Added Highlights: One of the three oldest caves in Napa. Art Gallery, Tours and Barrel Tastings done to explore the influence of different types of barrels on the wine's flavors.

Deux Amis Wines 1960 Dry Creek Rd. Healdsburg (Northern Sonoma)
707.431.7945 friends@deuxamiswines.com www.deuxamiswines.com
Hours: by appt only   Tasting Fee: Complimentary
Wine List: Zinfandel, Petite Sirah

Diamond Oaks 1595 Oakville Grade Oakville
707.948.3000 info@diamond-oaks.com www.diamond-oaks.com
Hours: 10am - 5pm daily   Tasting Fee: $5
Wine List: Chardonnay, Pinot Noir, Merlot, Cabernet Sauvignon
Added Highlights: Picnic Area
Notes: Great views, great picnic area

Domaine Carneros 1240 Duhig Rd. Napa   (Carneros)
707.257.0101 tours@domainecarneros.com www.domainecarneros.com
Hours: 10am - 6pm daily Closed Major Holidays Tasting Fee: table service by the glass
Wine List: Brut Cuvee, Brut Rosé, Le Reve Blanc de Blancs, Pinot Noir
Added Highlights: Architecture, Gardens, Gift Shop, Views
Notes: A destination winery, very convenient to San Francisco. Part of the Taittinger family wineries specializing in Sparkling Wines, they produce some of the most authentic 'Champagne' in the area, elegant, refined and beautiful, like their location and building. The building is based on one of their ancestral homes in France, but the extensive patios and inside tasting rooms are joys to relax in. Suitable for large groups.
Part of Tour on page: 69, 109, 125, 127, 163

Domaine Chandon 1 California Dr. Yountville
707.944.2280 www.domainechandon.com
Hours: 10am - 6pm daily   Tasting Fee: $10 or by the glass
Wine List: Brut, Blanc de Noirs, Rosé, Sparkling Chardonnay, Blanc de Blancs, Pinot Noir, Pinot Meunier, Chardonnay, Unoaked Pinot Noir Rosé, Unoaked Chardonnay
Added Highlights: Architecture, Gardens, Gift Shop, Restaurant
Notes: A great French sparkling wine house with lots of rooms for guests. Chandon was the first of the European companies to invest in Napa and they incorporated a top notch restaurant, Etoile, in their property. A lot of fun and their patio is a great place to finish the day.
Part of Tour on page: 117, 149, 195

Domaine Danica Winery 1960 Dry Creek Rd. Healdsburg (Northern Sonoma)
707.431.1902
Hours: by appt only shares bldg w/Wilson Winery Tasting Fee: none listed
Wine List: Chardonnay, Pinot Noir

Dominari 210 Camino Oruga Napa
707.226.1600 marieschultz@dominari.com www.dominari.com
Hours: by appt only daily located near Napa Airport Tasting Fee: Complimentary
Wine List: Cabernet Sauvignon, Merlot

Dry Creek Vineyard 3770 Lambert Bridge Rd. Healdsburg (Northern Sonoma)
707.433.1000 www.drycreekvineyard.com
Hours: 10:30am - 4:30pm Tasting Fee: $5 - $10 (CWP)
Wine List: Dry Chenin Blanc, Fumé Blanc, Zinfandel, Merlot, Cabernet Sauvignon, Meritage, Dessert wines, blends
Added Highlights: Gift Shop, Picnic Area
Notes: Right at the center of the Dry Creek Valley, they produce a wonderful array of wines and have for many years. Nice tasting room and good picnic area. Fun events.
Part of Tour on page: 179

Duckhorn Vineyards 3027 Silverado Trail N. St. Helena
707.963.7108 welcome@duckhorn.com www.duckhorn.com
Hours: 10am - 4pm by Tasting Fee: $20
Wine List: Sauvignon Blanc, Merlot, Cabernet Sauvignon
Added Highlights: Architecture, Gardens, Gift Shop
Notes: They do a wonderful sit down tasting in their Georgian style mansion tasting room. The wines are first class and the staff is very friendly once they get to know you. Duckhorn is very respected in the area as a mentor to other winemakers. The winery, along with its sister wineries, Paraduxx in Yountville and Goldeneye in Mendocino County were all sold by the family.
Part of Tour on page: 163, 201, 203

Dunn Vineyards 805 White Cottage Rd. N. Angwin
707.965.3642 dunnvineyards@sbcglobal.net www.dunnvineyards.com
Hours: by appt only   Tasting Fee: PIE
Wine List: 100% Cabernet Sauvignon - 2 labels One is 100% Howell Mountain grapes, the other adds 15% grapes from the Napa Valley floor.
Notes: Rustic winery on the top of Howell Mountain. Randy Dunn was one of the pioneers of producing top quality wines on Howell Mountain and acted as a mentor for other wine makers that followed, they are starting to open up to visitors. Great caves.

Dutch Henry Winery 4310 Silverado Trail Calistoga
707.942.5771 info@dutchhenry.com www.dutchhenry.com
Hours: 10am - 5pm   Tasting Fee: $10 (CWP)
Wine List: Cabernet Sauvignon, Syrah, Argos (Bordeaux Blend), Zinfandel, Pinot Noir, Cabernet Franc, Chardonnay
Added Highlights: Pet Friendly
Notes: Small winery with laid back style and well made wines.

Dutcher Crossing Winery 8533 Dry Creek Rd. Healdsburg (Northern Sonoma)
707.431.2700 www.dutchercrossingwinery.com
Hours: 11am - 5pm daily Tours & private groups by appt Tasting Fee: $5
Wine List: Zinfandel, Chardonnay, Cabernet Sauvignon, Merlot, Port, Petite Sirah, Sauvignon Blanc
Added Highlights: Picnic Area, Tours

Ehlers Estate 3222 Ehlers Ln. St. Helena
707.963.5972 info@ehlersestate.com www.ehlersestate.com
Hours: 10am - 4pm daily Tasting Fee: none listed
Wine List: Cabernet Sauvignon, Merlot, Sauvignon Blanc, Cabernet Franc, Zinfandel
Added Highlights: Biodynamic, Great Building, Bocce Court, Tours
Notes: Outdoor winery with interesting tasting room. Seminar-like tasting format with enthusiastic staff. Private tours & wine tasting are also available by appointment.

Elizabeth Spencer Wines 1165 Rutherford Rd. Rutherford
707.963.6067 tastingroom@elizabethspencerwines.com www.elizabethspencerwines.com
Hours: 10am - 6pm Tasting Fee: $5 - $10
Wine List: Chardonnay, Pinot Noir, Syrah, Cabernet Sauvignon
Added Highlights: Architecture
Notes: A cute little tasting room on Rutherford Road in the old Post Office. The grapes are from Sonoma and the winemakers are first rate. The staff is very friendly and knowledgeable and everyone has a great time there. Some excellent Pinot Noir and Chardonnay.
Part of Tour on page: 143

Elyse Winery 2100 Hoffman Ln. Rutherford
707.944.2900 appt www.elysewinery.com
Hours: 10am - 5pm by appt only Tasting Fee: $5 (CWP)
Wine List: Syrah, Petite Sirah, Zinfandel, Cabernet Sauvignon, Chardonnay, Rosé of Pinot Noir, Blend
Notes: Charming small winery with great Zinfandels

Envy Wines 1170 Tubbs Ln. Calistoga
707.942.4670 www.envywine.com
Hours: 10am - 4:30pm by appt only Tasting Fee: $10
Wine List: Cabernet Sauvignon, Petite Sirah, Sauvignon, Blanc, Blend

Eric Ross Winery 14301 Arnold Dr. Glen Ellen
707.939.8525 www.ericross.com
Hours: 11:30am - 6pm Wed. - Sun. Tasting Fee: none listed
Wine List: Viognier, Chardonnay, Pinot Noir, Carignane, Zinfandel, Syrah, Zin-Syrah Port
Notes: The tasting room is very convenient to down town Glen Ellen. Put this together on a tour with Benziger (for their tram tour and picnic tables) and Audelssa, picking up a picnic at the Glen Ellen Market. Also tasted at Locals Tasting Room, a collective.
Part of Tour on page: 48

Etude 1250 Cuttings Wharf Rd. Napa (Carneros)
707.257.5300 www.etudewines.com
Hours: 11am - 4pm Sat other days by appt Tasting Fee: $15 - $25
Wine List: Pinot Noir, Merlot, Cabernet Sauvignon, Pinot Blanc, Pinot Gris
Added Highlights: Tours
Notes: A Beautiful Carneros winery specializing in Pinot Noir

Everett Ridge Winery 435 W. Dry Creek Rd. Healdsburg (Northern Sonoma)
707.433.1637 Info@EverettRidge.com www.everettridge.com
Hours: 10am - 4:30pm daily appt req for groups of 8 or more Tasting Fee: none listed
Wine List: Zinfandel, Syrah, Cabernet Sauvignon, Sauvignon Blanc, Chardonnay, Pinot Noir, Pinot Gris, Port, Blend
Added Highlights: Great Views
Notes: They are a little bit off by themselves in Dry Creek but worth the short drive. Great views, good wine and nice people. Tasting on the patio is wonderful.
Part of Tour on page: 59

F. Teldeschi Winery 3555 Dry Creek Rd. Healdsburg (Northern Sonoma)
707.433.6626 dteldeschi@neteze.com www.teldeschi.com
Hours: 12pm - 5pm daily additional times by appt Tasting Fee: $2 - $5
Wine List: Zinfandel, Zinfandel Port, Pink Zinfandel, Petite Sirah, Blends

Failla   3530 Silverado Trail   St. Helena
707.963.0530   info@faillawines.com   www.faillawines.com
Hours: 11am - 4pm by appt   Thu - Sun by appt   Tasting Fee: $10
Wine List: Pinot Noir, Viognier, Syrah, Chardonnay
Added Highlights: Architecture, Caves
Notes: A small winery specializing in Pinot Noir and Chardonnay. They may do the best Pinot Noir in Napa, in part because the grapes come from Sonoma's Russian River Valley and Coastal region. Great caves & winery, wonderful staff in a charming bungalow tasting room. Right across from Rombauer.
Part of Tour on page: 195

Family Wineries   4791 Dry Creek Rd.   Healdsburg   (Northern Sonoma)
707.433.0100   tastingroom@familywines.com   www.familywineriesdrycreekvalley.com
Hours: 10:30am - 4:30pm daily   Tasting Fee: $5 glass purchase
Wine List: Cabernet Sauvignon, Merlot, Petite Sirah, Red Meritage Blends, Sangiovese, Syrah, Zinfandel, Chardonnay, Pinot Grigio, Sauvignon Blanc, Barbara, Charbono, Syrah Rosé, Zinfandel Port, Late Harvest Zinfandel
Added Highlights: Bocce Court, Picnic, Restaurant/Market
Notes: A collective tasting room for Collier Falls, Dashe Cellars, Mietz, Philip Staley, Lago di Merlo, Forth and more. Map on page 59.

Family Wineries of Sonoma Valley   9380 Sonoma Hwy.   Kenwood   (www.familywineries.com
Hours: 11am - 6pm daily   Tasting Fee: CWP
Wine List: Various wines from multiple wineries
Added Highlights: Art Gallery, Gift Shop
Notes: A collective tasting room for David Noyes, Deerfield Ranch, Mayo Family Winery, Noel Wine Cellars, Meredith Wine Cellars   Part of Tour on page: 48

Fantesca Estate & Winery   2920 Spring Mountain Rd.   St. Helena
707.968.9229   info@fantesca.com   www.fantesca.com
Hours: by appt only   Tasting Fee: none listed
Wine List: Cabernet Sauvignon, Chardonnay

Far Niente   1350 Acacia Dr.   Oakville
707.944.2861   info@farniente.com   www.farniente.com
Hours: 10am - 4pm by appt only Mon - Sat   Tasting Fee: $75
Wine List: Cabernet Sauvignon, Chardonnay
Added Highlights: Architecture, Gardens, Tours
Notes: One of the crown jewels of Napa architecture surrounded by wonderful gardens and grounds. An extensive tour comes with the tasting and the wines are world class. It is an expensive ticket but one you remember. The tour includes a visit to a fabulous collection of cars. Plan on 1 ½ hours as a minimum for your visit. And do not arrive late for your appointment.
Part of Tour on page: 167

Farella-Park Vineyards   2222 N. Third Ave.   Napa
707.254.9489   www.farella.com
Hours: by appt only   Tasting Fee: none listed
Wine List: Sauvignon Blanc, Merlot, Cabernet Sauvignon Blanc, Blends
Added Highlights: Picnic Area

Favero Vineyards   3939 Lovall Valley Rd.   Sonoma
707.935.3939   faverovineyards@vom.com   www.faverovineyards.com
Hours: by appt only   Also tasted at Sonoma Enoteca   Tasting Fee: none listed
Wine List: Super Tuscan style Blend, Sangiovese, Moscato

Ferrari-Carano Vineyards & Winery 8761 Dry Creek Rd. Healdsburg (Northern Sonoma)
800.831.0381 customerservice@ferrari-carano.com www.ferrari-carano.com
Hours: 10am - 5pm Tasting Fee: $5 (CWP >$25)
Wine List: Grenache Rosé, Chardonnay, Sangiovese, Syrah, Cabernet Sauvignon, Fumé Blanc, Zinfandel, Merlot, Blends
Added Highlights: Architecture, Caves, Gardens, Gift Shop, Tours
Notes: The crown jewel of the Dry Creek Valley. Beautiful buildings and gardens in a spectacular location. If you visit Dry Creek Valley you have to visit Ferrari-Carano. For a more intimate experience go downstairs to the Enoteca & don't miss the hidden gardens behind the wall to the right as you approach.
Part of Tour on page: 59, 177, 179, 183

Field Stone Winery & Vineyard 10075 Highway 128 Healdsburg (Northern Sonoma)
707.433.7266 www.fieldstonewinery.com
Hours: by appt only Tasting Fee: none listed
Wine List: Chardonnay, Pinot Noir

Fleury Winery 950 Galleron Rd. Rutherford
707.967.8333 www.fleurywinery.com
Hours: 9am - 5pm by appt only Tasting Fee: $25
Wine List: Bordeaux varietals
Notes: Very high energy tasting room

Flora Springs Winery 677 S. St Helena Hwy. St. Helena (TR next door to Dean & DeLuca)
707.967.8032 mmh@kswines.com www.florasprings.com
Hours: 10am - 5pm Tasting Fee: $5 - $12
Flora Springs Winery by Appt 1978 W. Zinfandel Ln. 707.963.5711 (Winery)
Wine List: Cabernet Sauvignon, Sangiovese, Merlot, Rosato, Chardonnay, Pinot Grigio, Blends: Trilogy (red blend of Cabernet Franc, Merlot, petit Verdot& Malbec), Soliloquy (white blend)
Added Highlights: Gift Shop, Picnic Area. Tasting Room under construction as of Spring 2008

Folie a Deux Winery 7481 St. Helena Hwy. Oakville
707.963.1160 www.folieadeux.com
Hours: 10am - 6pm Tasting Fee: none listed
Wine List: Blends, Zinfandel, Cabernet Sauvignon, Sangiovese, Syrah
Added Highlights: Picnic Area

Folio Winemaker's Studio 1285 Dealy Ln. Napa (Carneros)
707.256.2757 TR www.foliowine.com
Hours: 10am - 5pm daily Tasting Fee: $10
Wine List: Cabernet Sauvignon, Chardonnay, Merlot, Petite Sirah, Pinot Noir, Rosé, Sauvignon Blanc, Syrah, Zinfandel
Notes: A collective tasting room owned by Michael Mondavi for California winemakers, Hangtime Cellars, Hunterdon, I'M Wines, Mayro-Murdick, Medusa, Oberon, Rocinante, Spellbound; plus wines from France, Argentina, Spain, Austria, Italy & New Zealand 24 labels, 7 countries, 4 continents
Part of Tour on page: 69

Foppiano Vineyards 12707 Old Redwood Hwy. Healdsburg (Northern Sonoma)
707.433.7272 hospitality@oppiano.com www.foppiano.com
Hours: 10am - 4:30pm Self guided vineyard tour Tasting Fee: Complimentary
Wine List: Zinfandel, Merlot, Chardonnay, Sangiovese, Cabernet Sauvignon, Pinot Noir, Petite Sirah, White Zinfandel
Added Highlights: Picnic Area, Tours

Forchini Vineyards & Winery 5141 Dry Creek Rd. Healdsburg (Northern Sonoma)
707.431.8886 wine@forchini.com www.forchini.com
Hours: 11am - 4:30pm Fri - Sun Parties of 8 or more require reservations Tasting Fee: $5
Wine List: Cabernet Sauvignon, Chardonnay, Pinot Noir, Zinfandel, Tuscan & Bordeaux Style Blends
Added Highlights: Gardens, Tours

Forman Vineyards 1501 Big Rock Rd. St. Helena
707.963.3900 appt   www.formanvineyard.net
Hours: by appt only   Tasting Fee: PIE
Wine List: Cabernet Sauvignon, Cabernet Franc, Sauvignon Blanc, Chardonnay, Merlot, Petite Verdot
Added Highlights: Architecture
Notes: Very private, tucked away in its own canyon down a steep road, Forman makes wonderful wines

Forth Vineyards 4791 Dry Creek Rd. Healdsburg (Northern Sonoma)
707.433.0100 TR wine@forthvineyards.com www.forthvineyards.com
Hours: 10:30am - 4:30pm daily Tasting Fee: $5 glass purchase
Wine List: Sauvignon Blanc, Rose, Syrah, Cabernet Sauvignon
Notes: Tastings are at Family Wineries, a collective tasting room. The Forth family sometimes hosts tastings for collectors at their winery in the hills above Dry Creek.

Franciscan Oakville Estate 1178 Galleron Rd. St. Helena
707.963.7111 www.franciscan.com
Hours: 10am - 5pm   Tasting Fee: $10 - $15
Wine List: Cabernet Sauvignon, Chardonnay, Merlot, Meritage
Added Highlights: Gift Shop

Frank Family Vineyards 1091 Larkmead Ln. Calistoga
707.942.0859 info@frankfamilyvineyards.com www.frankfamilyvineyards.com
Hours: 10am - 4pm   Tasting Fee: Complimentary
Wine List: Sangiovese, Zinfandel, Cabernet Sauvignon, Chardonnay, Sparklers, Zinfandel Port
Added Highlights: Architecture, Picnic Area
Notes: One of the best tasting room staffs in the valley. Fantastic wines with a great story and a sparkling wine that they really could call Champagne and they'll tell you why. A fun time is had by all. Good picnic area and great history. They are in the middle of a major renovation and restoration of their historic Larkmead Winery building, so we expect them to be better than ever.
Part of Tour on page: 141, 149, 199, 201, 203

Frazier Winery 70 Rapp Ln. Napa
707.255.3444 x 107 appt sales@frazierwinery.com www.frazierwinery.com
Hours: 10am - 4pm by appt only Mon - Sat Tasting Fee: $20
Wine List: Cabernet Sauvignon, Merlot, Blend
Added Highlights: Architecture, Caves, Picnic Area
Notes: The whole tasting is done in their caves and it's a lot of fun. Located to the east of the city of Napa, it is out of the way but worth the ride. The wines are great, the story interesting and plan on at least a couple of hours to enjoy this winery. Tasting always includes crackers, cheese and chocolate.
Part of Tour on page: 129

Freemark Abbey Winery 3022 St. Helena Hwy. N. St. Helena
707.963.9698 x 241   www.freemarkabbey.com
Hours: 10am - 6pm Summer, 5pm Winter   Tasting Fee: $10 - $20
Wine List: Cabernet Sauvignon, Viognier, Chardonnay, Blends

Frick Winery 23072 Walling Rd. Geyserville (Northern Sonoma)
707.857.1980 frick@frickwinery.com www.frickwinery.com
Hours: 12pm - 4:30pm Sat & Sun Closed last weekend in April Tasting Fee: Complimentary
Wine List: Viognier, Cinsault, Syrah, Rosé, Merlot, Carignane, Blends

Fritz Cellars 24691 Dutcher Creek Rd. Cloverdale (Northern Sonoma)
707.894.3389 Hours: 10:30am - 4:30pm daily Tasting Fee: none listed
Wine List: Chardonnay, Pinot Noir

Frog's Leap Winery 8815 Conn Creek Rd. Rutherford
800.959.4704 TR & tours ribbit@frogsleap.com www.frogsleap.com
Hours: 10am - 4pm Mon - Sat Tasting includes a tour Tasting Fee: Complimentary
Wine List: Merlot, Zinfandel, Chardonnay, Sauvignon Blanc, Cabernet Sauvignon, Syrah, Blends
Added Highlights: Biodynamic/Organic, Gift Shop, Tours
Notes: Great tour. This organic winery has a new hospitality center with a very nice staff.

Front Street Wineries 51-61 Front St. Healdsburg (Northern Sonoma)
707.433.1290 www.frontstreetwineries.com
Hours: 11am - 6pm daily Tasting Fee: none listed
Wine List: Various wines from multiple wineries
Notes: A collective tasting room for Camellia Cellars, Holdredge Winery, Huntington, Davis Family
Vineyards, Sapphire Hill Winery

Gallo of Sonoma Winery 320 Center St. Healdsburg (Healdsburg Plaza) (Northern Sonoma)
707.433.2458 www.gallosonoma.com
Hours: 10am - 6pm daily Tasting Room is on the Plaza Tasting Fee: $0 - $12
Wine List: Barbera, Cabernet Sauvignon, Chardonnay, Merlot, Pinot Gris, Pinot Noir, Syrah, Zinfandel
Added Highlights: Gift Shop, Tours

Gargiulo Vineyards 575 Oakville Crossroad Napa
707.944.2770 sharon@gargiulovineyards.com www.gargiulovineyards.com
Hours: 10:30am - 3:30pm by appt only Two appts daily Tasting Fee: $25
Wine List: 90% Cabernet 10% Merlot Blend, 96% Sangiovese 4% Cabernet Blend
Added Highlights: Architecture, Gardens, Views
Notes: Very private, charming winery with great views and charming people.

Gary Farrell Vineyards & Winery 10701 Westside Rd. Healdsburg (Northern Sonoma)
707.473.2900 www.garyfarrellwines.com
Hours: 11am - 4pm daily Tasting Fee: $5 - $15
Wine List: Chardonnay, Pinot Noir, Zinfandel, Merlot, Cabernet Sauvignon, Blend
Added Highlights: Architecture, Views at the top of a high hill

Geyser Peak Winery 22281 Chianti Rd. Geyserville (Northern Sonoma)
707.857.9400 www.geyserpeak.com
Hours: 10am - 5pm daily Tasting Fee: $5 - $10
Wine List: Cabernet Sauvignon, Chardonnay, Merlot, Sauvignon Blanc, Shiraz

Girard Winery 1551 Sage Canyon Rd. St. Helena
707.968.9297 steve@girardwinery.com www.girardwinery.com
Hours: 11am - 4pm daily by appt limited to 30 visitors per week. Tasting Fee: $25
Wine List: Artistry - (Bordeaux Blend of 56% Cabernet Sauvignon, 21% Merlot, 9% Cabernet Franc, 9%
Malbec & 5% Petite Verdot), Cabernet Franc, Petite Sirah, Zinfandel, Chardonnay, Sauvignon Blanc

Gloria Ferrer Caves & Vineyards 23555 Carneros Hwy. 121 Sonoma   (Carneros)
707.996.7256 info@gloriaferrer.com www.gloriaferrer.com
Hours: 10am - 5pm daily   Tasting Fee: $4 - $10 by the glass
Wine List: Sparklers, Blanc de Blancs, Brut, Blanc de Noirs, Cuvee, Brut Rosé, Chardonnay, Pinot Noir, Syrah
Added Highlights: Architecture, Gardens, Gift Shop, Restaurant/Market, Views
Notes: Very convenient to San Francisco, they offer their sparkling wines by the glass. The views from their patio are wonderful and this is a great place to either begin or end a tour.
Part of Tour on page: 41, 93, 95, 109

Goosecross Cellars 1119 State Ln. Yountville
707.944.1986 hospitality@goosecross.com www.goosecross.com
Hours: 10am - 4:30pm daily   Tasting Fee: $5 - $10
Wine List: Viognier, Chenin Blanc, Sauvignon Blanc, Chardonnay, Sparkling Rosé, Cabernet Sauvignon, Zinfandel, Merlot, Pinot Noir, Syrah, Blends
Added Highlights: Gift Shop, Picnic Area
Notes: A small family-run winery with a great selection of well-made wines. The tasting room is the barrel room and you'll walk past the fermentation tanks to get to it. The staff is great, the experience informal and friendly. Everyone loves Goosecross.
Part of Tour on page: 117, 121, 141, 195

Grange Sonoma 23564 Highway 121 Sonoma, 707.933.8980 www.grangesonoma.com
Collective tasting room at Cornerstone featuring small, excellent Sonoma Wineries. Pgs. 97, 109, 123

Grgich Hills Cellar 1829 St. Helena Hwy. S. Rutherford
707.963.2784 info@grgich.com www.grgich.com
Hours: 9:30am - 4:30pm daily Tours $10 at 11am & 2pm daily Tasting Fee: $10 (logo glass)
Wine List: Chardonnay, Fumé Blanc, Violetta (botrytis dessert wine), Cabernet Sauvignon, Zinfandel, Merlot
Added Highlights: Biodynamic/Organic, Gift Shop, Tours
Notes: Mike Grgich is one of the grand old men of Napa. He produced Chateau Montelena's award winning Chardonnay that put Napa on the world map at the Judgment of Paris in 1976. Owners of the largest Biodynamic wineries in America. The tasting room is the barrel room, relaxed, earthy and fun. The wines are wonderfully made and a good value.
Part of Tour on page: 62, 115, 143, 149, 191

Groth Vineyards & Winery 750 Oakville Cross Rd. Oakville
707.754.4254 appt info@grothwines.com www.grothvineyards.com
Hours: 10am - 4pm by appt   Tasting Fee: $10 (CWP)
Wine List: Cabernet Sauvignon, Chardonnay, Sauvignon Blanc
Added Highlights: Architecture. A Grand building but a simple tasting.

Grove Street Winery 1441 Grove St. Healdsburg (Northern Sonoma)
707.433.6734 TR info@grovestreetwinery.com www.grovestreetwinery.com
Hours: 10am - 4pm Fri - Sun   Tasting Fee: none listed
Wine List: Cabernet Sauvignon, Chardonnay, Merlot, Meritage, Blend

Guilliams Vineyards 3851 Spring Mountain Rd. St. Helena
707.963.9059   Hours: by appt only   Tasting Fee: none listed Wine List: Bordeaux varietals

Gundlach Bundschu Winery 2000 Denmark St. Sonoma   (Carneros)
707.938.5277 info@gunbun.com www.gunbun.com
Hours: 11am - 4:30pm Tasting Fee: $5 - $10
Wine List: Zinfandel, Gewürztraminer, Chardonnay, Pinot Noir, N.V. Red Bearitage, Gamay Beaujolais, Cabernet Franc, Merlot, Cabernet Sauvignon, N.V. Sonoma Red (continued next page)

Added Highlights: Architecture, Gardens, Gift Shop, Picnic Area, Tours
Notes: Five generations of grape growers and winemakers, just minutes from the Sonoma Plaza. A beautiful location and completely authentic Sonoma with a great tasting room staff, a fun but short tour of the caves and nice picnic tables.
Part of Tour on page: 97

Hagafen Cellars 4160 Silverado Trail Napa
707.252.0781 info@hagafen.com www.hagafen.com
Hours: by appt only Tours by appt daily at 11am Tasting Fee: coupon available online
Wine List: Riesling, Syrah
Added Highlights: Tours, Kosher wines that have been served at the White House

Hall 401 St. Helena Hwy S. St. Helena
707.967.2620 www.hallwines.com
Hours: 10am - 5:30pm   Tasting Fee: $10
Wine List: Cabernet Sauvignon, Merlot, Sauvignon Blanc
Added Highlights: Architecture, Art Gallery, Gardens, Gift Shop, Picnic Area
Notes: On their way to becoming a destination winery, the Halls are a glamorous talented couple and their tasting room is charming. Pick up a lunch at Dean & DeLuca (right next door) and picnic under the mulberry trees. Noted architect Frank Gehry is designing their new winery and it should be spectacular. The wines are well made with huge potential considering the quality of grapes on their lands. Note: At the time of printing the construction is going full tilt. The tasting room is an oasis surrounded by this grand venture, so if you would like to see the 'in process' it will make your future visits that much more interesting. They also do tastings at their mountain top winery off Rutherford Hill Road by appointment in one of the most beautiful caves in America.
Part of Tour on page: 62, 153, 159, 163, 197

Hanna Winery & Vineyards 9280 Highway 128 Healdsburg (Northern Sonoma)
707.575.3371 appt.   www.hannawinery.com
Hours: 10am - 4pm private tours of winery and wetlands by appt Tasting Fee: $10
Wine List: Merlot, Zinfandel, Pinot Noir, Cabernet Sauvignon, Sauvignon Blanc, Syrah, Blends, Cabernet Franc, Rosé
Added Highlights: Architecture, Gardens, Tours
Notes: At the lower edge of Alexander Valley, this Asian style winery sits in a spectacular location. Wonderful wines, big reds with lots of depth and softness. And they have a good staff.
Part of Tour on page: 59, 181

Hanzell Vineyards 18596 Lomita Ave. Sonoma
707.996.3860 appt guests@hanzell.com www.hanzell.com
Hours: by appt only   Tasting Fee: $45 - $150
Wine List: Chardonnay, Pinot Noir
Added Highlights: Architecture, Views
Notes: Private tour and sit down tastings. Stunning views. They are the site of California's oldest Pinot Noit vineyards and some of the oldest Chardonnay. Very high quality wines from old vines, their vineyards can be seen from downtown Sonoma. Great old winery building based on traditional European designs, and newer caves and winery. A bit of a ride up a winding road but well worth the effort.

Hartford Family Wines 8075 Martinelli Rd. Forestville (Northern Sonoma)
707.887.8010 hartford.winery@hartfordwines.com www.hartfordwines.com
Hours: 10am - 4:30pm daily reservations req for 6 or more Tasting Fee: $5 - $15
Wine List: Pinot Noir, Chardonnay, Multiple Old Vine Zinfandel
Added Highlights: Architecture

Notes: Out of the way in the Russian River Valley but they produce wonderful wines. Nice people in a pretty location more than worth the visit.
Part of Tour on page: 185

Hart's Desire Wines 2062 Pinercrest Dr. Santa Rosa (Northern Sonoma)
707.579.1687 john@hartsdesirewines.com www.hartsdesirewines.com
Hours: by appt only   Tasting Fee: Complimentary
Wine List: Cabernet Franc, Cabernet Sauvignon, Chardonnay, Claret, Merlot, Pinot Noir, Sauvignon Blanc, Syrah, Zinfandel

Hartwell Vineyards 5795 Silverado Trail Napa
707.255.4269 info@hartwellvineyards.com www.hartwellvineyards.com
Hours: by appt only   Tasting Fee: $45
Wine List: Cabernet Sauvignon, Merlot
Added Highlights: A Stag's Leap District Winery, Architecture, Gardens

Harvest Moon Estate & Winery 2192 Olivet Rd. Santa Rosa (Northern Sonoma)
707.573.8711 info@harvestmoonwinery.com www.harvestmoonwinery.com
Hours: 10:30am - 5pm Tasting Fee: $0 - $5
Wine List: Zinfandel, Gewürztraminer, Sparkling Gewürztraminer, Pinot Noir
Notes: Charming small winery

Havens Wine Cellars 2055 Hoffman Ln. Napa
707.261.2000 info@havenswine.com www.havenswine.com
Hours: by appt only   Tasting Fee: Complimentary
Wine List: Albariño, Merlot, Syrah, Blends
Notes: Simple tasting room with very good wines, they are one of the few producers of the Spanish wine Albariño, a bright, white wine, which is grown at the edge of the wetlands in the Carneros District.

Heitz Wine Cellars 436 St. Helena Hwy. S. St. Helena
707.963.3542 www.heitzcellar.com
Hours: 11am - 4:30pm   Tasting Fee: $10 - $20
Wine List: Cabernet Sauvignon, Chardonnay, Grignolino, Rosé, Zinfandel, Port
Notes: Great wines with a long reputation

Hess Collection Winery 4411 Redwood Rd. Napa
707.255.8584 TR   www.hesscollection.com
Hours: 10am - 5pm daily Tasting Fee: $10
Wine List: Cabernet Sauvignon, Sauvignon Blanc, Chardonnay, Syrah, Late Harvest Riesling, Malbec, Cabernet Franc, Syrah Rosé, Petite Sirah, Zinfandel, Sauvignon Blanc, Viognier, Semillon, Shiraz, Blends, Olive Oil, Vinegar
Added Highlights: Architecture, Art Gallery, Gardens, Gift Shop
Notes: A world class modern art collection bonded to a wonderful winery tucked up on Mount Veeder. A bit out of the way but it works because it is a destination onto itself. Great gift shop and unique architecture, the old blends with the new in unique ways.
Part of Tour on page: 142

Holdredge Wines 51 Front St. Healdsburg (Northern Sonoma)
707.431.1424 www.holdredge.com
Hours: 11am - 4:30pm daily Tasting Fee: none listed
Wine List: Pinot Noir, Syrah, Zinfandel, Gewürztraminer, Pinot Gris
Notes: Tastings at Front Street Wineries, a collective tasting room.

Homewood Winery 23120 Burndale Rd.   Vineburg   (Carneros)
707.996.6353 www.homewoodwinery.com
Hours: 10am - 4pm daily   Tasting Fee: $0 - $5
Wine List: Sauvignon Blanc, Chardonnay, Pinot Noir, Grenache, Merlot, Syrah, Zinfandel, Blends
Added Highlights: Picnic Area
Notes: A friendly family winery that is completely authentic Sonoma. Good wines, a lot of fun and they do some of the best special events. David Homewood, the owner/winemaker is often on hand to chat about the wines. Small tasting room accommodates 6. Larger parties can be accommodated by tastings outdoors under the canopy
Part of Tour on page: 41, 95

Honig Cellars 850 Rutherford Rd.   Rutherford
707.963.5618 www.honigcellars.com
Hours: 10am - 4pm by appt   Tasting Fee: $10
Wine List: Sauvignon Blanc, Cabernet Sauvignon
Notes; Their tasting patio and room are relaxed and stylish and the mood is relaxed and gracious.

Hook & Ladder Winery 2134 Olivet Rd.   Santa Rosa
707.526.2255   info@hookandladderwinery.com www.hookandladderwinery.com
Hours: 10am - 4:30pm   Bus tours req advance appt   Tasting Fee: Complimentary
Wine List: Cabernet Sauvignon, Zinfandel, White Zinfandel, Pinot Noir, Chardonnay, Gewürztraminer, Rosé, Blends, Olive Oil

Hop Kiln Winery 6050 Westside Rd.   Healdsburg (Northern Sonoma)
707.433.6491 info@hopkilnwinery.com www.hopkilnwinery.com
Hours: 10am - 5pm   Tasting Fee: $5 - $10
Wine List: Cabernet Sauvignon, Chardonnay, Riesling, Zinfandel, Blends
Added Highlights: Architecture, Art Gallery, Gift Shop, Picnic Area
Notes: Placed along a curvy part of Westside Road, it is popular for its great building, a converted Hop Kiln from years past, its great gift shop, including snacks and chocolate, its well made, good value wines and its friendly staff. Nice place for a picnic.
Part of Tour on page: 177

Huntington Wine Cellars 53 Front St. Healdsburg   (Northern Sonoma)
707.433.5215 www.huntingtonwine.com
Hours: 11am - 6pm daily   Tasting Fee: none listed
Wine List: Sauvignon Blanc, Chardonnay, Merlot, Cabernet Sauvignon, Petite Sirah, Syrah
Added Highlights: Art Gallery
Notes: Tastings at Front Street Wineries, a collective tasting room.

Imagery Estate Winery 14335 Highway 12   Glen Ellen
877.550.4278 www.imagerywinery.com
Hours: 10am - 4:30pm   Tasting Fee: $10   Food & Wine Pairing Sat & Sun, Reservation Required $30
Wine List: Cabernet Franc, Petite Sirah, Barbera, Sangiovese, Malbec, White Burgundy, Pinot Blanc, Viognier, Petite Sirah Port, Interlude: Chocolate Infused Port, Blends
Added Highlights: Art Gallery, Biodynamic/Organic, Bocce Court, Gardens, Gift Shop, Picnic Area
Notes: One of the jewels of the Sonoma Valley and a personal favorite. This is where the Benziger family offers their small lot wines and it makes the tasting experience quite exceptional and unusual. And then there is the art work. Imagery has commissioned art work for their labels for over twenty years and they have the largest collection of art created for wine bottles in the world. The originals are on display here in their gallery. The Benziger Family was voted one of the best county employers by their staff.
Part of Tour on page: 48, 97, 99, 101, 103, 105, 107

Inman Family Wines 5793 Skylane Blvd. Ste C Windsor (Northern Sonoma)
707.395.0689 appt   www.inmanfamilywines.com
Hours: by appt only   Tasting Fee: Varies
Wine List: Pinot Gris, Pinot Noir

Iron Horse Vineyards 9786 Ross Station Rd. Sebastopol
707.887.1507   www.ironhorsevineyards.com
Hours: 11am - 3:30pm Tastings are outdoors Tasting Fee: $10
Wine List: Chardonnay, Pinot Noir, Viognier, Sangiovese, Merlot, Cabernet Sauvignon, Sparklers, Cuvee, Blanc de Blanc, Brut, Blanc de Noir
Added Highlights: Pet Friendly
Notes: Tucked off by itself, they produce good still and sparkling wines at a beautiful location down at the end of a skinny road. The tasting room is a lean-to covering a rough cut tasting bar. Taste the wines while looking out over the hills at the great view. Get there in the first part of the day because they close early. They make a good jumping-off point for the Russian River Valley and River Road.
Part of Tour on page: 55, 177

J Vineyards & Winery 11447 Old Redwood Hwy. Healdsburg (Northern Sonoma)
707.431.5430 reservations winefolk@jwine.com www.jwine.com
Hours: 11am - 5pm daily Tasting Fee: $10 - $20; $55 pairing
Wine List: Pinot Noir, Pinot Gris, Chardonnay, Vin Gris, Dessert wine Pear Liqueur, Rosé, Sparklers
Added Highlights: Architecture, Gardens, Gift Shop
Notes: A very classy sparkling wine producer in a gorgeous building. They offer wine and food pairings that are always popular and have various elegant rooms to enjoy them. Nice gift shop. Convenient to Healdsburg and Highway101. Same driveway as Rodney Strong.
Part of Tour on page: 173

J W Morris Winery 331 Healdsburg Ave. Healdsburg (Northern Sonoma)
707.431.7677
Hours: by appt only   also tasted at Front Street Wineries Tasting Fee: none listed
Wine List: Gewürztraminer, Chardonnay, Chenin Blanc, Cabernet Sauvignon

J. Rochioli Vineyards & Winery 6192 Westside Rd. Healdsburg (Northern Sonoma)
707.433.2305
Hours: Thursday through Monday 11:00 am to 4:00pm Tues & Wed by appt   Tasting Fee: none listed
Wine List: Sauvignon Blanc, Chardonnay, Pinot Noir

Jacuzzi Family Vineyards 24724 Arnold Dr. Sonoma   (Carneros)
707.931.7575 TR   www.jacuzziwines.com
Hours: 10am - 5:30pm   Tasting Fee: Complimentary to $5
Wine List: Chardonnay, Pinot Noir, Barbera, Sangiovese, Arneis, Merlot, Nebbiolo, Primitivo, Pinot Grigio, Moscato Blanc, Blends
Added Highlights: Architecture, Gardens, Gift Shop, Event Spaces
Notes: A new Italian style winery created by the Cline Family (The families are related) whose winery is across the street. Big spacious tasting room specializing in well made Italian varietals. The Olive Press shares the building and has an olive oil tasting bar and both sides have great gift shops. Very convenient to San Francisco. They make a great first or last stop on a tour originating in the city.
Part of Tour on page: 41, 95, 97, 109, 123

Jarvis Vineyards 2970 Monticello Rd. Napa
800.255.5280 x 150 TR info@jarviswinery.com www.jarviswines.com
Hours: 11am - 4pm by appt Tasting Fee: $20 - $30   (continued on next page)

Wine List: Chardonnay, Cabernet Sauvignon, Malbec, Merlot, Petit Verdot, Cabernet Franc, Blends
Added Highlights: Architecture, Caves, Tours
Notes: When you drive way out on Monticello Road, through the electronic gate and arrive at Jarvis all you see is a cave door. The entire winery is inside that cave and it is quite beautiful. An expensive tasting but a unique experience. Bring a sweater. Bacchus Tasting Tour: $20. pp (4 wines), Vintage Tasting Tour: $30 pp (6 wines). Cheese and crackers accompany both tastings. 24 hour cancellation policy
Part of Tour on page: 131

Jessup Cellars 6740 Washington St. Yountville (Downtown Yountville)
707.944.8523 TR info@jessupcellars.com www.jessupcellars.com
Hours: 10am - 6pm daily   Tasting Fee: $10 (CWP)
Wine List: Chardonnay, Rosé, Merlot, Zinfandel, Cabernet Sauvignon, Blends, Petite Sirah, Zinfandel Port

Johnson's Alexander Valley Wines 8333 Highway 128 Healdsburg (Northern Sonoma)
707.433.2319 www.johnsonavwines.com
Hours: 11am - 4pm daily   Tasting Fee: none listed
Wine List: Chardonnay, Johannisberg Riesling, White Zinfandel, Pinot Noir, Cabernet Sauvignon, Zinfandel, Late Harvest Zinfandel

Jordan Vineyard & Winery 1474 Alexander Valley Rd. Healdsburg (Northern Sonoma)
707.431.5250 Info@JordanWinery.com www.jordanwinery.com
Hours: by appt only Tours & Tastings Mon - Sat by appt Closed Sunday Tasting Fee: $20
Wine List: Cabernet Sauvignon, Chardonnay, Dessert Wine, Olive Oil
Added Highlights: Architecture, Gardens, Tours
Notes: A grand estate in the Alexander Valley, it is both elegant and gracious, with a wonderful staff and well regarded wines. Alexander Valley is known for Cabernet Sauvignon and Merlot and Jordan's wines are highly respected. The sign on Alexander Valley Road is small but the entrance to the driveway is quite broad and well done, so look for that on the up hill side of the road. They have had the same winemaker since the wineries inception.
Part of Tour on page: 59, 173, 181

Joseph Phelps Vineyards 200 Taplin Rd. St. Helena
707.967.3720 jpvwines@jpvwines.com www.jpvwines.com
Hours: appt only   9am - 5pm Mon - Fri Sat/Sun 10am - 4pm   Tasting Fee: $20 and up
Wine List: Cabernet Sauvignon, Chardonnay, Merlot, Pastiche, Sauvignon Blanc, Syrah, Viognier
Added Highlights: Architecture, Pet Friendly, Picnic Area
Notes: Tucked in their own little valley they offer both tastings by appointment and seminars. A lovely tasting room and patio, their wines are highly respected. Very nice, knowledgeable and relaxed staff. Beautiful building. The first Napa winery to create a Bordeaux-style blend.
Part of Tour on page: 133, 207

Joseph Swan Vineyards 2916 Laguna Rd. Forestville (Northern Sonoma)
 707.573.3747 rod@swanwinery.com www.swanwinery.com
Hours: 11am - 4:30pm Sat - Sun appt available for Mon & Fri Tasting Fee: Complimentary
Wine List: Zinfandel, Pinot Noir, Syrah

Judd's Hill Winery 2332 Silverado Trail Napa
707.255.2332 www.juddshill.com
Hours: 10am - 4pm by appt only   Tasting Fee: none listed
Wine List: Cabernet Sauvignon, Petite Sirah, Chardonnay, Merlot, Zinfandel, Pinot Noir

Juslyn Vineyards 5225 Solano Ave. Napa
707.299.3930 TR   www.juslynvineyards.com
Hours: 10am - 4pm daily Tasting Fee: $10 - $20
Wine List: Cabernet Sauvignon, Blends (red)
Notes: Tastings at Silenus, a collective tasting room.

Kaz Vineyards & Winery 233 Adobe Canyon Rd. Kenwood
707.833.2536 kaz@vom.com www.kazwinery.com
Hours: 11am - 5pm Fri - Mon   Tasting Fee: $5
Wine List: Chardonnay, Sauvignon Blanc , Nebbiola Rosa (Rosé), Grenache, Sangiovese, Barbera, Zinfandel, Syrah, Cabernet Franc, Port, Blends including ZAM - (Zinfandel, Alicante Bouschet & Mourvèdre) also including Carignane, Malbec
Added Highlights: Biodynamic/Organic, Gift Shop
Notes: A very small family winery down the street from Landmark. A bit eccentric, very local and always fun. They make a startling variety of wines so this will clearly expand your flavor horizons. Open Friday to Monday. Funky but fun tasting room.
Part of Tour on page: 48, 107

Keever Vineyards PO Box 2906 Yountville
707.944.910 www.keevervineyards.com
Hours: 10am - 3pm by appt only Tasting Fee: $10
Wine List: Cabernet Sauvignon
Added Highlights: Tours
Notes: Tastings include a tour. Last tour/tasting is at 3pm. Physical address given when appt is made. Max capacity of 8 people. Small private winery.

Kelham Vineyards & Winery 360 Zinfandel Ln. St. Helena
707.963.2000 info@kelhamvineyards.com www.kelhamvineyards.com
Hours: by appt only   Tasting Fee: $20
Wine List: Cabernet Sauvignon, Sauvignon Blanc, Merlot
Added Highlights: Architecture, Art Gallery, Gardens, Gift Shop,
Notes: Truly a family winery and a very class act. As gracious and charming as you hope to find in Napa, the Kelham's are wonderful hosts and produce wines with character and integrity. Sit down tasting with great art and friendly dogs.
Part of Tour on page: 157, 159

Keller Estate 5875 Lakeville Hwy. Petaluma
707.765.2117 kellerestate@kellerestate.com www.kellerestate.com
Hours: 10am - 5pm Tue - Sat Tours by appt $25 Tasting Fee: $10
Wine List: Rosé, Chardonnay, Pinot Gris, Pinot Noir, Syrah, Olive Oil
Added Highlights: Art Gallery, Tours, Spectacular Winery, Very Convenient to San Francisco.

Kendall-Jackson 5007 Fulton Rd. Fulton (Northern Sonoma)
707.433.7102 TR   www.kj.com
Hours: 10am - 5pm daily Complimentary Coupon Online Tasting Fee: $5 - $15 - $25 with food pairing
Wine List: Cabernet Sauvignon, Merlot, Syrah, Chardonnay, Pinot Noir, Riesling, Sauvignon Blanc, Zinfandel, Olive Oil
Added Highlights: Architecture, Gardens, Gift Shop
Notes: The crown Jewel of the Jess Jackson empire, the tasting room is very convenient to Highway 101 on Fulton Road just above River Road. A beautiful building, good tours and gift shop and of course well made, popular wines.
Part of Tour on page: 55, 185

Kenwood Vineyards Winery 9592 Sonoma Hwy. Kenwood
707.833.5891 info@kenwoodvineyards.com www.kenwoodvineyards.com
Hours: 10am - 4:30pm daily Tasting Fee: Complimentary
Wine List: Cabernet Sauvignon, Chardonnay, Sauvignon Blanc, Zinfandel, Pinot Noir, Merlot, Gewürztraminer
Added Highlights: Gift Shop
Notes: Right in the center of Kenwood, their big, rambling tasting room is relaxed and a bit rustic. However their wines are very well made and the gift shop selection is fun. The Jack London Vineyards wines are great. Taste up to four of wines free of charge
Part of Tour on page: 48

Kirkland Ranch Winery Jameson Canyon Rd. Napa (Carneros)
707.254.9100 info@kirklandwinery.com www.kirklandwinery.com
Hours: 10am - 4pm Tasting Fee: Complimentary w/2 bottle purchase
Wine List: Cabernet Sauvignon, Merlot, Sangiovese, Syrah, Pinot Noir, Pinot Grigio, Muscat Canelli, Viognier (sweet), Rosato di Sangiovese, Late Harvest White
Added Highlights: Tours
Notes: Across from the Chardonnay Golf Course - Ya gotta love wine country!

Korbel Champagne Cellars 13250 River Rd. Guerneville (Northern Sonoma)
707.824.7000 www.korbel.com
Hours: 9am - 5pm Tasting Fee: $5 - $10
Wine List: Sparklers, Blanc de Noirs, Chardonnay Champagne, Moscato Frizzante, Merlot Champagne, Brut Rosé, Pinot Grigio Sparkler
Added Highlights: Architecture, Gift Shop, Picnic Area, Restaurant/Market
Notes: As you travel west on River Road, Korbel is the final winery you encounter. A great history and a beautiful location, their tours are very enjoyable. A wonderful deli restaurant with seating outdoors among the redwood trees.
Part of Tour on page: 185

Kuleto Estate Family Vineyards 2470 Sage Canyon Rd. St. Helena
707.963.9750 info@kuletoestate.com www.kuletoestate.com
Hours: by appt only Mon - Sat 10:30am and 2:30pm Tasting Fee: $25
Wine List: Cabernet Sauvignon, Sangiovese, Syrah, Pinot Noir, Rosato, Chardonnay
Added Highlights: Architecture, Gardens, Views
Notes: Guests receive a map and gate code upon confirmation. Long winding driveway. Worth it!

Kunde Estate Winery & Vineyards 10155 Sonoma Hwy. Kenwood
707.833.5501 naomi@kunde.com www.kunde.com
Hours: 10:30am - 4:30pm daily Tasting Fee: $5 - $10
Wine List: Sauvignon Blanc, Chardonnay, Syrah, Zinfandel, Merlot, Cabernet Sauvignon, Primitivo, Meritage, Sangiovese, Barbera, Gewürztraminer, Grenache Rosé, Claret, Blends, Zinfandel Port
Added Highlights: Architecture, Caves, Gardens, Gift Shop, Picnic Area, Tours
Notes: Five generations of grape growers in one of the most beautiful expanses of the Valley of the Moon. They started making their own wines in the early 1990's and with two thousand acres of vineyards, they offer a wide variety of well made, good value wines. Reserve Wines and guided tours of aging caves Fri, Sat, Sun throughout the day by appt.
Part of Tour on page: 48, 93, 107

La Crema 235 Healdsburg Ave. Healdsburg (On the Plaza) (Northern Sonoma)
707.431.9400 TR service@lacrema.com www.lacrema.com
Hours: 10am - 5:30pm Tasting Fee: Complimentary
Wine List: Pinot Noir, Chardonnay, Syrah, Viognier Added Highlights: Gift Shop Map on page 186

Ladera   150 White Cottage Rd. S.   Angwin   (Howell Mountain)
707.965.2445   winery@laderavineyards.com   www.laderavineyards.com
Hours: by appt only Mon- Sat   Tasting Fee: Complimentary
Wine List: Cabernet Sauvignon
Added Highlights: Tours
Notes: Daily tastings only 11am, 1 pm, 3pm. Daily tours & tastings: 10am, 12 pm, 2pm. Groups of 10 or more are charged a tasting fee.

Lago di Merlo Vineyards & Winery   4791 Dry Creek Rd.   Healdsburg
707.433.0100 TR   wines@lagodimerlo.com   www.lagodimerlo.com
Hours: 10:30am - 4:30pm daily   Tasting Fee: $5 glass purchase
Wine List: Cabernet Sauvignon, Merlot, Zinfandel, Sangiovese, Syrah, Pinot Grigio, Sauvignon Blanc, Moscato, Vino Rosso
Notes: Tastings at Family Wineries, a collective tasting room.

Laird Family Estate   5055 Solano Ave.   Napa
707.257.0360 x 26   www.lairdfamilyestate.com
Hours: 10am - 5pm (instant appts)   Tasting Fee: $10 (CWP)
Wine List: Pinot Grigio, Chardonnay, Syrah, Cabernet Sauvignon, Merlot

Lake Sonoma Winery   340 Healdsburg Ave.   Healdsburg   (Northern Sonoma)
707.473.2999   info@lswinery.com   www.lakesonomawinery.net
Hours: 10am - 5pm   Tasting Fee: Complimentary
Wine List: Cabernet Sauvignon, Zinfandel and Chardonnay
Notes: Just a Tasting room. No winery at this location.

Lambert Bridge Winery   4085 W. Dry Creek Rd.   Healdsburg   (Northern Sonoma)
707.431.9600   wines@lambertbridge.com   www.lambertbridge.com
Hours: 10:30am - 4:30pm   Tasting Fee: $10 - $20
Wine List: Sauvignon, Blanc, Chardonnay, Zinfandel, Syrah, Cuvee, Petite Sirah, Merlot, Cabernet Franc, Cabernet, Sauvignon, Vinegar, Mustard, Mayonnaise, Grapeseed Oil
Added Highlights: Architecture, Gift Shop, Picnic Area, Restaurant/Market
Notes: Tucked on the sloping side of the Dry Creek Valley this is a beautiful little winery with a great picnic area. The staff is quite knowledgeable and best yet, the wines are spectacular. One of our personal favorites.
Part of Tour on page: 173, 177, 181, 183

Lancaster Estate Winery   15001 Chalk Hill Rd.   Healdsburg   (Northern Sonoma)
707.433.8178   guestrelations@lancaster-estate.com   www.lancaster-estate.com
Hours: Tue - Sat by appt only $25 cancellation fee   Tasting Fee: Complimentary
Wine List: Cabernet Sauvignon, Sauvignon Blanc, Blends
Added Highlights: Tours

Landmark Winery   101 Adobe Canyon Rd.   Kenwood
707.833.0218 TR   www.landmarkwine.com
Hours: 10am - 4:30pm   Tasting Fee: $5 - $10
Wine List: Chardonnay, Pinot Noir, Syrah
Added Highlights: Bocce Court, Gardens. Gift Shop
Notes: Part of the John Deere Tractor family, this lovely little winery specializes in Burgundy and Rhone wines, and they do them quite well. A wonderful staff, pretty tasting room and a good gift shop including model tractors of course. Nice gardens for picnics.
Part of Tour on page: 48, 107

Larkmead Vineyards   1100 Larkmead Ln.   Calistoga
707.942.0167   info@larkmead.com   www.larkmead.com
Hours: 10am - 5pm by appt only   Tasting Fee: none listed
Wine List: Cabernet Sauvignon, Merlot

Larson Family Winery   23355 Millerick Rd.   Sonoma   (Carneros)
707.938.3031   tr@larsonfamilywinery.com   www.LarsonFamilyWinery.com
Hours: 10am - 5pm daily   Tasting Fee: $5 (CWP)
Wine List: White table wine, Chardonnay, Gewürztraminer, Cuveé Rosé, Pinot Noir Rosé, Pinot Noir, Merlot, Red Table Wine, Meritage, Petite Sirah, Cabernet Sauvignon
Added Highlights: Bocce Court, Horses, Pet Friendly, Picnic Area, This was the Site of the Sonoma Rodeo for many years and the great Sea Biscuit trained here when in the area for a race.
Notes: Also tasted at Cornerstone's collective tasting room.

Ledson Winery & Vineyards   7335 Highway 12   Santa Rosa
707.537.3810   www.ledson.com   (Their wines are also tasted at their hotel on the Plaza, see page 18)
Hours: 10am - 5pm daily   Tasting Fee: $5 - $10
Wine List: Merlot, Pinot Noir, Sangiovese, Syrah, Petite Sirah, Zinfandel, Cabernet Sauvignon, Cabernet Franc, Malbec, Barbera, Mourvèdre, Primitivo, Grenache, Chardonnay, Sauvignon Blanc, Johannisberg Riesling, Rosé, Madera Port
Added Highlights: Architecture, Gift Shop, Picnic Area, Restaurant/Market
Notes: Known locally as The Castle, this mansion style tasting room is a favorite venue for weddings. A great deli with lots of outdoor seating to enjoy the food. Well made wines in a spacious group of tasting rooms. Nice staff.
Part of Tour on page: 48, 103

Limerick Lane Vineyards   1023 Limerick Ln.   Healdsburg   (Northern Sonoma)
707.433.9211   limerick@monitor.net   www.limericklanewines.com
Hours: 10am - 5pm daily   Tasting Fee: $6
Wine List: Zinfandel, Syrah

Little Vineyards   15188 Sonoma Hwy.   Glen Ellen
707.996.2750 appt   winery@littlevineyards.com   www.littlevineyards.com
Hours: by appt only   Tasting Fee: $5 - $50
Wine List: Zinfandel, Cabernet Sauvignon, Syrah, Blends

Locals   Hwy. 128 & Geyserville Ave.   Geyserville   (Northern Sonoma)
707.857.4900   yummy@tastelocalwines.com   www.tastelocalwines.com
Hours: 11am - 6pm Wed - Mon   (Tue by appt)   Tasting Fee: none listed
Wine List: Blends, Cabernet Sauvignon, Carignane, Chardonnay, Malbec, Meritage, Merlot, Muscat Blanc, Petite Sirah, Pinot Gris, Pinot Noir, Port, Riesling, Rosé, Sangiovese, Sauvignon Blanc, Syrah, Viognier, Zinfandel
Notes: A collective tasting room for Arbios & Praxis, Bluenose, Dark Horse, Eric Ross Winery, Hauck Cellars, Hawley Wines, Laurel Glen Winery, Martin Family Vineyards, McFadden Vineyard, Peterson Winery, Ramazzotti Wines, Topel Winery

Long Meadow Ranch Winery   1775 Whitehall Ln.   St. Helena
707.963.4555   info@longmeadowranch.com   www.longmeadowranch.com
Hours: by appt only   Tours: 10:30am sharp - 12:15pm Sat by appt   Tasting Fee: $35 (w/tour)
Wine List: Cabernet Sauvignon, Sauvignon Blanc, Sangiovese, Ranch House Red, Olive Oil, Beef Jerky
Added Highlights: Art Gallery, Biodynamic/Organic, Breeds & Sells Horses, Gardens, Tours

Long Vineyards 1535 Sage Canyon Rd. St. Helena
707.963.2496 bob@longvineyards.com www.longvineyards.com
Hours: by appt only   Tasting Fee: none listed
Wine List: Sangiovese, Cabernet Sauvignon, Chardonnay, Pinot Grigio, Riesling

Longboard Vineyards 5 Fitch St. Healdsburg (Northern Sonoma)
707.433.3473 info@longboardvineyards.com www.longboardvineyards.com
Hours: 11am - 7pm Thu - Sat, Sun 11am - 5pm   Tasting Fee: $5 (CWP)
Wine List: Syrah, Cabernet Sauvignon, Merlot
Added Highlights: Surf Boards
Notes: A Surfer's delight. After hours wine bar scene. Visit on Mon - Wed by appt or gate crashing.

Louis M. Martini Winery 254 St. Helena Hwy. S. St. Helena
800.321.WINE   www.louismartini.com
Hours: 11am - 5pm   Tasting Fee: $5
Wine List: Zinfandel, Cabernet Sauvignon
Added Highlights: Picnic Area
Notes: One of the grand old wineries of Napa, now owned by their family friends the Gallos. Don't let the stern exterior fool you, a very sleek tasting room and an expansive garden for picnics. Classic Napa wines of the highest quality. Central location.
Part of Tour on page: 155

Loxton Cellars 11466 Dunbar Rd. Glen Ellen
707.935.7221 chris@loxtonwines.com www.loxtoncellars.com
Hours: 11am - 5pm daily by appt only   Tasting Fee: $5
Wine List: Rosé, Vin Gris of Syrah, Zinfandel, Syrah, Cabernet Sauvignon, Syrah Port, Chardonnay, Shiraz
Added Highlights: Gift Shop, Picnic Area
Notes: A small winery where Chris Loxton, the owner/winemaker is often pouring for you. You have to walk past the winemaking equipment to reach the barrel room/tasting room. A personal favorite of ours. The wines are excellent and a good value. Visit Loxton when you want to know about the small wineries that are the backbone of Sonoma. Chris is a third generation Australian grape grower and former physics professor.
Part of Tour on page: 48, 97, 103, 105, 175

Luna Vineyards 2921 Silverado Trail Napa
707.255.2474 luna@lunavineyards.com www.lunavineyards.com
Hours: 10am - 5pm daily Tasting Fee: $5 - $10
Wine List: Sangiovese, Merlot, Petite Sirah, Pinot Grigio, Tocai Friulano, Chardonnay, Cabernet Sauvignon, Blends (Freakout)
Added Highlights: Architecture, Gift Shop, Tours
Notes: Specializing in Italian varietals, Luna is one of the most southern wineries on the Silverado Trail so it's very convenient for a day trip. A nice staff, pretty tasting room and good wines. A great first or last stop when touring along the Trail. Golfers will want to look for the Arnold Palmer signature wines. Special tours & tastings can be arranged by appointment.
Part of Tour on page: 121, 145

Lynmar Winery 9060 Graton Rd. Sebastopol (Northern Sonoma)
707.829.3374 info@lynmarwinery.com www.lynmarwinery.com
Hours: 10am - 5pm   Tasting Fee: $10 - $20
Wine List: Pinot Noir, Chardonnay, Vin Gris, Syrah
Added Highlights: Architecture, Gardens

Maboroshi Vineyard and Wine Estates 2970 Thorn Rd. Sebastopol (Northern Sonoma)
707.829.1216 rebecca@maboroshiwine.com www.maboroshiwone.com
Hours: by appt only   Tasting Fee: Complimentary
Wine List: Pinot Noir, Cabernet Sauvignon, Merlot
Notes: After living all over the world, their "dream" was to make wine. "Maboroshi", a Japanese term for extraordinary visions.

Madonna Estate 5400 Old Sonoma Rd. Napa   (Carneros)
707.255-8864 mail@madonnaestate.com www.madonnaestate.com
Hours: 10am - 5pm daily   Tasting Fee: $5 - $12
Wine List: Pinot Grigio, Chardonnay, Pinot Noir, Merlot, Dolcetto, Cabernet Sauvignon, Riesling, Gewürztraminer, Muscat Canelli
Added Highlights: Biodynamic/Organic, Picnic Area
Notes: Very convenient from San Francisco. A popular tour bus stop. 3rd generation Italian American winemakers. Organic, dry farmed vineyards.

Manzanita Creek Winery 1441-B Grove St. Healdsburg (Northern Sonoma)
707.433.4052 info@manzanitacreek.com www.manzanitacreek.com
Hours: by appt only   Also tasted at Sonoma Enoteca   Tasting Fee: none listed
Wine List: Petite Sirah, Syrah, Zinfandel, Pinot Noir, Muscat, Cabernet Sauvignon

Manzanita Ridge Wine Co. 347 Healdsburg Ave. Healdsburg (Northern Sonoma)
707.433.8333
Hours: 11am - 4pm by appt   Tasting Fee: Complimentary
Wine List: Chardonnay, Pinot Noir

Marimar Estate 11400 Graton Rd. Sebastopol (Northern Sonoma)
707.823.4365 info@marimarestate.com www.marimarestate.com
Hours: 11am - 4pm daily   Tours by appt   Tasting Fee: $10 groups of 10 or more
Wine List: Chardonnay, Pinot Noir, Syrah-Tempranillo
Added Highlights: Biodynamic/Organic, Tours

Mario Perelli-Minetti Winery 1443 Silverado Trail N. St. Helena
707.963.8762 andrewpmwine@yahoo.com www.mpmwinery.com
Hours: 10am - 4:30pm   Tasting Fee: none listed
Wine List: Cabernet Sauvignon, Chardonnay, Pinot Noir

Markham Vineyards 2812 St. Helena Hwy. N. St. Helena
707.963.5292 www.markhamvineyards.com
Hours: 10am - 5pm   Tasting Fee: $5 - $15
Wine List: Merlot, Cabernet Sauvignon, Sauvignon Blanc, Chardonnay
Added Highlights: Art Gallery

Martin Ray Winery 2191 Laguna Rd. Santa Rosa (Northern Sonoma)
707.823.2404 info@martinray-winery.com www.martinray-winery.com
Hours: 11am - 5pm daily   Tasting Fee: Complimentary
Wine List: Pinot Gris, Sauvignon Blanc, Chardonnay, Pinot Noir, Merlot, Cabernet Sauvignon. Under the Angeline Label: Gewürztraminer, Riesling, Sauvignon Blanc, Chardonnay, Pinot Noir, Cabernet Sauvignon, Merlot, Zinfandel
Notes: Winter hours: Nov - Mar Thu- Mon 11am – 4pm Closed Tue & Wed. Summer hours: Apr - Oct Open 7 days a week, 11am – 5pm

Martinelli Vineyards & Winery   3360 River Rd.   Windsor   (Northern Sonoma)
707.525.0570   vinoinfo@martinelliwinery.com   www.martinelliwinery.com
Hours: 10am - 5pm daily   more than 8 - require appt. No buses.   Tasting Fee: $5
Wine List: Chardonnay, Pinot Noir, Syrah, Zinfandel, Gewürztraminer, Muscat Alexandria, Sauvignon, Blanc
Added Highlights: Gift Shop, Picnic Area
Notes: After generations of grape growing the Martinelli Vineyards is finally getting the acclaim they deserve. Wonderful Russian River style wines. A very rustic tasting room with a great, down home style gift shop. A charming and very knowledgeable staff. Tremendously convenient on River Road just a short distance off of Highway 101 in a converted Hop Kiln. A good first stop for a Russian River tour.
Part of Tour on page: 55, 185

Matanzas Creek Winery   6097 Bennett Valley Rd.   Santa Rosa
800.590.6464 www.matanzascreek.com
Hours: 10am - 4:30pm   Tours Mon-Sat by appt   Tasting Fee: $5 - $10
Wine List: Merlot, Chardonnay, Sauvignon, Blanc, Cabernet Sauvignon, Syrah, Rosé
Added Highlights: Gardens, Gift Shop, Tours
Notes: The lavender fields are heady in season. Great gift shop with estate made lavender products in addition to very nice wines. Gorgeous property convenient to Glen Ellen.

Mauritson Family Winery   2859 Dry Creek Rd.   Healdsburg   (Northern Sonoma)
707.431.0804   info@mauritsonwines.com   www.mauritsonwines.com
Hours: 10am - 5pm daily   Tours by appt   Tasting Fee: $0 - $10
Wine List: Sauvignon Blanc, Chardonnay, Zinfandel, Cabernet Sauvignon, Petite Sirah, Syrah, Blends
Added Highlights: Picnic Area, Tours

Mayacamas Vineyards & Winery   1155 Lokoya Rd.   Napa
707.224.4030   mayacamas@napanet.com   www.mayacamas.com
Hours: by appt only 11am or 2pm   Tasting Fee: PIE
Wine List: Cabernet Sauvignon, Chardonnay, Sauvignon Blanc, Pinot Noir, Blend
Added Highlights: Gift Shop

Mayo Family Winery   13101 Arnold Dr.   Glen Ellen
707.938.9401   www.mayofamilywinery.com
Hours: 10am - 6:30pm daily   Tasting Fee: none listed
Wine List: A very wide variety of wines, thirty to forty
Added Highlights: Very convenient location at the light where Arnold Avenue meets Rt. 12. Gift Shop
Notes: The Mayo Family has two tasting rooms, the main one at the address above and the reserve room just north of there on the south-bound side of Rt 12 in Kenwood, along with several other tasting rooms. Their tasting room staff includes family members, quite knowledgeable and the wines are well made.
Part of Tour Maps on page: 18*, 48

Mazzocco Vineyards   1400 Lytton Springs Rd.   Healdsburg   (Northern Sonoma)
707.431.8159   vino@mazzocco.com   www.mazzocco.com
Hours: 11am - 5pm   Tasting Fee: $5 (CWP)
Wine List: Chardonnay, Viognier, Carignane, Pinot Noir, Zinfandel, Cabernet Sauvignon, Merlot, Blend

Meeker Vineyards   21035 Geyserville Ave.   Geyserville   (Northern Sonoma)
707.431.2148   gillian@meekerwine.com   www.meekervineyards.com
Hours: 11am - 4pm   Tasting Fee: none listed
Wine List: Bordeaux Blend, Cabernet Sauvignon, Merlot, Zinfandel, Petite Sirah, Syrah, Carignane, Ice wine style blend of Muscat, Chenin Blanc & Gewürztraminer
Notes: Tasting room is an historic bank - tasting in the vault!

Merryvale Vineyards 1000 Main St. St. Helena
707.963.7777 www.merryvale.com
Hours: 10am - 6:30pm   Tasting Fee: $10 - $20
Wine List: Sauvignon Blanc, Semillon, Chardonnay, Merlot, Cabernet Sauvignon, Dessert Wine (Muscat de Frontignan - fortified w/CA Brandy), Zinfandel, Pinot Noir, Blends
Added Highlights: Gift Shop
Notes: This festive tasting room is open till late so it makes a great last stop before dinner. Walk next door to Tra Vigne or Pizzeria Tra Vigne to complete the day. The advent of a new winemaker brought on the redesign of their winery, which was once owned by the Mondavi family.

Michel Schlumberger Fine Wine 4155 Wine Creek Rd. Healdsburg (Northern Sonoma)
707.433.7427 www.michelschlumberger.com
Hours: 11am - 5pm by appt only tours at 11am or 2pm Tasting Fee: $5 - $10
Wine List: Cabernet Sauvignon, Syrah, Pinot Noir, Merlot, Pinot Blanc, Chardonnay
Added Highlights: Just off West Dry Creek Rd, Gift Shop, Tours

Mietz Cellars 4791 Dry Creek Rd. Healdsburg (Northern Sonoma)
707.433.0100 TR info@mietzcellars.com www.mietzcellars.com
Hours: 10:30am - 4:30pm Tasting Fee: $5 glass purchase
Wine List: Sauvignon Blanc Pinot Noir, Cabernet Sauvignon, Merlot, Sangiovese, Zinfandel, Petit Verdot, Claret
Notes: Tastings at Family Wineries, a collective tasting room.

Milat Vineyards Winery 1091 St. Helena Hwy. S St. Helena
707.963.0758 info@milat.com www.milat.com
Hours: 10am - 5:30pm daily hours may vary in Winter Tasting Fee: $5 (CWP)
Wine List: Chenin Blanc, Chardonnay, Merlot, Zinfandel, Cabernet Sauvignon, Blends, Port, Chocolate Port Sauce

Mill Creek Vineyards & Winery 1401 Westside Rd. Healdsburg (Northern Sonoma)
707.431.2121 www.millcreekwinery.com
Hours: 10am - 5pm daily   Tasting Fee: $0 - $5
Wine List: Chardonnay, Syrah, Gewürztraminer, Sauvignon Blanc, Zinfandel, Blends
Added Highlights: Picnic Area

Miner Family Vineyards 7850 Silverado Trail Oakville
707.944.9500 x 17   www.minerwines.com
Hours: 11am - 5pm   Tasting Fee: $5 - $10
Wine List: Chardonnay, Viognier, Sauvignon Blanc, Cabernet Sauvignon, Pinot Noir, Merlot, Syrah, Petite Sirah, Zinfandel, Sangiovese, Rosato, Blends
Added Highlights: Gift Shop, Picnic Area, Views
Notes: Perched above the Silverado Trail, the views from their patio and tasting room are wonderful. Good wines and a nice staff, and you can picnic on the patio if it's not too cool. It gets breezy up there. Part of Tour on page: 123

Montemaggiore 2355 W. Dry Creek Rd. Healdsburg (Northern Sonoma)
707.433.9499 www.montemaggiore.com
Hours: by appt only (same day) Tasting Fee: Complimentary
Wine List: Specialize in Reds, especially Syrah
Added Highlights: Biodynamic/Organic, Tours, Views
Notes: Tasting includes a tour of organic vineyards and/or state of the art winery

Monticello Cellars 4242 Big Ranch Rd. Napa
707.253.2802 x 18   www.CorleyFamilyNapaValley.com
Hours: 10am - 4:30pm Blending seminars are $45. Tasting Fee: $10, Reserve $25
Wine List: Cabernet Sauvignon, Merlot, Blend
Added Highlights: Scaled Replica of Monticello, Picnic Area

Moon Mountain Vineyard 1700 Moon Mountain Dr. Sonoma
707.996.5870 www.moonmountainvineyard.com
Hours: by appt only Tue - Sat Tours at 2:30pm only. Tasting Fee: $5 - $10
Wine List: Cabernet Sauvignon, Sauvignon Blanc, Chardonnay
Added Highlights: Biodynamic/Organic, Historic Caves, Tours, Views, Long Winding Road

Moss Creek Winery 6015 Steele Canyon Rd. Napa
707.252.1295 info@mosscreekwinery.com www.mosscreekwinery.com
Hours: by appt only   Tasting Fee: $50 (CWP)
Wine List: Cabernet Sauvignon, Zinfandel, Merlot, Petite Sirah, Sauvignon Blanc

Mt Veeder Winery & Vineyards 1999 Mount Veeder Rd. Napa
707.967.3993 appt   www.mtveeder.com
Hours: by appt only Tasting Fee: $15
Wine List: Cabernet Sauvignon, Cabernet Franc, Zinfandel
Notes: Can also be tasted at Franciscan Oakville Estate

Mumm Napa Valley 8445 Silverado Trail Rutherford
707.967.7700 mumm_club@mummnapa.com www.mummnapa.com
Hours: 10am - 5pm Tasting Fee: $5 - $15 by the glass or flight
Wine List: Pinot Noir, Chardonnay, Santana, DVX, Demi Sec, Sparkling Pinot Noir, Cuvee M Red, Blanc de Blanc, Brut Prestige, Blanc de Noirs, Cuvee M, Brut Reserve
Added Highlights: Art Gallery, Gardens, Gift Shop, Pet Friendly, Views
Notes: Sparkling wines. A very fun place where tastings take place sitting down either in the glass enclosed tasting room or on the expansive patio. A festive staff, not surprising since they're pouring bubbly all day. They can handle larger parties. Great gift shop and the views from the patio over the vineyards as the sun sets are great. Chocolate is always available.
Part of Tour on page: 62, 69, 145, 153, 159, 196

Murphy-Goode Estate Vineyard & Winery 4001 Highway 128 Geyserville (Northern Sonoma)
707.431.7644 general@murphygoodewinery.com www.murphygoodewinery.com
Hours: 10:30am - 4:30pm   Tasting Fee: $5
Wine List: Fumé Blanc, Chardonnay, Cabernet Sauvignon, Merlot, Pinot Noir, Zinfandel, Claret, Petit Verdot, Rosé, Muscat Canelli
Notes: A very friendly winery in a slightly blocky building in the Alexander Valley. Good wines and consistently a nice experience.
Part of Tour on page: 59

Nalle Winery 2383 Dry Creek Rd. Healdsburg (Northern Sonoma)
707.433.1040 info@nallewinery.com www.nallewinery.com
Hours: 12pm - 5pm Sat Sun - Fri by appt Tasting Fee: $5 (CWP)
Wine List: Zinfandel, Pinot Noir, Sauvignon Blanc, Chardonnay

Napa Wine Company 7830-40 St. Helena Hwy. Oakville
707.944.1710 www.napawineco.com
Hours: 10am - 4:30pm   Tasting Fee: none listed (continued on next page)

Your Day in Wine Country

Wine List: Sauvignon Blanc, Pinot Noir, Petite Sirah, Zinfandel, Pinot Blanc, Cabernet Sauvignon
Notes: A collective tasting room. They stock 25 Boutique Wineries. Vintners included are Downing Family Vineyards, Lamborn Family Vineyards, Pavi Wines, Napa Wine Company, Ottimino, Volker Eisele, Falcor Wines, Showket Vineyards, Vinum Cellars, and Madrigal Vineyards

Newton Vineyard 2555 Madrona Ave. St. Helena
707.963.9000 winery@newtonvineyard.com www.newtonvineyard.com
Hours: 11am appts only Thu - Mon Tasting Fee: $30
Wine List: Chardonnay, Merlot, Cabernet Sauvignon, Cabernet Franc, Petit Verdot, Blends
Added Highlights: Architecture, Biodynamic/Organic, Gardens, Tours
Notes: Only one or two appointment slots daily, that are not easy to arrange, but worth the effort. Remarkable grounds and gardens, incredible views from the ridges of Spring Mountain. Seriously good wines. Knowledgeable staff.
Part of Tour on page: 207

Nichelini Winery 2950 Sage Canyon Rd. St. Helena (Chiles Valley)
707.963.0717 nichwine@nicheliniwinery.com www.nicheliniwinery.com
Hours: 10am - 5pm weekends   Tasting Fee: Complimentary
Wine List: Sauvignon Vert, Chardonnay, Zinfandel, Petite Sirah, Cabernet Sauvignon, Primitivo
Added Highlights: Bocce Court
Notes: Lovely wines from one of the oldest family wineries in Napa, the winery is perched on a hillside up Chiles Valley (Pronouced like Child). When you visit the place you can only imagine the effort that went into planting the vineyards and building the winery in such a difficult to reach place.

Nicholson Ranch 4200 Napa Rd. Sonoma   (On the edge of Carneros, but Sonoma Valley)
707.938.8822 info@nicholsonranch.com www.nicholsonranch.com
Hours: 10am - 6pm daily   Tasting Fee: $10 - $15
Wine List: Chardonnay, Pinot Noir, Syrah, Merlot
Added Highlights: Architecture, Art Gallery, Caves, Picnic Area, Views, Tours
Notes: Perched on top of their caves at the intersection of Napa Road and Carneros Highway, Nicholson is a bee hive of activity. Beautiful views, spacious tasting room, small gift shop, well made wines, local Sonoma flavor. They are across the road from Carneros but officially in the Sonoma Valley AVA.
Part of Tour on page: 41, 69, 97, 101

Nickel & Nickel 8164 St. Helena Hwy. Oakville
707.967.9600 www.nickelandnickel.com
Hours: 10am - 3pm by appt   Tasting Fee: $40
Wine List: Chardonnay, Cabernet Sauvignon, Merlot, Syrah, Zinfandel
Added Highlights: Architecture, Gardens
Notes: Associated with Far Niente, directly across the street from Robert Mondavi, between the beautiful buildings and gardens, wonderful tour and great single vineyard wines what's not to like. A class act that's worth the higher price.
Part of Tour on page: 62, 161

O'Brien Family Vineyard/Seduction Wine 1200 Orchard Ave. Napa
707.252.8463 (VINE) bart@obrienwines.com www.obrienfamilyvineyard.com
Hours: by appt only Tasting Fee: $25
Wine List: Chardonnay, Merlot, Bordeaux Blend (Seduction)
Added Highlights: Biodynamic/Organic, Tours
Notes: They do 2 tours per day at 2pm & 4pm at $40 pp which can be credited against 6 bottle purchase or 2 per case

OnThEdge Winery 1255 Lincoln Ave. Calistoga (Downtown Calistoga)
707.942.7410 info@onthedgewinery.com www.OnThEdgewinery.com
Hours: 10am - 5 pm   Tasting Fee: none listed
Wine List: Charbono, Cabernet Franc, Cabernet Sauvignon, Zinfandel
Added Highlights: Gift Shop
Notes: Superb gifts and candle shop. Taste the label from Philadelphia Eagles football coach Dick Vermiel's family vineyard. Some unique wines available. This downtown Calistoga location is just a tasting room. No winery at this location.

Optima Wine Cellars 498-C Moore Ln. Healdsburg (Northern Sonoma)
707.431.8222 info@optimawinery.com www.optimawinery.com
Hours: by appt only   Tasting Fee: none listed
Wine List: Petite Sirah, Zinfandel Port, Cabernet Sauvignon, Chardonnay

Opus One Winery 7900 St. Helena Hwy. Oakville
707.944.9442 guest relations info@OpusOneWinery.com www.OpusOneWinery.com
Hours: 10am - 4pm daily   1 hour tour available by appt at 10:30am   Tasting Fee: $25
Wine List: Blends of: Cabernet Sauvignon, Cabernet Franc, Merlot. Recent vintages add Malbec and/or Petit Verdot
Added Highlights: Architecture, Tours, Views
Notes: Making only 25,000 cases per year Opus is a standard known internationally as a Cabernet Sauvignon blend. They pour a small glass for a hefty price so enjoy it in the small tasting room or the upstairs loggia with its views of Oakville. The Opus One building is styled like an Aztec temple. The sign on the gate is tiny. Look for it immediately north, past the Oakville market.
Part of Tour on page: 62, 69, 133, 165

Outpost Wines 2075 Summit Lake Dr. Angwin   (Howell Mountain)
707.965.1718 outpost@starband.net www.outpostwines.com
Hours: by appt only   Tasting Fee: PIE
Wine List: Zinfandel, Grenache, Petite Sirah, Cabernet Sauvignon
Added Highlights: Views
Notes: These vineyards and winery sit on top of Howell Mountain across from Spring Mountain.

Paloma Vineyard 4013 Spring Mountain Rd. St. Helena
707.963.7504 www.palomavineyards.com
Hours: by appt only   Tasting Fee: PIE
Wine List: Merlot
Added Highlights: Great Views
Notes: They are at the top of Spring Mountain with incredible views of the valley. The vineyards are so steep that they have to hold onto the wires to work them. The wine is extrodinarily good and only after recieving international acclaim did they hire someone to help them. The tastings are poured by the owners either in their kitchen or on their porch. Their drive is gated and only marked by a number.

Papapietro-Perry 4791 Dry Creek Rd. Healdsburg (Northern Sonoma)
707.433.0422 info@papapietro-perry.com www.papapietro-perry.com
Hours: 11am - 4:30pm daily Tasting Fee: $5
Wine List: Pinot Noir, Zinfandel
Notes: A small rustic tasting room, they produce some great Zinfandel. A friendly local staff are on hand plus you get a chance to wander around to their neighbors, Family Wineries and Amphora, in the same complex of farm buildings.
Part of Tour on page: 59

Paradigm Winery 683 Dwyer Rd. Oakville
707.944.1683 info@paradigmwinery.com www.paradigmwinery.com
Hours: by appt only Tasting Fee: PIE
Wine List: Merlot, Cabernet Sauvignon, Zinfandel, Cabernet Franc
Added Highlights: Tours
Notes: Tours w/Tasting usually scheduled for 11am and 2pm but other times can be arranged. A sign on the road that says, "No Wineries this Road" lets you know you are almost there!

Paradise Ridge Winery 4545 Thomas Lake Harris Dr. Santa Rosa Winery (Northern Sonoma)
Additional Tasting Room 8860 Sonoma Hwy Kenwood
707.528.9463 info@prwinery.com www.paradiseridgewinery.com
Hours: 11am - 5pm daily Jan - Mar Fri - Mon Tasting Fee: $5 - $10
Wine List: Sauvignon Blanc, Chardonnay, Blanc de Blanc Sparkler, Pinot Noir, Syrah, Zinfandel, Cabernet Sauvignon, Merlot, Pinot Noir
Added Highlights: Art Gallery, Gardens, Picnic area, Views
Notes: What a lovely tasting room at the winery. It is no wonder that so many weddings are held here. Lovely people, great views and a wonderful garden sculpture collection. Their new Tasting Room is shown on Page 48 in Kenwood close to some other wonderful tasting rooms. Opening Spring 2008.

Paraduxx 7257 Silverado Trail Yountville
707.945.0890 tastings@paraduxx.com www.paraduxx.com
Hours: 11am - 4pm by appt Tasting Fee: $20 - $40 w/cheese plate
Wine List: Bordeaux Blends, Cabernet/Zinfandel, coming soon, Rhone twist blend
Added Highlights: Gardens
Notes: Created by Duckhorn to feature their unique blend, it has a charming style and a good location. Vertical tastings of their only blend and food pairings options.

Passalacqua Winery 3805 Lambert Bridge Rd. Healdsburg (Northern Sonoma)
707.433.5550 info@passalacquawinery.com www.passalacquawinery.com
Hours: 11am - 5pm   Tasting Fee: $5 - $10
Wine List: Sauvignon Blanc, Chardonnay, Zinfandel, Merlot, Cabernet Sauvignon
Added Highlights: Gardens, Gift Shop, Picnic Area, Views
Notes: A real jewel and one of our personal favorites. Recently voted best winery in the North Bay, this very small family winery sits on a great site at the center of the Dry Creek Valley. A top notch winemaker produces elegant, complex wines. Best picnic area. Very convenient for a picnic since it is within sight of the Dry Creek General Store where you can pick up sandwiches and other picnic items. Wonderful staff.
Part of Tour on page: 59, 173, 181, 183

Pastori Winery 23189 Geyserville Ave. Cloverdale (Northern Sonoma)
707.857.3418
Hours: by appt only   Tasting Fee: none listed
Wine List: Chardonnay, Pinot Noir

Patz & Hall Wine Co. 851 Napa Valley Corporate Way Ste. A Napa
707.265.7700 info@patzhall.com www.patzhall.com
Hours: by appt only tasting includes food pairings Tasting Fee: $40
Wine List: Pinot Noir, Chardonnay

Peacock Family Vineyard 1241 Adams St. #10 St. Helena
707.967.0770 info@peacockfamilyvineyard.com www.peacockfamilyvineyard.com
Hours: by appt only   Tasting Fee: none listed
Wine List: Cabernet Sauvignon

Pedroncelli Winery 1220 Canyon Rd. Geyserville (Northern Sonoma)
800.836.3894 shirley@pedroncelli.com www.pedroncelli.com
Hours: 10am - 4:30pm   Tasting Fee: none listed
Wine List: Sauvignon Blanc, Chardonnay, Sangiovese, Merlot, Zinfandel, Cabernet Sauvignon, Syrah, Petite Sirah, Port   Added Highlights: Bocce Court

Peju Province Winery 8466 St. Helena Hwy. Rutherford
707.963.3600 x 309 info@peju.com www.peju.com
Hours: 10am - 6pm   Closed Thanksgiving & Christmas   Tasting Fee: $5 - $10
Wine List: Sauvignon Blanc, Chardonnay, French Colombard, Syrah, Merlot, Cabernet Franc, Zinfandel, Cabernet Sauvignon, Blends
Added Highlights: Architecture, Art Gallery, Gardens, Gift Shop
Notes: Peju is a very pretty and entertaining winery, with a great building and gardens, art collection and gift shop. Get there early in the day if you can. They stay open until 6pm, but they can really load up with visitors. People are brought into the tasting bar in groups from a queue, as space is available, so on busy days be prepared to wait.
Part of Tour on page: 62, 149

Pellegrini Family Vineyards 4055 W. Olivet Rd. Santa Rosa (Northern Sonoma)
707.575.8465 info@pellegrinisonoma.com www.pellegrinisonoma.com
Hours: 10:30am - 4:30pm daily   Tasting Fee: none listed
Wine List: Pinot Noir, Chardonnay, Cabernet Sauvignon, Merlot, Rosato, Carignane, Sauvignon Blanc, Zinfandel, Unoaked Chardonnay
Added Highlights: Gift Shop

Peters Family Winery 2064 Gravenstein Hwy. Ste. 102 Sebastopol (Northern Sonoma)
707.829.3111 info@petersfamilywinery.com www.petersfamilywinery.com
Hours: by appt only weekends   Tasting Fee: none listed
Wine List: Chardonnay, Pinot Noir, Cabernet Sauvignon, Syrah

Peterson Family Winery 4791 Dry Creek Rd. Bldg. #7 Healdsburg (Northern Sonoma)
707.431.7568 friends@petersonwinery.com www.petersonwinery.com
Hours: 11am - 4:30pm daily   Tasting Fee: $0 -$5
Wine List: Cabernet Sauvignon, Syrah, Zinfandel, Merlot, Muscat Blanc, Sangiovese, Blend
Part of Tour on page: 59

Petroni Vineyards 990 Cavedale Rd. Sonoma
707.935.8311 www.petronivineyards.com
Hours: 10am - 4pm weekdays 10AM - 12N Sat   Tasting Fee: $20
Wine List: Poggio Alla Pietra (Sangiovese Grosso), Cabernet Sauvignon, and Syrah
Notes: Tasting Room is in a cave at the owner's weekend home

Pezzi King Vineyards 3225 West Dry Creek Rd. Healdsburg (Northern Sonoma)
707.431.9388 www.pezziking.com
Hours: by appt only with a few days advance notice   Tasting Fee: Complimentary
Wine List: Cabernet Sauvignon, Zinfandel, Chardonnay, Sauvignon Blanc

Philip Staley Vineyards & Winery 4791 Dry Creek Rd. Healdsburg (Northern Sonoma)
707.433.0100 TR   www.staleywines.com
Hours: 10:30am - 4:30pm daily   Tasting Fee: $5 glass purchase
Wine List: Chardonnay, Pinot Noir
Notes: Tastings at Family Wineries, a collective tasting room.

Piña Cellars 8060 Silverado Trail Rutherford
707.738.9328 info@pinanapavalley.com www.pinacellars.com
Hours: 10am - 4pm by appt only Mon - Sun Tasting Fee: $10
Wine List: Cabernet Sauvignon, Tasting includes 5 Cabs from 5 different vineyards

Pine Ridge Winery 5901 Silverado Trail Napa
707.944.8111 www.pineridgewinery.com
Hours: 10:30am - 4:30pm   Tasting Fee: $10 - $20
Wine List: Chenin Blanc-Viognier, Rosé, Merlot, Cabernet Franc, Malbec, Cabernet Sauvignon
Notes: Excellent wines from this corporate venture. A nice stop in the Stag's Leap District.
Part of Tour on page: 144

Plaza Farms 106 Matheson St. Healdsburg (Northern Sonoma)
707.433.2345 www.plazafarms.com
Hours: 10am - 6pm daily   Tasting Fee: none listed
Wine List: Various wines from multiple wineries
Added Highlights: Gift Shop, Restaurant/Market
Notes: A collective tasting room for Davero Olive Oil & Wine, Tandem Winery - also contains vendor restaurants, a chocolatier, teas, ceramics, and more

Plumpjack Winery 620 Oakville Cross Rd. Oakville
707.945.1220 www.plumpjack.com
Hours: 10am - 4pm Reservations required for groups of 8 or more. Tasting Fee: $5 - $10
Wine List: Cabernet Sauvignon, Chardonnay, Merlot
Added Highlights: Gift Shop
Notes: Down a long driveway just off Oakville Cross Road, Plumpjack is popular for its charming tasting room and excellent wines. A very friendly staff and a nice gift shop. The winery is just across the way from the tasting room. Limited parking.
Part of Tour on page: 117, 147, 167

Pope Valley Cellars 6613 Pope Valley Rd. Pope Valley
707.965.1246 info@popevalleywinery.com www.popevalleywinery.com
Hours: by appt only   Tasting Fee: Complimentary
Wine List: Chenin Blanc, Sangiovese, Sangiovese Rosé, Zinfandel, Merlot, Cabernet Sauvignon, Zinfandel Port Added Highlights: Picnic Area

Porter Creek Vineyards 8735 Westside Rd. Healdsburg (Northern Sonoma)
707.433.6321 info@portercreekvineyards.com www.portercreekvineyards.com
Hours: 11am - 4pm daily 8 people max - no buses Tasting Fee: Complimentary
Wine List: Chardonnay, Viognier, Pinot Noir, Syrah, Carignane
Added Highlights: Biodynamic/Organic

Prager Winery & Port Works 1281 Lewelling Ln. St. Helena
707.963.7678 www.pragerport.com
Hours: 10:30am - 4:30pm Mon - Sat Closed Sundays Tasting Fee: none listed
Wine List: Late Harvest Riesling, Petit Sirah, Port

Preston of Dry Creek 9282 W. Dry Creek Rd. Healdsburg (Northern Sonoma)
707.433.3372 www.prestonofdrycreek.com, www.prestonvineyards.com
Hours: 11am - 4:30pm daily no groups larger than 8 Tasting Fee: $5 (CWP)
Wine List: Petite Sirah, Syrah, Sauvignon Blanc, Barbera, Mourvèdre, Cinsault, Carignane, Rousanne, Viognier, Vin Gris, Blends, Olive Oil, Olives

Added Highlights: Bocce Court, Gift Shop, Picnic Area
Notes: After starting off as a much larger production winery Preston chose to focus on smaller, organic, and high quality. The in house bakery, olive oil and gracious grounds make for a relaxed, friendly experience. Around the corner from Ferrari Carano.
Part of Tour on page: 59

Pride Mountain Vineyards 4026 Spring Mountain Rd. St. Helena
707.963.4949 www.pridewines.com
Hours: by appt only   Tours & tastings by appt only. Wed -Sat, Mon. Tasting Fee: $20
Wine List: Merlot, Cabernet Sauvignon, Cabernet Franc, Viognier, Chardonnay
Added Highlights: Architecture, Gift Shop, Picnic Area, Tours
Notes: All the way at the top of Spring Mountain, not only do they make great wines, but also they offer spectacular views and one of the best picnic areas around. Allow twenty five minutes to reach them from downtown St Helena. Winding road.
Part of Tour on page: 205

Provenance Vineyards 1695 St. Helena Hwy. St. Helena
707.968.3633 info@provenancevineyards.com www.provenancevineyards.com
Hours: 10am - 4:30pm   Tasting Fee: $10 ($5 applied to purchase)
Wine List: Sauvignon Blanc, Merlot, Cabernet Sauvignon, NV Port
Added Highlights: Gift Shop

Quintessa 1601 Silverado Trail Rutherford
707.967.1601 info@quintessa.com www.quintessa.com
Hours: by appt only   Tasting Fee: $65
Wine List: Bordeaux Style Blend
Added Highlights: Architecture, Biodynamic/Organic
Notes: Remarkable building and they have a great tour. Allow one hour for "The Experience". Includes 2 block samples, 1 current release, 2 bite sized food pairings

Quivira Vineyards 4900 W. Dry Creek Rd. Healdsburg (Northern Sonoma)
707.431.8333 www.quivirawine.com
Hours: 11am - 5pm daily   Tasting Fee: CWP
Wine List: Zinfandel, Sauvignon Blanc, Syrah, Petite Sirah, Grenache and other Rhone-style blends
Added Highlights: Art Gallery, Biodynamic/Organic, Gift Shop
Notes: On West Dry Creek above the Lambert Bridge crossing, this very 'green' building reflects the Biodynamic commitment that Quivira maintains. A friendly staff, a small map museum, a gift shop and some very good wines. Quivira was the name of a mythical Chinese city thought to be located in California's North Coast!
Part of Tour on page: 59, 179

Ravenswood Winery 18701 Gehricke Rd. Sonoma
707.933.2332 www.ravenswood-wine.com
Hours: 10am - 4:30pm   receive a logo glass w/tasting fee   Tasting Fee: $10 - $15
Wine List: Zinfandel, Merlot, Cabernet Sauvignon, Cabernet Franc, Carignane, Petite Sirah, Icon (blend of Syrah, Grenache, Mourvèdre, Viognier) They are famous for their old vine Zinfandel.
Added Highlights: A great gift shop filled with unique items based on their famous label.
Notes: Very convenient to the Plaza in Sonoma, this well-known label is sure to please. Map on page 95.

Raymond Burr Vineyards 8339 W. Dry Creek Rd. Healdsburg (Northern Sonoma)
888.900.24 www.raymondburrvineyards.com
Hours: 10am - 5pm by appt only Tasting Fee: Complimentary   (continued on next page)

Wine List: Cabernet Sauvignon, Cabernet Franc, Chardonnay
Added Highlights: Orchids, Picnic Area, Tours
Notes: Orchid tour by appt at 11am on Sat

Raymond Vineyard & Cellar 849 Zinfandel Ln. St. Helena
707.963.3141 www.raymondvineyards.com
Hours: 10am - 4pm groups of 6 or more req appt (small TR) Tasting Fee: $7.50 - $15 (CWP)
Wine List: Cabernet Sauvignon, Merlot, Chardonnay, Sauvignon Blanc, Blends

Redmon Family Vineyards 1185 Starr Ave. St. Helena
707.968.9252 www.redmonvineyards.com
Hours: by appt only Tasting Fee: none listed
Wine List: Cabernet Sauvignon, Merlot, Blends. Also Starr Cellars Label.
Notes: Panoramic view of Napa Valley, taste RFV wine in their custom wine cellar.

Regusci Winery 5584 Silverado Trail Napa
707.254.403 www.regusciwinery.com
Hours: 10am - 4pm Tasting Fee: $5 - $10
Wine List: Cabernet Sauvignon, Merlot, Zinfandel, and Chardonnay
Added Highlights: Architecture, Gift Shop, Picnic Area, Tours
Notes: Old time Napa, the barrel building is a stone winery from the late 1800's, the oldest winery building in the Stag's Leap district. Charming, friendly, informal setting on a real working farm. Good wines & a good value too. A favorite picnic spot. Cute dogs.
Part of Tour on page: 119, 121, 129, 131, 153

Revana Family Vineyard 2930 St. Helena Hwy. N. St. Helena
707.967.8814 info@revanawine.com www.revanawine.com
Hours: 10am - 4pm by appt Tasting Fee: none listed
Wine List: Cabernet Sauvignon

Reverie Vineyard & Winery 1520 Diamond Mountain Rd. Calistoga
707.942.6800 Tasting Fee: $20
Hours: 10am - 5pm by appt only
Wine List: Bordeaux varietals, Cabernet Franc, Cabernet Sauvignon, Sauvignon Blanc, Barbera, Rousanne
Notes: Tastings done in the caves and outdoors in a beautiful fairy circle of Redwood Trees

Reynolds Family Winery 3266 Silverado Trail Napa
707.258.2558 info@reynoldsfamilywinery.com www.reynoldsfamilywinery.com
Hours: 10am - 4:30pm daily (instant appts) Tasting Fee: $10 - $20
Wine List: Cabernet Sauvignon, Pinot Noir, Chardonnay, Persistence, Blend

Rezonja Wine Cellars 31969 Pine Mountain Cloverdale (Northern Sonoma)
707.431.1449 steve@rezonjawinecellars.com www.rezonjawinecellars.com
Hours: by appt only Tasting Fee: none listed
Wine List: Cabernet Sauvignon

Richard L. Graeser Winery 255 Petrified Forest Rd. Calistoga
707.942.4437 richard@graeserwinery.com www.graeserwinery.com
Hours: 10am - 5pm (instant appts) Tasting Fee: $10
Wine List: Cabernet Franc, Merlot, Zinfandel, Cabernet Sauvignon, Semillon, Blends
Added Highlights: Pet Friendly, Picnic Area, Tours
Notes: Charmingly rustic & dog friendly. Romantic picnic spot with a view. Perfect for popping the question!

Ridge Lytton Springs 650 Lytton Springs Rd. Healdsburg (Northern Sonoma)
707.433.7721 www.ridgewine.com
Hours: 11am - 4pm daily   Tasting Fee: $5
Wine List: Zinfandel
Added Highlights: Architecture, Views
Notes: The northern branch of the well-respected Ridge Winery. Behind the stunning building are acres of old vines in the classic field blend style of Zinfandel, Petite Syrah, Alicante Bouschet etc. Larger groups and limousines need to call ahead.
Part of Tour on page: 59

Ritchie Creek Vineyard 4024 Spring Mountain Rd. St. Helena
707.963.4661 rev@napanet.net www.ritchiecreek.com
Hours: by appt only   Tasting Fee: Complimentary
Wine List: Cabernet Sauvignon, Pinot Noir, Blaufrankisch
Added Highlights: Tours

River Road Vineyards 5220 Ross Rd. Sebastopol   (Northern Sonoma)
707.887.8130 wine@riverroadvineyards.com www.riverroadvineyards.com
Hours: by appt only   Tasting Fee: Complimentary
Wine List: Chardonnay, Cabernet Sauvignon, Merlot, Pinot Meunier, Pinot Noir
Notes: They do custom labels for events, business promotion, etc.

Robert Craig Wine Cellars 880 Vallejo St. Napa
707.252.2250 x 1 appts rachel@robertcraigwine.com www.robertcraigwine.com
Hours: Mon - Sat by appt only No Sundays Tasting Fee: PIE - 1 case minimum
Wine List: Cabernet Sauvignon, Chardonnay, Syrah, Zinfandel

Robert Hunter Winery 15655 Arnold Dr. Sonoma
707.996.3056 wineclub@roberthunterwinery.com www.roberthunterwinery.com
Hours: by appt only   Tasting Fee: $15 - $25
Wine List: Sparklers, Brut de Noirs, Pinot Noir
Added Highlights: Great gardens, private winery, tasting on the owner's patio

Robert Keenan Winery 3660 Spring Mountain Rd. St. Helena
707.963.9177 appt   www.keenanwinery.com
Hours: by appt only   Tasting Fee: Complimentary
Wine List: Cabernet Sauvignon, Merlot, Zinfandel, Syrah, Chardonnay
Added Highlights: Tours

Robert Mondavi Winery 7801 St. Helena Hwy. Oakville
707.226.1395;1335 info@robertmondaviwinery.com www.robertmondaviwinery.com
Hours: 10am - 5pm Closed Major Holidays. Tasting Fee: $15 - $50+ tastings & pairings
Wine List: Fumé Blanc, Chardonnay, Pinot Noir, Merlot, Cabernet Sauvignon, Moscato d'Oro, Sauvignon Blanc, Zinfandel, Dry Rosé
Added Highlights: Architecture, Art Gallery, Gardens, Gift Shop, Tours
Notes: A big, sprawling Spanish style winery, known throughout the world. Good tours. For a special treat bypass the main tasting room and go to the To Kalon Reserve room for world class Cabernet Sauvignon from vineyards just outside the door. Pricey but worth it. The wines are heady so share the tasting. Great gift shop. There is a variety of tours available; it is recommended that you make tour arrangements in advance.
Part of Tour on page: 69, 147, 165

Robert Rue Vineyard 1406 Wood Rd. Fulton (Northern Sonoma)
707.578.1601 carlene@robertruevineyard.com www.robertruevineyard.com
Hours: by appt only   Tasting Fee: Complimentary
Wine List: Zinfandel

Robert Sinskey Vineyards 6320 Silverado Trail Napa
707.944.9090 rsv@robertsinskey.com www.robertsinskey.com
Hours: 10am - 4:30pm daily   Tasting Fee: $10 - $60 w/ food pairings
Wine List: Pinot Blanc, Rosé of Pinot Noir, Pinot Gris, Vin Gris of Pinot Noir, Pinot Noir, Merlot, Cabernet Franc, Cabernet Sauvignon, Blends, Late Harvest Zinfandel
Added Highlights: Architecture, Biodynamic/Organic, Gift Shop
Notes: On the Silverado Trail at the top of the Stag's Leap District, this is a favorite with the younger set. A very modern building, Biodynamic wines, the aroma of a commercial kitchen and the best bar snacks. A delightful working garden supplies the kitchen. A fun place with good wines including some interesting varieties.
Part of Tour on page: 69, 119, 129, 131

Robert Stemmler Winery/Donum Estate 35 E. Napa St. Sonoma
707.935.1200 TR tastingroom@robertstemmlerwinery.com www.robertstemmlerwinery.com
Hours: by appt only   Tasting Fee: none listed
Wine List: Pinot Noir
Notes: The winery is by appt only but the address listed is for the Sonoma Enoteca, a collective tasting room where you can taste these and other wines daily on the Plaza in downtown Sonoma.

Robert Young Estate Winery 4960 Red Winery Rd. Geyserville (Northern Sonoma)
707.431.4811 info@ryew.com www.ryew.com
Hours: 10am - 4:30pm daily   Tasting Fee: $5
Wine List: Chardonnay, Merlot, Cabernet Sauvignon, Cabernet Franc, Blends

Robinson Family Vineyards 5880 Silverado Trail Napa
707.944.8004 www.robinsonfamilyvineyards.com
Hours: by appt only   Tasting Fee: $10
Wine List: Cabernet Sauvignon, Merlot

Robledo Family Winery 21901 Bonness Rd. Sonoma   (Carneros)
707.939.6903 www.robledofamilywinery.com
Hours: by appt only Mon - Sat 10am - 5pm, Sun 11am - 4pm   Tasting Fee: none listed
Wine List: Chardonnay, Pinot Grigio, Blends, Muscato, Cabernet Sauvignon, Merlot, Pinot Noir, Pinot Blanc, Sauvignon Blanc
Notes: From vineyard workers to winemakers this is a great family story. Visit them during Carneros Passport Events for a great time.

Roche Carneros Estate Winery 28700 Arnold Dr. Sonoma (Carneros)
800.825.9475 www.rochewinery.com
Hours: 10am - 6pm Summer; 5pm Winter Tasting Fee: Complimentary (10 or more, $5pp)
Wine List: Chardonnay, Pinot Noir, Merlot, Syrah, Cabernet Sauvignon, Muscat Cannelli, Tamarix (a blend of Chardonnay, Syrah & Pinot Noir: the name Tamarix comes from the color of a bush that grows on the property. Serve ice cold with spicy foods.)
Added Highlights: Horse Tours, Views, including Infineon Raceway
Notes: Down home tastings in a building on a hill that overlooks Infineon Raceway. Hear the roar of the cars and even catch a glimpse at the high turn on race day while sipping your wine.
Part of Tour on page: 41

Rodney Strong Vineyards 11455 Old Redwood Hwy. Healdsburg (Northern Sonoma)
707.433.6511 www.rodneystrong.com
Hours: 10am - 5pm Tours 11am & 3pm; self guided tours: 10am – 5pm Tasting Fee: $5 - $10
Wine List: Sauvignon Blanc, Chardonnay, Pinot Noir, Merlot, Syrah, Cabernet Sauvignon, Meritage, Zinfandel, Port
Added Highlights: Architecture, Gardens, Gift Shop, Tours
Notes: A very unique building and good solid wines from the Russian River Valley. Sharing the same driveway as the J Winery, it is convenient to both Highway 101 and Healdsburg. The self-guided tour is great and the staff is consistently friendly and fun.
Part of Tour on page: 173

Rombauer Vineyards 3522 Silverado Trail N. St. Helena
707.963.5170 www.rombauervineyards.com
Hours: 10am - 5pm by appt only Tasting Fee: $10
Wine List: Cabernet Sauvignon, Merlot, Chardonnay, Zinfandel, Port, Blend
Added Highlights: Architecture, Caves, Gardens, Picnic Area, Views
Notes: Perched on their hill and sitting on a mile of caves, Rombauer is a long time favorite. Very appealing wines, a friendly staff, great picnic area, wonderful views. For a special treat call ahead for a private tour. Aviation memorabilia.
Part of Tour on page: 151, 191, 193, 195, 203

Rosenblum Cellars 250 Center St. Healdsburg (Northern Sonoma - Downtown)
707.431.1169 www.rosenblumcellars.com
Hours: 10am - 6pm daily Tasting room is on the Plaza Tasting Fee: none listed
Wine List: Zinfandel, Syrah, Petite Sirah, Phone Blends, Chardonnay, Bordeaux Blends, Pinot Noir, Rosé, Dessert wines Map on page 186

Roshambo Winery & Gallery 23564 Arnold Dr. Sonoma
707.431.2051 www.roshambowinery.com
Hours: 10am - 5pm daily Tasting Fee: $5 (CWP)
Wine List: Zinfandel, Chardonnay, Syrah, Sauvignon Blanc, Table Red, Table White, Rosé
Notes: Currently Tasted at Cornerstone, a collective tasting room, while their facility is rebuilt. Roshambo is the name of the game we know as rock, paper, scissors! Fun wines!

Rosso & Bianco 300 Via Archimedes Geyserville (Northern Sonoma - Alexander Valley)
707.857.1400 www.rossobianco.com
Hours: 10am - 5pm daily Tasting Fee: $10 - $15 (some wines are Complimentary)
Wine List: Chardonnay, Pinot Noir, Syrah, Viognier, Cabernet Sauvignon, Zinfandel, Claret, Merlot, Malbec, Syrah-Shiraz, Pinot Grigio, Sparklers, Rosé
Added Highlights: Architecture, Gift Shop, Restaurant/Market, Views
Notes: Francis Ford Coppola's redux of the classic Chateau Souverain. One focus here is the brunch and luncheon restaurant for Italian comfort foods that are favorites of the Coppola family. Grand Estate.
Part of Tour on page: 59

Round Pond Estate 875 Rutherford Rd. Rutherford
707.302.2575 roundpond@roundpond.com www.roundpond.com
Hours: 11am - 4pm by appt Thu-Mon Tasting Fee: $25
Wine List: Cabernet Sauvignon, Nebbiolo
Added Highlights: Tours, great building. These wines are the 5% of grapes that they don't sell to others.
Notes: Credit Card required to reserve a tasting. Estate Tasting: $25. Guided Winery Tour & Tasting (1.5 hours): $35 at 11am, 1pm, 3pm by appt Thu - Mon. Twilight Tour, Tasting & Dinner: $175, per person 4th Sat of month by reservation

Rubicon Estate   1991 St. Helena Hwy.   Rutherford
707.968.1100 www.rubiconestate.com
Hours: 10am - 5pm daily, till 6pm Fri & Sat Memorial Day - Labor Day   Tasting Fee: $25
Wine List: Cabernet Sauvignon, Merlot, Cabernet Franc, Syrah, Blanc de Blanc, Rosé, Sauvignon Blanc, Pinot Noir, Zinfandel, Rubicon Blends
Added Highlights: Biodynamic/Organic, Gardens, Gift Shop, Restaurant/Market, Tours
Notes: This Inglenook Castle was the center of the Niebaum Estate that Francis Ford Coppola spent years reassembling to its original scope. Picture Nicholas Cage and Sofia Coppola playing around the fountains in their childhood. It has one of the most elegant gift shops in the Valley and the cafe/espresso bar is a wonderful place to relax amid a day of tasting. You can even sail a boat in the fountains.
Part of Tour on page: 62, 69, 127, 155, 165

Rudd   500 Oakville Cross Rd.   Oakville
707.944.8577 info@ruddwines.com www.ruddwines.com
Hours: by appt only Tue – Sat Closed Sun-Mon   Tasting Fee: $35 - $60
Wine List: Cabernet Sauvignon, Chardonnay, Sauvignon, Blanc, Blends
Added Highlights: Architecture, Gardens, Tours
Notes: Very private, very beautiful, excellent, expensive wines. Leslie Rudd is the owner the of Dean and DeLuca chain, among other enterprises. This is a winery for the serious. Tours at 10am limited to a max of 8 guests. Credit card charged when appt is scheduled. No refund w/o 48 hrs notice. A "Request for Visit Form" is found on the website.
Part of Tour on page: 207

Russian Hill Estate Winery   4525 Slusser Rd.   Windsor   (Northern Sonoma)
707.575.9428 www.russianhillestate.com
Hours: 10am - 4pm Thu - Mon   Tasting Fee: Complimentary (groups 6 or more $10pp)
Wine List: Pinot Noir, Syrah, Chardonnay, Port

Russian River Vineyards   5700 Gravenstein Hwy.   Forestville   (Northern Sonoma)
707.887.3344 TR info@russianrivervineyards.com www.russianrivervineyards.com
Hours: 11am - 5pm daily   Tasting Fee: none listed
Wine List: Pinot Noir, Syrah, Zinfandel, Petite Sirah, Sparklers, Barbera, Pinot Noir
Added Highlights: Restaurant/Market
Notes: Their restaurant serves lunch & dinner as well as brunch on Sundays

Ruston Family Vineyards   2798 Spring St.   St. Helena
707.967.8025 john@rustonvines.com www.rustonvines.com
Hours: by appt only   Tasting Fee: Complimentary
Wine List: Blends, Cabernet Sauvignon, Cabernet Franc, Merlot, Sauvignon Blanc, Semillon

Rustridge Ranch Vineyards   2910 Lower Chiles Valley Rd.   St. Helena
707.963.9503; 707.965.9353
Hours: by appt only   Tasting Fee: none listed
Wine List: Cabernet Sauvignon, Chardonnay, Zinfandel, Sauvignon Blanc, Blend
Notes: This winery also has a Bed & Breakfast

Rutherford Grove Winery & Vineyards   1673 Highway 29   Rutherford
707.963.544 www.rutherfordgrove.com
Hours: 10am - 4:30pm   Tasting Fee: $10
Wine List: Cabernet Sauvignon, Merlot, Sauvignon Blanc, Petite Sirah, Sangiovese
Added Highlights: Picnic Area

Rutherford Hill Winery 200 Rutherford Hill Rd. Rutherford
707.963.7194 info@rutherfordhill.com www.rutherfordhill.com
Hours: 10am - 5pm   Tasting Fee: $10
Wine List: Zinfandel Port, Merlot, Cabernet Sauvignon, Sangiovese, Blends, Petite Verdot, Chardonnay, Syrah, Malbec, Sauvignon Blanc
Added Highlights: Caves, Gardens, Gift Shop, Picnic Area, Views
Notes: Perched on side of the mountain above the hotel Auberge du Soleil, it is a fun place with great views, picnic grounds under the hundred year old olive trees. A great tour and of course good wines. A friendly staff and nice indoor & outdoor tasting areas.
Part of Tour on page: 117, 147, 161, 195

Rutherford Ranch Vineyards 1680 Silverado Trail St. Helena
707.967.5120 www.rutherfordranch.com
Hours: 10am - 4:30pm Tasting Fee: $10
Wine List: Cabernet Sauvignon, Chardonnay, Merlot, Sauvignon Blanc, Zinfandel, White Zinfandel, Port, Muscato, Blends
Notes: Other labels that can be tasted here include Story Ridge, Scott Family Estate, Grand Pacific, Round Hill

Sable Ridge Vineyards 6320 Jamison Rd. Santa Rosa (Northern Sonoma)
707.542.3138 wine@sableridge.com www.sableridge.com
Hours: by appt only   Tasting Fee: none listed
Wine List: Syrah, Viognier, Petite Sirah

Saddleback Cellars 7802 Money Rd. Oakville
707.944.1305 hillery@saddlebackcellars.com www.saddlebackcellars.com
Hours: by appt only   Tasting Fee: $5 for 6 wines
Wine List: Pinot Blanc, Pinot Grigio, Chardonnay, Viognier, Merlot, Old Vine Zinfandel, Cabernet Sauvignon
Notes: The tastings are done outside on the picnic tables and the wines are quite good. Money Rd. is just across from the Silver Oak Winery off of Oakville Cross Road so it is convenient to a number of great wineries that you can combine into a tour.

Saintsbury Vineyard 1500 Los Carneros Ave. Napa   (Carneros)
707.252.0592 info@saintsbury.com www.saintsbury.com
Hours: by appt only   Tasting Fee: Complimentary
Wine List: Pinot Noir, Pinot Gris, Syrah, Chardonnay
Added Highlights: Tours

Salvestrin Vineyard & Winery 397 Main St. St. Helena
707.963.5105 sales@salvestrinwinery.com www.salvestrinwinery.com
Hours: by appt only   Tasting Fee: $10
Wine List: Cabernet Sauvignon, Sangiovese, Retaggio (Red Blend), Sauvignon Blanc, Petite Sirah
Added Highlights: Tours

Sausal Winery 7370 Highway 128 Healdsburg (Northern Sonoma)
707.433.2285 www.sausalwinery.com
Hours: 10am - 4pm daily   Tasting Fee: $5
Wine List: Chenin Blanc, Zinfandel, Cabernet Sauvignon, Sangiovese, Italian Blend
Added Highlights: Picnic Area
Notes: A charming, small family-run winery in the Alexander Valley. Good wines, a good value, pretty, intimate tasting room and friendly staff that make you feel at home. Nice picnic area.
Part of Tour on page: 59

Sawyer Cellars 8350 St. Helena Hwy. Rutherford
707.963.1980 appts   www.sawyercellars.com
Hours: 10am - 5pm daily (instant appts) Tasting Fee: $7.50 - $15
Wine List: Cabernet Sauvignon, Merlot, Sauvignon Blanc, Meritage, Blend
Added Highlights: Gift Shop, Tours
Notes: A small family-run jewel of a winery tucked among some of Napa's most famous. Authentic Rutherford, tremendously well made wines, pretty tasting room with small gift shop and friendly staff. Larger groups should call ahead.
Part of Tour on page: 62, 69, 157

School House Vineyards 3549 Langtry Rd. St. Helena
707.963.4240 Sales@SchoolHouseVineyard.com www.SchoolHouseVineyard.com
Hours: by appt only   Tasting Fee: PIE
Wine List: Pinot Noir, Chardonnay, Mescolanza (mixed black field-blend derives its character from mountain-grown Zinfandel (76%), Petite Sirah (17%) and Carignane (7%))
Added Highlights: Views, Some of the only Burgundy-style fruit on Spring Mountain
Notes: Charming "Mom and Pop Winery" gives a nice patio tasting.

Schramsberg Vineyards 1400 Schramsberg Rd. Calistoga
707.942.2414 tours reception@schramsberg.com www.schramsberg.com
Hours: 10am - 4pm daily by appt Tasting Fee: $25
Wine List: Sparklers; Brut Rosé, Cremant, Blanc de Noirs, Blanc de Blanc, Mirabelle
Added Highlights: Architecture, Caves, Gardens, Gift Shop, Tours
Notes: Sparkling wines. The site of the original winery that Robert Louis Stevenson visited and said "and their wine is bottled poetry..." It has a wonderful mix of old and new. Tasting appointments include a tour. It is up a long and winding, but well paved road. Allow extra time and be sure to arrive early. Going north Schramsberg Rd. is on the left just past Larkmead Lane and before Dunaweal Lane.
Part of Tour on page: 125

Schug Carneros Estate Winery 602 Bonneau Rd. Sonoma   (Carneros)
707.939.9363 david@schugwinery.com TR www.schugwinery.com
Hours: 10am - 5pm daily Tours by appt Tasting Fee: $5, $10 for reserve
Wine List: Sauvignon Blanc, Chardonnay, Pinot Noir, Merlot, Cabernet Franc, Cabernet Sauvignon, Syrah, Blanc de Noirs Sparkling Pinot Noir
Added Highlights: Architecture, Gift Shop, Picnic Area, Tours, Views
Notes: Wonderfully convenient to San Francisco and just off of Route 121 North of the first group of wineries in Carneros. Schug is highly respected for their Chardonnay and Pinot Noir. Charming location and building, small tasting room that spreads out to the great barrel room when busy. Makes a great first or last stop on a tour from San Francisco.
Part of Tour on page: 41, 109

Schweiger Vineyards 4015 Spring Mountain Rd. St. Helena
707.963.4882 svwine@schweigervineyards.com www.schweigervineyards.com
Hours: 11am - 4pm by appt   Tasting Fee: $10
Wine List: Sauvignon Blanc, Chardonnay, Merlot, Cabernet Sauvignon, Dedication™, Petite Sirah, Port, Estate Red Wine
Added Highlights: Views
Notes: On the top of Spring Mountain, this family-run winery is getting better by leaps and bounds. Long time grape growers turned winemakers, they have a beautiful location and a charming staff. Tastings are conducted downstairs in the barrel room. Nice dogs.
Part of Tour on page: 205

Seavey Vineyard 1310 Conn Valley Rd. St. Helena
707.963.8339 info@seaveyvineyard.com www.seaveyvineyard.com
Hours: by appt only   Tasting Fee: Complimentary
Wine List: Cabernet Sauvignon, Merlot

Sebastiani Vineyards and Winery 389 - 4th St. E. Sonoma
707.938.5532 www.sebastiani.com
Hours: 10am - 5pm daily   Tasting Fee: $5 - $10
Wine List: Cabernet Sauvignon, Merlot, Barbera, Zinfandel, Pinot Noir
Added Highlights: Architecture, Gift Shop
Notes: Located within walking distance of the Sonoma Plaza, Sebastiani is old time Sonoma remade for modern tastes. Wonderful well-priced wines, great gift shop, historic barrels and equipment and a beautiful, gracious visitor center. Their old barrel room is a favorite event site.
Part of Tour on page: 41, 95

Sebastopol Vineyards 8757 Green Valley Rd. Sebastopol (Northern Sonoma)
707.829.9463 www.sebastopolvineyards.com
Hours: weekends   Tasting Fee: none listed
Wine List: Chardonnay, Sauvignon Blanc, Syrah

Seghesio Winery 14730 Grove St. Healdsburg (Northern Sonoma - Downtown)
707.433.3579 www.seghesio.com
Hours: 10am - 4:30pm daily Tasting Fee: $5 (CWP)
Wine List: Zinfandel, Arneis, Pinot Grigio, Barbera, Sangiovese
Added Highlights: Bocce Court, Gift Shop
Notes: Walking distance from downtown Healdsburg their gracious grounds and stunning tasting room, with its views of the barrels, is home to some wonderfully made wines. Their Italian varietals are greatly respected and their Passport parties are famous. They also do tastings with food pairings, $25 to taste 4 library wines plus 4 small plates.
Part of Tour on page: 59

Selby Winery 215 Center St. Healdsburg (Northern Sonoma)
707.431.1288 www.selbywinery.com
Hours: 11am - 5:30pm   Tasting Fee: $0 - $5
Wine List: Chardonnay, Sauvignon Blanc, Rosé of Syrah, Syrah, Pinot Noir, Old Vine Zinfandel, Zinfandel Port, Merlot, Dessert Wine

Sequoia Grove Vineyards 8338 St. Helena Hwy. S. Rutherford
707.944.2945 www.sequoiagrove.com
Hours: 10:30am - 5pm   Tasting Fee: $10 - $20
Wine List: Cabernet Sauvignon, Chardonnay, Syrah
Added Highlights: Gardens, Sequoia Trees
Notes: Tucked amidst some of the most famous wineries of Oakville and Rutherford, they can clearly hold their own for quality and excellence. A charming, relaxed tasting room and a good staff make for a great experience. Look for the grove of Sequoias.
Part of Tour on page: 62, 141, 145

Shafer Vineyards 6154 Silverado Trail Napa
707.944.2877 www.shafervineyards.com
Hours: by appt only   Tasting Fee: $35
Wine List: Chardonnay, Cabernet, Blends
Added Highlights: Views, Famous Wines   (continued on the next page)

Notes: Their recent Cabernet Sauvignon Stags Leap Hillside Select was given a perfect score. fSerious wine buyers will love this winery. One of Napa's great Ultra-Premium producers.

Sherwin Family Vineyards 4060 Spring Mountain Rd. St. Helena
707.963.1154 info@sherwinfamilyvineyards.com www.sherwinfamilyvineyards.com
Hours: by appt only Tasting Fee: Complimentary (groups of 8 or more $25pp)
Wine List: Cabernet Sauvignon
Added Highlights: Architecture   Notes: Their Cabernet gets consistently high marks in Wine Spectator.

Siduri Wines 980 Airway Ct. Ste. C Santa Rosa (Northern Sonoma - Corporate Park)
707.578.3882 appt pinot@siduri.com www.siduri.com
Hours: 10am - 3pm daily by appt   Tasting Fee: Complimentary
Wine List: single vineyard Pinot Noir

Signorello Vineyards 4500 Silverado Trail Napa
707.255.5990 info@signorellovineyards.com www.signorellovineyards.com
Hours: 10:30am - 5pm   Tasting Fee: $5
Wine List: Cabernet Sauvignon, Zinfandel, Pinot Noir, Syrah Seta: is a Sauvignon-Semillon Blend
Added Highlights: Gardens, Gift Shop, Views
Notes: A charming, small family winery perched on the hillsides of Silverado just north of Darioush. Very well made wines in small production from vineyards in site of the charming tasting room. Great patio and views. Wonderful staff that makes you feels at home. A personal favorite.
Part of Tour on page: 69, 121, 129, 195

Silenus Vintners 5225 Solano Ave. Napa
707.299.3930 www.silenusvintners.com
Hours: 10am - 4pm daily   Tasting Fee: $10 - $20
Wine List: Barbera, Blends, Cabernet Sauvignon, Chardonnay, Dolcetto, Grenache, Merlot, Petite Sirah, Port, Rosé, Sauvignon Blanc, Syrah, Viognier, Zinfandel
Notes: A collective tasting room for Ahnfeldt, B Cellars, Bialla Vineyards, Brookdale, Due Vigne di famiglia, Ilsley Vineyards, Juslyn Vineyards, MacLean vineyards, Modus Operandi Cellars, Ramian Estate, Renard, Robert Williamson Family Estate Wines, Scott Harvey Wines

Silver Oak Cellars 915 Oakville Cross Rd. Oakville
707.944.8808 www.silveroak.com
Hours: 9am - 4pm   Tasting Fee: $10
Wine List: Cabernet Sauvignon
Added Highlights: Architecture, Gift Shop
Notes: Known for its very appealing Cabernet Sauvignon blend, this is a popular destination. They taste two blends, one from Napa Valley and the other from Alexander Valley in Sonoma County. They are just building a new visitor center which will have the same friendly staff and should open Fall 2008.
Part of Tour on page: 133, 167 Note: They are currently tasting in a double wide trailer.

Silver Oak Wine Cellars 24625 Chianti Rd. Geyserville (Northern Sonoma - Alexander Valley)
707.944.8808 info@silveroak.com www.silveroak.com
Hours: 9am - 4pm Mon - Sat   Tasting Fee: $10 per wine
Wine List: Cabernet Sauvignon
Added Highlights: Gift Shop
Notes: Known for its very appealing Cabernet Sauvignon blend, this is a less visited cousin of their more accessible Napa winery. They taste two blends, one from Napa Valley and the other from Alexander Valley in Sonoma County. Pretty building, friendly staff.
Part of Tour on page: 59

Silverado Vineyards 6121 Silverado Trail   Napa
707.257.1770 www.silveradovineyards.com
Hours: 10:30am - 4:30pm   Tasting Fee: $10 - $20
Wine List: Sauvignon Blanc, Chardonnay, Merlot, Sangiovese, Cabernet Sauvignon
Added Highlights: Architecture, Gift Shop, Views
Notes: Perched on its own hill in the Stag's Leap district along the Silverado Trail, they are very popular for their beautiful building, location and views. Well made wines, great tasting room and patio. Fun staff. Owned by Walt Disney's Daughter.
Part of Tour on page: 123, 127, 159

Simi Winery 16725 Healdsburg Ave.   Healdsburg (Northern Sonoma)
707.433.6981 www.simiwinery.com
Hours: 10am - 5pm   Tours: 11am & 2pm. Large groups req appt   Tasting Fee: none listed
Wine List: Sauvignon Blanc, Chardonnay, Merlot, Cabernet Sauvignon
Added Highlights: Gift Shop, Picnic Area, Tours
Notes: One of the great, old family wineries of Healdsburg with its roots put down before Prohibition. Great wines and friendly staff.
Part of Tour on page: 59

Smith-Madrone Vineyards 4022 Spring Mountain Rd.   St. Helena
707.963.2283 www.smithmadrone.com
Hours: by appt only Mon - Sat   Tasting Fee: PIE
Wine List: Riesling
Added Highlights: Tours

Sonoma Enoteca 35 E. Napa St.   Sonoma (On the Sonoma Plaza)
707.935.1200 info@sonoma-enoteca.com www.sonoma-enoteca.com
Hours: daily   Tasting Fee: none listed
Wine List: A collective tasting room for Abundance Vineyards, Brutocao Cellars, Compass, Dreyer Sonoma, Favero, Manzanita Creek, Madrone Ridge, Il Cuore, Robert Stemmler, Seabiscuit Ranch, Trios/Brion. Plus Stonehouse Olive Oil
Added Highlights: Gift Shop
On map on page: 18

Souverain 308B Center Street   Healdsburg (On the Healdsburg Plaza)
707-433-2822   info@Souverain.com   www.Souverain.com
Hours: 11am to 6pm   Tasting Fee: $5 - $25 (The higher fee is for the Wine and Cheese Pairing)
Wines: Sauvignon Blanc, Chardonnay and Voignier. Cabernet Sauvignon and Merlot. Pinot Noir, Syrah, Petite Sirah and Zinfandel. Map on page 186

Spottswoode Winery 1902 Madrona Ave. St. Helena
707.963.0134 tours@spottswoode.com www.spottswoode.com
Hours: 10am by appt only Tue & Fri   Tasting Fee: PIE
Wine List: Cabernet Sauvignon, Sauvignon Blanc, Blends
Added Highlights: Biodynamic/Organic, Tours
Notes: Book your appointment 4 – 6 weeks in advance.

Spring Mountain Vineyards 2805 Spring Mountain Rd. St. Helena
707.967.4188 info@springmtn.com www.springmtn.com
Hours: 10am - 5pm by appt only   Tasting & Tour Fee: $25 (applied to purchase)
Wine List: Syrah, Cabernet Sauvignon, Sauvignon Blanc, Blend
Added Highlights: Architecture, Caves, Gardens, Tours   (continued on next page)

Notes: One of the Grand Estates of Napa, sitting at the foot of Spring Mountain with their vineyards reaching up the mountain. The tour/tasting is worth the price, the mansion and grounds are magnificent. Wonderful staff, great wines. Allow two hours for the tour and tasting. It is very convenient to downtown, St. Helena, just a few minutes up Spring Mountain Road before it begins to climb.
Part of Tour on page: 205

St. Clement Vineyards 2867 N. St. Helena Hwy. St. Helena
800.331.8266 www.stclement.com
Hours: 10am - 4pm   Tasting Fee: $10 - $25
Wine List: Cabernet Sauvignon, Merlot, Sauvignon Blanc, Chardonnay, Syrah
Added Highlights: Gift Shop, Picnic Area
Notes: The Victorian tasting room perched on its own hill on Route 29 north of St. Helena was built as a home in the late 1800's. Nice staff, cute gift shop and great views. Good wines and wonderful picnic tables on the patio that you have to call ahead to reserve.
Part of Tour on page: 151

St. Francis Vineyard & Winery 100 Pythian Rd. Santa Rosa (Northern Sonoma)
707.833.0242 info@stfranciswine.com www.stfranciswine.com
Hours: 10am - 5pm   Tasting Fee: $5 - $20
Wine List: Chardonnay, Cabernet Sauvignon, Merlot, Zinfandel, Syrah
Added Highlights: Architecture, Gift Shop, Picnic Area, Tours, Views
Notes: Beautiful Spanish style visitor's center and tasting room that overlooks the vineyards and mountains beyond. Wonderful wines and nice staff. The traffic light at the intersection makes it a great 'northern limit' for a Sonoma Valley tour on a busy day.
Part of Tour on page: 48, 103, 107, 175

St. Supéry Vineyards & Winery 8440 St. Helena Hwy. Rutherford
707.963.4507 x 36   www.stsupery.com
Hours: 10am - 5:30pm   Tasting Fee: $10 - $25
Wine List: Sauvignon Blanc, Cabernet Sauvignon, Merlot, Chardonnay, Unoaked Chardonnay, Syrah, Cabernet Franc
Added Highlights: Art Gallery, Gift Shop, Tours
Notes: Very modern, spacious tasting room, beautiful art gallery and good self-tour. Well made European style wines, knowledgably staff, small gift shop. Limousines and larger groups must call ahead. Tours are $45 pp but the Art Gallery can be viewed free of charge. What is less well-known is their charming reserve tasting done upstairs, which is quite elegant and requires advance reservations.
Part of Tour on page: 62, 69, 159, 191

Stagecoach Vineyard 3265 Soda Canyon Rd. Napa
707.259.1198 www.stagecoachvineyard.com
Hours: by appt only   Tasting Fee: PIE
Wine List: Cabernet Sauvignon, Cabernet Franc, Merlot, Malbec, Petit Verdot, Syrah, Petite Sirah, Chardonnay, Marsanne, Viognier, Tempranillo, Sangiovese and Zinfandel
Added Highlights: Exclusive tasting, Vineyards are just below Atlas Peak, Views. The Stagecoach Vineyards name appears on many high-quality wine labels.

Staglin Family Vineyard 1570 Bella Oaks Ln. Rutherford
707.944.477 www.staglinfamily.com
Hours: 11am - 3pm by appt only Mon - Fri   Tasting Fee: $25
Wine List: Chardonnay, Cabernet Sauvignon, Sangiovese
Added Highlights: Architecture, Biodynamic/Organic

Stag's Leap Wine Cellars 5766 Silverado Trail Napa
707.261.6441 retail@cask23.com www.cask23.com
Hours: 10am - 4:30pm Tasting Fee: $10 - $30
Wine List: Riesling, Sauvignon Blanc, Chardonnay, Merlot, Cabernet Sauvignon
Added Highlights: Gift Shop, Tours
Notes: One of the wineries that put Napa on the Map during the 1976 Judgment of Paris for their Cabernet Sauvignon. Recently sold by its founder. The tank room tasting room is rather bare. Basic tasting is to the left, reserve to the right. Not a famous tasting experience but the long reputation keeps the place busy. Pretty grounds. Tours (1 hour) by appt $20 pp for up to 10 people. Wine sampling included in the tour. Larger groups accommodated by special arrangement. In 2008 it was reportedly sold to a consortium including Beringer Blass and Antinori for 171 million dollars.
Part of Tour on page: 115, 119, 133, 157

Stags' Leap Winery 6150 Silverado Trail Napa
707.944.1303 www.stagsleapwinery.com
Hours: by appt only Tasting Fee: $25 includes tour (no TR) Tours are at 10:30am or 2:30pm
Wine List: Viognier, Chardonnay, Merlot, Cabernet Sauvignon, Petite Syrah
Added Highlights: Tours
Notes: This is not the winery involved in the Judgment of Paris. There was some controversy about the use of such a similar name and these wineries are often confused. This winery is by appointment only.

Steltzner Vineyards 5998 Silverado Trail Napa
707.252.7272 retailsales@steltzner.com www.steltzner.com
Hours: 10:30am - 4:30pm by appt only (same day) Tasting Fee: $10 (7 or more, $15 - $25 pp)
Wine List: Sauvignon Blanc, Rosé of Syrah, Chardonnay, Claret, Merlot, Cabernet Sauvignon, Cuvee, Pinotage, Sangiovese, Merlot Port
Added Highlights: Tours, Caves

Sterling Vineyards 1111 Dunaweal Ln. Calistoga
707.942.3344 www.sterlingvineyards.com
Hours: 10am - 4:30pm Tasting Fee: $15 - $20
Wine List: Cabernet Sauvignon, Merlot, Chardonnay, Pinot Noir, Shiraz, Sauvignon Blanc, Blends
Added Highlights: Architecture, Gift Shop, Tours, Views
Notes: Just south of Calistoga and famous for their tramway that brings you up to the mountain top winery, Sterling was the first winery to charge for tastings. A fun time, great views, good gift shop, nice wines. Allow two hours. Visitor Center: $15 adults, $10 child < 21, (child under 3 is free). Weekends & Holidays: $20 for adults. Includes: Tram, self-guided tour, 5 wine seated tasting. Reserve Tour & Tasting $45. pp (no one under 21) at 11am, limit of 8 or less.
Part of Tour on page: 203

Stone Creek Tasting Room (Family Wineries) 9380 Sonoma Hwy. Kenwood
707.833.5070 info@slcellars.com www.slcellars.com
Hours: 10:30am - 5pm daily   Tasting Fee: none listed
Wine List: Various wines from multiple wineries
Added Highlights: Gift Shop, Picnic Area
Notes: Collective Tasting Room for: Simon Levi Cellars, Cuttings Wharf, Pour La Vie
Part of Tour on page: 48

Stoneheath Winery PO Box 626 Napa
707.257.0701 ciao@stoneheath.com www.stoneheath.com
Hours: by appt only Tasting Fee: none listed
Wine List: Nebbiola Riserva, Barbera,   Added Highlights: Tours

Stonestreet Winery 7111 Highway 128 Healdsburg (Northern Sonoma)
707.433.7102 info@stonestreetwines.com www.stonestreetwinery.com
Hours: 10am - 5pm daily Jul – Oct; Nov – Jun till 4pm &closed Tue. Tasting Fee: $5 - $12
Wine List: Merlot, Cabernet Sauvignon, Chardonnay, Sauvignon Blanc, Bordeaux Style Blend
Added Highlights: Bocce Court
Notes: Complimentary tasting coupon available on the website; $20 w/food pairing

Stony Hill Vineyard 3331 N. St. Helena Hwy. St. Helena
707.963.2636 www.stonyhillvineyard.com
Hours: 9am - 5pm Mon - Fri by appt (except holidays) Tasting Fee: Complimentary
Wine List: Chardonnay
Added Highlights: Tours
Notes: Visits average about 1 hour & include a tour of the winery and a wine tasting at the house.

Storybook Mountain Winery 3835 Highway 128 Calistoga
707.942.5310 appt sigstory@storybookwines.com www.storybookwines.com
Hours: by appt only (closed Sun) Tasting Fee: Complimentary (groups of 8 or more $10 pp)
Wine List: Zinfandel, Cabernet Sauvignon, Blend
Added Highlights: Views

Stryker Sonoma Winery 5110 Highway 128 Geyserville (Northern Sonoma)
707.433.1944 donna@strykersonoma.com www.strykersonoma.com
Hours: 10:30am - 5pm daily (Mon-Wed by appt Jan - Mar) Tasting Fee: $5 - $10
Wine List: Cabernet Sauvignon, Merlot, Syrah, Zinfandel, Pinot Noir, Blend, Chardonnay, Semillon
Added Highlights: Architecture, Gift Shop
Notes: An ultra modern building in the center section of the Alexander Valley. A popular location with great views and wonderful picnic areas. Good wines, nice staff.
Part of Tour on page: 59

Stuhlmuller Vineyards 4951 W. Soda Rock Ln. Healdsburg (Northern Sonoma)
707.431.7745 info@stuhlmullervineyards.com www.StuhlmullerVineyards.com
Hours: by appt only Tasting Fee: Complimentary
Wine List: Cabernet Sauvignon, Chardonnay, Zinfandel

Sullivan Vineyards Winery 1090 Galleron Rd. St. Helena
877.BIG.REDS (244-7337) appt info@sullivanwine.com www.sullivanwine.com
Hours: 10am - 5pm by appt only Tasting Fee: $10 - $45
Wine List: Rosé, Chardonnay, Bordeaux Blend, Cabernet Sauvignon, Merlot

Summers Winery 1171 Tubbs Ln. Calistoga
707.942.5508 info@summerswinery.com www.sumwines.com
Hours: 10:30am - 4:30pm daily Tasting Fee: $7
Wine List: Cabernet Sauvignon, Chardonnay, Merlot, Charbono, Zinfandel, Muscat Canelli, Petite Sirah
Added Highlights: Bocce Court, Gift Shop, Picnic Area, Tours

Summit Lake Vineyards & Winery 2000 Summit Lake Dr. Angwin (Howell Mountain)
707.965.2488 appt www.summitlakevineyards.com
Hours: by appt only daily Tasting Fee: $10
Wine List: Cabernet Sauvignon, Zinfandel, Zinfandel Port

Suncé Winery 1839 Olivet Rd. Santa Rosa (Northern Sonoma)
707.526.9463 info@suncewinery.com www.suncewinery.com

Hours: 10:30am - 5pm daily   pronounced Soon-say!   Tasting Fee: none listed
Wine List: Chardonnay, Sauvignon Blanc, Blends, Pinot Noir, Zinfandel, Rhone, Bordeaux, Cabernet Sauvignon, Meritage, Barbera, Port, Sangiovese, Super Tuscan, Blends, Cabernet Franc, Malbec, Syrah, Syrah Port, Petite Sirah
Added Highlights: Bocce Court

Sutter Home Winery 277 St. Helena Hwy. S.   St. Helena
707.963.3104 www.sutterhome.com
Hours: 10am - 5pm   Tasting Fee: Complimentary
Wine List: White Zinfandel, Moscato, Chardonnay, Pinot Grigio, Cabernet Sauvignon, Merlot, Sauvignon Blanc, Chenin Blanc, Merlot, White Cabernet Sauvignon, Pinot Noir, Zinfandel, Gewürztraminer
Added Highlights: Architecture, Gardens
Notes: One of the biggest wineries in Napa yet mostly known for their White Zinfandel, generally considered a light weight wine, but still the biggest selling wine in America. Beautiful building and grounds, friendly staff and good wines at a good price.
Part of Tour on page: 155

Swanson Vineyards & Winery 1271 Manley Ln.   Rutherford
707.944.1642 www.swansonvineyards.com
Hours: by appt only   Tasting Fee: $25
Wine List: Merlot, Pinot Grigio, Rosato, Petite Sirah, Sangiovese, Syrah, Chardonnay, Blends, Muscat
Added Highlights: Architecture
Notes: This winery is owned by the family that began the Swanson Frozen dinner empire. They make excellent wines to be tasted in an elegant tasting room. No TV dinners here.

Taft Street Winery 2030 Barlow Ln. Sebastopol (Northern Sonoma)
707.823.2049 tastingroom@taftstreetwinery.com www.taftstreetwinery.com
Hours: 11am - 4pm M-F, 4:30pm weekends   Tasting Fee: none listed
Wine List: Merlot, Chardonnay, Pinot Noir, Sauvignon Blanc, Zinfandel, Syrah

Tamber Bey Yount Mill Rd. Yountville
707.945.0483 wine@tamberbey.com www.tamberbey.com
Hours: by appt only   Tasting Fee: Collectors Only PIE
Wine List: Cabernet Sauvignon, Merlot, Chardonnay
Added Highlights: Architecture, Gardens, Horses
Notes: Not open for casual tastings. Named for the owners now retired Arabian performance race horses, Tamborina & Bayamo

Tantalus Winery 19320 Orange Ave. Sonoma
707.933.8218 info@tantaluswinery.com. www.tantaluswinery.com
Hours: by appt only Tue - Sat   Tasting Fee: Complimentary
Wine List: Pinot Noir, Zinfandel, Tempranillo, Syrah, Cabernet Sauvignon, Merlot, Syrah

Tara Bella Winery 3701 Viking Rd. Santa Rosa (Northern Sonoma)
707.544.9049 www.tarabellawinery.com
Hours: by appt only   Tasting Fee: Complimentary
Wine List: Cabernet Sauvignon

Terra Valentine 3787 Spring Mountain Rd. St. Helena
707.967.8340 kathy@terravalentine.com www.terravalentine.com
Hours: by appt only   Tasting Fee: $20 (CWP)
Wine List: Pinot Noir, Cabernet Sauvignon, Bordeaux Blends   (continued on next page)

Added Highlights: Architecture, Art, Tours, Views
Notes: Don't miss this extraordinary building. Their story is also amazing and the wines are well made.

The Wine Room 9575 Sonoma Hwy.   Kenwood
707.833.6131 www.the-wine-room.com
Hours: 11am - 5pm daily   Tasting Fee: $5 (CWP)
Wine List: Sauvignon Blanc, Gewürztraminer, Sangiovese, Pinot Noir, Merlot, Zinfandel, White Zinfandel, Cabernet Sauvignon, Port, Muscat, Cream Sherry
Added Highlights: Pet Friendly, Picnic Area, Wine Maker often pours, great staff and gift shop.
Notes: A collective tasting room featuring Moondance Cellars, Smothers/Remick Ridge Vineyards, Sonoma Valley Portworks, Orchard Station Winery & The Friendly Dog Winery
Part of Tour on page: 48

Trecini Cellars 1107 Sonoma Ave. Santa Rosa (Northern Sonoma)
707.528.8668 www.trecini.com
Hours: by appt only   Tasting Fee: none listed
Wine List: Syrah, Sauvignon Blanc, Merlot, Zinfandel
Notes: also tastings at the Wine Annex, Healdsburg & Vine & Barrel, Petaluma

Trefethen Vineyards & Winery 1160 Oak Knoll Ave.   Napa
707.255.7700 www.trefethen.com
Hours: 10am - 4:30pm   Tasting Fee: $10 - $20
Wine List: Dry Riesling, Viognier, Chardonnay, Pinot Noir, Cabernet Franc, Merlot, Cabernet Sauvignon, Late Harvest Riesling, Blends
Added Highlights: Gift Shop, Tours
Notes: Estate Tastings: $10 - taste 4 current release estate wines. Reserve Tastings: $20 - taste 3 Library & Reserve wines. Tours of historic winery approx. 30 mins by appt.

Trentadue Winery 19170 Geyserville Ave. Geyserville   (Northern Sonoma)
707.433.3104 www.trentadue.com
Hours: 10am - 5pm   Tasting Fee: $0 - $5
Wine List: Cuvee Sparkler, Chardonnay, Zinfandel, Syrah, Merlot, Cabernet Sauvignon, Petite Sirah, Port, Blends
Added Highlights: Gift Shop
Notes: One of the great Italian family wineries of the Alexander Valley who make great wine and hospitality a way of life. Don't miss them.
Part of Tour on page: 59

Tres Sabores 1620 S. Whitehall Ln. St. Helena
707.967.8027 jaj@tressabores.com www.tressabores.com
Hours: by appt only   Tasting Fee: PIE
Wine List: Zinfandel, Cabernet Sauvignon, Petite Sirah, Petite Verdot, Sauvignon Blanc
Added Highlights: Biodynamic/Organic
Notes: Charming family winery with spectacular wines in a beautiful setting. Tucked up against the Mayacamus mountains on prime benchland with old vine Zinfandel and Cabernet Sauvingnon vines.

Trespass Vineyard 424 Crystal Springs Rd. St. Helena
707.963.0804 wine@trespassvineyard.com www.trespassvineyard.com
Hours: by appt only   Tasting Fee: PIE
Wine List: Cabernet Sauvignon, Cabernet Franc
Notes: The Tastings are done at the Venge Winery where the owner/winemaker creates his wine.

Trinchero Family Estates 3070 St. Helena Hwy. St. Helena
707.963.3104 x 4208 info@trincherowinery.com www.trincherowinery.com
Hours: 10am - 5pm   Tasting Fee: $10
Wine List: Cabernet Sauvignon, Chardonnay, Meritage, Pinot Noir, Sauvignon Blanc, Merlot, Petit Verdot
Notes: At the time of this writing, their new hospitality center is just being completed. It is sure to become a wonderful destination that will help showcase the best of the Trinchero wines, one of the great families of Napa.
Part of Tour on page: 155

Trinitas Cellars 875 Bordeaux Way. Napa
707.251.1956 www.trinitascellars.com
Hours: 12:00pm - 8pm   Tasting Fee: $10 Waived with purchase of wine
Wine List: Chardonnay, Pinot Noir, Pinot Blanc, Sauvignon Blanc, Mataro, Petit Sirah, Zinfandel, Blends
Added Highlights: Their tasting room, which includes a nice gift shop, is located in the cave at the Meritage Resort in the Carneros region of Napa. The wines are made at Folio, just a few miles away. The grapes are brought in from a number of great locations, and the collection is remarkable for the number of old vine wines, including Petite Sirah, Zinfandel and Mataro, a rarely seen grape.

Truchard Vineyard 3234 Old Sonoma Rd. Napa
707.253.7153 www.truchardvineyards.com
Hours: by appt only Sat   Tasting Fee: Complimentary (Larger groups charged TF)
Wine List: Chardonnay, Roussanne, Pinot Noir, Syrah, Zinfandel, Merlot, Cabernet Franc, Cabernet Sauvignon, Petit Verdot, Tempranillo, Olive Oil
Added Highlights: Tours

Trust Winery Limited 243 Healdsburg Ave. Healdsburg (Northern Sonoma)
707.431.8749   Hours: 10am - 6pm   Tasting Fee: none listed
Wine List: Dry Creek Zinfandel, Howell Mountain Cabernet Sauvignon, Monterey Pinot Noir, Mendocino Port.

Tudal Family Winery 1015 Big Tree Rd. St. Helena
707.484.3413 appt   www.tudalwinery.com
Hours: by appt only   Tasting Fee: Complimentary
Wine List: Cabernet Sauvignon, Sauvignon Blanc, Blends

Turnbull Wine Cellars 8210 St. Helena Hwy. Oakville
707.963.5839 info@turnbullwines.com www.turnbullwines.com
Hours: 10am - 4:30pm daily   Tasting Fee: $10 - $20
Wine List: Sauvignon Blanc, Old Bull Red, Viognier, Toroso, Cabernet Sauvignon, Merlot, Barbera, Syrah
Added Highlights: Art Gallery, Tours
Notes: Tucked amidst some of the most famous wineries of Oakville and Rutherford, good quality wines and a great photography gallery in the barrel room. A charming, relaxed tasting room and a good staff make for a great experience. Give at least 48 hours notice if you want to arrange a tour.
Part of Tour on page: 62, 151

Twomey Cellars 1183 Dunaweal Ln. Calistoga
707.942.2489 www.twomeycellars.com
Hours: 9am - 4pm Mon - Sat (closed Sun)   Tasting Fee: $5 inc complimentary glass
Wine List: Merlot, Pinot Noir, Sauvignon Blanc
Added Highlights: Gift Shop, Part of the Silver Oak Family of Wineries

Twomey Healdsburg 3000 Westside Rd. Healdsburg
800-505-4850 www.twomeycellars.com
Hours: 9am - 4pm Mon - Sat (closed Sun)   Tasting Fee: $5 inc complimentary glass
Wines: Pinot Noir. Notes: This is a great location with fantastic architecture and ourdoor seating.

Ty Caton Vineyards & Muscardini Cellars 8910 Sonoma Hwy.   Kenwood
707.833.526   www.MuscardiniCellars.com   Part of Tour on page: 48
Hours: 11am - 6pm daily   Tasting Fee: $5 (CWP)
Wine List: Rosato di Sangiovese, Zinfandel, Barbera, Syrah, Cabernet Sauvignon, Merlot, Petite Sirah
Notes: Joint tasting room for two very different winemaking styles & varietals. Tastings with the winemakers.

Unti Vineyards 4202 Dry Creek Rd.   Healdsburg (Northern Sonoma)
707.433.5590   www.untivineyards.com
Hours: 10am - 4pm by appt only   Tasting Fee: none listed
Wine List: Barbera, Syrah, Petite Sirah, Barbera Port, Blends

V. Sattui Winery 1111 White Ln.   St. Helena
707.963.7774   info@vsattui.com   www.vsattui.com
Hours: 9am - 6pm 9AM - 5PM in Winter   Tasting Fee: $5 - $10
Wine List: Sparklers, Sauvignon Blanc, Semillon, Chardonnay, Riesling, Gamay Rouge, White Zinfandel,
Rosato, Gewürztraminer, Pinot Noir, Merlot, Zinfandel, Cabernet Sauvignon, Sangiovese, Grappa, Port,
Madeira, Muscat, Petite Sirah, Syrah, Blends
Added Highlights: Gardens, Gift Shop, Pet Friendly, Picnic Area, Restaurant/Market
Notes: One of the most visited wineries in Napa thanks to their deli, picnic grounds, gift shop & central
location. The wines are only sold there & tastings are free, but sales are brisk & they are super busy on
the weekends. The success of this location led to the vision and now reality that is Castello di Amorosa.
Part of Tour on page: 62, 69, 125, 156

Valley of the Moon Winery 777 Madrone Rd.   Glen Ellen
707.996.6941   luna@valleyofthemoonwinery.com   www.valleyofthemoonwinery.com
Hours: 10am - 4:30pm   Tours daily at 10:30AM & 2PM   Tasting Fee: $0 - $8
Wine List: Pinot Blanc, Chardonnay, Pinot Noir, Sangiovese, Syrah, Zinfandel, Cuvee, Sparklers, Vintage Port
Added Highlights: Gift Shop, Tours

Van Der Heyden Vineyards 4057 Silverado Trail   Napa
707.257.130   www.vanderheydenvineyards.com
Hours: 10am - 6pm   Tasting Fee: $10
Wine List: Cabernet Sauvignon, Merlot, Chardonnay

Venge Vineyards 424 Crystal Springs Rd.   St. Helena
707.967.1008 appt   info@vengevineyards.com   www.vengevineyards.com
Hours: 10am - 5pm daily by appt only   Tasting Fee: $25 (CWP >$100)
Wine List: Blends, Syrah, Sangiovese, Late Harvest Zinfandel, Merlot, Cabernet Sauvignon
Added Highlights: Tours, Sit Down Tasting

Vérité 4611 Thomas Rd.   Healdsburg (Northern Sonoma)
707.433.9000 www.veritewines.com
Hours: 10am - 5pm by appt only closed Sunday   Tasting Fee: $25
Wine List: Bordeaux style blends
Notes: Archipel wines also tasted here.

Viansa Winery & Italian Marketplace 25200 Arnold Dr.   Sonoma (Carneros)
707.935.5738   tuscan@viansa.com   www.viansa.com
Hours: 10am - 5pm   Tasting Fee: $5 - $15
Wine List: Cabernet Sauvignon, Chardonnay, Barbera, Merlot, Nebbiolo Sangiovese, Dolcetto, Aleatico,
Primitivo, Vernaccia, Pinot Grigio, Tocai, Cabernet Franc, Arneis, Rosato, Aleatico, Sweet Wines, Blends
Added Highlights: Architecture, Gift Shop, Picnic Area, Restaurant/Market, Tours, Views

Notes: Started by Sam and Vicki Sebastiani, although now in other hands, this is one of the first wineries you see as you make your way north from San Francisco, via the Golden Gate. They make Italian style wines and have a wonderful gift shop, a great deli and an outdoor seating area with great views. The wines are surprisingly good and the staff is knowledgeable, although they are sometimes overwhelmed with visitors. Their location makes them very popular for tour buses.
Map on page: 41

Vincent Arroyo Winery 2361 Greenwood Ave.   Calistoga
707.942.6995 www.vincentarroyo.com
Hours: 10am - 4pm   Tasting Fee: $0 - $5
Wine List: Cabernet Sauvignon, Merlot, Petite Sirah, Chardonnay, Sangiovese, Port, Blends

Vine Cliff Winery 7400 Silverado Trail   Yountville
707.944.1364   share@vinecliff.com   www.vinecliff.com
Hours: 10am - 5pm daily by appt   Tasting Fee: $25
Wine List: Cabernet Sauvignon, Chardonnay, Merlot
Added Highlights: Architecture, Caves, Gardens, Views
Notes: A jewel of a winery situated in its own canyon on the Silverado Trail just North of the Yountville Cross Rd. A charming building with beautiful gardens, great caves and the tasting room is in the barrel room. The tour is small but very informative. Great staff and excellent wines. Often open to last minute appointments. This is the part of the Valley where George Yount, who first brought grapes to Napa, planted his vines. He had bought a thousand vines from the Mission Fathers in Sonoma and in gratitude Yountville was named for him.
Part of Tour on page: 69, 157, 159, 167

Vineyard 29 2929 Highway 29 N.   St. Helena
707.963.9292 www.vineyard29.com
Hours: by appt only   Tue - Sat for up to 6 guests. Tasting Fee: $50
Wine List: Cabernet Sauvignon, Cabernet Franc, Sauvignon Blanc, Zinfandel, Blends
Added Highlights: Architecture, Tours
Notes: Allow 1 ½ hrs for tasting and tour and they need 2-4 weeks notice. No children, no pets allowed.

Vintner's Collective Tasting Room 1245 Main St.   Napa
707.255.7150 info@vintnerscollective.com www.vintnerscollective.com
Hours: 11am - 6pm   Tasting Fee: $15 - $25
Wine List: Blends, Cabernet Sauvignon, Chardonnay, Merlot, Petite Sirah, Pinot Gris, Pinot Noir, Rosato, Sangiovese, Sauvignon Blanc, Syrah, Viognier, Zinfandel
Notes: A collective tasting room for Ahnfeldt, Ancien, Buoncristiani, Chiarello, D Cubed, Destino, Gregory Graham, JC Cellars, Longfellow, Melka, Mi Sueno, Parallel, Phelan, Richard Perry, Showket, Spelletich, Vinoce. Also Patz and Hall, Judd's Hill, Melka, and Mason

VJB Vineyards & Cellars 9077 Sonoma Hwy.   Kenwood
707.833.2300 ljohn@vjbcellars.com www.vjbcellars.com
Hours: 10am - 5pm   Tasting Fee: $5 (CWP)
Wine List: Cabernet Sauvignon, Syrah, Montepulciano
Added Highlights: Gift Shop
Notes: A very convenient tasting room opposite Kenwood Vineyards. Nice wines and great gift shops with wonderful food items produced by the chef owners. They have an espresso bar which always makes it a good stop. Next door to Café Citti. Their home, where they often host events in just to the north behind the Ledson Winery. The vines behind Ledson are owned by VJB.
Part of Tour on page: 48

Volker Eisele Family Estate 7830-40 St. Helena Hwy. Oakville
707.944.1710 TR info@volkereiselevineyard.com www.volkereiselevineyard.com
Hours: same as collective Tasting Fee: none listed
Wine List: Cabernet Sauvignon, Blends
Added Highlights: Biodynamic/Organic
Notes: Tastings at are at the Napa Wine Company

von Strasser Winery 1510 Diamond Mountain Rd. Calistoga
707.942.930 www.vonstrasser.com
Hours: 10:30am - 4:30pm by appt only Tasting Fee: $20 - $30
Wine List: Cabernet Sauvignon, Cabernet Franc, Zinfandel, Blends
Added Highlights: Wonderful cave tour and tasting including chocolate. Lovely outdoor patio for events, great wines and views. Very easy to reach up Diamond Mountain Road. A real jewel.

Wellington Vineyards 11600 Dunbar Rd. Glen Ellen
707.939.0708 wv@wellingtonvineyards.com www.wellingtonvineyards.com
Hours: 11am - 5pm daily Tasting Fee: $5
Wine List: Cabernet Sauvignon, Viognier, Merlot, Zinfandel, Syrah, Rousanne, Chardonnay
Added Highlights: Gift Shop Notes: Just off Route 12 down the street from Loxton, a friendly staff in a quaint tasting room. Some unusual wines, well made, with an emphasis on organic methods.
Part of Tour on page: 48, 99

Westwood 11 E. Napa St. #3 Sonoma (On the Sonoma Plaza)
707.480.2251 cell info@westwoodwine.com www.westwoodwine.com
Hours: by appt only Tasting Fee: $10
Wine List: Pinot Noir, Syrah
Added Highlights: Gift Shop
Notes: Boutique winery with fantastic wines, poured by the winemaker right on the Plaza in Sonoma. Makes a great stop on a tour of the Plaza where you can taste at 5 locations in one square block area.
Part of Tour on page: 18, 105

White Oak Vineyards 7505 Highway 128; 208 Haydon St. Healdsburg
707.433.8429 tastingroom@whiteoakwinery.com www.whiteoakwinery.com
Hours: 10am - 5pm Tasting Fee: $5 (CWP) Reserve tastings: $10
Wine List: Sauvignon Blanc, Chardonnay, Merlot, Cabernet Sauvignon, Syrah, Zinfandel
Added Highlights: Art Gallery, Tours
Notes: In the lower section of Alexander Valley, a charming tasting room, good wines and very convenient for a tour started in Napa, up through Knight's Valley. Good wines, friendly staff.
Part of Tour on page: 59

Whitehall Lane Winery 1563 St. Helena Hwy. S. St. Helena
707.963.7035 greatwine@whitehalllane.com www.whitehalllane.com
Hours: 11am - 5:45pm Tasting Fee: $10
Wine List: Cabernet Sauvignon, Merlot, Chardonnay, Belmuscato Dessert Wine
Added Highlights: Architecture, Gift Shop, Tours
Notes: A fun winery with a great staff and excellent wines. The very modern tasting room has a bit of a bar feel, but it allows diverse groups to mix. It feels like a smaller winery than it actually is in reality.
Part of Tour on page: 147, 195

William Harrison Vineyards 1443 Silverado Trail St. Helena
707.963.8310 www.whwines.com
Hours: 11am - 5pm Thu - Mon Tasting Fee: $7.50
Wine List: Cabernet Sauvignon, Cabernet Franc, Chardonnay, Blend

William Hill Estate   1761 Atlas Peak Rd.   Napa
707.265.3024 appt   www.williamhillestate.com
Hours: 10:30am - 4pm daily by appt only   Tours at 10:30am by appt.   Tasting Fee: $15
Wine List: Chardonnay, Merlot, Cabernet Sauvignon, Cabernet Franc, Malbec, Petit Verdot, Aura (Bordeaux blend)
Added Highlights: Great Building and Grounds, Tours, Recently purchased by Gallo

Wilson Winery   1960 Dry Creek Rd.   Healdsburg   (Northern Sonoma)
707.433.4355   dee@wilsonwinery.com   www.wilsonwinery.com
Hours: 11am - 5pm daily   Tasting Fee: $5 - $10
Wine List: Cabernet Sauvignon, Cabernet Franc, Zinfandel, Merlot, Syrah, Petite Sirah, Blends

Work Vineyard   3190 Highway 128   Calistoga
707.942.0251   Karen@workvineyard.com   www.workvineyard.com
Hours: by appt only   Tasting Fee: $15
Wine List: Sauvignon Blanc, Botrytised Sauvignon Blanc

X Winery   1405 - 2nd St.   Napa
707.204.9522 x 9 appt   cmac@xwinery.com   www.xwinery.com
Hours: by appt only   Tasting Fee: $5 - $15
Wine List: Cabernet Sauvignon, Sauvignon Blanc, Chardonnay, Petite Sirah, Zinfandel
Notes: The wines from Amicus Cellars label can also be tasted here.

Yoakim Bridge Winery   7209 Dry Creek Rd.   Healdsburg   (Northern Sonoma)
707.433.8511   www.virginia@yoakimbridge.com   www.yoakimbridge.com
Hours: 11am - 4pm Fri - Sun   weekdays by appt   Tasting Fee: $10 (CWP)
Wine List: Old Vine Zinfandel
Added Highlights: Tours
Notes: Charming Mom and Pop winery at the top of the Dry Creek Valley. Notice the old vine Zinfandel out in front of the intimate tasting room.
Part of Tour on page: 59

Zahtila Vineyards   2250 Lake County Hwy.   Calistoga
707.942.9251   www.zahtilavineyards.com
Hours: 10am - 5pm by appt only   Tasting Fee: $5 (logo glass)
Wine List: Cabernet Sauvignon, Zinfandel, Chardonnay
Added Highlights: Picnic Area

ZD Wines   8380 Silverado Trail   Napa
707.963.5188   www.zdwines.com
Hours: 10am - 4:30pm   Tasting Fee: $10 - $15
Wine List: Chardonnay, Pinot Noir, Cabernet Sauvignon, Blends
Added Highlights: Gardens, Gift Shop
Notes: Tucked down the hill just south of Mumm Napa on the Silverado Trail, ZD's tasting room is friendly and relaxed, and nice for a small group. Good wines, convenient location.
Part of Tour on page: 195

Zichichi Vineyard & Winery   8626 W. Dry Creek Rd.   Healdsburg   (Northern Sonoma)
707.433.4410   www.zichichifamilyvineyard.com
Hours: 11am - 4pm   Tasting Fee: none listed
Wine List: Zinfandel, Petite Sirah
Added Highlights: Picnic Area

About the Authors

Ralph & Lahni DeAmicis are authors, professional speakers and tour guides. After spending many years in the splendor of Philadelphia they moved to the wilds of Sonoma and Napa. When they arrived they realized there was Wine! In their quest to visit all of the wineries in those two counties, they started writing a book.

As they traveled around to the wineries, they kept noticing big black cars parked out front. They suddenly realized that the limousine drivers were visiting all of the wineries that Ralph and Lahni wanted to visit, but the drivers were getting paid to do that. What a concept! So, Ralph went down the street from their home in downtown Sonoma and got a job driving wine tours. For the next two years, he talked with absolutely everyone, read absolutely everything and generally absorbed everything he could about Wine Country. In the process, he brought back huge piles of information for Lahni to organize, including the maps of his tours, complete with his client's reactions. The result is their eleventh book, 'Your Day in Wine Country'.

After two years, they had enough information for the book so Ralph tried to stop touring. Then he realized that he missed it too much, so Ralph and Lahni started their own tour company, Amicis Tours, that specializes in creating tours based on the clients' needs, visiting wineries both big and small in Napa and Sonoma, and whose slogan is "You've Got Friends in Wine Country".

Ralph & Lahni do their Tours in English, Spanish, Italian, French & German

Cuore Libre Publishing & Amicis Tours
divisions of Space and Time Designing Inc.
19201 Sonoma Hwy. #125, Sonoma, CA 95476
Office: 707-320-4274, Cell: 707-235-2364, Fax 707-320-0572
Ralph@SpaceAndTime.com   Lahni@SpaceAndTime.com
www.YourDayInWineCountry.com